VMWARE® VI AND VSPHERE SDK

MANAGING THE VMWARE INFRASTRUCTURE AND VSPHERE

STEVE JIN

PRENTICE
HALL

Upper Saddle River, NJ • Boston • Indianapolis • San Francisco

New York • Toronto • Montreal • London • Munich • Paris • Madrid

Cape Town • Sydney • Tokyo • Singapore • Mexico City

The publisher offers excellent discounts on this book when ordered in quantity for bulk purchases or special sales, which may include electronic versions and/or custom covers and content particular to your business, training goals, marketing focus, and branding interests. For more information, please contact

U.S. Corporate and Government Sales
(800) 382-3419
corpsales@pearsontechgroup.com

For sales outside the United States, please contact

International Sales
international@pearson.com

Visit us on the Web: informit.com/ph

The Library of Congress Cataloging-in-Publication data is on file.

ISBN-13: 978-0-137-15363-3
ISBN-10: 0-137-1563-5
Text printed in the United States on recycled paper at R.R. Donnelly in Crawfordsville, Indiana.
First printing September 2009

Editor-in-Chief
Karen Gettman
Acquisitions Editor
Jessica Goldstein
Development Editor
Sheri Cain
Managing Editor
Kristy Hart
Project Editor
Jovana San Nicolas-Shirley
Copy Editor
Karen A. Gill
Indexer
Erika Millen
Proofreader
Williams Woods Publishing Services
Publishing Coordinator
Romny French
Cover Designer
Chuti Prasertsith
Compositor
Jake McFarland

VMWARE® VI AND VSPHERE SDK

To Maggie and Melody

Table of Contents

Table of Contents

Acknowledgments

I thank VMware founders Dr. Mendel Roseblum, Diane Greene, Scott Devine, Dr. Edward Wang, and Edouard Bugnion for creating the great technology that I can write about today. I also thank the many engineers who have followed their footsteps to push the virtualization technology to state-of-the-art, and the many other colleagues who brought the company to its dominant position in the marketplace.

I'd like to thank Carter Shanklin, Mark Menkhus, Robert D. Petruska, and Cody Bunch for reading early drafts of this manuscript and working hard to improve its clarity and accuracy. I could not have written this book without their help, and any mistakes that remain are my own.

I'd also like to thank those teachers, colleagues, and managers who have done so much for me: Cheng Wu, Jun Li, Liman Deng, Jincai Xu, Wenjian Chen, Jeane Chen, Shauchi Ong, George Hung, Steve Nameroff, Frank Yang, Charles Yan, Bingxue Xu, Yingqiu Sui, Sujit Panikatt, Lawrence Jocobs, Marianna Tessel, Carter Shanklin, Alan Tan, Luke Dion, Jeff Hu, Beng-Hong Lim, Colleen Lam, Pablo Roesch, Gilbert Lau, Melissa Ercoli Cotton, Budianto Bong, Tobin Edwards, Lucas Nguyen, Kimberly Wang, Prasad Pimplaskar, Giampiero Caprino, Andrew Zhu, Frank Li, Mike Chen. Without their support, I would not be where I am in my career today and would never have been in a position to write this book. For their teaching, mentoring, inspiration, and support, I am truly grateful.

I thank Jessica Goldstein, Karen Gettman, Romny French, Sheri Cain, Jovana San Nicolas-Shirley, Karen Gill, Kristy Hart, Doug Ingersoll, Chuti Prasertsith, Jake McFarland, and the entire team at Prentice Hall for their great support and professionalism. I feel so blessed to have worked with the best publishing team.

About the Author

Steve Jin is a senior member of technical staff at VMware, where he provides guidance to strategic partners, such as IBM, HP, Dell, NetApp, and BEA, who build applications using VI (vSphere) SDK. In his spare time, he created VI (vSphere) Java API opensource project (http://vijava.sf.net), which is widely used by various commercial companies and developers. Jin received his BA, MS, and Ph.D. degrees in control theory (EE) from prestigious Tsinghua University in Beijing. Prior to his current job, Jin worked at IBM Research, Rational Software, and ASDC in various engineering and management roles.

Jin is the author of two software engineering books published for the Springer Tsinghua Press and the China Electronics Industry Press.

Preface

Virtualization is not a new concept, but it is changing the computing industry in a profound way. Server virtualization is now #1 on enterprises' budget lists. According to analysts, it will continue to be the highest impact trend, changing infrastructure and operations through 2012.

Virtualization became popular for two reasons. First, the hardware (especially x86–based servers) capacity has increased so much that most servers are under utilized. The market demand is strong for consolidating servers and saving operation and management cost. Virtualization has clearly provided a proven solution for this demand. Second, the social awareness of environment protection and energy saving has put green technology into the spotlight. Virtualization addresses this social requirement well by saving electricity consumption.

Today, more than 4 million virtual machines are installed. With the acceleration of hypervisor toward commodity because of increased competition, even more virtual machines will be running along the way.

In this virtualization game, VMware is by far the market leader, with 100 percent coverage of Fortune 100 enterprises. In 2007, the company achieved $1.3 billion revenue and has been growing steadily about 80 percent since its inception in 1998. There were 100,000 customers and 10,000 partners in 2008. The VMware annual conference, VMworld, attracted more than 14,000 attendees in 2008.

With the proliferation of the VMware platform, the demand for management of the virtualization environment is clear. In general, for every dollar spent on the initial infrastructure investment, $6 or more is needed for management and operation. VMware has done a great job of providing best-of-the-breed management products, including VirtualCenter server and other value-added solutions, such as Site Recovery Manager.

Clearly, VMware cannot do everything. As a platform company, VMware needs to enable partners and customers to come up with solutions to the integration, customization, and automation of VMware platforms. To achieve these, you need a solid understanding and hands-on expertise of VI SDK. This is where this book fits into the big picture of whole virtualization technology and industry.

This book helps you with the basic concepts of virtualization, the VMware VI SDK, and how to effectively use the SDK in your projects.

Who Should Read This Book

This book is for anyone interested in virtual system management of VMware platforms. It specifically targets the following audiences:

- System administrators who want to automate, customize, and optimize the VMware virtualization platforms. This book uncovers many interfaces under the hook of VI Client, RCLI, VI PowerShell, and so on.

- Software architects, engineers, and solution developers who want to design and develop applications with VI SDK. Possible vendors include the following:

  - Hardware vendors who use the VI SDK for developing management software to manage their specific system or device

  - Independent software vendors who develop applications or components using the SDK

  - System integrators who develop solutions targeting specific industry sectors

  - VMware competitors who use VI SDK as a reference for their own designs

- Technical managers, including program managers, who oversee virtualization projects for a good sense of the SDK.

- Researchers and students interested in VMware virtualization technology and might use it in their projects.

- Anyone interested in system management of virtualization platforms.

Prerequisites

To read this book, you need to have the following skills and knowledge:

- **Basic Java programming skills**—Most of our code samples are written in Java. It's not because VI SDK favors Java over others, but because Java is a popular programming language that runs on all major platforms and has the widest audience today.

  If you use other programming languages, the samples are still helpful even though they cannot be used as they are. The methods and data objects don't change much across the languages. Reading the Java sample for these can help you develop in other languages as well.

- **OS virtualization basics, especially the VMware virtualization platforms**—They are the management target of the SDK; therefore, a solid understanding of how things work in the virtual world offers an advantage toward understanding the model behind the APIs.

- **Web Services**—It's optional, and only needed to understand the VI SDK Web Services interfaces. This book covers a little background when it gets there.

This book gives you in-depth knowledge, the best practices of VMware VI SDK development, and hands-on experience with many useful samples that can be easily modified for your own automation or application development.

Structure of This Book

This book takes a pragmatic approach to show you how to program or script VI SDK for your work. As a long-time software professional, I know how software engineers think and work. We don't start a new technology by reading hundreds of pages of documents. Instead, we start with samples and read some documents when we have doubts with some concepts and API usages. With this in mind, this book provides you with many useful samples[1] that you can use as is or adapt to your projects.[2]

Although samples are important, so are the basic concepts and best practices. I show you both the big pictures and details that can be easily ignored or missed. While helping VMware strategic partners with their development projects and

---

[1] For easy reading, I highlighted all Java keywords in bold in the samples.

[2] These samples are intended to illustrate the usage and best practices of the APIs. They are not necessarily comprehensive or production ready.

community members with their questions, I have seen how the SDK can be mis-used. I explain some of these pitfalls and how to effectively avoid them. I also intro-duce how to best use these APIs. This book is not just another reference book.

Better than a typical SDK book, this book introduces the VI Java API I have created. With the API, you can build much shorter, faster, and more importantly much more readable and maintainable code. Most of the samples used in this book are written using this higher-level API.

Most chapters are organized around various management tasks, which are supported by VI SDK managed objects. When applicable, the related managed objects involved are listed in the following overview as well as the beginning of each chapter so that you can easily locate a chapter given a managed object.

This book contains 18 chapters and 6 appendixes:

- **Chapter 1, "VMware Infrastructure Overview"**—This chapter introduces the virtualization basics and VMware products, especially VMware Infrastructure. It explains how VI SDK fits in the big picture.

- **Chapter 2, "VI SDK Basics"**—Here, you examine the VI SDK from the bot-tom up. This chapter covers the Web Services API, the object model, and various tools that help to familiarize you with the SDK.

- **Chapter 3, "Hello VI"**—In this chapter, you learn how to set up the develop-ment environment and run your first "Hello World" sample code. Debugging techniques are also included here.

- **Chapter 4, "Using `PropertyCollector` and `SearchIndex`"**—Exclusive attention is devoted in this chapter to how to retrieve properties and search managed entities using `PropertyCollector` and `SearchIndex`. `PropertyCollector` is one of the most often-used services; it's also regard-ed as one of the most difficult ones in the SDK.

- **Chapter 5, "Introducing the VI Java API"**—This chapter examines the open source Java API, which is built on top of the Web Services API. Using this API instead of Web Services, you can have much shorter, faster, and more readable code.

- **Chapter 6, "Managing Inventory"**—The structure of inventory and how to manage it are covered here. Also covered are the View family of managed objects, which can be used in GUI applications.

  The managed objects covered include `ManagedEntity`, `Folder`, `Datacenter`, `CustomFieldsManager`, `View`, `ManagedObjectView`, `ViewManager`, `ContainerView`, `InventoryView`, and `ListView`.

- **Chapter 7, "Managing Host Systems"**—In this chapter, focus is on the hypervisor on which virtual machines are running. It covers all the aspects except networking and storage, which are covered in detail in Chapters 10 and 11, respectively.

  The managed objects discussed are `HostSystem`, `HostDateTimeSystem`, `HostBootDeviceSystem`, `HostDiagnosticSystem`, `HostCpuSchedulerSystem`, `HostFirmwareSystem`, `HostHealthStatusSystem`, `HostAutoStartManager`, `HostMemorySystem`, and `HostPatchManager`.

- **Chapter 8, "Managing Virtual Machines, Snapshots, and VMotion"**—A virtual machine is the equivalent of a physical machine in the virtual world. This chapter shows how to manage its life cycle, change its configuration, find out more about the guest OS running on it, and migrate it and its storage live. Also covered are the virtual machine snapshots, including how they are structured and how to manage them.

  This chapter focuses on three managed objects: `VirtualMachine`, `CustomizationSpecManager`, and `VirtualMachineSnapshot`.

- **Chapter 9, "Managing Clusters and Resource Pools"**—Clustering is an advanced feature in which multiple hosts are grouped for high availability, load balancing, and energy saving, among other things. This chapter introduces how to manage VMware HA and DRS/DPM clusters. Resource pools and various resource allocation policies are also introduced here.

  This chapter covers three managed objects: `ComputeResource`, `ClusterComputeResource`, and `ResourcePool`.

- **Chapter 10, "Managing Networking"**—Networking is an important and sometimes confusing aspect of virtualization. This chapter guides you through the basic concepts of how to manage the virtual switches, port groups, virtual NIC, and network policies, as well as how to manage SNMP, network services, firewalls, and more.

  This chapter covers these managed objects: `HostNetworkSystem`, `Network`, `HostFirewallSystem`, `HostSnmpSystem`, `HostServiceSystem`, and `HostVMotionSystem`.

- **Chapter 11, "Managing Storage and Datastores"**—Storage is one of the most confusing parts because it involves many enterprise-level storage systems and how ESX virtualizes them. This chapter introduces basic concepts and how to perform various tasks from storage to datastore and files.

This chapter discusses the following managed objects:
`HostStorageSystem`, `HostDatastoreSystem`, `Datastore`,
`HostDatastoreBrowser`, and `FileManager`.

- **Chapter 12, "Events and Alarms"**—This chapter introduces what events and alarms are. It also shows how to retrieve events and how to set up alarms to monitor the virtual systems.

  The managed objects in focus are `EventManager`,
  `EventHistoryCollector`, `Alarm`, and `AlarmManager`.

- **Chapter 13, "Performance Monitoring"**—Performance is one of the biggest concerns people have when coming to virtualization. This chapter introduces the basic concepts of performance monitoring and how to retrieve performance statistics and monitor performance in real time.

  The sole managed object covered is `PerformanceManager`.

- **Chapter 14, "Task and `ScheduledTask`"**—This chapter introduces tasks and scheduled tasks. It shows how to monitor/cancel a task and how to set up scheduled tasks for automation.

  The managed objects covered are `Task`, `TaskManager`,
  `TaskHistoryCollector`; `ScheduledTask`, and `ScheduledTaskManager`.

- **Chapter 15, "User and License Administration"**—Here, you learn how user and license management work in VMware Infrastructure and how you can manage them using the SDK.

  The managed objects discussed are `AuthorizationManager`,
  `HostLocalAccountManager`, `UserDirectory`, `SessionManager`, and
  `LicenseManager`.

- **Chapter 16, "Extending the VI Client"**—The VI SDK provides an extension API. This chapter introduces how it works and what it takes to plug into the VI Client.

  The managed object involved is `ExtensionManager`.

- **Chapter 17, "Scripting the VI SDK with Jython, Perl, and PowerShell"**—This chapter introduces development of scripts with three major scripting languages that are commonly used in system administration: VI Perl, PowerShell, and Jython (Python).

- **Chapter 18, "Advanced Topics"**—This chapter covers topics that are important but do not fit in previous chapters (for example, multithreading, versioning, best practices for performance and scalability, and I18N).

The managed objects involved are `OptionManager`, `DiagnosticManager`, and `HostSystem`.

- **Appendix A, "The Managed Object Types"**— This appendix lists all the managed object types in VI SDK 2.5 and vSphere 4.

- **Appendix B, "The Performance Counters"**— This appendix lists all the performance counters you might need to retrieve performance statistics.

- **Appendix C, "Cmdlets in the VI Toolkit (for Windows)"**— This appendix includes the cmdlets in the toolkit 1.0.

- **Appendix D, "Unified Modeling Language"**—This appendix provides you with the basic knowledge to understand this book's UML diagrams.

- **Appendix E, "VI SDK Web Services"**— This appendix examines the Web Services in greater detail than Chapter 2.

- **Appendix F, "What Is New in vSphere 4 SDK?"**—This appendix summarizes the changes in the newly released vSphere 4 SDK, which is the next version after VI SDK 2.5.

How to Read This Book

This book is organized in an order best for most readers. It starts with an overview of virtualization technology and VMware VI products, trying to give you the big picture of virtualization and the importance of system management in a virtualized environment. Chapter 1 is recommended, but it's not required.

This book then covers the VI SDK basics (Chapter 2), how to set up the development environment (Chapter 3), and the basic managed objects `PropertyCollector` and `SearchIndex` (Chapter 4). Chapter 3 is a must-read if you want to get hands on with the samples. Chapter 4 is optional, but crucial to understand the implementation of VI Java API discussed in the chapter after.

Chapter 5 is a must-read for Java developers, because after this chapter, the Java API is used primarily. You don't necessarily read how the API is designed, but definitely how it should be used.

The chapters following Chapter 5 cover different parts/aspects of the VI SDK, from inventory management, host and virtual machine management, and storage to networking, performance statistics, and event management. You can randomly read these chapters, which are in braces ({}) in the following list, depending on your interest and preference.

Not all readers are application developers. More often than not, system administrators write scripts to automate daily tasks. If you're only looking for scripting, you can jump directly to Chapter 17, where three basic scripting languages are covered.

The following summarizes the critical reading paths based on your interests:

- **General knowledge**—Chapters 1 and 2

- **Java development**—Chapters 3, 5, {2, 4, 6, 7, 8, 9, 10, 11, 12, 13, 14, 15, 16, 17, 18}

- **Jython development**—Chapters 2, 5, 17, {6, 7, 8, 9, 10, 11, 12, 13, 14, 15, 16, 18}

- **VI PowerShell development**—Chapter 17, Appendix C, {6, 7, 8, 9, 10, 11, 12, 13, 14, 15, 16, 18}

- **VI Perl development**—Chapters 2, 17, {6, 7, 8, 9, 10, 11, 12, 13, 14, 15, 16, 18}

Chapter 1

VMware Infrastructure Overview

This chapter first introduces the basics of virtualization, including its definition, history, benefits, and various VMware products/solutions. It then focuses on the VMware Infrastructure family of products, covering ESX/ESXi hypervisor, VirtualCenter management server, and the VI Client. Finally, this chapter discusses various VMware management APIs, including the VMware Infrastructure SDK (VI SDK), which is the major focus of this book.

This chapter shows how the VI SDK fits into the big picture of the VMware strategy of virtualization management.

Introducing OS Virtualization

Virtualization has been a buzzword in the IT industry for the past couple of years, and it will continue to be so in the coming years. This section examines virtualization's definition, history, and benefits.

What Virtualization Is

Before defining virtualization, let's look at how a computer system works without virtualization in place. Figure 1-1 shows a typical stack of a physical system. As you can see,

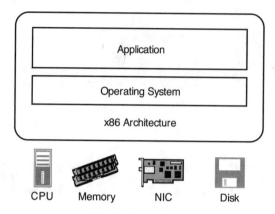

Figure 1-1 A typical stack of a physical system

the operating system runs directly on top of the hardware, including the CPU, memory, NIC, and disk. In this case, the operating system and hardware are tightly coupled, and applications often interfere with each other. Given the boundary of the physical machine, expensive resources cannot be shared and often are underutilized.

Now let's look at a virtualized system. As you can see from Figure 1-2, the operating system is detached from physical hardware and is running on a virtual machine. Multiple operating systems can be installed and run simultaneously on the same machine.

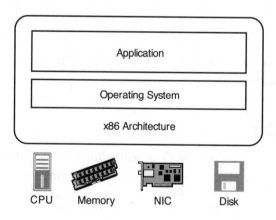

Figure 1-2 A typical stack of a virtualized system

A virtual machine is a software abstraction of the hardware. It has all the virtual hardware components, just like its physical equivalent. You can manage the OS and application as a single unit by encapsulating them in VMs.

Because of the separation of the OS and hardware, virtualization breaks hardware dependencies. The standard, hardware-independent environments can be provisioned anywhere. Virtualization also allows you to choose the right OS for your applications. In addition, you can easily have a new dedicated OS for an application to avoid interference between applications. This form of virtual machine is also called a virtual appliance.

> Virtualization is not simulation or emulation. You have "real" machines that can do the same as their physical counterparts; you can expect the same from a virtual machine as you would from a physical one.
>
> Neither is a virtual machine a session, as with Windows Terminal Service or Citrix MetaFrame. Each virtual machine runs its own OS, whereas a session shares an OS instance.

The architecture shown in Figure 1-2 is the one used in VMware ESX. It's also referred to as the "bare metal" approach, in which the hypervisor runs directly on top of hardware.

Another architecture, known as the "hosted" approach, implements the virtualization layer on top of an operating system. The "hosted" hypervisor is an application on the underlying OS. This means more layers, of course, which affects performance. But on a positive side, it's not necessary to develop another set of hardware drivers; vendors have to do this with the "bare metal" approach. VMware Server and Workstation use the "hosted" architecture.

History of Virtualization

Virtualization has a long history that dates back to the 1960s. At that time, IBM first implemented virtualization as a way to logically partition mainframe computers into separate virtual machines. These partitions allowed mainframes to multitask, or run multiple applications and processes at the same time. Mainframes were expensive; they were designed for partitioning as a way to fully leverage the investment. Virtualization was effectively ignored during the 1980s and 1990s when client server architecture and inexpensive x86 servers with Windows and Linux started to dominate the computing world.

The growth in x86 server and desktop deployments has introduced new IT infrastructure and operational challenges. Essentially, these x86-based computers faced the same problems of rigidity and underutilization that mainframes faced in the 1960s.

- **Low utilization rate**—According to a market research survey, typical x86 server deployments achieve utilization of only 10 percent to 15 percent of their total capacity. Organizations typically run one application per server to avoid the risk of vulnerabilities in one application affecting the availability of another application on the same server.

- **Increasing physical infrastructure costs**—The operational costs to support the growing physical infrastructure have steadily increased. Most computing infrastructure must remain operational at all times, resulting in power consumption, cooling, and facilities costs that do not vary with utilization levels.

- **Increasing IT management costs**—As computing infrastructures have become more complex, the levels of specialized education and experience required for infrastructure management personnel and the associated costs of such personnel have increased. Organizations spend disproportionate time and resources on manual tasks associated with server maintenance; thus, more personnel are required to complete these tasks.

- **Insufficient failover and disaster protection**—Organizations are increasingly affected by the downtime of mission-critical applications and the inaccessibility of critical end user desktops. The threat of security attacks, natural disasters, health pandemics, and terrorism has elevated the importance of business continuity planning for both desktops and servers.

- **High maintenance end-user desktops**—The process of managing and securing enterprise desktops presents numerous challenges. Controlling a distributed desktop environment and enforcing management, access, and security policies without impairing users' ability to work effectively is complex and expensive. Numerous patches and upgrades must be continually applied to desktop environments to eliminate security vulnerabilities.

VMware invented virtualization for the x86 platform in the 1990s to address underutilization and other issues, overcoming many challenges in the process. Today, VMware is the global leader in x86 virtualization and has achieved success that is building momentum for virtualization in all x86 computers.

Besides VMware, several other players have emerged along the way, including XEN, Microsoft, and KVM in the hypervisors space, and many more in the application and solution space.

Benefits

Virtualization has brought many distinguishing technical advantages to the computing infrastructure:

- **Compatibility**—Just like a physical computer, a virtual machine runs its own guest operating system and applications and has all the components you can find in a physical computer (CPU, memory, NIC, disk, and so on). As a result, virtual machines are completely compatible with all the standard x86 operating systems, applications, and device drivers, so you can run all the same software that you would run on a physical x86 computer on a virtual machine.

- **Isolation**—Although multiple virtual machines can share one physical computer, they are completely isolated from each other as if they were running on multiple physical machines. On these virtual machines, you can run different operating systems and applications. They don't interfere with each other at all. If one of them crashes, the others remain available. Isolation is an important factor that makes applications running on a virtual machine far superior to those running on a traditional, nonvirtualized system.

- **Encapsulation**—A virtual machine is essentially a software container that bundles a complete set of virtual hardware resources, as well as an operating system and all its applications, inside a software package. When it's not running, a virtual machine is just several files.

  This encapsulation makes virtual machines incredibly portable and easy to manage. For example, you can move and clone a virtual machine from one location to another just like any other files, or store a virtual machine on any standard data storage medium, from a pocket-sized USB flash memory card to an enterprise storage area network (SAN).

- **Hardware independence**—A virtual machine is completely independent from its underlying physical hardware. You can, for example, configure a virtual machine with virtual components—say CPU, NIC, and SCSI controller—that are completely different from the physical components on the underlying hardware.

Hardware independence gives you the freedom to move a virtual machine from one type of x86 computer to another without changing the device drivers, operating system, or applications.

- **Resource sharing**—Whereas multiple virtual machines run on the same server, physical resources are shared across them. Advanced techniques such as memory over commitment, storage thin provisioning, and so on can significantly maximize the resource usage. Memory over commitment, for example, allows a virtual machine to borrow other virtual machines' unused memory; therefore, virtual machines seemingly have more memory than physical machines.

  This effective resource sharing reduces the overall requirement for physical resources and saves infrastructure costs.

These technical advantages benefit both the customers and the environment:

- **Cost savings**—One of the immediate benefits of virtualization is the consolidation of data centers. It means less hardware investment, physical space, utility usage, and administration efforts. All these are reflected in final cost savings.

- **Management flexibility**—When physical machines are converted into virtual machines, fewer machines are involved, which makes the process more flexible and easier to move virtual machines around, back them up, provision them, patch them, and manage them.

- **Robust infrastructure**—Virtualization makes it easier and cheaper to implement advanced features such as high availability, fault tolerance, and disaster recovery; therefore, virtualization is emerging even into small data centers. With these powerful features, the computing infrastructure becomes more robust than ever.

- **Environmental friendliness**—Servers run at 75 percent or higher of maximum power consumption even when idle. Also, every watt a server uses normally requires about the same in cooling. Therefore, it's critical that underused servers are eliminated, lending to virtualization.

  As VMware estimates, companies can reduce power consumption and cost by 80 to 90 percent by implementing its technology. The company claims that for every server virtualized, customers can save about 7,000 kilowatt hours, or four tons of carbon dioxide emissions, every year. It also claims that PCs virtualized and hosted on servers can reduce power consumption and cost by 35 percent. By using virtualization, you reduce energy consumption and increase your score on the green scorecard.

Solutions

Virtualization is a revolutionary technology that opens many new areas and changes the way things are done with new mechanisms. You can build many different types of applications on top of it. Following are some of the examples:

- **Business continuity and disaster recovery**—With the flexibility that virtualization brings in, testing and executing disaster recovery plans no longer require huge investment and effort and disruption to daily operations. A running virtual machine, not just data, can be replicated to a remote site and boot there instantaneously.

- **Test automation**—You can easily create multiple testing environments and manage them across their life cycles. You can run these testing environments simultaneously, which results in big savings on equipment as well as space and utility bills.

- **Virtual desktop**—It's yet another try after the network computer in the enterprise desktop market. Given the market size and impact the virtual desktop could create for people, it might be the next big thing in virtualization space.

- **Capacity and performance management**—This helps to measure the performance and better plan and manage the computing infrastructure for business needs. Although the infrastructure is expanding, the urgency for such management tools will only increase.

- **System security**—Virtualization has changed the way the computing infrastructure is constructed and runs. It also challenges system security. As an example, you can externalize the security software and run it in the host or a dedicated virtual system, which could mean better security.

- **System and application life cycle management**—It's where you can manage your system and application's life cycle from development to testing to production. Virtualization makes it easy to switch and track these stages.

This solution list could go on and on, especially when it comes to vertical industries where you tailor solutions just for the industry's specific requirement and business workflows.

VMware Products

The following gives you an overview of what is available from VMware and how the VI and VI SDK fit into the big picture. This book only covers programming VMware Infrastructure.

In Table 1-1, all the products whose names are followed by an asterisk (*) are actually built on top of the VMware Infrastructure; these represent more than half the products. VMware Infrastructure plays a pivotal role in the company strategy.

Table 1-1

VMware Product Overview		
Targeted Domain	**Products**	**Description**
Datacenter	VMware Infrastructure 3	Runs virtual data centers with a suite of ESX/ESXi, VirtualCenter servers, and other add-on components such as DRS, HA, and VMware Consolidated Backup
	VMware Site Recovery Manager*	Automates and tests end-to-end disaster recovery in the data center
Development and testing	VMware Workstation	Runs multiple OSs simultaneously on a single PC with the Windows or Linux host OS
	VMware Lab Manager*	Pools servers, networking, storage, and other resources and shares them across the development and test teams
	VMware Stage Manager*	Streamlines and accelerates the transition of complex, multitier IT services through the preproduction stages into production
	VMware Lifecycle Manager*	Allows companies to implement a consistent and automated process for requesting, approving, deploying, updating, and retiring virtual machines

Table 1-1   continued

VMware Product Overview		
Targeted Domain	**Products**	**Description**
Enterprise desktop	VMware Virtual Desktop Infrastructure*	Hosts desktop environments inside virtual machines running in the data center, enabling end users to gain remote access from a PC or thin client terminal
	VMware ACE	Deploys and manages secure, platform-independent virtual machines that end users can use on their work PC, personal computer, or even on a portable USB media device
Free virtualization	VMware Server	Similar to Workstation with fewer functionalities
	VMware Player	Read-only version of the VMware server
Consumer	VMware Fusion	Runs Windows XP or Vista on an Intel-based Mac

As the technology progresses and the company strategy evolves, more members could come into the product family. Be sure to check the VMware company Web site for up-to-date product information.

VMware Infrastructure

VMware VI is the flagship product in its product offering, representing the biggest revenue stream to the company. It is essentially a suite of products, composed of three key components:

- **ESX server**—The core virtualization platform
- **vCenter server (also known as VirtualCenter)**—The central management platform
- **VI Client**—The standard user interface to interact with either ESX or VC server

VI is not only a leading virtualization product for datacenters, but a platform for building many other value-added products, such as VMware Lab Manager and Virtual Desktop.

It's imperative that you understand the basic features and how they operate before you work on an SDK project. After all, like any SDK, the VI SDK just exposes management interfaces to what is available and capable in VI.

ESX Server

ESX server is the core hypervisor where virtual machines are running. The name came from the music band Elastic Sky, which was composed of VMware employees. To make it a three-letter acronym for easy pronunciation, the name ESX was created.

Before ESX, VMware offered a hosted hypervisor, which ran on top of a host OS. With ESX, the underlying OS is no longer needed. Therefore, ESX performs better and has become the choice of datacenters.

ESXi is a new addition to the ESX. It's only 32MB and can be preinstalled with the physical servers when it's shipped from the vendors. ESXi reflects the VMware philosophy that virtualization is part of the hardware,[1] not the software as in Microsoft products. In this book, ESX and ESXi are used interchangeably.

The major difference between Classic ESX and ESXi is the service console, which is a typical Linux OS for management purpose. The service console is a running OS; therefore, many vendors use it to run their integration software or agents. You can find more details in Table 1-2 and the KB article 1006543.[2]

Table 1-2

Differences between ESX and ESXi		
	VMware ESX	**VMware ESXi**
Service console	Yes.	No.
VI Client	Yes.	Yes.
API support	Yes.	Yes on the license version; however, it's limited to read-only on the free version.

---

[1] http://redmondmag.com/reports/article.asp?EditorialsID=679
[2] http://kb.vmware.com/selfservice/documentLink.do?externalID=1006543. Given the competition in the marketplace, the product feature can change from time to time. Be sure to check out the latest documents from VMware. Table 1-2 is based on the information of early 2009.

Table 1-2   continued

Differences between ESX and ESXi

	VMware ESX	**VMware ESXi**
Remote CLI	Host CLI is supported. ESX 3.5 Update 2 supports RCLI.	Yes through a virtual appliance. Limited to read-only access for the free version.
Scriptable installation	Yes through utilities such as KickStart.	No. But you can run a post installation configuration script using RCLI.
Boot from SAN	Yes. Booting from SAN requires one dedicated LUN per server.	No need.
Serial cable connectivity	Yes.	No.
SNMP	Yes.	No for the free version.
Active Directory integration	Yes with third-party agents installed on the service console.	No for the free version. When licensed and with VirtualCenter, you can log in directly to an ESXi host and authenticate using a local username and password.
HW instrumentation	Through agents in the service console.	Through CIM providers.
Software patches and updates	Similar to traditional Linux-based patches and updates.	More like firmware patches and updates.
VI Web access	Yes.	No.
Licensing	Licensed as part of VI.	Free edition or licensed as part of VI.

VirtualCenter Server

The management server manages multiple ESX servers. Beyond what is available in ESX server, the VC server provides much more advanced management features, including these:

- VMotion and storage VMotion features to allow live migration of a running virtual machine from one ESX host to another, and relocating virtual machine files from one storage location to another.

- Clustering, a feature to group many ESX hosts to achieve high availability or distributed resource scheduling.

- Provisioning new virtual machines based on templates for fast and large-scale deployment.

- Alarm and scheduled task management.

- Monitoring much more and longer statistics than the ESX server.

The server runs on Microsoft Windows and Linux and requires database management systems: either Oracle or Microsoft SQL Server.

VI Client

The VI Client is the standard GUI to manage the VI, both ESX server and VC server. It is a Windows application built on top of .NET using C#.

Interestingly, the VI Client uses the same interfaces as the VI SDK to communicate with the two types of servers. It is, in fact, the most complete SDK application because it touches almost every aspect of the management.

Whatever you can do with a VI Client, you can almost do the same in your own application using the VI SDK. Observing what the VI Client does is a good way to become familiar with basic concepts behind the VI SDK.

VMware Management APIs

For a platform company like VMware, it's critical to have an ecosystem around the core virtualization platforms. To enable partners and customers, VMware has released a full set of APIs besides management APIs, including VMsafe API, Virtual Disk Development Kit, ESX Device Development Kit, and CIM Provider Development Kit. You can check out the details from the VMware developer site.[3]

---

[3] http://communities.vmware.com/community/developer

Given the focus of this book, only the management APIs are introduced. These APIs can be used together for a comprehensive solution. For example, you can have a solution in which you use GuestSDK to develop an agent, the VI SDK for the backend server, and CIM to collect hardware information such as fan temperatures.

Each API/toolkit has its own focus, strengths, and weaknesses. Some of them provide duplicate information. You have to make a best choice for your own requirements and design constraints.

VI SDK

The VI SDK facilitates development of applications that target the VI API. The VI API is exposed as a Web service on VMware Infrastructure 3 platforms (ESX Server, VirtualCenter Server).

The VI SDK is based on Web Services, so it is platform/programming language independent. You can use any major programming language to develop your application or automation scripts.

Most VI SDK applications are client-side applications, but the VI SDK actually provides more than that. A few interfaces are really for server integrations, which will be highlighted along the way. You can also integrate your server application or agent with the VMware Infrastructure using the VI SDK.

The VI SDK works with both ESX and VC now, and in the future it might work with more virtualization platforms like VMware Server and Workstation.[4] In the long run, it's not only about VMware Infrastructure, but a standardized management API for other virtualization platforms.

In addition to the VI SDK, VMware has released the VI Perl toolkit and the VI Toolkit (for Windows) (see Chapter 17, "Scripting the VI SDK with Jython, Perl, and PowerShell"). Both use scripting languages; the latter uses Microsoft PowerShell. There is open source VI Java API that I created (see Chapter 5, "Introducing the VI Java API").

---

[4] VMware Server 2.0 has experimental support on the interface.

CIM APIs

The VMware CIM APIs provide Common Information Model (CIM) interfaces for developers to build management applications. With the VMware CIM APIs, developers can use the standards-based CIM-compliant applications to manage ESX servers. Unlike the VI SDK, CIM APIs work only with ESX hosts including ESXi, not VC server.

Two sets of profiles are supported in two different packages:

- The Storage Management Initiative Specification (SMI-S) profiles in the VMware CIM SDK, for ESX 3.0/3.5. The profiles allow CIM clients to explore the virtual machines on an ESX host, along with associated storage resources.
- The DMTF's System Management Architecture for Server Hardware (SMASH) compatible profiles in the CIM SMASH/Server Management API, for ESX(i) 3.5. The profiles allow CIM clients to monitor the system health of a managed server.

VIX API

The VIX API enables you to develop scripts and programs that automate virtual machine operations. The API is high level, easy to use, and practical for both script writers and application developers. It runs on VMware Server and Workstation products, both Windows and Linux. Bindings are provided for C, Perl, and COM (Visual Basic, VBScript, C#). As of version 1.6.2, the VIX API supports VI.

GuestSDK

GuestSDK is a set of read-only APIs for monitoring various statistics of a virtual machine, such as memory usage, CPU speed and CPU shares, elapsed time since last virtual machine power-on or reset, and ESX Server host system CPU time scheduled for specific virtual machine CPUs. Management agents or other software running in the guest operating system on the virtual machine can use this data at the application layer.

GuestSDK is available on Windows and Linux guest OSs with VMware Tools installed. You can use C or Java (supported via wrapper classes) as your programming language.

VMware VMCI

The Virtual Machine Communication Interface (VMCI) supports fast and efficient communication between a virtual machine and the host operating system and between two or more virtual machines on the same host. This API is available in VMware Server 2.0 and Workstation 6.5.

Legacy APIs

These APIs include VMware Perl API for Linux (Perl on ESX 3.x, ESX Server 2.x, and GSX Server), VMware Perl API for Windows, and VMware COM API for Windows. These APIs are deprecated in favor of the VI SDK and toolkits are built around it.

Other APIs

Another set of management APIs are designed for products built on top of VI, such as Lab Manager SOAP API,[5] and Site Recovery Manager API.[6] Most of these APIs are based on Web Services, and they're relatively smaller and simpler than the VI SDK. They can help you to manage, customize, and automate the target products.

Summary

This chapter introduced the basic concepts and history of virtualization and how you might benefit from this virtual computing. In addition, it provided an overview of various families of products that VMware provides, and different management APIs. As you have found, the VI SDK plays a pivotal role in the virtualization of system management.

---

[5] http://www.vmware.com/support/pubs/labmanager_pubs.html
[6] http://www.vmware.com/support/pubs/srm_pubs.html

Chapter 2

VI SDK Basics

This chapter introduces the basic concepts of the VI SDK and lays the foundation for you to move forward to programming in successive chapters. These basic concepts include Web Services, the VI SDK object model from managed objects to data objects, and faults. This chapter also illustrates several basic tools to familiarize you with the object model and how the objects are related. The object model is critical to mastering the programming interfaces along the way, because these interfaces are simply "views" to these objects in the model. Finally, this chapter shows you how to effectively use the VI SDK API reference and get help from various resources, such as online communities.

Overview of the VI SDK

The VI SDK provides a complete set of management interfaces to the VMware Infrastructure. Everything is centered on Web Services, a popular communication method after RPC, CORBA, and Java RMI. Unlike its predecessors, Web Services uses XML to describe the request and response messages; therefore, it's easier for people to read the messages and for it to be supported on almost all the platforms and programming languages.

Web Services defines the interfaces and can be supported by different underlying communication protocols. Simple Object Access Protocol (SOAP) is the underlying protocol in the VI SDK (see Figure 2-1).

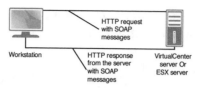

Figure 2-1   The Web Services request and response

As a developer, you don't need to know too many details about how SOAP works, because most of the time you work with methods generated from Web Services Definition Language (WSDL). But it's a big help if you can understand the SOAP messages while debugging and analyzing logs from the servers or other applications. Appendix E, "VI SDK Web Services," provides a detailed introduction.

What Is Included in VI SDK 2.5?

Included in the VI SDK 2.5 package are WSDL files, pregenerated client stub JAR files, documentation, and samples. The `wsdl` directory includes two subdirectories: `vim` and `vim25`. The `vim` subdirectory contains two WSDL files of SDK 2.0 for managing ESX3.0/VirtualCenter 2.0. The `vim25` subdirectory contains two WSDL files of SDK 2.5 for managing ESX3.5/VirtualCenter 2.5. Two namespaces are used for each set of WSDL files. You'll read more details about these WSDL files in Appendix E.

To save developers time, two pregenerated and compiled Java client libraries (`vim.jar` and `vim25.jar`) from WSDL using AXIS 1.4 are included. So you don't need to regenerate these client stubs for development and testing purposes.

The documentation includes an API reference, Javadoc for sample code, a porting guide, an installation guide, and more. The most important one is the API reference. More details on how to use it effectively come at the end of this chapter.

Two sets of samples are included. One set is written in Java using the AXIS-generated stubs, and the other set is written in C# using stubs generated from Microsoft tools.

Object Model

The core part of the VI SDK is the object model behind the Web Services interfaces. Given the procedural nature of Web Services, object type definition is not available in the WSDL, nor is it in the generated stubs from the WSDL. Even so, you have to know the missing information to use the VI SDK effectively. How do you accomplish this?

Fortunately, the API reference has provided a complete picture of the object model. Through your development, the API reference is your best source of the object model.

The VI SDK object model contains three types of objects:

- **Managed objects**—Server-side object representing either a manageable entity or a service

- **Data objects (including enumeration)**—An aggregate of information for either passing parameters to the Web Services call or getting returns from the Web Services call

- **Faults**—A data structure representing an exceptional case that applications should handle

There is one special type called ManagedObjectReference, which is indeed a data object type, but it's used to represent managed objects on the client side. Given its importance and possible confusion, it has its own dedicated section in this chapter.

The managed object type is the most confusing part of the entire VI SDK. On one hand, people talk a lot about managed objects. Basically nothing meaningful can be done without a managed object. On the other hand, you don't see a single managed object in the VI SDK sample code. Most users wonder what is happening when they first come to use the VI SDK. Why are managed objects missing? What should you do with them? The section "Managed Objects" answers these questions.

Unified Interface with Different Support

One key decision by the VI SDK designers was to keep the interfaces the same for both the VC server and the ESX server. Of course, there is a big difference in functionalities between VC and ESX. Some interfaces are not implemented or supported in one or the other. Overall, the VC has much broader functionalities than ESX or ESXi.

To make the API consistent between ESX and VC, the inventory structure has the same design. So the tree navigation process is identical. The difference comes with quantities and the exact types of managed objects in the hierarchy. Figure 2-4 (shown later in this chapter) shows the hierarchy of ESX inventory. Figure 6-1 (in Chapter 6, "Managing Inventory") shows the hierarchy of VirtualCenter inventory.

The advantage of this design is that you can use the same code to work with both the VC server and the ESX server, whichever best meets your requirement.

As a rule of thumb, connecting to the VirtualCenter server is better than connecting directly to the host. As mentioned, the VirtualCenter server has much broader support of the interfaces than the ESX server does. Cross-host features and advanced features are available only in the VirtualCenter server. Instead of having multiple sessions to the ESX servers, you can have one session for all, which creates fewer management hassles. Furthermore, because VirtualCenter manages old versions of ESX servers, you don't need to worry about versioning in a heterogeneous environment. Lastly, you just need to authenticate with VirtualCenter rather than with multiple ESX servers, so things are more secure.

Managed Objects

Managed objects are server-side objects, representing real managed entities or services provided by the servers. A managed entity can be a virtual machine or a physical host system. A service can be an authentication service or a performance management service.

Inheritance Hierarchy

VI SDK 2.5 has about 63 types of managed object types defined. All these managed object types relate to each other in an inheritance hierarchical structure, which is shown in Figure 2-2.

More managed objects will be added in future releases of the VI SDK when additional functionalities are added into the core platforms. At that time, the new managed object types will further crowd the UML diagram and make it hard to fit into one page.

Although the concept of managed object is there, the SDK API reference doesn't have an explicit type defined as ManagedObject. To make the hierarchy complete, it is added to the top of the entire structure. In the VI Java API covered in Chapter 5, "Introducing the VI Java API," ManagedObject is a key type that encapsulates several common properties and behaviors.

Among all the managed objects, ServiceInstance is one of the most important because it is the starting point of all the managed objects when you connect to a

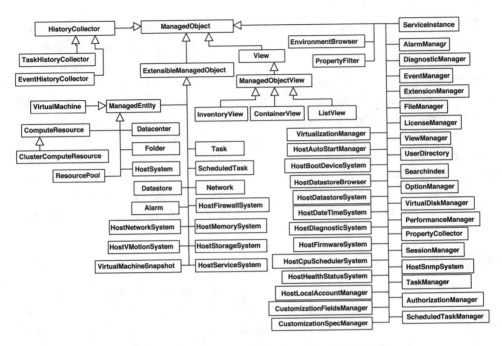

Figure 2-2 The inheritance hierarchy of managed object types in VI SDK 2.5

server; it's either an ESX or a VC server. From the ServiceInstance object, you can get its property serviceContent, which aggregates all the ManagedObjectReference (MOR) objects to the 21 managed objects on the right side of the UML diagram. All these managed objects are singleton objects, meaning there is only one instance of the managed type under one ServiceInstance object. Some of these singleton managed objects might not be present depending on the type of server. For example, ExtensionManager is not available on the ESX(i) server.

> If you are connected to VirtualCenter, you cannot get hold of the ServiceInstance for the ESX servers that are managed by that VirtualCenter.

A similar pattern is repeated with HostSystem. From a HostSystem object's property configManager, you can get all the MORs to the 16 singleton objects closely attached to it, such as HostFirewallSystem and HostHealthStatusSystem. If you connect to the VirtualCenter server, there can be multiple instances of these singleton objects in the whole system scope, but there is only one instance in the scope of a single HostSystem.

The HostLocalAccountManager is a managed object that manages the user accounts at the ESX server. It is available only when you connect to an ESX server. Interestingly enough, it's attached to ServiceInstance, but it really should be attached to the HostSystem.

You can get the MOR of the root folder of the inventory tree from the ServiceInstance. From that root folder, you can navigate to all the entities you want to manage or retrieve information from. See Chapter 6 for more details on the inventory tree structure and navigation.

ManagedEntity is also an important managed object type. Everything you can find in the inventory tree is a subtype of ManagedEntity. The subtypes include VirtualMachine, HostSystem, ComputerResource, ResourcePool, Datacenter, and Folder. ComputerResource is further inherited by ClusterComputerResource to support advanced features such as HA and DRS. To do something meaningful with the VI SDK, you will most likely work with these managed entities. The managed entities are also the only managed objects you can exercise permission control over. Given managed objects' importance, Chapters 6-11 cover them exclusively in detail.

Appendix A, "The Managed Object Types," describes all the managed object types in VI SDK 2.5. Note that all the types with * after the names are experimental in the 2.5 release and subject to change in the future release. You should be aware of the implications while using these managed objects in your application.

Inventory Hierarchy

The inventory is structured like a tree in which various ManagedEntity objects are linked with a parent-child relationship. This relationship is an association between two instances, not two types.

Figure 2-3 shows the hierarchy of inventory in an ESX server. The inventory of the VC server is similar in structure but different in quantities and possibly nesting structures. One obvious difference is that there is one and only one HostSystem in an ESX inventory tree, and zero to many HostSystem instances in the VC server inventory tree. See Chapter 6 for more details.

Properties

Like any other object in an object-oriented programming language, each managed object has properties and methods defined. Only a few managed objects do not have either a property or a method defined on themselves.

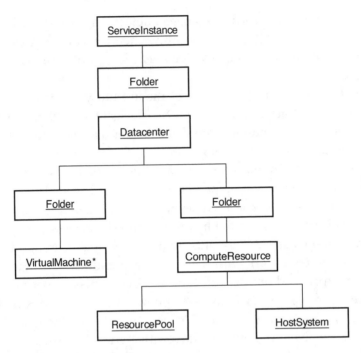

Figure 2-3   The inventory tree structure of an ESX server

The properties of managed objects can be as follows:

- Primitive data types such as integer, string, Boolean, and byte.
- Data object types. These are the most common types for properties defined on managed object types. The name comes from a well-known design pattern in which multiple primitive data types are aggregated together and passed over the network to save bandwidth and calls from the client to the server.

  This aggregation also helps to group similar information for easy management. For example, the VirtualMachineRuntimeInfo data object groups all the runtime information of a virtual machine.

- ManagedObjectReference pointing to another managed object. To represent and identify a managed object, a ManagedObjectReference object is used on the client side. ManagedObjectReference is essentially a data object that can be easily passed back and forth between the client and the server.
- Array of any of the above.

In the VI SDK, most properties are well named after their purposes. Most of them follow naming conventions. You can easily tell their meanings and intended usages from their names.

Some naming conventions are different from industry general practices. For example, the designers could have used plural forms for an array type of data, perhaps using Datastores instead of Datastore for an array of Datastore objects. One of the reasons for not using the plural is that the variable names are serialized into XML tag names in the SOAP message. Using plural names makes the SOAP messages look awkward. For example, if Datastores was used as the name for an array of datastores, the SOAP message would look like the following. Each tag essentially holds the information of only one datastore.

```
<datastores>...</datastores> ... <datastores>...</datastores>
```

You can find a few naming inconsistencies. For instance, in some places "obj" is used for a managed object, whereas in other places "key" is used. These issues are minor and do not affect your understanding of the whole SDK.

Note the existence of some duplicate information among the properties of the same managed object. For example, the VirtualMachine object has a property called summary that contains a superset of the information in the runtime property. If you already have the summary retrieved, you don't need to get the runtime anymore. This duplication pattern is repeated with several other managed entities that have summary and runtime properties defined.

Unlike a typical object in an object-oriented programming language, a managed object doesn't provide you direct access to these properties or any getter/setter method. To obtain any property of any managed object, you have to use the PropertyCollector, which is itself a managed object. The PropertyCollector is powerful yet hard to use. More details will be covered in Chapter 4, "Using PropertyCollector and SearchIndex."

In contrast to most modern object-oriented environments, the VI SDK does not use setter methods. There are 11 methods whose names seem like setters, but they really are not. For example, CustomFieldsManager has a property field of type CustomFieldDef[] and a method SetField. From the following signature of the method, you can tell it's not a setter to change the property field.

```
public void setField(com.vmware.vim25.ManagedObjectReference _this,
com.vmware.vim25.ManagedObjectReference entity, int key, java.lang.String value)
throws java.rmi.RemoteException, com.vmware.vim25.RuntimeFault;
```

The closest setter method is the method SetLocale defined on SessionManager, which is used to change the property defaultLocal. For some reason, it doesn't follow the setter convention to be named SetDefaultLocal. Other than this, it's a perfect setter method.

In general, you don't use setter methods to change the properties directly. All the properties are self-maintained by the managed objects. If you do want to change their values, just call defined methods to change them indirectly. Some methods named as reconfig*(), such as reconfigVM_Task(), are obviously for this purpose.

Methods

VI SDK 2.5 has 375 methods defined on all the managed object types. These methods cover all the major aspects of VI management. Each method defines the parameters, return type, and faults that can be raised. Most of the parameters and return values are of data object types to be covered in the next section.

> The method names in the API reference always start with uppercase, whereas in Java the equivalent methods start with lowercase. They mean the same thing and are used interchangeably in later discussions.

You can sometimes find the managed object type names in the method names, which is not necessary in the object-oriented world. But the managed object type is missing in the WSDL, and all the methods are flattened. To avoid method name clashing or to make the method explicit, the managed object type is added to the method name. For example, the reconfigVM_Task() method has VM as part of its name.

Because some methods have complicated data objects as parameters, their usage becomes complicated as well. On one hand, you might have to prepare complicated data objects nested with other data objects for layers. On the other hand, the parameters can actually change the behavior of the method. For example, the updateNetworkConfig() method defined on HostNetworkSystem takes in changeMode to specify whether it's a "modify" or "replace." Furthermore, the properties in the

HostNetworkConfig parameter, such as HostVirtualNicConfig, have changeOperation to specify whether it's "add," "edit," or "remove." Combined, they are much more complicated than any method you can find from conventional interfaces. They may take more than ten times the effort to understand them.

For these methods, it's crucial to understand the data object types for the parameters. To get there, you need to understand VI basic concepts. If you are familiar with how VI works in related management areas, you will find it much easier to understand these data object types. I will explain additional basic concepts while discussing these methods and data object types along the way.

The API reference also indicates the required privileges for the methods. Normally one method requires one privilege, but it might require different privileges depending on the target and input. If the login user does not have the permission, the method cannot be completed. Even if a method can be executed, the result might be different depending on the permissions the user has on the managed entities on which that method operates.

In the WSDL and generated stub, this information is lost. No formal way exists to validate the required privileges from the language. You have to check the API reference for the privileges. See Chapter 15, "User and License Administration," for more details about the security model in the VI SDK.

Some methods are sensitive to the state of the managed entity when they are called. For instance, the powerOnVM_Task() method should not be called when the virtual machine is already in the powered on state or the InvalidState fault is thrown.

On the ManagedEntity, there is a disabledMethod property that holds an array of disabled methods of the entity. This list takes into account the state of the entity but not the privilege of the login user over the entity. You cannot rely on this information to validate the privilege.

Like other APIs, the VI SDK might provide more than one method to get your work done. For example, to change the name of a virtual machine, you can use either rename_Task() defined on ManagedEntity or reconfigVM_Task() on the VirtualMachine.

The VI SDK also has a few methods that work on multiple entities or items at a time. These methods are not atomic, however, which means they do not roll back when returning due to errors in the middle. All the entities or items already processed and to be processed keep their states as the errors happened. You have to handle the issue on your own. The easiest and, unfortunately, the slowest way to take care of this is to work on only one entity or item at a time.

Some of the methods are really for server integration in which another server application can leverage the existing infrastructure of the VirtualCenter. Without this context in mind, some methods might be hard to understand and justify.

For example, the updateProgress() method defined on the Task managed object is never used by a client application; therefore, it's not interesting for a client-side application developer. Together with the createTask() method defined on TaskManager, a server application can post a new Task that can be tracked by all the clients and update its progress continuously.

Synchronous versus Asynchronous Methods

Some methods defined on managed objects are asynchronous, meaning they return right away whether the operations are done successfully or not. That makes sense for long-running operations; you don't want to block your current thread by waiting for the return of the call, and you might want to cancel it before it's done.

For these asynchronous methods, the VI SDK provides a way to track the progress and results after the invocation is returned. As a naming convention, a long-running asynchronous method has _Task as a suffix in the method name, and it returns MOR to a Task.[1] With MOR pointing to the Task object, you can track the progress and even get the result of the operation. For example, the cloneVM_Task() method defined in VirtualMachine is a long-running method that returns MOR pointing to a Task managed object.

In your application code, you can choose to ignore the MOR task and move on to other things, wait for the task to be finished before moving on, or spawn a thread to monitor the task and move on.[2]

---

[1] All these methods incur Task objects on the server side. But there are other methods with no Task in name and returning no Task can also incur Tasks as well. For example, the renameSnapshot() method doesn't return a Task, but it does create one. You can find more with description.methodInfo property of the TaskManager.

[2] When implementing a GUI application, you should always spawn a new thread from the main thread. Failing to do so may result in the GUI freezing while your application is running. You can use different techniques and utilities to handle this. Find out the details in the specific programming language and GUI toolkit you are using.

The asynchronous methods lead to an interesting phenomenon with fault handling. Because the asynchronous method returns right away, it doesn't give you a runtime fault. But the signature has the fault, so you have to handle it even though it doesn't happen in the asynchronous call. The asynchronous method does do preliminary checking of the parameters, so you still get faults such as InvalidArgument. If the fault occurs after the Task is returned, you can get hold of the info.error property of the Task. The property is of LocalizedMethodFault; it's not a fault type but a data type wrapping a fault.

For the asynchronous methods, you can get more when the Task is finished. You can tell whether the operation is successful and if so retrieve a result from the info property of the Task managed object. Chapter 14, "Task and ScheduledTask," goes into detail about how to achieve this.

Not all the long operations are designed as asynchronous methods. For example, querying huge performance data using the queryPerf() method could be a long operation. But it's not an asynchronous method. To avoid performance problems, you should query as little information as possible with these calls. Of course, most synchronous methods take no time to finish. You can use them comfortably.

It is worthwhile to mention the waitForUpdate() method of PropertyCollector, which is designed to block and returns only when the object it watches has a change. This method allows you to be notified instead of requiring you to keep polling. Because it blocks, you should have a separate thread for this method in your GUI application.

ManagedObjectReference

The most often used data object type in the entire VI SDK is the ManagedObjectReference, which represents managed objects. Although the ManagedObjectReference is closely associated with managed objects, it is indeed a data object. Its WSDL definition is shown as follows:

```
<complexType xmlns="http://www.w3.org/2001/XMLSchema"
xmlns:vim25="urn:vim25" name="ManagedObjectReference">
   <simpleContent>
      <extension base="xsd:string">
         <attribute name="type" type="xsd:string"/>
      </extension>
   </simpleContent>
</complexType>
```

The type attribute can only be one of the 63 managed object types in VI SDK 2.5. In that sense, the "type" should have been defined as an enumeration type instead of the freestyle string. The following is part of SOAP message for a property obj defined as a type of ManagedObjectReference:

```
<obj type="VirtualMachine">272</obj>
```

As you can tell, this line points to a VirtualMachine managed object whose value is 272. In this case, the value looks like an integer, but it really is a string. Some other ManagedObjectReference object might have a pure string or a mixed value. For example, a MOR pointing to a ServiceInstance has a ServiceInstance value; a MOR to Datacenter has a value of datacenter-2.

You can think of a MOR as a pointer in some sense because it uniquely identifies a managed object. Even better, you can think of the "type" and "value" defined in the MOR in the SQL way. The type is like a table name, and the value is like the primary key that can uniquely identify a managed object in its type. It explains why key is used as the property name for the ManagedObjectReference type in some data objects like AutoStartPowerInfo.

A MOR object is guaranteed to be unique within one server but not across different servers. You should not compare the MORs from two different servers. Even if they are equal in type and value, they might not be referring to the same managed object. In fact, many managed objects use the same MOR. For example, the MORs representing all ServiceInstance objects from all the servers are identical.

Regardless of whether two MORs are different or the same, the managed object they represent might or might not be the same. They could be referring to the same managed object. For example, when connecting to an ESX server directly, you will get its MOR with a value of ha-host. When a VC server manages the ESX server, the MOR retrieved from VirtualCenter has to be something like host-2596 simply because a VC server cannot distinguish several ESX servers that all have ha-host. So when you connect to the VC server and ESX server at the same time, two different MORs might refer to the same managed object. Even so, you must not use them interchangeably; for example, you should not use the MOR from the ESX server for the method calls to the VC server.

Even with the same server, if you remove one managed entity and add it back again, the MOR value might be different. That means your application might work at one time but not later if you hard-code the MOR value into your code.

There is no easy way to tell whether a MOR is still valid from the client side. If you really need to, you can retrieve a property or invoke a simple method on it and catch the exception. If it works fine, the MOR is still valid.

Some managed objects are closely related to the user session. In the MORs, session IDs are included in the values. For example, a MOR pointing to a PropertyFilter object might look like the following. Similar managed objects include these View objects that are discussed in Chapter 6.

```
<filter type="PropertyFilter">session[52e6d0f7-486b-7bab-338b-
a63a924a4098]52470a71-1250-a2c3-8c88-9b6260c7acf0</filter>
```

You should not use these MORs across different sessions, either due to a different login user or the same user logging in for a second time. In your application, you need to re-create these managed objects and use the new MORs after reconnecting to the server.

In short, MOR is really intended to be used by software and should be carefully limited to the scope of where it comes from. I will show you how to hide it from application developers in the VI Java API.

You can get MOR objects using several approaches:

- **By using its constructor and setting its type and value**—Except for these managed objects whose MOR value is well known, it is hard to obtain the value of a MOR before the object instance is available. Therefore, this approach is not used as often as the others even though it's pretty straightforward.

  The ServiceInstance is a special managed object in that it's the starting point to all other managed objects and always present. Its type and value are well known and can be used to construct a MOR as follows:

  ```
  ManagedObjectReference si_mor = new ManagedObjectReference();
  si_mor.setType("ServiceInstance");
  si_mor.set_value("ServiceInstance");
  ```

  Some other managed objects—especially these singleton ones closely attached to the ServiceInstance—also have predefined MOR values. For example, the MOR value of a TaskManager on an ESX server is normally ha-taskmgr. The MOR value of the HostSystem on an ESX server is ha-host.

The only object guaranteed is ServiceInstance. It's safer to get the objects from the content property of ServiceInstance or to retrieve them from the inventory tree in your application.

The Managed Object Browser (MOB), which is covered later in this chapter, is an excellent tool to find out the type and value of a specific managed object. With the MOB, you can call the related method without navigating to it from the ServiceInstance. Again, if you use the values from the MOB, the code can be fragile because of the reasons mentioned earlier. Nevertheless, it's not bad if you just want to code a quick sample.

- **From the return of a method call**—One good example is the createAlarm() method defined on AlarmManager, which returns a MOR to the newly created Alarm object. All six methods of SearchIndex are good examples here.

- **From the PropertyCollector**—As noted, MOR is used as the type for properties in both managed objects and data objects. Retrieving any of these properties can get you a MOR object or an array of MOR objects.

Because MOR is so closely related to a managed object, it can be interchangeable with a managed object in the discussion. A "managed object" might mean the MOR to the managed object in the code, and vice versa.

Data Objects

The data objects are an aggregation of primitive data types that can be nested within each other. They define the properties of managed objects, as well as parameters passed to the server or information returned from the server. Unlike with primitive data types, passing around these data objects can avoid multiple calls and save network traffic. This handling technique has been summarized as the Data Transfer Object (also known as Value Object) design pattern.[3]

Another advantage of using these data objects is that similar information can be grouped for better understanding and management, which reduces the learning

---

[3] http://en.wikipedia.org/wiki/Data_Transfer_Object

curve. For example, VirtualMachineRuntimeInfo is defined to group all the information that is related to a virtual machine's runtime information, including its boot time, power state, and connection state. Several other data objects are named *ConfigInfo to represent the configuration-related information associated with their corresponding managed objects.

Many more data object types are available besides managed object types. In VI SDK 2.5, about 900 data objects are defined,[4] not including the enumeration types.

Even more data objects are created in the generated client stub. So don't be surprised when you cannot find a data object called ArrayOfDynamicProperty or other array types in the API reference. These data objects are created in WSDL to handle arrays of data objects. These new types are really simple wrappers around the array of data objects.

The VI SDK API reference does provide a detailed introduction and explanation for each of the data objects, as well as its properties. When any property is defined as another data object type, you can easily navigate to that data object type by clicking the hyperlink on it. You can easily drill down to the data objects you want to know.

There are simply too many of these data object types to be covered individually. Let's focus on the general principles here. More details of the key data objects are introduced using UML diagrams in later chapters.

- Many data objects' properties are optional and need not be set, as indicated with a red asterisk in the API reference.[5] When a data object is a parameter passed in a Web Service call to the server, it means you can set only these properties you would like to change and forget about the other optional properties.

- Quite a few of the data object types are inherited from DynamicData, which has two properties defined: dynamicProperty and dynamicType. The dynamicProperty is defined as an array of the DynamicProperty data object, which has two properties—name and val—both of string type and optional.

---

[4] Some of the data objects are duplicated. For example, the TypeDescription and ElementDescription have the same definitions.

[5] When a data object is returned from the server, its properties might be null, so you need to check before you use these parameters. In Java, you can easily get a NullPointerException if you forget to do so.

The dynamicType is defined as an optional string type. Figure 2-4 shows the UML diagram for this super type.

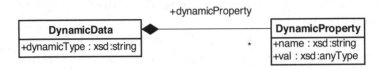

Figure 2-4   The DynamicData data object

The intention for this design was to have a scalable data structure to add more properties while sticking to the same structure. It is, however, not implemented as such consistently. The side effect is that every data object inherited from there has inherited extra properties. This is not really a big deal given that languages like Java are not really memory conscientious.

In general, all the data object types are named according to their purpose. For example, the *Spec data objects, such as VirtualMachineConfigSpec, are normally used to hold change specification sent to the servers. To change anything on the server side, you most likely need a Spec object. The other obvious group of data objects is *Info, such as ClusterRuleInfo, which usually represents one aspect of information of a managed object.

A property of a data object can be any of the following types:

- Primitive data type such as string, integer, Boolean, or byte.
- Data object type, including itself. Some of the data object types can recursively include themselves to many levels. For example, the VirtualMachineSnapshotTree data object includes an array of the same type as the child snapshots.
- Enumeration type, to be discussed soon.
- Array of primitive data or data objects.
- Any type. This is a special XML type (xsd:anyType), meaning it can be any data type. It can be considered as the topmost type that is extended by other types, such as the java.lang.Object in Java. You really need to pay attention when a property is claimed as such. In general, you need to know what the possible types are and check the real type at runtime before you use it.

Property Path Notation

Data objects can be nested within each other or even within themselves. Some of the complicated data objects can have several layers of nesting before you can obtain the primitive data.

To identify a property nested in layers of data objects starting from a managed object, use property path notation as in the following format:

```
x.y.z
```

Each part of the path that is separated by the dot is a property name, not the type of the property. The type of the path is determined by the last property in the path. The following is a quick example of a property path that points to an integer defined in ShareInfo embedded all the way up to VirtualMachineConfigInfo:

```
config.cpuAllocation.shares.shares
```

In general, a property path starts with an immediate property of a managed object and can stop anywhere down to the primitive data types. For example, config.cpuAllocation points to a data object of type ResourceAllocationInfo.

If there is a property in an array of some objects, you can represent one of them by specifying the index or key of the property, as in the following. To use the second notation, the data object type z must have a property named key.

```
x.y.z[0]
```

or

```
x.y.z["123"]
```

Note that the property path works only with data objects, and it cannot pass through a managed object. Therefore, if you have any property in the path of type ManagedObjectReference, you should stop there. For example, the following path with VirtualMachine is illegal, because currentSnapshot is a ManagedObjectReference pointing to a VirtualMachineSnapshot managed object.[6]

---

[6] The VI SDK API reference has a page for each data object and managed object type. Check the type before the type name. The page for VirtualMachineSnapshot shows "Managed Object— VirtualMachineSnapshot" at the top of the page.

`snapshot.currentSnapshot.alternateGuestName`

More than one path might be available to the information you want. For example, with the `HostSystem`, the `summary.runtime` and `runtime` actually give you the same information.

Also, different managed objects' property paths can point to the same information. For example, when connecting to an ESX server, the `content.about` from `ServiceInstance` and `summary.config.product` from `HostSystem` return you the same `AboutInfo` data object.

Property path notation is helpful while it's used with `PropertyFilterSpec`. `PropertyCollector` can then fetch the primitive data or a data object embedded deeply in another data object without grabbing all the upper-level data objects. It can save quite some bandwidth and processing power when it comes to big data objects like `VirtualMachineConfigInfo`.

A path with an index or key does not work with `PropertyCollector`. You have to stop at the array and locate the element on your client side. Also, you cannot include a subproperty that is specific to an extended type. For example, the `Datastore` object has a property called `info` whose type `DatastoreInfo` is extended by `VmfsDatastoreInfo` and others. `VmfsDatastoreInfo` has one extra property called `vmfs`. You cannot use `info.vmfs` with the property collector even though the real type of the info is `VmfsDatastoreInfo`. But it's okay to include any property defined in the base type, such as `info.name`.

Enumeration Types

One special type of data object is the enumeration type. About 108 enumeration types are defined in VI SDK 2.5.

Unlike the typical data object, these enumeration types predefine a set of values. You have to choose one from these values. For example, `TaskInfoState` is an enumeration type that defines four constants: error, queued, running, and success.

These four constant names should be self-explanatory. The WSDL definition for the `TaskInfoState` is as follows:

```
<simpleType xmlns="http://www.w3.org/2001/XMLSchema"
xmlns:vim25="urn:vim25" name="TaskInfoState">
  <restriction base="xsd:string">
  <enumeration value="queued"/>
  <enumeration value="running"/>
  <enumeration value="success"/>
  <enumeration value="error"/>
  </restriction>
</simpleType>
```

Some of the properties in data objects have to be set with one of the predefined values, but they are not defined as an enumeration type. One such example is the `type` of `ManagedObjectReference` data object.

Fault Types

A fault is like an exception in Java or another modern programming language. It's a data structure that holds information about an exceptional situation. Most of the faults are raised by the server; you can normally determine the cause from their fault names.

Approximately 247 fault types are defined in the VI SDK 2.5. Let's look at the overall hierarchy shown in Figure 2-5.

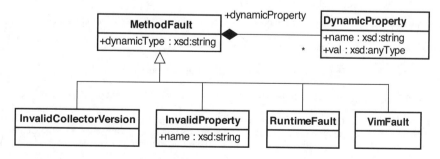

Figure 2-5   The fault type overview in VI SDK 2.5

The supertype for all faults is MethodFault. It is extended by InvalidCollectorVersion, InvalidProperty, RuntimeFault, and VimFault. The first two faults are not further extended to any other fault types.

Each of the last two fault types has a pretty big subtype hierarchy underneath. RuntimeFault is the base for all runtime faults that a method can throw. Please don't confuse RuntimeFault with RuntimeException in Java. RuntimeException does not require you to catch it explicitly. RuntimeFault does, even though it is intended to be like RuntimeException. Optionally, you can declare to throw it in the containing method signature.

When client-side stubs are generated from WSDL, the faults are mapped to language-specific exception types. In the AXIS-generated Java stubs, the MethodFault type becomes a subclass of java.rmi.RemoteException, while the hierarchy underneath remains the same. If you catch RemoteException in your code, you are going to catch all the possible faults. In general, you should not catch RemoteException or MethodFault unless you don't want to handle the specific fault types. It's a good practice, though, to catch RemoteException after you catch the more specific fault types, but not the other way around.

To understand exception handling, you should look at these basic fault types so that you can understand the scenarios in which the faults are thrown and handle them accordingly in your application. Table 2-1 lists several common fault types.

Table 2-1

Common Fault Types in VI SDK 2.5	
Name	**Causes**
InvalidArgument	The set of arguments passed to the function is not specified correctly.
InvalidState	The operation failed due to the current state of the system.
InvalidName	The name contains an invalid character or format.
NoPermission	An operation is denied because of a privilege not held on a managed object.
NotSupported	The method is not supported on the server. Not all methods are supported on all servers. An ESX server host supports less functionality than a VirtualCenter server. A feature might also be disabled due to missing licenses.
TaskInProgress	An operation tries to access an entity that already has another (long) operation in progress.

Table 2-1   continued

Common Fault Types in VI SDK 2.5

Name	Causes
Timedout	A server abandons an operation that is taking longer than expected.
OutOfBounds	A parameter exceeds the acceptable range of values.
NotFound	A referenced component of a managed object cannot be found. The referenced component can be a data object type (such as a role or permission) or a primitive (such as a string).
AlreadyExists	An attempt is made to add an element to a collection, if the element's key, name, or identifier already exists in that collection.

The concrete fault types sometimes have extra properties defined to show you the information specific to the fault. For example, TaskInProgress defines a property called task to hold the MOR to the task already in progress. With this information you can tell with which task your last invocation was in conflict.

LocalizedMethodFault is a misleading type. Although its name suggests it's a fault type, it's in fact a data object that wraps a fault along with a localized display message for the fault. The localized message is optional so that clients are not required to send a localized message to the server, but servers are required to send the localized message to clients.

Using Tools to Become Familiar with Object Model

You can take advantage of several tools to familiarize yourself with the VI SDK object model, including the VI Client, Web Access, MOB, and the Web-based datastore browser. Each one of them has pros and cons. Used collectively, they can sharpen your understanding of the object model.

VI Client

The VI Client is the standard graphical user interface to manage either ESX server or VirtualCenter server. It comes with the product by default. After you install the ESX server or VC server, you can point your browser to the VI Client and download the VI Client binary there.

As mentioned earlier, the VI Client is built on top of the .NET platform using C#. It's the most complete application you can find that uses Web Service interfaces, because it touches almost every aspect of VI management.

The VI Client GUI looks like any other typical Windows application with a main menu and toolbars, a left pane with various types of hierarchical trees, and a main content pane in the middle. The content pane is normally equipped with multiple tabs, reflecting different aspects of contents associated with the managed object selected from the left tree.

> The path you see in the inventory tree of the VI Client is *not* the path that many VI SDK methods expect. To make the tree visually friendly, the VI Client ignores part of the standard inventory path. For example, you don't see a vm folder in the inventory path as expected by a VI SDK call. To make sure you get the path right, check the MOB.

Because the functionalities of the ESX and VC servers are different, the GUI of the VI Client looks slightly different when connecting to them. Figure 2-6 and Figure 2-7 are two screenshots of the VI Client connecting to an ESX and a VC server, respectively. As you would expect, the VC one has many more GUI components than the ESX one.

The VI Client has a very good help system, as you would expect from a typical Windows application. Just click Help, Help Topics to bring up the Help window.

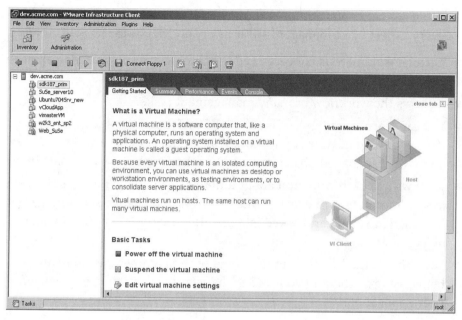

Figure 2-6 A screenshot of the VI Client when it connects to an ESX server

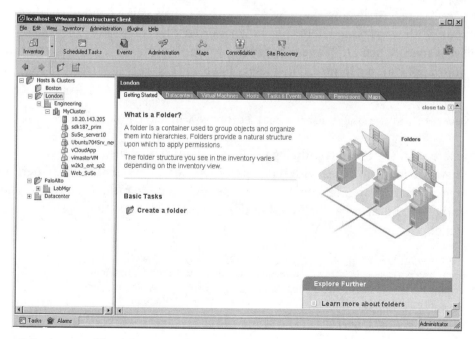

Figure 2-7 A screenshot of the VI Client when it connects to a VirtualCenter server

The VI Client is important for end users and even for VI SDK users, because it covers every aspect of VI management. It has many values for VI SDK developers:

- It explains numerous concepts and terminologies from a user's perspective, which makes them easier to understand.
- It shows the workflow of many management tasks.
- You can learn from the VI Client what SOAP operations are invoked and do the same thing in your application. It's extremely helpful when you don't know what managed object and what methods to use to get what you want.
- It shows lots of information about different managed objects, and it asks lots of information in wizards when you want to change something. The information shown and asked is more often than not mapped to data objects and their properties.
- You can use the VI Client to test some of the parameter combinations before you put them in your code. That can save you time on debugging your application.

If you would like to see what SOAP messages are sent and received at the VI client, you can run your client with the -log +n option to turn on the logging of SOAP messages. Analyzing these SOAP messages gives you a good idea of what methods, with what parameters, and in what order they should be called to achieve a specific task. In some sense, you can think of the VI Client as a giant, and your application can just follow its footsteps.

The log files are in the following directory:

```
C:\Documents and Settings\<user>\Local Settings\Application Data\VMware\vpx
```

where <user> is the currently logged in Windows username.

There are many log files with name patterns such as viclient-*.log, where * is an integer number ranging from 0 to the maximum log file number minus 1. The currently used number can be found in the viclient-index.xml file, as shown in the following:

```
<?xml version="1.0"?>
<LogSettings xmlns:xsi="http://www.w3.org/2001/XMLSchema-instance"
xmlns:xsd="http://www.w3.org/2001/XMLSchema" xmlns="www.vmware.com">
  <MaxLogFiles>10</MaxLogFiles>
  <NextIndex>5</NextIndex>
</LogSettings>
```

The tag there is NextIndex, which means you should subtract the number by 1 to get the real current number. If it's 0, the current number is the maximum log file number minus 1.

To monitor the complete communication between the VI Client and the server, you can configure the server to use HTTP instead of the default HTTPS. (See Chapter 3, "Hello VI," for details.) In the VI Client login dialog box, enter a full URL starting with http in the IP Address / Name combo box. The URL can include the port number as well. You can use a network sniffer to monitor the HTTP traffic between the VI Client and the server. Optionally, you can find similar information in server-side logs. Again, see Chapter 3 for more details.

The VI Client is also a powerful platform. You can extend it with the ExtensionManager managed object to include your application in the GUI. You can find more in Chapter 16, "Extending the VI Client."

Web Access

Web Access is very much like the VI Client, but it's purely Web based. This means easy access from any Web browser; it also means less functionality compared to the rich VI Client in the same release. Typically, Web Access is about 18 months or one major release behind what is available in the VI Client. Figure 2-8 shows a screen shot of the Web Access user interface.

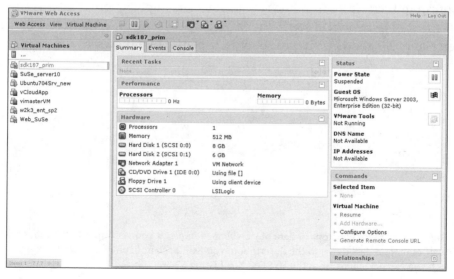

Figure 2-8   Web Access

Because Web Access is similar to the VI Client, most descriptions and discussions regarding the VI Client still hold true for Web Access. Normally you would not consider Web Access unless you didn't have the VI client installed.

Managed Object Browser (MOB)

The MOB is a Web-based application that allows you to navigate all the managed objects in the hierarchy. In fact, it covers not only the managed objects, but also data objects that are properties of the managed objects. For the nested data objects, you can drill down anywhere as you like.[7]

The MOB is a critical tool for VI SDK developers because it can display information per object base and show the associations of all the managed objects and data objects. Better than the VI Client, it can also show you information invisible on the VI Client, such as the ManagedObjectReference value.

The inventory path in the MOB is different from what you see in the VI Client inventory tree. The navigation of these objects in the MOB is the same as in the VI SDK. When you are not sure how to get a piece of information using the VI SDK, find it with the MOB first and then repeat your discovery path with the VI SDK.

The MOB is easily accessible. To use it, just enter the link as the following:

```
https://<hostname_or_IP_address>/mob
```

The MOB then challenges you with username and password. When it asks you to confirm the certificate from the server, you can simply ignore it.

The first object you will see in the MOB is always the ServiceInstance managed object. Figure 2-9 shows a screenshot of it displayed in a browser.

---

[7] In some cases, the MOB stops at data objects. For example, if you visit the AlarmManager on the VirtualCenter and drill down to the description, you won't see action and expr there, even though you can get values from the VI SDK. See Listing 12-3.

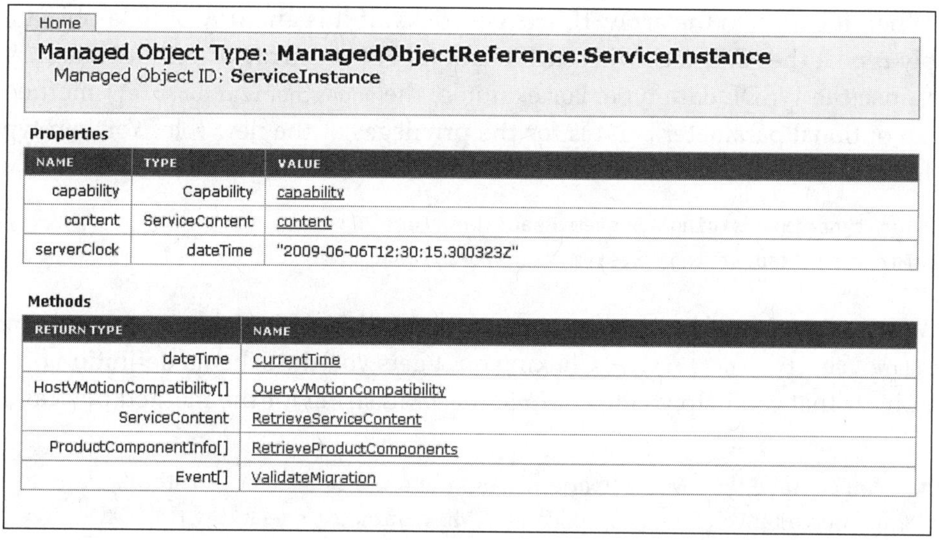

Figure 2-9 A screenshot of the MOB

Unlike what is suggested by its name, the MOB is not just about browsing and navigating around the managed objects. You can also click the hyperlinks on the methods to invoke them.[8] For example, you can click the CurrentTime method shown in the screenshot to get the time on the server.

A few methods do not require parameters, but most do. If the parameter is a primitive type, just enter its value directly. If the parameter is a data object, you need to manually compile the XML representation. For example, if a method expects a parameter called entity defined as a MOR type, the XML string you can input is like this:

```
<entity type="HostSystem">272</entity>
```

---

[8] In some cases, the methods you see in the MOB are slightly different from what you find in API reference. For example, the VirtualDiskManager has several methods whose names end with Task. Some of them don't return you Task or MOR, but void or String. When in doubt, check the API reference.

When it comes to the array, things get tricky. If it is an array of data objects, simply repeat the XML tags with each element. For the array of primitive data types, use the WSDL data type. For example, the `addAuthorizationRole()` method has an optional parameter `privIds` for the privileges of the new role. You can type the following:

```
<privIds type="xsd:string">System.Read</privIds>
<privIds type="xsd:string">System.View</privIds>
```

Within the page of each data object in the VI SDK API reference, you can find a link `Show WSDL type definition`. Clicking on it gets you the schema definition of the data object that can help you to compile the XML string for the method invocation.

> When you compile the XML, pay attention to the order of the nodes within a parent node. Before you invoke on a complicated XML parameter, check it with an XML tool. Or simply save it to a file and open it with Internet Explorer, which can help to catch common errors. Overall, the XML can be pretty error prone.

The MOB can be hacked as REST API in some sense. Table 2-2 lists several URLs to "resources" to an ESX server.[9] The returned pages include well formatted XML data which you can easily parse. The VI Java API version 2.0 (discussed in Chapter 5) includes a light-weight package that supports RESTful client API.

Table 2-2

Resource URLs Using the MOB	
Resource	**Sample URL**
ServiceInstance	GET https://<host_ip>/mob
Host	GET https://<host_ip>/mob/?moid=ha%2dhost
Virtual Machine	GET https://<host_ip>/mob/?moid=1120
Property	GET https://<host_ip>/mob/?moid=1120&doPath=config%2ehardware
Method	POST https://<host_ip>/mob/?moid=48&method=rename

---

[9] Several sample URLs are not part of a public API; therefore, they are subject to change in the future.

Given its importance, you should take the time to become familiar with the MOB. Time you spend on this now can save you more time in the future.

Web-Based Datastore Browser

This tool allows you to use a standard Web browser to browse the datastores. You can access it using the following URL:

```
https://<hostname_or_IP>/folder
```

After logging in using your username and password, you see a list of datacenters, as shown in Figure 2.10. Clicking on one of them yields the list of datastores in the datacenter. After clicking on any datastore, you can browse the virtual machine folders in the datastores. Further navigation shows the list of files in the folder.

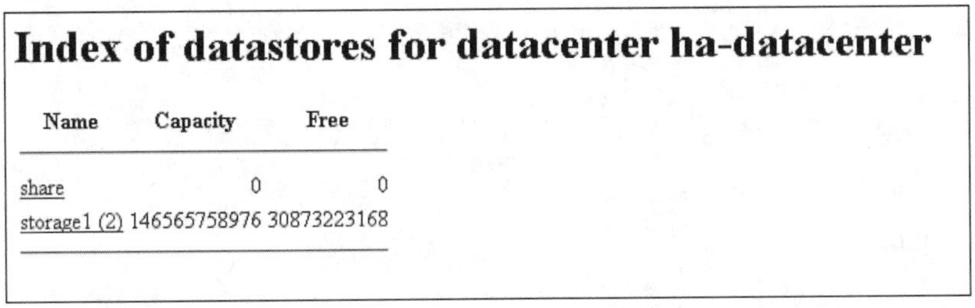

Index of datastores for datacenter ha-datacenter

Name	Capacity	Free
share	0	0
storage1 (2)	146565758976	30873223168

Figure 2-10   Web-based datastore browser

The datastore browser supports the following URL pattern:

```
http(s)://<hostname>/folder[/<path>]?dcPath=<datacenter_path>[&dsName=<datastore
_name>]
```

You can download and upload files using the URLs. Some VI SDK APIs, such as `FileManager`, use the URLs as parameters. These URLs are not easy to type in correctly, but this datastore browser helps avoid those typos.

Using the API Reference

The API reference covers almost everything and is the most complete documentation on the VI SDK. It looks very much like a typical API reference created by Javadoc.

Figure 2-11 shows the API reference in a browser. At the top left are the navigation links for different categories of types. When you click any of them, all the types in that category are shown into the bottom part of the left pane. If there are too many types to browse, you can type in part of the type name, and the matched types will appear in a pop-up window for you to choose from.

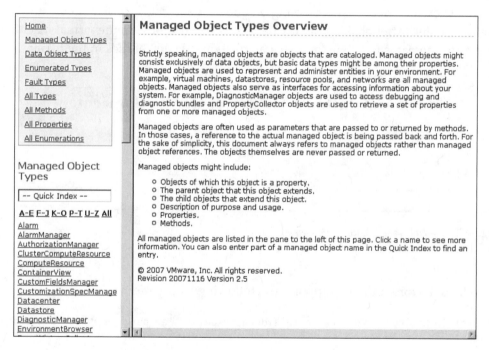

Figure 2-11   The API reference in a browser

When a type is selected, the content of that type is shown in the major content frame on the right side. All the related types, such as property or parameter types, supertypes, and subtypes, have hyperlinks so you can navigate to these related types easily.

Most of the content in the API reference was written by the designers and developers of the VI SDK, so it's the most direct and authoritative source of information. Because it's not coming from one person, the writing style and detail level are not consistent across different types. Occasionally the descriptions are not as clear as you would expect.

You just need a little time with the API reference before you can find the type you're looking for. During development, you should always have the API reference accessible. It's a good idea to bookmark it in your browser.

VMware Online Communities and Conferences

Beyond the previous resources, you can also find other resources online. The most important one is, of course, the VMware communities.[10]

VMware has many different subcommunities focusing on different products and solutions. The most relevant subcommunity is the management API community, where you can find many useful discussions about the VMware APIs. You can post a question if you cannot find an answer in any previous discussion. And it's only fair to help others when you have answers to other questions asked. It's a community where people seek help and help each other. On the open source front, the VI Java API project (http://vijava.sf.net) has an active community where you can get help.

Besides the community, VMware has set up a Developer Center Web site[11] where you can find links to all the resources you need as a developer, including various documentation, FAQs, Webinars, a knowledge base, sample code, and blogs.

---

[10] http://www.vmware.com/communities/content/
[11] http://www.vmware.com/communities/content/developer/

VMware has an annual conference, VMworld (http://www.vmworld.com/), which attracted more than 14,000 attendees in 2008. In fact, it's more than a VMware annual conference. It's open to any player in the virtualization industry. VMworld is a great opportunity for anyone to learn new virtualization technologies, share experiences, network with peers, and promote products.

For VMware partners, there are TechnologyExchange conferences where more information is shared. If you are with a VMware partner, please make sure to contact VMware for the upcoming conferences.

Summary

This chapter introduced all the basics of the VI SDK, from the Web Services interfaces to object model, including managed objects, `ManagedObjectReference`, data objects, enumeration, and faults. It also discussed the managed object inheritance hierarchy and the inventory tree structure.

To familiarize you with the basic concepts and object model, this chapter showed several tools, such as the VI Client, Managed Object Browser, Web Access, and the Web-based datastore browser.

The end of this chapter introduced the VI SDK API reference and various resources such as online communities so that you can find more information and help on VI SDK–related questions.

Chapter 3

Hello VI

This chapter introduces setting up an environment to start your VI SDK application development in Java, including VMware Infrastructure, JDK, VI SDK, and Eclipse IDE. After that, it shows the first sample code in the book followed by a brief introduction of a typical application flow. Finally, it discusses several debugging techniques, use of various logs, and common bugs you might encounter.

Setting Up the Environment

This section shows how to set up a development environment from scratch. The environment requires VMware Infrastructure, VI SDK, Java JDK, Eclipse IDE, and AXIS.

Setting Up the VMware Infrastructure

To properly set up the VMware Infrastructure, you need at least one physical server-based x86 architecture that is supported by the VMware ESX hardware compatibility list (HCL). The Systems Compatibility Guide for ESX Server 3.5 and ESX Server 3i[1] gives you a complete list of servers from various vendors that run VMware ESX.

---

[1] http://www.vmware.com/pdf/vi35_systems_guide.pdf

Optionally, you can install ESX 3.5 on VMware Player or Workstation as a VM. It can be a huge saving on your initial hardware investment. You can check out white papers from Xtravirt at http://knowledge.xtravirt.com/white-papers/esx-3x.html.

After you get your server, your ESX, and your VC software installed, you are ready to move forward. You can find instructions on how to install an ESX server in the ESX Server 3 Installation Guide—ESX Server 3.5 and VirtualCenter 2.5.[2] Just follow these instructions to set up the environment.

Optionally, you can install your VirtualCenter server on a virtual machine on the ESX server; the VC server then manages the ESX server. It's not recommended for your production environment, but it's good for development given the savings you can get. You can also create a virtual machine as your development workstation. The SDK being able to power off the virtual machine and ESX server might cause problems in some scenarios.

Installing a Java JDK

Java is our primary language for most samples across the book. To try the samples on your own machine, download a Java Development Kit (Standard edition) version 6 or newer from Sun's Java download site.[3] JDK SE 6.0_12 is used to test all the Java samples in this book.

Downloading the VI SDK, AXIS, and the VI Java API

Having successfully installed the ESX server, you can enter a URL pointing to your ESX server, such as https://192.168.218.174/, and see a welcome page as shown in Figure 3-1. Just click the Download the SDK link to download the SDK. The SDK provides JAR files pregenerated from WSDL, the API reference, and code samples.

To download AXIS, visit the AXIS Web site at http://ws.apache.org/axis/. We use AXIS 1.4. You can regenerate the JAR files from VI SDK WSDL with AXIS, but this is usually not necessary.

To download the VI Java API, visit the project at http://vijava.sf.net. This chapter uses 1.0u1, which must be used with AXIS 1.4.

---

[2] http://www.vmware.com/pdf/vi3_35/esx_3/r35/vi3_35_25_installation_guide.pdf

[3] http://java.sun.com/javase/downloads/index.jsp

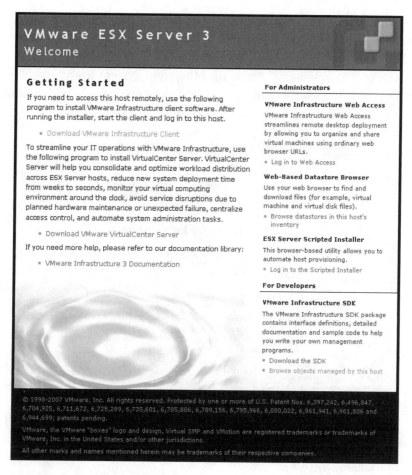

Figure 3-1 Welcome page of an ESX server

If you plan to use the new VI Java API 2.0 and beyond, you don't need to download VI SDK and AXIS. Version 2.0 includes everything that you need to get started. The samples in this and the next chapter still need 1.0.

Setting Up the Eclipse IDE

The Eclipse JDT (Java Development Tool) is one of the most popular Integrated Development Environments (IDEs) for Java development. It has all the basic and advanced features you need to develop, refactor, debug, and unit-test your Java applications. At no cost, you can download version 3.3.2 or newer, stable releases from the Eclipse download site.[4]

---

[4] http://www.eclipse.org/downloads/

The installation process is easy—just unzip the files from the zip file to a directory. After double-clicking on eclipse.exe, you see a Welcome page after the IDE is initialized.

If you are new to Eclipse, you may find the Help system useful. Just click Help, Help Contents to bring up the Help dialog box as in Figure 3-2. Take a moment to browse through Workbench User Guide and Java Development User Guide.

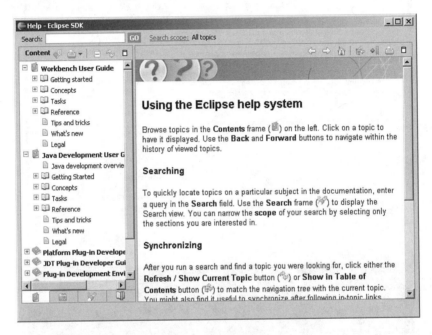

Figure 3-2 The Eclipse help system

For additional reference, you can browse the Eclipse foundation Web site. You can find many good articles at http://www.eclipse.org/articles/.

Creating Your First Application

After the environment is set up, you can start to code your first application.

1. Create a Java project with the New Project Wizard, as shown in Figure 3-3 and Figure 3-4.

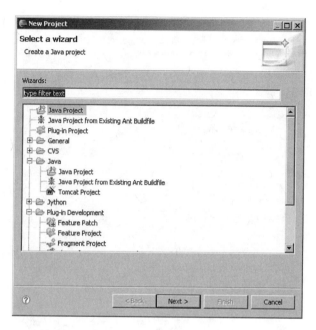

Figure 3-3 The New Project Wizard

2. Right-click the newly created project and choose Properties. In the dialog box shown in Figure 3-5, add all the needed JAR files: `activation.jar`, `axis-ant.jar`, `axis.jar`, `commons-discovery-0.2.jar`, `commons-httpclient-3.0-rc2.jar`, `commons-logging-1.0.4.jar`, `jaxrpc.jar`, `mailapi.jar`, `mo_*.jar`, `saaj.jar`, `vim25.jar`, `wsdl4j-1.5.1.jar`, `xalan.jar`, `xerces.jar`, `xml-apis.jar`. The `mo_*.jar` file is the latest JAR of the VI Java API 1.0.

   Depending on the nature of your project, you might need other JARs as well. For example, if you are developing a Java servlet, you need `servlet.jar`.

   In VI Java API 2.0 and beyond, only two JAR files are needed. Figure 3-6 shows the required Java build path in Eclipse using VI Java API 2.0. Given the simplification and performance boost, 2.0 is highly recommended for samples after Chapter 5, "Introducing the VI Java API," and your development.

3. Type in the code as listed in Listing 3-1.

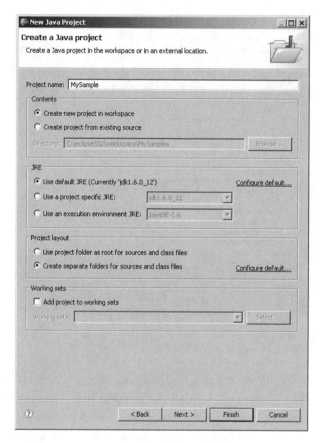

Figure 3-4 The New Project Wizard (continued)

Listing 3-1
HelloVI.java

```java
package vim.samples.ws;
import java.net.URL;
import com.vmware.vim25.*;

public class HelloVI
{
  public static void main(String[] args) throws Exception
  {
    if(args.length != 1)
    {
```

```
    System.out.println("Usage: java HelloVI <url>");
}

//ignore the SSL certificate
System.setProperty(
    "org.apache.axis.components.net.SecureSocketFactory",
    "org.apache.axis.components.net.SunFakeTrustSocketFactory"
    );

//create the interface on which services are defined
VimServiceLocator vsl = new VimServiceLocator();
VimPortType vimService = vsl.getVimPort(new URL(args[0]));

//create a ManagedObjectReference to the ServiceInstance
ManagedObjectReference siMOR = new ManagedObjectReference();
siMOR.set_value("ServiceInstance");
siMOR.setType("ServiceInstance");

//retrieve ServiceContent data object from ServiceInstance
ServiceContent sc = vimService.retrieveServiceContent(siMOR);

//get the AboutInfo object from ServiceContent
AboutInfo ai = sc.getAbout();

//print out just one of the many properties here
System.out.println("Hello " + ai.getName());
System.out.println("API type: " + ai.getApiType());
    }
}
```

4. Right-click the Java code in your Eclipse package explorer and select Run
As, Java Application. You get a line of output showing the command
usage, but then it goes nowhere. Don't worry; just go to the main menu
and select Run, Open Run Dialog. Then add the program parameter as
shown in Figure 3-7. You should change the IP address In parameter to
your server's IP. When you are done, click the Run button at the bottom of
your dialog box.

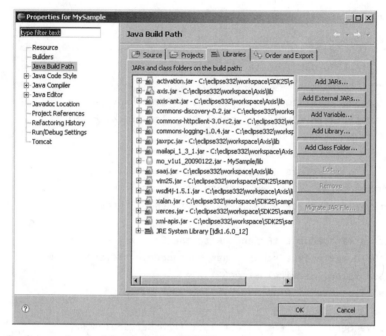

Figure 3-5   Configure a Java build path for the VI SDK project.

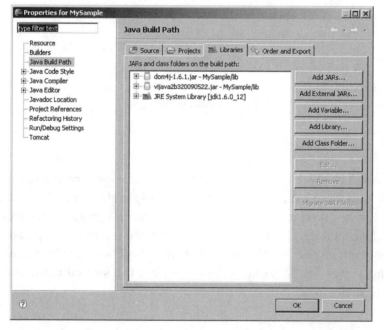

Figure 3-6   Configure a Java build path for the VI SDK project using VI Java API 2.0.

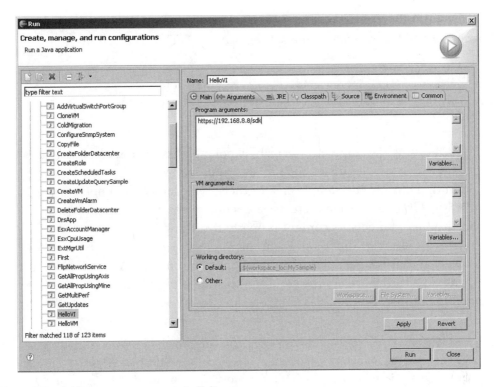

Figure 3-7 Add program arguments in Eclipse.

The URL to your ESX server or VC server is in the following format:

```
https://<target_IP_or_DNS_name>/sdk
```

Here is the output while connecting to an ESX server:

```
Hello VMware ESX Server
API type: HostAgent
```

The following is the output while connecting to a VC server:

```
Hello VMware VirtualCenter
API type: VirtualCenter
```

Now let's take a close look at the code. The following line tells the Java code to ignore the SSL certificate while setting up the HTTPS connection.

```
System.setProperty(
    "org.apache.axis.components.net.SecureSocketFactory",
    "org.apache.axis.components.net.SunFakeTrustSocketFactory"
    );
```

In fact, during development, security is not a big issue. You can just ignore the certificate with a simple line of code as shown previously.

From that line on, the sample creates the service locator and obtains the VimPortType interface. Then it creates a MOR object pointing to the top ServiceInstance and gets its content property by calling the retrieveServiceContent() method. From the ServiceContent, it gets the AboutInfo data object and prints part of the information to the console. You can easily print out many other properties in the ServiceContent data object, such as the API version, build number, vendor, productLineId, and localVersion.

Surprisingly, this first program doesn't require you to provide a username and password as most of the following samples do. That is because it is not necessary. But to use other managed objects or drill down the inventory tree, you need to log in with SessionManager as shown in the next few samples.

Debugging VI SDK Applications

Debugging a program is never easy. You need to have basic debugging skills as well as a solid understanding of the program, from its use cases to its system architecture and algorithm. The following sections focus on the techniques specific to VI SDK application debugging.

Using Logs

Chapter 2, "VI SDK Basics," discussed VI client logs. The logs are helpful for you to understand the SOAP communications associated with common management tasks, but not so much in debugging your application where VI Client is normally out of the picture. It can, however, be a reference application so that you can compare and analyze messages and results from both your application and the VI Client.

The logs from the server side are more relevant to your debugging. Many logs are used in both the VC server and the ESX server and virtual machine. The following discussion focuses on those that are related to VI SDK application development and debugging.

> It's critical to synchronize the time of all the components involved, especially when you care about the sequences of actions and messages. You can configure NTP on ESX, Guest OS, and Windows on which VirtualCenter is running.

You can use the VI Client to read these logs, read them in the file system, or create log bundles[5] for downloading.

VirtualCenter Logs

There are about ten log files in the following directory:

```
%ALLUSERSPROFILE%\Application Data\VMware\VMware VirtualCenter\Logs
```

Most likely, the `%ALLUSERSPROFILE%` is `C:\Documents and Settings\All Users\`.

The log files share a common name pattern, like `vpxd-?.log`, where `?` is a single digit from 0 to 9. The system automatically jumps to the next log file when it starts or the current log file has reached a predefined size, such as 5M.[6] To find out which log file is currently used, just take a look at `vpxd-index` file in the same directory.

Each log entry follows this format:

```
[Date Time '<ThreadName>' <ThreadID> <logLevel>] [COMPONENT] INFORMATION
```

where the COMPONENT is optional.

---

[5] On VirtualCenter, you can use the Start, All Programs, VMware, Generate VirtualCenter Server log bundle program, and the resulting bundle will be on VC desktop. On ESX server, manually run the `vm-support` command; the program will tell where resulting *.tgz is. To save space, you should delete it when it is no longer needed.

[6] You can change the default in the vpxd.cfg file, same for the total number of log files to retain.

The following is a sample entry from the VC server log:

```
[2008-06-21 14:00:34.303 'SOAP' 3736 trivia] Received soap request from
[127.0.0.1]: retrieveContents
```

The component to pay attention to is VpxVmomi, as shown in the following log entry:

```
[2008-06-21 14:00:34.303 'App' 3736 verbose] [VpxVmomi] Invoking
[retrieveContents] on [vmodl.query.PropertyCollector:propertyCollector] session
[BC00F87C-0A43-49D3-B06B-E06C21BC3F8E]
```

You can change the log level in the configuration file to give you as much detail as you want. The full path to the configuration file is this:

```
C:\Documents and Settings\All Users\Application Data\VMware\VMware
VirtualCenter\vpxd.cfg
```

Look for a section like the following:

```
<log>
<level>trivia</level>
</log>
```

You can change the log level to any one of these values: none, error, warning, info, verbose, or trivia, in an order from less to more detailed messages. The more messages you log, the less performant your system will be. It's helpful for a development setting to turn on the trivia level, but not for your production system.

When you are done changing the configuration, restart the VirtualCenter server from Windows Services.

ESX Server Logs

There are about ten log files in the ESX server for the hostd agent with the same naming pattern as hostd-?.log under the /var/log/vmware directory. The hostd-index file has the number of currently used log files.

The log entry has a similar format to that of VC server logs. Following is a quick sample:

```
[2008-06-21 07:24:40.769 'SOAP' 64834480 trivia] Received soap request from []:
checkForUpdates
```

The log level can be configured in the /etc/vmware/vpxa.cfg file. Just look for a section like the following. The possible levels are the same as those of VC logs.

```
<log>
  <directory>/var/log/vmware/</directory>
  <name>hostd</name>
  <outputToConsole>false</outputToConsole>
  <level>verbose</level>
</log>
```

After saving the configuration, you need to restart the hostd with the following command line:

```
service mgmt-vmware restart
```

VM Logs

The virtual machines can have their logs as well, mainly for low-level device, I/O-related events. As an SDK developer, you don't need to look at these log files most of the time. If you do, just find them in the virtual machine's home directory.[7] The log-enabling state, filename, and rotate size can be configured in the .vmx file. For example, the following lines can be added:

```
logging=[true | false]
log.filename="/vmfs/volumes/vol1/myVM/myVM.log"
log.rotateSize=1000000
```

Check out the Knowledge Base article "Log Rotation and Logging Options for vmware.log"[8] for more details. The VI SDK API can make the changes programmatically.

---

[7] If a log file is configured to some other location in the datastore, you should follow the pointer and find it.

[8] http://kb.vmware.com/selfservice/documentLink.do?externalID=8182749

See Chapter 8, "Managing Virtual Machines, Snapshots, and VMotion," in the section "Reconfiguring Virtual Machine."

Monitoring SOAP Messages with HTTP

The SOAP message is one of the most important artifacts for your debugging. In most of the cases, HTTPS is the underlying transportation for security reasons. The encryption makes the message almost impossible to be intercepted for analysis.[9]

The good news is that VMware has provided HTTP as an alternative to HTTPS. For VI SDK 2.5, you should consult the Developer Setup Guide,[10] in the section "Modifying the Server Configuration to Support HTTP."

If you use VI SDK 2.0.1, read the VMware Infrastructure SDK Programming Guide,[11] in the chapter "Developing Client Applications," section "Setting Up the VMware Infrastructure SDK Client."

With that configured, you can use any network sniffer or use a proxy to log the SOAP messages sent back and forth from your application to the server. Wireshark[12] and Apache TCPMon[13] are great tools to monitor the network traffic. The latter also has an Eclipse plug-in that can be easily integrated with your debugging environment.

Common Bugs

A bug can sneak into your code in many different ways. Covered here are several common bugs. Other bugs that are closely related to specific areas, such as performance monitoring, are covered in related chapters.

Null Pointer

The null pointer is a historically famous bug from C/C++ days in which you could get an application or even a system crash. In Java, C#, things are not that extreme, but it still raises an exception and disrupts your normal application flow.

---

[9] It's possible to intercept the SOAP messages at the underlying Web Services engine even using HTTPS. In AXIS, for example, you can change configuration to log the messages, or you can set break points to inspect the messages in debug mode. Tools like Wireshark can be configured to intercept the HTTPS traffic if keys are provided.

[10] http://www.vmware.com/support/developer/vc-sdk/visdk25pubs/visdk25setupguide.pdf

[11] http://www.vmware.com/pdf/ProgrammingGuide201.pdf

[12] http://www.wireshark.org

[13] http://ws.apache.org/commons/tcpmon/index.html

In a VI SDK application, it's quite easy to get such a null pointer bug. For example, many data objects' properties are optional. If they are missing in a SOAP message, the corresponding properties in the data object are null. That is mostly okay if the properties are primitive data, but it becomes a problem if the properties are data objects and you try to access their subproperties.

It's always a good practice to check whether a data object is null before further accessing its properties or invoking its methods. The same is true for the array type.

Connection Timeout

By default, a session is alive only 30 minutes before the server terminates it. For most applications, that is not an issue. For others, it can cause a problem that is hard to debug, because the problem might manifest itself in a different form. For example, you might get a fault complaining of no permission or an authenticated user. It's difficult to trace the facial faults to the root cause of session timeout.

The timeout comes for a good reason—you simply don't want the inactive sessions to add up to the extent that hurts the performance. Timing out the inactive sessions is a good way to prevent that from happening.

Arguably, the default 30 minutes should be longer to mitigate this problem. In fact, this issue is not hard to overcome. If your application expects no activity for 30 minutes, you should fake some activity from your main application flow or have a low-priority thread send out a quick call once in a while, just to keep the session alive.

If a session is timed out, you need to reconnect to the server. Some managed objects, such as `PropertyFilter`, are closely associated with a session. They become invalid after reconnection, so make sure you create them again after a new session is established.

Yet another kind of timeout happens with extra long (greater than 15 minutes) running operations. Check out Chapter 14, "Task and `ScheduledTask`," in the section "Fixing Task Timeout."

No Permission

Most methods in the VI SDK require one or more privileges. For example, `createSnapshot_Task()` requires the privilege `VirtualMachine.State.CreateSnapshot`. In some exceptional cases, a method requires different privileges depending on the target it operates on and the arguments. The `cloneVM_Task()` method, for example, requires `VirtualMachine.Provisioning.Clone` for cloning from one virtual machine to another, `VirtualMachine.Provisioning.DeployTemplate` for cloning from a template to a virtual machine, and so on. If the current user's role doesn't have the privilege, the operation cannot be done and a fault is returned upon invocation.

More often than not, developers use "root" (ESX) or "administrator" (VC server) to log in the server, and they are granted with every privilege. Therefore, you don't see the `NoPermission` fault until it's tested or even deployed.

The `NoPermission` fault itself is not an issue. It's actually good for protecting the system. The problem is the handling of the fault when it happens. Don't assume it's not happening and let the exception pop up all the way to the top and abort your application.

> To catch the problem as early as possible, test your application with various users with different privilege combinations before it's handed over for deployment.

Invalid Arguments

This bug is caused by the `InvalidArgument` fault, which can be thrown by many different methods. In theory, it should be an easy one to debug because it contains an `invalidProperty` property in the `InvalidArgument` telling what property caused the fault.

The reality is that `invalidProperty` is not always set with a value telling which property is the troublemaker. For the methods with huge data objects as parameters, that issue could be quite problematic.

To start with the debugging, first check whether `invalidProperty` is set. If it is, just check the property it points to: whether it's set, the value, and so on. If it's not, move on.

Second, check the API reference to see if you forgot to set a required parameter. Because some data objects are used in more than one method, one optional parameter may be required for the other.

Third, try different combinations of the parameters. It is also helpful to do the same task from the VI Client. It's even better if you can monitor the SOAP messages with HTTP.

Overall, this type of bug can be difficult to debug. You should check the online forum and other's samples as well.

Invalid State

A method can return with an InvalidState fault or its subtype if it's called on a managed entity in the "wrong" state. For example, you can get an InvalidPowerState (subtype of InvalidState) when calling defragmentAllDisks() on a virtual machine that is still powered on.

To handle this type of error, you can have two options. The first is to check the state requirement before calling the method. The second is to wrap the call with a try/catch block so that the fault does not interfere with the normal execution path.

Summary

The first sample code in this book introduced how to set up the development environment step by step. Similar to many other HelloWorld samples, the sample is pretty simple, just illustrating what a VI SDK application looks like.

In the end, this chapter discussed debugging skills and techniques, such as how to use the logs and how to monitor the SOAP messages. Several common mistakes were covered so that you could learn to avoid them in your VI SDK applications.

Chapter 4

Using PropertyCollector and SearchIndex

The first half of this chapter introduces you to the `PropertyCollector`, which provides universal services to retrieve any property from any set of managed objects from the server side. Several samples are provided to demonstrate how to get properties, traverse the inventory, monitor changes, and retrieve notifications.

The second half of this chapter introduces you to `SearchIndex`, which helps you search for a managed entity in the inventory based on various criteria. `SearchIndex` is not used as often as `PropertyCollector`, but it provides a quick way to obtain a managed entity. To help you decide when to use which, this chapter analyzes the differences.

The next chapter introduces you to the VI Java APIs, in which the `PropertyCollector` is made transparent to the developers under the getter methods. Therefore, you don't necessarily need to know all the details of `PropertyCollector` unless you want to use its advanced features. These details help you understand the VI Java API design and implementation.

Because all the samples after the next chapter use VI Java API, you don't see `PropertyCollector` that much in sample code. But, underlying every getter method, `PropertyCollector` is there doing the real work.

Managed Objects: `PropertyCollector`, `SearchIndex`

PropertyCollector

`PropertyCollector` is a managed object that you can easily get from `ServiceInstance`. It's almost the only way[1] to get any property of any managed object in the VI SDK. Therefore, it is one of the most often used managed objects. You can find `PropertyCollector`-related code in almost every sample that directly uses the VI SDK Web Service.

    `PropertyCollector` comes with a sophisticated design that does more than retrieve a single property from a managed object. It can retrieve multiple properties across multiple managed objects. Beyond that, you can use it to check for updates or wait for update notifications from the server.

    Five methods are defined on the `PropertyCollector`. These methods take one to three parameters and return a value just as any other typical method. The complexity is with the parameter or return types.

    Let's look at a quick sample using the `PropertyCollector`.

Getting Properties from a Single Managed Object

Getting properties from a single managed object is a basic use case for `PropertyCollector`. Listing 4-1 shows a sample to retrieve the name and `overallStatus` properties from the inventory tree root folder.

Listing 4-1
The Sample to Retrieve Properties from a Single Managed Object

```
package vim.samples.ws;
import java.net.URL;
import com.vmware.vim25.*;

public class PropertyCollector1
{
  public static void main(String[] args) throws Exception
  {
```

---

[1] The only exception is with `ServiceInstance`, which provides a method called `retrieveServiceContent()` to get its property "content."

```
if(args.length != 3)
{
  System.out.println("Usage: java PropertyCollector1 <url> "
      + "<username> <password>");
}

//ignore the SSL certificate
System.setProperty(
  "org.apache.axis.components.net.SecureSocketFactory",
  "org.apache.axis.components.net.SunFakeTrustSocketFactory"
  );

//create the interface on which services are defined
VimServiceLocator vsl = new VimServiceLocator();
vsl.setMaintainSession(true);
VimPortType vimService = vsl.getVimPort(new URL(args[0]));

//create a ManagedObjectReference to the ServiceInstance
ManagedObjectReference siMOR = new ManagedObjectReference();
siMOR.set_value("ServiceInstance");
siMOR.setType("ServiceInstance");

//retrieve ServiceContent data object from ServiceInstance
ServiceContent sc = vimService.retrieveServiceContent(siMOR);

//log in with SessionManager
ManagedObjectReference sessionMOR = sc.getSessionManager();
vimService.login(sessionMOR, args[1], args[2], null);

// get PropertyCollector MOR
ManagedObjectReference pcMOR = sc.getPropertyCollector();
// get inventory root folder
ManagedObjectReference rootFolderMOR = sc.getRootFolder();

// prepare the parameter to retrieveProperties method
ObjectSpec oSpec = new ObjectSpec();
oSpec.setObj(rootFolderMOR);

PropertySpec pSpec = new PropertySpec();
pSpec.setAll(false);
```

```
pSpec.setType(rootFolderMOR.getType());
pSpec.setPathSet(new String[] {"name", "overallStatus"});

PropertyFilterSpec[] pfss = new PropertyFilterSpec[1];
pfss[0] = new PropertyFilterSpec();
pfss[0].setObjectSet(new ObjectSpec[] { oSpec });
pfss[0].setPropSet(new PropertySpec[] { pSpec });

// retrieve the property
ObjectContent[] objs;
objs = vimService.retrieveProperties(pcMOR, pfss);

// get the value from the returned value
if (objs!=null && objs[0]!=null)
{
  DynamicProperty[] dps = objs[0].getPropSet();
  for(int i=0; i<dps.length; i++)
  {
    System.out.println(dps[i].getName()
        + ": " + dps[i].getVal());
  }
}
}
}
}
```

When this sample runs against an ESX server, it prints the following to the console:

```
Name:ha-folder-root
overallStatus: green
```

Notice that the name of this root folder happens to be the same as the value in the ManagedObjectReference.

Look closely at the code. The first half of it is doing the basic initialization, login, and so on. Skip those code lines until it gets to the PropertyCollector.

The following lines prepare an array of `PropertyFilterSpec`, which is then passed into the `retrieveProperties()` method. Figure 4-1 shows the data structure of `PropertyFilterSpec` with a UML diagram.

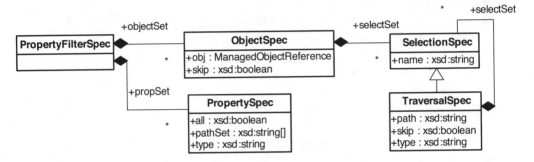

Figure 4-1   The `PropertyFilterSpec` data object and its sub data objects

```
// prepare the parameter to retrieveProperties method
ObjectSpec oSpec = new ObjectSpec();
oSpec.setObj(rootFolderMOR);

PropertySpec pSpec = new PropertySpec();
pSpec.setAll(false);
pSpec.setType(rootFolderMOR.getType());
pSpec.setPathSet(new String[] {"name", "overallStatus"});

PropertyFilterSpec[] pfss = new PropertyFilterSpec[1];
pfss[0] = new PropertyFilterSpec();
pfss[0].setObjectSet(new ObjectSpec[] { oSpec });
pfss[0].setPropSet(new PropertySpec[] { pSpec });
```

To retrieve a property, you need to specify at least two parts:

- **What managed object you want to collect properties**—This information is held in `ObjectSpec`. The sample uses the `setObj()` method to set the `rootFolderMOR`. You can also specify complicated traversal to include more than one managed object.

- **What properties you want to collect**—You can indicate that you want all the properties by typing the following code. When you do so, you don't need to call setPathSet any more. If you repeatedly retrieve all the properties from managed objects that have many big data object properties, the performance can suffer.

```
pSpec.setAll(true);
```

The sample code sets it to be false and specifies the properties by names like the following:

```
pSpec.setPathSet(new String[] {"name", "overallStatus"});
```

You can include more than one property in the array at a time. Make sure you have the property name spelled and capitalized correctly, because it is case-sensitive. If you don't, an InvalidPropertyFault is thrown.

To reduce network traffic, specify the path to exactly what you need. The inventory tree root folder is not really a good example to illustrate this. Let's pick a HostSystem managed object as an example. You can specify capability.vmotionSupported for a single Boolean value, instead of capability for the entire HostCapability data object with all the rest of the subproperties you may not need. To find what properties and subproperties are there for a managed object, check the VI SDK API reference.

Again, the property path cannot transverse any managed object. If you see any property in the path defined as ManagedObjectReference, you need to stop there. After you get the MOR object, use PropertyCollector again to specify the properties in the rest of the path.

After calling retrieveProperties(), you get an array of ObjectContent, which is yet another complicated data object whose structure is shown in Figure 4-2. Each managed object returned has one corresponding ObjectContent instance, which has three properties:

- **obj**—Managed object these properties are associated with.
- **missingProperty**—Array for the properties wanted but not available for various reasons.
- **propSet**—Array for the properties that have been successfully fetched.

For the missing properties, you can further drill down to the associated fault to find out why it failed to be fetched.

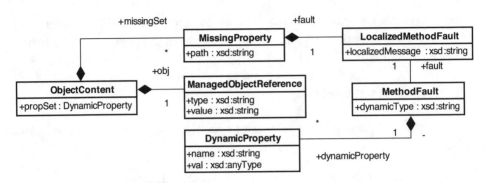

Figure 4-2 The `ObjectContent` data object and its nested data objects

In most cases, you care mostly about the `propSet` array. The element in the `propSet` array is of the type `DynamicProperty`, which has `name` and `val` defined. The interesting part is that the `val` property is of type `anyType`, which means that it can be any primitive data types, data objects, or an array of them. This makes `propSet` flexible enough to hold almost anything. At the same time, it makes it difficult to figure out what the real type is.

The following code snippet handles `anyType`. In WSDL, extra types are defined to encapsulate arrays of data objects (for example, `ArrayOfManagedObjectReference` for `ManagedObjectReference`). The code uses reflection to get the real array. If an object is `ArrayOfXXX`, get the `XXX[]` by invoking `getXXX()` on the object. For example, `ArrayOfManagedObjectReference.getManagedObjectReference()` returns `ManagedObjectReference[]`.

```
Object convertProperty(Object dynaPropVal)
{
  Object propertyValue = null;

  Class propClass = dynaPropVal.getClass();
  String propName = propClass.getName();
  if (propName.indexOf("ArrayOf") != -1)
  {
    String methodName = propName.substring(propName.indexOf(
        "ArrayOf") +"ArrayOf".length());
    try
    Method getMethod = null;
    try
  {
    getMethod = propClass.getMethod("get"
        + methodName, (Class[])null);
```

```
      } catch(NoSuchMethodException nsme)
      {
        getMethod = propClass.getMethod("get_"
          + methodName.toLowerCase(), (Class[])null);
      }
      propertyValue = getMethod.invoke(dynaPropVal,
          (Object[])null);
    }
    catch(Exception e)
    {
      e.printStackTrace();
    }
  }
  else if (dynaPropVal.getClass().isArray())
  { //Handle the case of an unwrapped array being deserialized
    propertyValue = dynaPropVal;
  }
  else
  {
    propertyValue = dynaPropVal;
  }
  return propertyValue;
}
```

Getting Properties of Multiple Managed Objects

The previous section showed a sample to retrieve properties from a single managed object. PropertyCollector can do more than that; it can traverse the inventory tree to include more managed objects so that you can get properties from multiple managed objects. The trick is using SelectionSpec and TraversalSpec, as you have seen in the PropertyFilterSpec, shown in Figure 4-1.

Listing 4-2 shows sample code to list all the items in the inventory tree, including the subtypes of ManagedEntity, such as VirtualMachine, HostSystem, and Folder. You can easily change the type from ManagedEntity to any subtype name (for example, VirtualMachine) to get all the virtual machines in the inventory.

Listing 4-2
The **PropertyCollector2.java**

```java
package vim.samples.ws;
import java.net.URL;
import com.vmware.vim25.*;

public class PropertyCollector2
{
  public static void main(String[] args) throws Exception
  {
    if(args.length != 3)
    {
      System.out.println("Usage: java PropertyCollector2 <url> "
          + "<username> <password>");
    }

    //ignore the SSL certificate
    System.setProperty(
      "org.apache.axis.components.net.SecureSocketFactory",
      "org.apache.axis.components.net.SunFakeTrustSocketFactory"
      );

    //create the interface on which services are defined
    VimServiceLocator vsl = new VimServiceLocator();
    vsl.setMaintainSession(true);
    VimPortType vimService = vsl.getVimPort(new URL(args[0]));

    //create a ManagedObjectReference to the ServiceInstance
    ManagedObjectReference siMOR = new ManagedObjectReference();
    siMOR.set_value("ServiceInstance");
    siMOR.setType("ServiceInstance");

    //retrieve ServiceContent data object from ServiceInstance
    ServiceContent sc = vimService.retrieveServiceContent(siMOR);

    //log in with SessionManager
    ManagedObjectReference sessionMOR = sc.getSessionManager();
```

```
        vimService.login(sessionMOR, args[1], args[2], null);

        // get PropertyCollector MOR
        ManagedObjectReference pcMOR = sc.getPropertyCollector();
        // get inventory root folder
        ManagedObjectReference rootFolderMOR = sc.getRootFolder();

        // prepare the parameter to retrieveProperties method
        PropertySpec pSpec = new PropertySpec();
        pSpec.setAll(false);
        pSpec.setType("ManagedEntity");
        pSpec.setPathSet(new String[] {"name"});

        ObjectSpec oSpec = new ObjectSpec();
        oSpec.setObj(rootFolderMOR);
        oSpec.setSelectSet(buildFullTraversal());

        PropertyFilterSpec[] pfss = new PropertyFilterSpec[1];
        pfss[0] = new PropertyFilterSpec();
        pfss[0].setObjectSet(new ObjectSpec[] { oSpec });
        pfss[0].setPropSet(new PropertySpec[] { pSpec });

        // retrieve the property
        ObjectContent[] objs;
        objs = vimService.retrieveProperties(pcMOR, pfss);

        // get the value from the returned value
        if (objs!=null && objs[0]!=null)
        {
          for(int i=0; i<objs.length; i++)
          {
            DynamicProperty[] dps = objs[i].getPropSet();
            System.out.println("Name:" + dps[0].getVal());
          }
        }
      }

/**
 * This method creates a SelectionSpec[] to traverses the
 * entire inventory tree starting at a folder
```

```
    */
    public static SelectionSpec [] buildFullTraversal()
    {
      // Recurse through all ResourcePools
      TraversalSpec rpToRp = createTraversalSpec( "rpToRp",
          "ResourcePool", "resourcePool",
          new String[]{ "rpToRp", "rpToVm"});


      // Recurse through all ResourcePools
      TraversalSpec rpToVm = createTraversalSpec( "rpToVm",
          "ResourcePool", "vm", new SelectionSpec[] {});


      // Traversal through ResourcePool branch
      TraversalSpec crToRp = createTraversalSpec( "crToRp",
          "ComputeResource", "resourcePool",
          new String[]{ "rpToRp", "rpToVm" });


      // Traversal through host branch
      TraversalSpec crToH = createTraversalSpec( "crToH",
          "ComputeResource",  "host",
          new SelectionSpec[] {});


      // Traversal through hostFolder branch
      TraversalSpec dcToHf = createTraversalSpec( "dcToHf",
          "Datacenter", "hostFolder",
          new String[] {"visitFolders"});


      // Traversal through vmFolder branch
      TraversalSpec dcToVmf = createTraversalSpec( "dcToVmf",
          "Datacenter", "vmFolder",
          new String[] {"visitFolders"});


      // Recurse through all hosts
      TraversalSpec hToVm = createTraversalSpec( "HToVm",
          "HostSystem", "vm",
          new String[] {"visitFolders"});


      // Recurse through the folders
      TraversalSpec visitFolders = createTraversalSpec(
          "visitFolders", "Folder",  "childEntity",
```

```
      new String[] {"visitFolders", "dcToHf", "dcToVmf",
          "crToH", "crToRp", "HToVm", "rpToVm"});

    // Note: include all the TraversalSpec objects even though
    // they are associated in their definitions
    return new SelectionSpec [] {visitFolders,dcToVmf,dcToHf,
        crToH,crToRp,rpToRp,hToVm,rpToVm};
}

public static TraversalSpec createTraversalSpec(String name,
    String type, String path, SelectionSpec[] selectSet)
{
  return  new TraversalSpec(null, null,
    name, // Name of the selection specification
    type, // Name of the object type containing the property
    path, // Name of the property to additional objects
    Boolean.FALSE, //include the object in the "path" field
    selectSet );
}

public static TraversalSpec createTraversalSpec(String name,
    String type, String path, String[] selectPath)
{
  return  createTraversalSpec(name, type, path,
      createSelectionSpec(selectPath));
}

public static SelectionSpec[] createSelectionSpec(String[] names)
{
  SelectionSpec[] sss = new SelectionSpec[names.length];
  for(int i=0; i<names.length; i++)
  {
    sss[i] = new SelectionSpec(null, null, names[i]);
  }
  return sss;
}
}
```

The most important part of this example is how to create TraversalSpec objects, which basically tell the PropertyCollector how to get onto other managed objects from the current one. You need to specify which properties to search on what managed objects. The `buildFullTraversal()` methods should have explained all the details with the code and comments.

The `TraversalSpec` is not easy to get right, and it's among the top mistakes developers make in their VI SDK application development.

Note that because of a full inventory traversal, the performance could be a serious problem especially when the inventory becomes bigger. You can remove some of the traversal paths that are not really needed (see Listing 4-3).

Monitoring Changes Using `PropertyFilter`

The `PropertyCollector` can not only get the properties, it can monitor their changes. You can either poll for changes or wait for them with a method like `CheckForUpdates()` or `WaitForUpdates()`.

Before you do this, you have to create a `PropertyFilter` with the `createFilter()` method. You need to pass in a `PropertyFilterSpec` object (not an array of `PropertyFilterSpec` as in the `retrieveProperty()` method) and a Boolean value indicating whether you want a partial update. If the Boolean value is `true`, a change reports only the nested property. If the value is `false`, a change reports the enclosing property named in the filter.

The `createFilter()` method returns a `PropertyFilter`, which is a managed object. After `createFilter()` is called, the MOR to the newly created `PropertyFilter` is added to the property filter of `PropertyCollector`.

With a `PropertyFilter` object, you can and should call its only method `destroyPropertyFilter()` when you no long need to monitor the associated properties.

You can create one or more `PropertyFilter` instances to monitor properties of various managed objects. Both `checkForUpdates()` and `waitForUpdates()` get the results for all the `PropertyFilter` objects you have created.

The more property filters you have, the more workload on the server. There is no way to bypass or temporarily disable any of them. So make sure that you create only those you really need, and destroy immediately those you don't. Whenever necessary, you can re-create those destroyed filters.

The `waitForUpdate()` method is a synchronous one that returns when a change comes up. If you don't want to wait for an outstanding `waitForUpdates()` call, you can call `cancelWaitForUpdates()` to cancel it. Upon the call, the `waitForUpdates()`

method completes and throws a RequestCanceled fault. The same fault can be thrown if you call waitForUpdate() before the outstanding one returns.

By default, the socket times out in 10 minutes with AXIS-generated stubs. If there is no change for 10 minutes, waitForUpdate() returns with RemoteException caused by SocketTimeOutException. You can extend it like the following code with a timeout of 20 minutes or longer:

```
VimPortType vimService = serviceLocator.getVimPort(url);
((org.apache.axis.client.Stub)vimService).setTimeout(1200000);
```

Another timing constraint is that the server side terminates an inactive SOAP session in 30 minutes. This termination is important because the inactive sessions can add up to hurt system performance. In most of the cases, 30 minutes is long enough for an application. If it's not, you can always fake some activity (for example, spawn out a thread to invoke inexpensive methods periodically).

Both checkForUpdates() and waitForUpdates() return an UpdateSet data object, which is yet another complicated data object. (Figure 4-3 shows the UML diagram.)

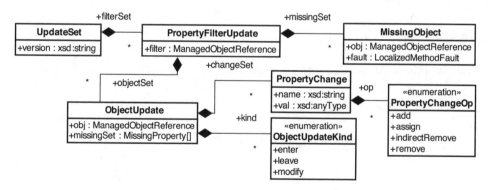

Figure 4-3 The UpdateSet data object and its nested data objects

As you can see, each UpdateSet has a version string that identifies the version of change. When you check or wait for an update, you pass in a version number as the base point from which you want the update. For the first time, you can simply pass in an empty string. After you get the first UpdateSet, always use the version string returned from a previous call to avoid duplicated updates.

The UpdateSet includes multiple PropertyFilterUpdate objects whose filter property holds the MOR of the corresponding PropertyFilter. The PropertyFilterUpdate has an array of `MissingObject` and an array of `ObjectUpdate`. Each `ObjectUpdate` object represents all changes to a single managed object, where an `ObjectUpdateKind` object indicates the change type, a `PropertyChange` object corresponds to a single property change, and a `MissingProperty` object represents a property wanted but not found. Note that missing objects are reported only once. In other words, if they have been reported in a previous version, they are not to be reported in a version thereafter.

Listing 4-3 is an example to get updates on the first `VirtualMachine` in the inventory.

Listing 4-3
`MonitorVM.java`

```java
package vim.samples.ws;
import com.vmware.vim25.*;
import java.util.*;
import java.io.*;
import java.net.URL;

public class MonitorVM
{
  public static void main(String [] args) throws Exception
  {
    if(args.length != 3)
    {
      System.out.println("Usage: java MonitorVM <url> "
        + "<username> <password>");
    }

    //ignore the SSL certificate
    System.setProperty(
      "org.apache.axis.components.net.SecureSocketFactory",
      "org.apache.axis.components.net.SunFakeTrustSocketFactory"
    );

    //create the interface on which services are defined
    VimServiceLocator vsl = new VimServiceLocator();
    vsl.setMaintainSession(true);
```

```
VimPortType vimService = vsl.getVimPort(new URL(args[0]));

//create a ManagedObjectReference to the ServiceInstance
ManagedObjectReference siMOR = new ManagedObjectReference();
siMOR.set_value("ServiceInstance");
siMOR.setType("ServiceInstance");

//retrieve ServiceContent data object from ServiceInstance
ServiceContent sc = vimService.retrieveServiceContent(siMOR);

//log in with SessionManager
ManagedObjectReference sessionMOR = sc.getSessionManager();
vimService.login(sessionMOR, args[1], args[2], null);

// get PropertyCollector MOR
ManagedObjectReference pcMOR = sc.getPropertyCollector();
// get inventory root folder
ManagedObjectReference rootFolderMOR = sc.getRootFolder();

ManagedObjectReference vmMOR = getFirstVM(vimService,
    pcMOR, rootFolderMOR);
if(vmMOR==null)
{
  System.out.println("no VM found.");
  return;
}

PropertySpec pSpec1 = new PropertySpec();
pSpec1.setType("VirtualMachine");
 pSpec1.setPathSet(new String[] {"name", "runtime"});

ObjectSpec oSpec1 = new ObjectSpec();
oSpec1.setObj(vmMOR);

PropertyFilterSpec pfSpec = new PropertyFilterSpec();
pfSpec.setObjectSet(new ObjectSpec[] {oSpec1});
pfSpec.setPropSet(new PropertySpec[] {pSpec1});

ManagedObjectReference pfMOR = null;
```

```java
    pfMOR = vimService.createFilter(pcMOR, pfSpec, false);

    String version = "";
    UpdateSet update;
    BufferedReader console = new BufferedReader(new
        InputStreamReader(System.in));

    while(true)
    {
      update = vimService.checkForUpdates(pcMOR, version);
      if(update != null && update.getFilterSet() != null)
       {
        printUpdate(update.getFilterSet());
        version = update.getVersion();
        System.out.println("version is:" + version);
      }
      else
      {
        System.out.println("No update is present!");
      }
      if(console.readLine().trim().equalsIgnoreCase("exit"))
        break;

    }
    //destroy this PropertyFilter
    vimService.destroyPropertyFilter(pfMOR);

    //log off with SessionManager
    vimService.logout(sc.getSessionManager());
}

public static ManagedObjectReference getFirstVM(
    VimPortType vimService,
    ManagedObjectReference pcMOR,
    ManagedObjectReference rootFolderMOR) throws Exception
{
  // prepare the parameter to retrieveProperties method
  PropertySpec pSpec = new PropertySpec();
  pSpec.setAll(false);
```

```java
pSpec.setType("VirtualMachine");
pSpec.setPathSet(new String[] {"name"});

ObjectSpec oSpec = new ObjectSpec();
oSpec.setObj(rootFolderMOR);
oSpec.setSelectSet(buildVMTraversal());

PropertyFilterSpec[] pfss = new PropertyFilterSpec[1];
pfss[0] = new PropertyFilterSpec();
pfss[0].setObjectSet(new ObjectSpec[] { oSpec });
pfss[0].setPropSet(new PropertySpec[] { pSpec });

// retrieve the property
ObjectContent[] objs;
objs = vimService.retrieveProperties(pcMOR, pfss);

ManagedObjectReference vmMOR = null;
if (objs!=null && objs[0]!=null)
{
  vmMOR = objs[0].getObj();
  DynamicProperty[] dps = objs[0].getPropSet();
  System.out.println("VM Name:" + dps[0].getVal());
  return vmMOR;
}
else
{
  return null;
}
}

public static SelectionSpec [] buildVMTraversal()
{
  // Traversal through vmFolder branch
  TraversalSpec dcToVmf = createTraversalSpec( "dcToVmf",
    "Datacenter", "vmFolder", new String[] {"visitFolders"});

  // Recurse through the folders
  TraversalSpec visitFolders = createTraversalSpec(
    "visitFolders", "Folder",  "childEntity",
     new String[] {"visitFolders", "dcToVmf" });
```

```
    return new SelectionSpec [] {visitFolders,dcToVmf,};
}

public static TraversalSpec createTraversalSpec(String name,
    String type, String path, String[] selectPath)
{
  return  new TraversalSpec(null, null,
       name, // Name of the selection specification
       type, // Name of the object type containing the property
       path, // Name of the property to additional objects
       Boolean.FALSE, //include the object in the "path" field
       createSelectionSpec(selectPath) );
}

public static SelectionSpec[] createSelectionSpec(
String[] names)
{
  SelectionSpec[] sss = new SelectionSpec[names.length];
  for(int i=0; i<names.length; i++)
  {
    sss[i] = new SelectionSpec(null, null, names[i]);
  }
  return sss;
}

static void printUpdate(PropertyFilterUpdate[] pfus)
{
  if(pfus!=null && pfus[0]!=null)
  {
    ObjectUpdate[] ou = pfus[0].getObjectSet();
    PropertyChange[] changes = ou[0].getChangeSet();

    for(int i=0; i < changes.length; i++)
    {
      String name = changes[i].getName();
      Object value = changes[i].getVal();
      if(changes[i].getOp() != PropertyChangeOp.remove)
      {
        System.out.println("  Property Name: " + name);
```

```
    if("runtime".equals(name))
    {
      VirtualMachineRuntimeInfo vmri;
      vmri = (VirtualMachineRuntimeInfo)value;
      System.out.println("   Power  State: "
          + vmri.getPowerState().toString());
      System.out.println("   Connection  State: "
          + vmri.getConnectionState().toString());
      Long moh = vmri.getMemoryOverhead();
      System.out.println("   Memory Overhead: " + moh);
    }
    else if("name".equals(name))
    {
      System.out.println("    "+value);
    }
  }
  else
  {
    System.out.println("Property: " + name + " removed.");
  }
      }
    }
  }
}
```

You might have noticed that the traversal specification has been simplified to traverse on VirtualMachine objects and ignore others in the inventory tree. To change this sample to monitor other types of managed objects, you need to modify the TraversalSpec part in addition to the managed object type string. The good news is that you have seen how to build a full traversal path. Just pick up whatever makes sense for your traversal, or simply use the full traversal path with a little performance penalty.

Some properties cannot be monitored via PropertyFilter because they change too fast. For example, summary.quickStats is a set of statistics that are typically updated in near real time. This data object does not support notification for scalability and performance reasons. Therefore, changes in QuickStats do not generate property collector updates. To monitor statistics values, poll them or use the performance manager and alarms instead.

SearchIndex

The `SearchIndex` service allows a client to efficiently query the inventory for a specific managed entity by attributes, such as name, UUID, IP address, DNS name, datastore path, and inventory path. Such searches typically return a reference to a `VirtualMachine`, `HostSystem`, or other managed entities.

While searching, only objects for which the user has sufficient privileges are considered. `findByInventoryPath` and `findChild` only search on entities for which the user has view privileges; all other methods only search virtual machines and hosts for which the user has read privileges.

If a user does not have sufficient privileges for an object that matches the search criteria, that object is not returned. Instead, `null` is returned. So when `null` is returned, it might be that there is no such managed object that matches the criteria, or simply that the user doesn't have enough privileges.

One big difference between `SearchIndex` and `PropertyCollector` is that `SearchIndex` only returns one entity, whereas `PropertyCollector` returns a collection of entities. A full comparison of these two and when to use which comes later in this section.

Listing 4-4 shows a sample that demonstrates the usage of all six methods defined on the `SearchIndex` managed object. After the sample gets the MOR of a managed object, it prints out the MOR without further exploring its properties or invoking a method. You can try all these methods in your application code.

When running this code in your environment, change all the hard-coded strings, such as the names of the datacenter, IP address, inventory path, and so on. You can also change the order of these six methods, or comment some of them out.

Listing 4-4

`SearchIndexSample.java`

```
package vim.samples.ws;
import java.net.URL;
import com.vmware.vim25.ManagedObjectReference;
import com.vmware.vim25.ServiceContent;
import com.vmware.vim25.VimPortType;
import com.vmware.vim25.VimServiceLocator;
```

```java
public class SearchIndexSample
{
  public static void main(String[] args) throws Exception
  {
    if(args.length != 3)
    {
      System.out.println("Usage: java SearchIndexSample <url> "
          + "<username> <password>");
    }

    //ignore the SSL certificate
    System.setProperty(
      "org.apache.axis.components.net.SecureSocketFactory",
      "org.apache.axis.components.net.SunFakeTrustSocketFactory"
      );

    //create the interface on which services are defined
    VimServiceLocator vsl = new VimServiceLocator();
    vsl.setMaintainSession(true);
    VimPortType vimService = vsl.getVimPort(new URL(args[0]));

    //create a ManagedObjectReference to the ServiceInstance
    ManagedObjectReference siMOR = new ManagedObjectReference();
    siMOR.set_value("ServiceInstance");
    siMOR.setType("ServiceInstance");

    //retrieve ServiceContent data object from ServiceInstance
    ServiceContent sc = vimService.retrieveServiceContent(siMOR);

    //log in with SessionManager
    ManagedObjectReference sessionMOR = sc.getSessionManager();
    vimService.login(sessionMOR, args[1], args[2], null);

    //get SearchIndex
    ManagedObjectReference searchMOR = sc.getSearchIndex();
    // get inventory root folder
    ManagedObjectReference rootFolderMOR = sc.getRootFolder();
```

```
//get the datacenter named "ha-datacenter"
ManagedObjectReference dcMOR = vimService.findChild(
    searchMOR, rootFolderMOR, "ha-datacenter");
printMOR(dcMOR);


ManagedObjectReference mor;

mor = vimService.findByDatastorePath(searchMOR, dcMOR,
    "[storage1 (2)] SuSe_server10/SuSe_server10.vmx");
printMOR(mor);

mor = vimService.findByDnsName(searchMOR, null,
    "dev.acme.com", false);
printMOR(mor);

mor = vimService.findByInventoryPath(searchMOR,
    "ha-datacenter/vm/SuSe_server10");
printMOR(mor);

mor = vimService.findByIp(searchMOR, null,
    "10.17.218.228", true);
printMOR(mor);

mor = vimService.findByUuid(searchMOR, null,
    "564d1c11-6768-4152-14da-3c95f044d6cc", true);
printMOR(mor);
}

public static void printMOR(ManagedObjectReference mor)
{
  if(mor!=null)
  {
    System.out.println(mor.getType() + ":" + mor.get_value());
  }
  else
  {
    System.out.println("ManagedObjectReference is null");
  }
}
}
```

The first part of the code checks the parameters and sets up a Web Services port and logins with the session manager. When all these are done, the code grabs the MOR to the SearchIndex from the ServiceContent data object like the following. The searchMOR is thereafter passed in as the first parameter to all the methods defined in SearchIndex.

```
ManagedObjectReference searchMOR = sc.getSearchIndex();
```

Now let's go over each of the six methods:

- **findChild()**—The method takes in three parameters: SearchIndex MOR, the parent managed object, and the name of the managed object to be searched. In the sample, it searches a datacenter called ha-datacenter. Note that this name happens to be the same as the MOR value, which is normally different from the name.

```
ManagedObjectReference dcMOR = vimService.findChild(
    searchMOR, rootFolderMOR, "ha-datacenter");
```

This method only searches the immediate children in the inventory tree. As mentioned earlier, the real structure of the inventory tree is slightly different from what you see in the VI Client. When in doubt, you can use MOB to find out what the real inventory structure is like.

- **findByDatastorePath()**—This method takes in three parameters: SearchIndex MOR, the datacenter, and the datastore path. It returns a VirtualMachine.

```
mor = vimService.findByDatastorePath(searchMOR, dcMOR,
    "[storage1 (2)] SuSe_server10/SuSe_server10.vmx");
```

The data store path has two parts: the datastore name and the path to the VirtualMachine's .vmx file. Make sure you include a space between the two parts; otherwise, it returns null.

- **findByDnsName()**—This method takes in four parameters: the SearchIndex MOR, a datacenter, the DNS name, and a Boolean switch. The datacenter could be null, meaning it searches all the inventory. The Boolean switch specifies finding a VirtualMachine when true and a HostSystem otherwise.

```
mor = vimService.findByDnsName(searchMOR, null,
        "dev.acme.com", false);
```

When trying to find a VirtualMachine, the DNS name is the one returned from VMware tools. It implies that you have to install the VMware Tool in the VirtualMachine if you want it to be searched using this method.

Even though DNS names are case insensitive, you should use a lowercased DNS name as the argument to this method. There is a bug whereby the method fails to return a valid entity when the DNS name is not lowercased.

■ **findByInventoryPath()**—This method finds a managed entity based on its location in the inventory, and it takes in two methods: the SearchIndex MOR and an inventory path:

```
mor = vimService.findByInventoryPath(searchMOR,
        "ha-datacenter/vm/SuSe_server10");
```

The path is separated by slashes (/). For example, a path to a VM should be of the form My Folder/My datacenter/vm/VM_name. A leading slash or trailing slash is ignored. The root folder should *not* be included in the path. You can have space in your path like the following:

```
"ha-datacenter/vm/SuSe Enterprise"
```

Again, the inventory path is *not* the same path that you see in a VI client. Using a path from what you see in the VI client may fail to find a managed object. For a better user experience, the VI client hides some of the elements. For example, you don't see an element called vm in a VI Client inventory tree. To find out the exact inventory path, use MOB.

Also, make sure all the strings in the path are names of entities, not the object IDs of the entities. For some managed entities at the top of the inventory tree, these two might be the same.

- **findByIp()**—This method finds a `VirtualMachine` or a `HostSystem` based on the IP address. It takes in three parameters: the `SearchIndex` `MOR`, the IP address, and a Boolean switch. When the Boolean switch is `true`, `findByIp()` looks for a `VirtualMachine`, or a `HostSystem` otherwise.

```
mor = vimService.findByIp(searchMOR, null, "10.17.218.228", true);
```

The IP address for a virtual machine is the one returned from VMWare Tools. It means you should install the VMware Tool if you want the virtual machine to be searched using the IP address.

Similar to the DNS name, you should not add extra digits to the IP argument. For example, 010.17.218.228 gets you nothing even though you might think it's the same as 10.17.218.228.

- **findByUuid()**—This method finds a virtual machine or host by UUID. It takes three parameters: the `SearchIndex`, the UUID, and a Boolean switch. When the Boolean switch is `true`, it looks for a `VirtualMachine`, or a `HostSystem` otherwise.

```
mor = vimService.findByUuid(searchMOR, null,
        "564d1c11-6768-4152-14da-3c95f044d6cc", true);
```

As the name of UUID suggests, it is a unique identifier for a `VirtualMachine` or a `HostSystem`. Normally, you don't have the UUID before you obtain the managed object. The use case for this method is special.

When to Use Which

`PropertyCollector` and `SearchIndex` are singleton managed objects that can be easily accessed from the `ServiceInstance`. They are different in many aspects and should be used to their best strength. Table 4-1 compares these two managed objects.

Overall, the `PropertyCollector` is more powerful and can do almost everything `SearchIndex` can do directly or indirectly. However, just like any other powerful tool, it is complex. The code using it is long for its purpose.

Table 4-1

Comparison of PropertyCollector and SearchIndex

	PropertyCollector	SearchIndex
Managed object	Yes	Yes
Fetch properties	Yes	No
Get managed objects	Yes	Yes; only to managed entities in inventory
Multiple managed objects	Yes	No; only the first managed object that meets criteria
Easy to use	No	Yes
Search criteria	Not directly	Limited to IP, inventory path, and so on
Performance	Normal	Good

SearchIndex is different. Its functionality is limited to searching only the managed entities in the inventory tree and can obtain only one item at a time. Yet, it's easier to use than PropertyCollector and performs well.

In general, consider SearchIndex over PropertyCollector. Given the limited functionality of SearchIndex, you'll still need to use PropertyCollector a lot, directly or indirectly.

Summary

This chapter showed how to retrieve properties and monitor property changes using PropertyCollector, and how to search for a managed entity from the inventory tree using SearchIndex. It also summarized the difference between these two managed objects so you can decide when to use which in your applications.

Chapter 5

Introducing the VI Java API

This chapter first reviews the challenges with the VI SDK Web Services interface. It then introduces the design objectives of the VI Java API and how it is architected. After the discussion, you see yet another sample converted from the previous `HelloWorld` sample using the VI Java API, followed by an introduction on how to use the VI Java API.

The chapter then digs into the VI Java API, with detailed discussion of key managed object types and the new high-performance Just Enough Web Service Engine. This part is optional. You can safely skip it and jump to the next chapter.

The API has created a full set of managed objects on the client side so that you can take full advantage of object-oriented programming and compile time–type checking. As a result, you have more readable and shorter code. Based on the observation of converting samples using Web Services in the VI SDK, the average reduction of code is about 70 percent. This boosts productivity for your development, meaning less investment for the product and shorter time to market.

The API has been open sourced at sourceforge.net (http://vijava.sf.net) under BSD license, which is lenient. Anyone can use it as it is or modify it as needed as long as they meet the license conditions.

Version 2.0 and beyond includes a new high-performance engine. You don't need AXIS any more to use the VI Java API.

Challenges with the VI SDK

Web Services is a great technology because it overcomes platform and language dependency. Having solved one big problem, it creates new problems. In nature, Web Services is procedural with only methods defined. It doesn't have an object-oriented concept built in. This section analyzes several issues with VI SDK Web Service interfaces.

Lack of Managed Object Types

Managed object types exist in the VI SDK API reference but not in the WSDL because of the limitation of Web Services. Therefore, any stub generated from the WSDL does not have a managed object type defined. So while you're developing your application, you don't have managed objects to work with. This big step back hurts code readability and productivity.

To represent a managed object on the client side, a ManagedObjectReference object is used for all types of managed objects. Therefore, type checking cannot catch errors at compile time.

To make it clear, consider the following lines from our first sample code in Listing 3-1 from Chapter 3, "Hello VI":

```
ManagedObjectReference siMOR = new ManagedObjectReference();
siMOR.set_value("ServiceInstance");
siMOR.setType("ServiceInstance");

//retrieve ServiceContent data object from ServiceInstance
ServiceContent sc = vimService.retrieveServiceContent(siMOR);
```

As you can see, the retrieveServiceContent() method expects a ManagedObjectReference variable pointing to a ServiceInstance object. If, for whatever reason, the variable is assigned with a ManagedObjectReference object pointing to any other managed object, such as HostSystem in the following code, the code still compiles without a problem. In fact, you don't even need a valid MOR object with correct type for it to compile as follows. Unfortunately, the problem can only be found in runtime.

```
siMOR.set_value("HostSystem"); // wrong type here
siMOR.setType("host123");
```

Confusing Method Signatures

For each method in WSDL, the first parameter is always _this, which is of type
ManagedObjectReference. You have to read the API reference to figure out what real
type is expected for the particular method.

In generated stubs, all the Web Services interfaces are flattened out in a jumbo
interface. In the VI SDK 2.5, this means all 375 methods are defined in a single
interface. It's not easy to browse them, let alone to pick one. You need to know
what real managed object type is behind the ManagedObjectReference parameter for
each method.

Also, given too many methods defined in one interface, the chance of method
name clashing is high. That is why you'll find many long method names, including
extra info that should have been avoided otherwise. For example, you can find
many reconfigure*() methods, such as reconfigureAlarm(),
reconfigureCluster_Task(), and so on. Alarm, Cluster, and such show up in the
method name to avoid the name clashing that would happen otherwise.

Extra Long Code for Its Purpose

In a typical VI SDK application, the code is cluttered with ManagedObjectReference,
PropertyCollector, and so on. As discussed in Chapter 4, "Using PropertyCollector
and SearchIndex," PropertyCollector is powerful but hard to use. It usually takes
more than ten lines of code to get a single property back.

As a result, the real interesting logic of application is buried in many long,
tedious code blocks that are not only hard to read and maintain, but more expensive to build. With the VI Java API, the lines of code can be significantly reduced
while code readability actually increases.

Design Objectives

While designing the VI Java API, I had the following objectives in mind:

- Reconstruct all the managed object types. This is the key to enabling real
  object-oriented application development using the VI SDK.

- Hide ManagedObjectReference as much as possible. Because it is used to represent managed objects, it should be encapsulated into the managed
  object types.

- Hide the `PropertyCollector` behind accessor methods. As its name suggests, the `PropertyCollector` should be used to retrieve properties of managed objects; it's natural to make the `PropertyCollector` transparent under the accessors of the managed objects.

- Build the API on top of the VI SDK and make it flexible and easy to switch between the two.

Unfortunately, the VI Java API cannot get away from all the `ManagedObjectReference` objects because some data objects hold `ManagedObjectReference` type properties. You can create a layer for data objects so that you can convert these properties to real managed object types. However, I decided not to take this approach for two reasons:

- It is too much work to create all these extended data object types, each of which is a wrapper around the 900+ data object types. Even though they can be automatically generated, it adds complexity to the system.

- When the data object or extended data object has getter methods to return real managed objects, it establishes a dependency on managed object types. Because the managed objects already depend on the data objects, this new dependency just makes a bidirectional dependency, so either of them can be safely taken away. This coupling makes the two modules tie together, which is not good from a software design point of view.

In fact, the `ManagedObjectReference` defined in managed objects can be handled in a fairly simple way. A utility method can be implemented to convert a `ManagedObjectReference` object to a real managed object. For the users, it's just one line of code.

API design is, of course, a complicated task. The designer has to work hard to get something that is good for most developers. It's an art to balance different aspects of requirement and constraints.

The following principles are followed during the designing process:

- **Simple, but no simpler**—Arguably, simplicity is the top criteria for designing an API. It means the API should hide everything that is tedious or hard to get right or not necessarily exposed, and present the API users a set of clean and easy-to-use programming interfaces. The things that are made transparent in the Java API include SOAP, Web Services, `PropertyCollector`, and so on.

As the UML father, Grady Booch pointed out, "Don't underestimate the importance of keeping things simple, or the difficulty of getting there. It requires energy to develop simple things."[1]

- **Easy to learn and use**—A coherent concept model must be provided behind the API and exposed in a natural way that is close to the domain knowledge and existing terminologies. No long documentation is needed for good APIs.

Architecture Overview

Architecture is the high-level blueprint for the software system. It's key to the implementation as well as understanding of the system. The following explains where the Java API is in the overall software stack and how different types are organized.

Layered Structure

Figure 5-1 illustrates the architecture of the whole stack of a VI SDK application. The ESX server and VC server both connect to the network cloud that links to the client-side application. On the client side, the AXIS engine and generated client stub provide high-level interfaces. Note that VI Java API 2.0 has included a new Web Service engine to replace AXIS, so the layers are slightly different from what Figure 5-1 shows.

Built on top of the stub is the Java API. For the applications, there can be two choices[2]: to solely build on top of the Java API, or to build partially on the Java API and partially on the Web Services interfaces.

From a technical point of view, there is no advantage to build on Web Services when there is a better choice. The hybrid approach is sometimes necessary if you already have a legacy system and just want to use the Java API for new features.

---

[1] http://www.cio.com/article/373215/
_Things_Grady_Booch_Has_Learned_About_Complex_Software_Systems/1
[2] To be completely logical, there is one more which is solely based on Web Services. Given the context of this chapter, it's just ignored.

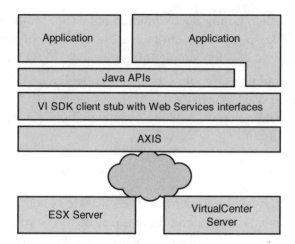

Figure 5-1 Layered architecture of applications

Object Hierarchy

Figure 2-3 in Chapter 2, "VI SDK Basics," showed all the managed object types and their inheritance relationships. All these can be inferred from our VI SDK API reference. Given the limitation of page size, only the names of the types are displayed, not properties and methods.

> There isn't a managed object type called ManagedObject in the VI SDK API reference. This is a type defined only in VI Java API to capture all the common properties and behaviors of all managed objects.

On the right side of Figure 2-3 are the ServiceInstance class and various singleton Manager classes like AuthorizationManager. From the ServiceInstance, you can get any object of these types with a single call, such as getAuthorizationManager().

In the middle, you can find the ManagedEntity class and its subclasses, such as HostSystem and VirtualMachine. These classes represent all the items you could find in the inventory tree from the VI client. They are the most important managed objects in the whole model. Without them, you can barely do anything useful to manage your VMware Infrastructure environment.

The HostSystem is like ServiceInstance in that it has many System or Manager types closely attached to it (for example, HostDatastoreSystem). You can obtain any of these objects with a single method call from a HostSystem object. This is a similar pattern you can find with the ServiceInstance and its attached singleton classes.

Most managed object types of the VI Java API except the top ManagedObject type have no property defined. They do have getter methods, though. Behind each method, PropertyCollector retrieves properties from the server side. For a real object-oriented design, it shouldn't matter how the information is stored and where the information is from as long as the accessor method is provided. The API is an excellent showcase of this principle.

As discussed earlier, managed object properties are mostly read-only. So you don't find getter methods for the properties in the API. You can change some of them indirectly by invoking other normal methods.

The API does not define new types of faults or change the fault types at all. Whatever faults are thrown from the Web Services interfaces are thrown again in the corresponding methods defined in the VI Java API.

Yet Another Hello VM

You've gone through the basics of the API. Now let's look at application code built on top of it, as shown in Listing 5-1.

The sample code obtains the first virtual machine in the inventory and prints out its name, guest OS name, and whether multiple snapshots are supported. As you can see, no ManagedObjectReference or PropertyCollector is present. All you have are managed object types on which you can get their properties in a single line of code. This leads to much shorter, more readable, and easier to maintain code compared to using the VI SDK Web Service API.

Listing 5-1
HelloVM.java

```java
package vim25.samples.mo;
import java.net.URL;


import com.vmware.vim25.VirtualMachineCapability;
import com.vmware.vim25.VirtualMachineConfigInfo;
import com.vmware.vim25.mo.Folder;
import com.vmware.vim25.mo.InventoryNavigator;
```

```java
import com.vmware.vim25.mo.ManagedEntity;
import com.vmware.vim25.mo.ServiceInstance;
import com.vmware.vim25.mo.VirtualMachine;
import com.vmware.vim25.mo.util.CommandLineParser;
import com.vmware.vim25.mo.util.OptionSpec;

public class HelloVM
{
  public static void main(String[] args) throws Exception
  {
    CommandLineParser clp = new CommandLineParser(
        new OptionSpec[]{}, args);
    String urlStr = clp.get_option("url");
    String username = clp.get_option("username");
    String password = clp.get_option("password");

    ServiceInstance si = new ServiceInstance(new URL(urlStr),
        username, password, true);
    Folder rootFolder = si.getRootFolder();
    ManagedEntity[] mes = new InventoryNavigator(
        rootFolder).searchManagedEntities("VirtualMachine");
    if(mes==null || mes.length ==0)
    {
      si.getServerConnection().logout();
      return;
    }
    VirtualMachine vm = (VirtualMachine) mes[0];

    VirtualMachineConfigInfo vminfo = vm.getConfig();
    VirtualMachineCapability vmc = vm.getCapability();
    System.out.println("Hello " + vm.getName());
    System.out.println("GuestOS: " + vminfo.getGuestFullName());
    System.out.println("Multiple snapshot supported: "
        + vmc.isMultipleSnapshotsSupported());

    si.getServerConnection().logout();
  }
}
```

When running the program,[3] you use the following arguments:

```
--url https://<ip_address>/sdk --username root --password mypass
```

The console output is like this:

```
Hello sdk_dev
GuestOS: Microsoft Windows Server 2003, Enterprise Edition (32-bit)
Multiple snapshot supported: true
```

How to Use the VI Java API

The VI Java API is clean and easy to use. This section briefly summarizes how to use the Java API and how to switch between the Java API and the Web Services interfaces.

Typical Application Flow

The API is consistent with the object models described in the VI SDK API reference. It is straightforward and easy to learn and use.

A typical application built using the Java API has the following logical flow:

First, it always starts with a ServiceInstance with the URL/username/password or URL/sessionID parameter combination. For example,

```
ServiceInstance si = new ServiceInstance(new URL(urlStr),
    username, password, true);
```

The last parameter is a Boolean type indicating whether to ignore the SSL certificate. During development, you can always say true to it. If it's set to false, you should have configured the SSL certificate into your Java key store and used the key store when running your code. It's recommended that you set false for applications targeted for the production environment.

---

[3] If you haven't set up the environment, read Chapter 3. I highly recommend VI Java API 2.0 and beyond for the samples in this chapter and after.

Second, from the `ServiceInstance` object, you can perform several tasks as follows:

- Get its properties such as capability, from which you further explore the subproperties of the `Capability` data object:

```
Capability cap = si.getCapability();
```

- Get the `rootfolder` object of the inventory tree. With the root, you can further search any managed entity or a group of managed entities. Optionally, you can explore the `root folder` as a `Folder` object (discussed later).

```
Folder rootFolder = si.getRootFolder();
```

- Get all different `Manager` objects, such as the `SearchIndex` object:

```
SearchIndex searchIndex = si.getSearchIndex();
EventManager em = si.getEventManager();
```

The property content (type: `ServiceContent`) only holds `AboutInfo` and `ManagedObjectReference` to all different managers that are moved up in the VI Java API. Getter methods such as `getAboutInfo` and various getter methods are provided to obtain the `AboutInfo` and manager objects directly.

After you obtain managed objects like `EventManager`, you can further get their properties and call their methods to accomplish various things.

Now look at how you can use the root folder of the entire inventory tree. Because the root is a `Folder` object, you can call its getter methods or normal methods as any other managed object, as well as `Folder`-specific methods. For example, you can call the `createFolder()` method to create a sub folder.

You can go down the path into the main part of the inventory for any interested managed objects. To get hold of these managed objects, you have two approaches:

- Call related methods to get immediate children of that managed object. `Folder`, for example, has a property called `childEntity`. You can then call the getter method `getChildEntity()` for the managed entities attached below it.

Another managed entity, Datacenter, is not that obvious in terms of its children. It actually has two possible ways underneath. One is a folder called vmFolder, which is only for VirtualMachine object children; the other is a folder called hostFolder, which is only for ComputerResource object children. The hostFolder is a little confusing, but the ComputerResource and its subtype ClusterComputeResource can contain HostSystem objects. This explains why the folder is called hostFolder.

From the rootFolder, you can have recursive folders and therefore make the traversing a little bit harder than otherwise. Chapter 6, "Managing Inventory," discusses these details.

- Use the InventoryNavigator class to find any type of managed objects (for example, the VirtualMachine named linux_vm_dev, or all the VirtualMachine objects below any node in the inventory tree). It's a powerful way to maneuver the inventory. You don't need to worry about recursion at all. The TraversalSpec used by PropertyCollector has taken care of that already.

The HostSystem managed object is a little special in that it has many managed objects attached to it. Most of these attached managed objects start with Host in their names. It's a repeated pattern as the ServiceInstance, and it's handled similarly in the VI Java API. Getter methods are there to obtain them from the HostSystem class.

You can now obtain all the managed objects, and it's good to play with them by yourself. A limited number of methods are defined in each type; it's much easier to pick one of those than pick one from the jumbo interface with all methods in the VI SDK.

Some methods return managed objects. For example, a Task object is returned upon calling the createVM_Task() on a Folder object. The returned managed objects are no different from others, and you can call any method on them.

Switching Between the API and Web Services

One of the design objectives is to make the API flexible enough for the users who want to switch between the Java API and the Web Services interfaces. Let's look at the two ways this can be done.

First, switch from the API to Web Services. The following is a quick example:

```
vm.getVimService().powerOffVM_Task(vm.getMOR);
```

instead of

```
vm.powerOffVM_Task();
```

The `vm.getVimService()` just gets the `VimPortType` jumbo interface. The `vm.getMOR()` gets the `ManagedObjectReference` pointing to the `VirtualMachine`.

In general, it's unnecessary for you to invoke the service this way. However, the Java API is flexible enough to make it happen.

Second, switch from the Web Services to the API. In the Web Services, you have `VimPortType` and `ManagedObjectReference`. You can get the `ServerConnection` from an existing managed object such as `ServiceInstance`. You can simply use the utility method as follows:

```
MorUtil.createExactManagedObject(
        serviceInstance.getServerConnection(), mor);
```

Upon the return of the method, you have a `ManagedObject` typed object. The burden is on you to explicitly cast it to the real type.

Even before casting, the object is already in its real type at runtime. Still, you need to cast it in your code before you can use any specific method of the casted type.

Getting Help

Because the Java API creates all the managed object types, it's a step closer to the VI SDK API reference than the VI SDK.

If you need to find out more about one getter method, just check out the related managed object for the property description. The getter methods comply with the naming convention; for example, `getXXX()` gets property XXX. So this is a fairly straight mapping.

If it's a normal method, just look for the managed object for the corresponding method in the API reference. When you read the API reference, keep in mind the following differences:

- Always forget about the first _this parameter because no Java API method has any such parameter.

- If a parameter is a `ManagedObjectReference` type in the reference, the Java API provides a real type behind it. The meaning of the parameter is the same.

- If a return type is a `ManagedObjectReference` type in the API reference, the Java API instead has a real type as return. Again, the meaning of the parameter remains the same.

The released API source package includes sample code that I and others have created to showcase the usage of the API. Studying these samples is an excellent way to familiarize yourself with the API and get up to full speed for your development.

Key Managed Object Types

This section closely looks at the system architecture. The most structurally important classes relating to the API architecture are shown in Figure 5-2. That doesn't mean that other classes, such as `HostSystem` and `VirtualMachine`, are not important. In fact, they are far more important in terms of functionality and frequency of usage than any class discussed here. However, because they are not structurally important, they are deferred to later chapters.

The UML diagram in Figure 5-2 is actually extracted from the overall model, but it adds many more details of individual classes with properties and methods. If you can understand this diagram, you can easily understand all the other managed object types.

The top of Figure 5-2 is the superclass `ManagedObject` for all the managed object classes in the Java API. It's associated with `ServerConnection`, which has a reference to the `ServiceInstance` object. With this design, every managed object, no matter where it is in the inventory tree, can easily get hold of the `ServiceInstance` object, which is the starting point of all managed objects. It provides a lot of flexibilities in navigating among these managed objects.

At the right side of the diagram are the `ExtensibleManagedObject` and its subclass `ManagedEntity`. `ExtensibleManagedObject` has defined two property getter methods and one normal method. As shown in Figure 2-3 in Chapter 2, it has many other subclasses, such as `Alarm`, `Datastore`, `Task`, `Network`, and so on.

`ManagedEntity` is one of the most important managed object types because `VirtualMachine`, `HostSystem`, and so on are inherited from it. To search the inventory, the Java API provides a utility class `InventoryNavigator` to group all the search

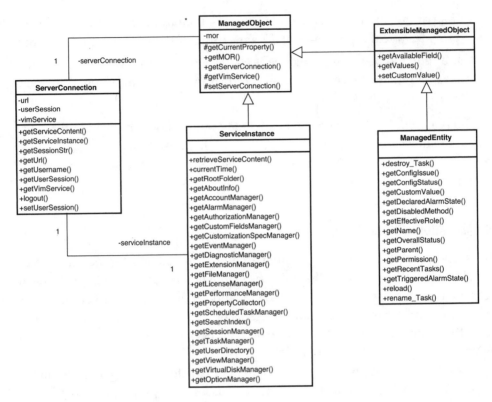

Figure 5-2   The key classes in the VI Java API

methods for retrieving items in the inventory tree from a specified node. For example, you can easily find all the virtual machines in the inventory with one single call.

The UML diagrams in Figures 2-3 and 5-2 show you the big picture of the object model and how key types are related. Let's examine these key classes in the following sections.

ManagedObject

The ManagedObject abstract class is the superclass for all the managed objects. As a type, it is not defined or mentioned in the API reference or anywhere else in the VI SDK. But it's indeed an important class to capture all the common properties and behaviors of all the managed objects.

For a managed object, it must know the answers to two questions: Where am I? and How do I identify myself?

The first question is answered by the ServerConnection class whose reference is held as a property in every managed object. It's not only the server but also the user who logs into the system that can make a difference for the behaviors of the managed object due to the security model of the VI SDK. Users have different roles and different privileges. A method call cannot be completed if the required privilege is not granted to the login user. Therefore, two users can get different results by invoking the same method. The unique combination of server and user is captured by the ServerConnection class.

The second question is answered by the ManagedObjectReference object that points to it. Like a primary key to a SQL database table, a valid ManagedObjectReference object serves as a unique identifier to a managed object within the specific server. Its value doesn't vary from user to user.

These two properties are defined as private, with public getter methods.

Given the fact that every managed object can have one or more properties, it's a good place to encapsulate the generic code to get properties from a managed object. Several methods are defined in ManagedObject to achieve this goal. In the subclasses, the property accessor method can be as simple as one line by providing a property name to the method defined in the ManagedObject class. One method is getPropertyByPath(), which is used in almost all subtypes that have a property defined.

The following is a sample access method defined in ManagedEntity to get a property named disabledMethod. It returns an array of disabled method names. Because the return of getPropertyByPath() is an object, it has to cast it to the String[] type.

```
public String[] getDisabledMethod()
{
  return (String[]) getPropertyByPath("disabledMethod");
}
```

getPropertyByPath() is marked as public. The reason for it to be public is that it supports path notation, and in some of cases, you don't need to retrieve the whole data object if you're just interested in a sub data object embedded. This might be a huge savings while you iterate through many managed entities for a subproperty under a property of a big data object. It's made possible with getPropertyByPath() method.

Overall, the property retrieving is made quite easy and straightforward with the getter methods in every managed object, with the supporting infrastructure provided in the ManagedObject class.

How about the methods? They are also well encapsulated and polished. Take a method from the ManagedEntity class:

```
public void reload() throws RuntimeFault, RemoteException
{
  getVimService().reload(getMOR());
}
```

As you can see, API users no longer need to worry about the Web Services port and ManagedObjectReference. The API has taken care of these. All they need to do is to invoke the method on an object.

What if there are parameters to a method? Take this example:

```
public Task rename_Task(String name) throws InvalidName,
              DuplicateName, RuntimeFault, RemoteException
{
  ManagedObjectReference taskMor = getVimService().rename_Task(
                              getMOR(), name);
  return new Task(getServerConnection(), taskMor);
}
```

In this example, you see that a parameter name is passed into the method, which is further passed into the Web Services call. The Web Services call actually returns a ManagedObjectReference referring to a Task managed object. To encapsulate it with a real type, just call Task's constructor, and it returns a real Task type. The alternative is to use the utility class to convert it.

Some methods take in ManagedObjectReference as parameters. Consider the following example from the VirtualMachine class:

```
public Task powerOnVM_Task(HostSystem host) throws VmConfigFault,
            TaskInProgress, FileFault, InvalidState,
            InsufficientResourcesFault, RuntimeFault,
            RemoteException
{
  ManagedObjectReference mor = getVimService().powerOnVM_Task(
        getMOR(), host==null? null : host.getMOR());
  return new Task(getServerConnection(), mor);
}
```

The new method now takes a real type HostSystem. Because it is an optional parameter, meaning it can be null, the method tests its nullity before calling its getMOR() method. For some other methods that require non-null parameters, first check them before passing them to the Web Services method. Like the previous example, the task MOR returned from the Web Services call is wrapped up with a real type before it's returned.

Source code is the ultimate blueprint of a software system. Look at the source code of the ManagedObject class in Listing 5-2.

Listing 5-2
ManagedObject.java

```java
package com.vmware.vim25.mo;
import java.lang.reflect.Array;
import java.lang.reflect.Constructor;
import java.rmi.RemoteException;
import java.util.Hashtable;

import com.vmware.vim25.DynamicProperty;
import com.vmware.vim25.InvalidProperty;
import com.vmware.vim25.ManagedObjectReference;
import com.vmware.vim25.ObjectContent;
import com.vmware.vim25.ObjectSpec;
import com.vmware.vim25.ObjectUpdate;
import com.vmware.vim25.PropertyChange;
import com.vmware.vim25.PropertyChangeOp;
import com.vmware.vim25.PropertyFilterSpec;
import com.vmware.vim25.PropertyFilterUpdate;
import com.vmware.vim25.PropertySpec;
import com.vmware.vim25.RuntimeFault;
import com.vmware.vim25.UpdateSet;
import com.vmware.vim25.VimPortType;
import com.vmware.vim25.mo.util.MorUtil;
import com.vmware.vim25.mo.util.PropertyCollectorUtil;

/**
```

```
* This class is intended to provide a wrapper around a managed
* object class. The abstraction will hide the Web Services
* details and make the managed objects OO style in the client-
* side programming. Every managed object class can inherit from
* this and take advantage of this abstraction.
*
* @author Steve JIN (sjin@vmware.com)
*/

abstract public class ManagedObject
{
  private static String MO_PACKAGE_NAME = null;
  static
  {
    MO_PACKAGE_NAME = ManagedObject.class.getPackage().getName();
  }

  /** holds the ServerConnection instance */
  private ServerConnection serverConnection = null;
  /** holds the ExtensionManager managed object reference */
  private ManagedObjectReference mor = null;

  protected ManagedObject()
  {}

  /**
   * Constructor that reuses exiting Web Services connection; Use
   * this constructor when you can reuse existing Web Services
   * connection.
   *
   * @param serverConnection
   * @param mor
   */
  public ManagedObject(ServerConnection serverConnection,
      ManagedObjectReference mor)
  {
    this.serverConnection = serverConnection;
    this.mor = mor;
  }
```

```
/**
 * Set the ManagedObjectReference object pointing to the
 * managed object
 */
protected void setMOR(ManagedObjectReference mor)
{
  this.mor = mor;
}

/**
 * get the ManagedObjectReference object pointing to the
 * managed object
 *
 * @return
 */
public ManagedObjectReference getMOR()
{
  return this.mor;
}

/**
 * Get the Web Service
 *
 * @return
 */
protected VimPortType getVimService()
{
  return serverConnection.getVimService();
}

public ServerConnection getServerConnection()
{
  return serverConnection;
}

/**
 * Set up the ServerConnection, only when it hasn't been set
 * yet.
```

```
    *
    * @param sc
    */
   protected void setServerConnection(ServerConnection sc)
   {
     if (this.serverConnection == null)
     {
       this.serverConnection = sc;
     }
   }

   protected ObjectContent retrieveObjectProperties(
       String[] properties)
   {
     ObjectSpec oSpec = PropertyCollectorUtil.createObjectSpec(
         getMOR(), Boolean.FALSE, null);

     PropertySpec pSpec = PropertyCollectorUtil
         .createPropertySpec(getMOR().getType(),
             properties == null || properties.length == 0,
// if true, all props of this obj are to be read
// regardless of propName
             properties);

     PropertyFilterSpec pfSpec = new PropertyFilterSpec();
     pfSpec.setObjectSet(new ObjectSpec[] { oSpec });
     pfSpec.setPropSet(new PropertySpec[] { pSpec });

     PropertyCollector pc = getServerConnection()
         .getServiceInstance().getPropertyCollector();

     ObjectContent[] objs;
     try
     {
       objs = pc
           .retrieveProperties(new PropertyFilterSpec[] { pfSpec });
     }
     catch (Exception e)
     {
```

```java
      throw new RuntimeException(e);
    }

    if (objs == null || objs[0] == null)
      return null;
    else
      return objs[0];
  }


  /**
   * @param propertyName
   *           The property name of current managed object
   * @return it will return either an array of related data
   *           objects or an data object itself.
   *           ManagedObjectReference objects are data objects!!!
   * @throws RemoteException
   * @throws RuntimeFault
   * @throws InvalidProperty
   */
  protected Object getCurrentProperty(String propertyName)
  {
    ObjectContent objContent = retrieveObjectProperties(new String[] {
propertyName });

    Object propertyValue = null;

    if (objContent != null)
    {
      DynamicProperty[] dynaProps = objContent.getPropSet();

      if ((dynaProps != null) && (dynaProps[0] != null))
      {
        propertyValue = PropertyCollectorUtil
            .convertProperty(dynaProps[0].getVal());
      }
    }
    return propertyValue;
  }
```

```java
public Object getPropertyByPath(String propPath)
{
  return getCurrentProperty(propPath);
}


/**
 * Get multiple properties by their paths
 *
 * @param propPaths
 *           an array of strings for property path
 * @return a Hashtable holding with the property path as key,
 *           and the value.
 * @throws InvalidProperty
 * @throws RuntimeFault
 * @throws RemoteException
 */
public Hashtable getPropertiesByPaths(String[] propPaths)
    throws InvalidProperty, RuntimeFault, RemoteException
{
  Hashtable[] pht = PropertyCollectorUtil.retrieveProperties(
      new ManagedObject[] { this }, getMOR().getType(),
      propPaths);
  if (pht.length != 0)
    return pht[0];
  else
    return null;
}


protected ManagedObject[] getManagedObjects(String propName,
    boolean mixedType)
{
  Object object = getCurrentProperty(propName);
  ManagedObjectReference[] mors = null;
  if (object instanceof ManagedObjectReference[])
  {
    mors = (ManagedObjectReference[]) object;
  }

  if (mors == null || mors.length == 0)
```

```
{
  return new ManagedObject[] {};
}

Object mos = new ManagedObject[mors.length];
;

try
{
  Class moClass = null;

  if (mixedType == false)
  {
    moClass = Class.forName(MO_PACKAGE_NAME + "."
        + mors[0].getType());
    mos = Array.newInstance(moClass, mors.length);
  }

  for (int i = 0; i < mors.length; i++)
  {
    if (mixedType == true)
    {
      moClass = Class.forName(MO_PACKAGE_NAME + "."
          + mors[i].getType());
    }
    Constructor constructor = moClass
        .getConstructor(new Class[] {
            ServerConnection.class,
            ManagedObjectReference.class });

    Array.set(mos, i, constructor.newInstance(new Object[] {
        getServerConnection(), mors[i] }));
  }
}
catch (Exception e)
{
  e.printStackTrace();
}
```

```java
  return (ManagedObject[]) mos;
}


protected ManagedObject[] getManagedObjects(String propName)
{
  return getManagedObjects(propName, false);
}


protected Datastore[] getDatastores(String propName)
{
  Object[] objs = getManagedObjects(propName);
  if (objs.length == 0)
  {
    return new Datastore[] {};
  }
  return (Datastore[]) objs;
}


protected Network[] getNetworks(String propName)
{
  Object[] objs = getManagedObjects(propName, true);
  if (objs.length == 0)
  {
    return new Network[] {};
  }
  Network[] nets = new Network[objs.length];
  for (int i = 0; i < objs.length; i++)
  {
    nets[i] = (Network) objs[i];
  }
  return nets;
}


protected VirtualMachine[] getVms(String propName)
{
  ManagedObject[] objs = getManagedObjects(propName);
  if (objs.length == 0)
  {
    return new VirtualMachine[] {};
```

```
  }
  return (VirtualMachine[]) objs;
}

protected PropertyFilter[] getFilter(String propName)
{
  Object[] objs = getManagedObjects(propName);
  if (objs.length == 0)
  {
    return new PropertyFilter[] {};
  }
  return (PropertyFilter[]) objs;
}

protected ResourcePool[] getResourcePools(String propName)
{
  Object[] objs = getManagedObjects(propName);
  if (objs.length == 0)
  {
    return new ResourcePool[] {};
  }
  return (ResourcePool[]) objs;
}

protected Task[] getTasks(String propName)
{
  Object[] objs = getManagedObjects(propName);
  if (objs.length == 0)
  {
    return new Task[] {};
  }
  return (Task[]) objs;
}

protected ScheduledTask[] getScheduledTasks(String propName)
{
  Object[] objs = getManagedObjects(propName);
  if (objs.length == 0)
  {
```

```
      return new ScheduledTask[] {};
  }
  return (ScheduledTask[]) objs;
}


protected View[] getViews(String propName)
{
  Object[] objs = getManagedObjects(propName);
  if (objs.length == 0)
  {
    return new View[] {};
  }
  return (View[]) objs;
}


protected HostSystem[] getHosts(String propName)
{
  Object[] objs = getManagedObjects(propName);
  if (objs.length == 0)
  {
    return new HostSystem[] {};
  }
  return (HostSystem[]) objs;
}


protected ManagedObject getManagedObject(String propName)
{
  ManagedObjectReference mor =
    (ManagedObjectReference) getCurrentProperty(propName);
  return MorUtil.createExactManagedObject(
      getServerConnection(), mor);
}


/**
 * Handle updates for a single object. Waits until expected
 * values of properties to check are reached. Destroys the
 * ObjectFilter when done.
 *
 * @param filterProps Properties list to filter
```

```
 * @param endWaitProps
 *          Properties list to check for expected values these
 *          be properties of a property in the filter
 *          properties list
 * @param expectedVals
 *          values for properties to end the wait
 * @return true indicating expected values were met, and false
 *          otherwise
 * @throws RemoteException
 * @throws RuntimeFault
 * @throws InvalidProperty
 */
protected Object[] waitForValues(String[] filterProps,
    String[] endWaitProps, Object[][] expectedVals)
    throws InvalidProperty, RuntimeFault, RemoteException
{
  String version = "";
  Object[] endVals = new Object[endWaitProps.length];
  Object[] filterVals = new Object[filterProps.length];

  ObjectSpec oSpec = PropertyCollectorUtil.createObjectSpec(
      getMOR(), Boolean.FALSE, null);

  PropertySpec pSpec = PropertyCollectorUtil
      .createPropertySpec(getMOR().getType(),
          filterProps == null || filterProps.length == 0,
          // if true, all props of this obj are to be read
          // regardless of propName
          filterProps);

  PropertyFilterSpec spec = new PropertyFilterSpec();
  spec.setObjectSet(new ObjectSpec[] { oSpec });
  spec.setPropSet(new PropertySpec[] { pSpec });

  PropertyCollector pc = serverConnection.getServiceInstance()
      .getPropertyCollector();
  PropertyFilter pf = pc.createFilter(spec, true);

  boolean reached = false;
```

```java
while (!reached)
{
  UpdateSet updateset = pc.waitForUpdates(version);
  if (updateset == null)
  {
    continue;
  }
  version = updateset.getVersion();
  PropertyFilterUpdate[] filtupary = updateset
      .getFilterSet();
  if (filtupary == null)
  {
    continue;
  }

  // Make this code more general purpose when PropCol changes
  // later.
  for (int i = 0; i < filtupary.length; i++)
  {
    PropertyFilterUpdate filtup = filtupary[i];
    if (filtup == null)
    {
      continue;
    }
    ObjectUpdate[] objupary = filtup.getObjectSet();
    for (int j = 0; objupary != null && j < objupary.length; j++)
    {
      ObjectUpdate objup = objupary[j];
      if (objup == null)
      {
        continue;
      }
      PropertyChange[] propchgary = objup.getChangeSet();
      for (int k = 0; propchgary != null
          && k < propchgary.length; k++)
      {
        PropertyChange propchg = propchgary[k];
        updateValues(endWaitProps, endVals, propchg);
```

```
      updateValues(filterProps, filterVals, propchg);
      }
    }
  }


  // Check if the expected values have been reached and exit
  // the loop if done.
  // Also exit the WaitForUpdates loop if this is the case.
  for (int chgi = 0; chgi < endVals.length && !reached; chgi++)
  {
    for (int vali = 0; vali < expectedVals[chgi].length
        && !reached; vali++)
    {
      Object expctdval = expectedVals[chgi][vali];
      reached = expctdval.equals(endVals[chgi]) || reached;
    }
  }
}


pf.destroyPropertyFilter();


return filterVals;
}


private void updateValues(String[] props, Object[] vals,
    PropertyChange propchg)
{
  for (int i = 0; i < props.length; i++)
  {
    if (propchg.getName().lastIndexOf(props[i]) >= 0)
    {
      if (propchg.getOp() == PropertyChangeOp.remove)
      {
        vals[i] = "";
      }
      else
      {
        vals[i] = propchg.getVal();
      }
```

```
        }
      }
    }

    public String toString()
    {
      return mor.getType() + ":" + mor.get_value() + " @ "
          + getServerConnection().getUrl();
    }

    protected ManagedObjectReference[] convertMors(
        ManagedObject[] mos)
    {
      ManagedObjectReference[] mors = null;
      if (mos != null)
      {
        mors = MorUtil.createMORs(mos);
      }
      return mors;
    }
}
```

ServerConnection

The ServerConnection represents a connection to the server under a specific login user. It holds information such as the URL to the server, the userSession with username, and an instance of VimPortType, which is the jumbo interface with 375 methods. It does not hold the password, though.

As mentioned earlier, every managed object has a reference to an instance of this class. Now the ManagedObject has both key elements to make a Web Services call: the VimPortType instance and its ManagedObjectReference. It cannot make a call without these two elements.

For convenience, ServerConnection also has a reference to a ServiceInstance object. In this way, every managed object can easily obtain the ServiceInstance object, which is the root of the hierarchy of all the managed objects. This provides flexibilities in navigating the managed objects.

ServerConnection is relatively simple. Its source code is shown in Listing 5-3.

Listing 5-3

ServerConnection.java

```java
package com.vmware.vim25.mo;
import java.net.URL;

import com.vmware.vim25.*;
import com.vmware.vim25.ws.WSClient;

/**
 * The class representing the connection to a server: either VC
 * server or ESX
 *
 * @author Steve JIN (sjin@vmware.com)
 */
final public class ServerConnection
{
  private URL url = null;
  private UserSession userSession = null;
  private ServiceInstance serviceInstance = null;
  private VimPortType vimService = null;

  public ServerConnection(URL url, VimPortType vimService,
      ServiceInstance serviceInstance)
  {
    this.url = url;
    this.vimService = vimService;
    this.serviceInstance = serviceInstance;
  }

  /**
   * @return the current session string in format like:
   *         vmware_soap_session="B3240D15-34DF-4BB8-B902-A844FDF42E85"
   */
  public String getSessionStr()
  {
    WSClient wsc = vimService.getWsc();
    return wsc.getCookie();
```

```java
}

/**
 * Disconnect from the server and clean up
 */
public void logout()
{
  if (vimService != null)
  {
    try
    {
      serviceInstance.getSessionManager().logout();
    }
    catch (Exception e)
    {
      System.err.println("Failed to disconnect...");
    }
    vimService = null;
    serviceInstance = null;
  }
}

public ServiceInstance getServiceInstance()
{
  return serviceInstance;
}

public VimPortType getVimService()
{
  return vimService;
}

public URL getUrl()
{
  return url;
}

public String getUsername()
{
```

```
    return userSession.getUserName();
  }

  public UserSession getUserSession()
  {
    return userSession;
  }

  void setUserSession(UserSession userSession)
  {
    this.userSession = userSession;
  }
}
```

ServiceInstance

ServiceInstance is a special managed object because it is the first managed object seen in a typical application logic flow.

You can create a new ServiceInstance object by providing the URL/username/password or URL/sessionID[4] combination. The latter is not used as much as the first constructor, but it's helpful when you develop a VI Client plug-in in Java or when sharing sessions across multiple clients. The tedious login process, as you've seen previously, is encapsulated into these constructors.

As a managed object, the ServiceInstance has three properties and five methods. Getter methods are provided for these three properties. Among the five methods, the method retrieveServiceContent() does essentially the same thing as the getter method for content, but it is marked as private. All the other four methods are handled as usual.

Because many managed objects are closely attached to the ServiceInstance by holding their MORs in the content property of ServiceInstance, the Java API simply bypasses the content property and provides getter methods for each of the managed objects. (For example, the getEventManager() method gets you the EventManager object.)

---

[4] The sessionID is a hash string like 9241E7B8-A37B-4264-A8D2-945628F9E0D6.

Besides the MORS, a data object typed as AboutInfo is included in the
ServiceContent. A getter method getAboutInfo() is provided to get it directly from
ServiceInstance.

A similar design pattern is repeated with HostSystem. These two managed
objects are different from their equivalent types in API reference for good reason:
MORS are encapsulated in real types and therefore hidden from API users.

Listing 5-4 shows all the source code of the ServiceInstance class.

Listing 5-4
ServiceInstance.java

```
package com.vmware.vim25.mo;
import java.net.MalformedURLException;
import java.net.URL;
import java.rmi.RemoteException;
import java.util.Calendar;

import com.vmware.vim25.*;
import com.vmware.vim25.mo.util.*;
import com.vmware.vim25.ws.WSClient;

/**
 * The managed object class corresponding to the one defined in
 * the VI SDK API reference.
 *
 * @author Steve JIN (sjin@vmware.com)
 */

public class ServiceInstance extends ManagedObject
{
  private ServiceContent serviceContent = null;
  final static ManagedObjectReference SERVICE_INSTANCE_MOR;
  public final static String VIM25_NAMESPACE = " xmlns=\"urn:vim25\">";
  public final static String VIM20_NAMESPACE = " xmlns=\"urn:vim2\">";

  static
  {
    SERVICE_INSTANCE_MOR = new ManagedObjectReference();
```

```
  SERVICE_INSTANCE_MOR.set_value("ServiceInstance");
  SERVICE_INSTANCE_MOR.setType("ServiceInstance");
}

public ServiceInstance(URL url, String username,
    String password) throws RemoteException,
    MalformedURLException
{
  this(url, username, password, false);
}

public ServiceInstance(URL url, String username,
    String password, boolean ignoreCert)
    throws RemoteException, MalformedURLException
{
  this(url, username, password, ignoreCert, VIM25_NAMESPACE);
}

public ServiceInstance(URL url, String username,
    String password, boolean ignoreCert, String namespace)
    throws RemoteException, MalformedURLException
{
  if (url == null || username == null)
  {
    throw new NullPointerException(
        "None of url, username can be null.");
  }

  setMOR(SERVICE_INSTANCE_MOR);

  VimPortType vimService = new VimPortType(url.toString(),
      ignoreCert);
  vimService.getWsc().setVimNameSpace(namespace);

  serviceContent = vimService
      .retrieveServiceContent(SERVICE_INSTANCE_MOR);
  setServerConnection(new ServerConnection(url, vimService,
      this));
  UserSession userSession = getSessionManager().login(
```

```
        username, password, null);
    getServerConnection().setUserSession(userSession);
}


public ServiceInstance(URL url, String sessionStr,
    boolean ignoreCert) throws RemoteException,
    MalformedURLException
{
    this(url, sessionStr, ignoreCert, VIM25_NAMESPACE);
}


// sessionStr format:
// "vmware_soap_session=\"B3240D15-34DF-4BB8-B902-A844FDF42E85\""
public ServiceInstance(URL url, String sessionStr,
    boolean ignoreCert, String namespace)
    throws RemoteException, MalformedURLException
{
    if (url == null || sessionStr == null)
    {
        throw new NullPointerException(
            "None of url, session string can be null.");
    }

    setMOR(SERVICE_INSTANCE_MOR);

    VimPortType vimService = new VimPortType(url.toString(),
        ignoreCert);
    WSClient wsc = vimService.getWsc();
    wsc.setCookie(sessionStr);
    wsc.setVimNameSpace(namespace);

    serviceContent = vimService
        .retrieveServiceContent(SERVICE_INSTANCE_MOR);
    setServerConnection(new ServerConnection(url, vimService,
        this));
    UserSession userSession = (UserSession) getSessionManager()
        .getCurrentProperty("currentSession");
    getServerConnection().setUserSession(userSession);
}
```

```
public ServiceInstance(ServerConnection sc)
{
  super(sc, SERVICE_INSTANCE_MOR);
}

public Calendar getServerClock()
{
  return (Calendar) getCurrentProperty("serverClock");
}

public Capability getCapability()
{
  return (Capability) getCurrentProperty("capability");
}

public ClusterProfileManager getClusterProfileManager()
{
  return (ClusterProfileManager) createMO(getServiceContent()
      .getClusterProfileManager());
}

public Calendar currentTime() throws RuntimeFault,
    RemoteException
{
  return getVimService().currentTime(getMOR());
}

public Folder getRootFolder()
{
  return new Folder(this.getServerConnection(), this
      .getServiceContent().getRootFolder());
}

public HostVMotionCompatibility[] queryVMotionCompatibility(
    VirtualMachine vm, HostSystem[] hosts,
    String[] compatibility) throws RuntimeFault,
    RemoteException
{
```

```
    if (vm == null || hosts == null)
    {
      throw new IllegalArgumentException(
          "Neither vm or hosts can be null.");
    }
    return getVimService().queryVMotionCompatibility(getMOR(),
        vm.getMOR(), MorUtil.createMORs(hosts), compatibility);
}


public ProductComponentInfo[] retrieveProductComponents()
    throws RuntimeFault, RemoteException
{
  return getVimService().retrieveProductComponents(getMOR());
}


private ServiceContent retrieveServiceContent()
    throws RuntimeFault, RemoteException
{
  return getVimService().retrieveServiceContent(getMOR());
}


public Event[] validateMigration(VirtualMachine[] vms,
    VirtualMachinePowerState state, String[] testType,
    ResourcePool pool, HostSystem host) throws InvalidState,
    RuntimeFault, RemoteException
{
  if (vms == null)
  {
    throw new IllegalArgumentException("vms must not be null.");
  }

  return getVimService().validateMigration(getMOR(),
      MorUtil.createMORs(vms), state, testType,
      pool == null ? null : pool.getMOR(),
      host == null ? null : host.getMOR());
}


public ServiceContent getServiceContent()
{
```

```
  if (serviceContent == null)
  {
    try
    {
      serviceContent = retrieveServiceContent();
    }
    catch (Exception e)
    {
      System.out.println("Exceptoin: " + e);
    }
  }
  return serviceContent;
}

public AboutInfo getAboutInfo()
{
  return getServiceContent().getAbout();
}

public AlarmManager getAlarmManager()
{
  return (AlarmManager) createMO(getServiceContent()
      .getAlarmManager());
}

public AuthorizationManager getAuthorizationManager()
{
  return (AuthorizationManager) createMO(getServiceContent()
      .getAuthorizationManager());
}

public CustomFieldsManager getCustomFieldsManager()
{
  return (CustomFieldsManager) createMO(getServiceContent()
      .getCustomFieldsManager());
}

public CustomizationSpecManager getCustomizationSpecManager()
{
```

```
  return (CustomizationSpecManager) createMO(getServiceContent()
      .getCustomizationSpecManager());
}

public EventManager getEventManager()
{
  return (EventManager) createMO(getServiceContent()
      .getEventManager());
}

public DiagnosticManager getDiagnosticManager()
{
  return (DiagnosticManager) createMO(getServiceContent()
      .getDiagnosticManager());
}

public DistributedVirtualSwitchManager getDistributedVirtualSwitchManager()
{
  return (DistributedVirtualSwitchManager) createMO(getServiceContent()
      .getDvSwitchManager());
}

public ExtensionManager getExtensionManager()
{
  return (ExtensionManager) createMO(getServiceContent()
      .getExtensionManager());
}

public FileManager getFileManager()
{
  return (FileManager) createMO(getServiceContent()
      .getFileManager());
}

public HostLocalAccountManager getAccountManager()
{
  return (HostLocalAccountManager) createMO(getServiceContent()
      .getAccountManager());
}
```

```
public LicenseManager getLicenseManager()
{
  return (LicenseManager) createMO(getServiceContent()
      .getLicenseManager());
}

public LocalizationManager getLocalizationManager()
{
  return (LocalizationManager) createMO(getServiceContent()
      .getLocalizationManager());
}

public PerformanceManager getPerformanceManager()
{
  return (PerformanceManager) createMO(getServiceContent()
      .getPerfManager());
}

public ProfileComplianceManager getProfileComplianceManager()
{
  return (ProfileComplianceManager) createMO(getServiceContent()
      .getComplianceManager());
}

public PropertyCollector getPropertyCollector()
{
  return (PropertyCollector) createMO(getServiceContent()
      .getPropertyCollector());
}

public ScheduledTaskManager getScheduledTaskManager()
{
  return (ScheduledTaskManager) createMO(getServiceContent()
      .getScheduledTaskManager());
}

public SearchIndex getSearchIndex()
{
```

```java
    return (SearchIndex) createMO(getServiceContent()
        .getSearchIndex());
}


public SessionManager getSessionManager()
{
    return (SessionManager) createMO(getServiceContent()
        .getSessionManager());
}


public HostSnmpSystem getHostSnmpSystem()
{
    return (HostSnmpSystem) createMO(getServiceContent()
        .getSnmpSystem());
}


public HostProfileManager getHostProfileManager()
{
    return (HostProfileManager) createMO(getServiceContent()
        .getHostProfileManager());
}


public IpPoolManager getIpPoolManager()
{
    return (IpPoolManager) createMO(getServiceContent()
        .getIpPoolManager());
}


public VirtualMachineProvisioningChecker getVirtualMachineProvisioningChecker()
{
    return (VirtualMachineProvisioningChecker) createMO(getServiceContent()
        .getVmProvisioningChecker());
}


public VirtualMachineCompatibilityChecker
getVirtualMachineCompatibilityChecker()
{
    return (VirtualMachineCompatibilityChecker) createMO(getServiceContent()
        .getVmCompatibilityChecker());
}
```

```
public TaskManager getTaskManager()
{
  return (TaskManager) createMO(getServiceContent()
      .getTaskManager());
}

public UserDirectory getUserDirectory()
{
  return (UserDirectory) createMO(getServiceContent()
      .getUserDirectory());
}

public ViewManager getViewManager()
{
  return (ViewManager) createMO(getServiceContent()
      .getViewManager());
}

public VirtualDiskManager getVirtualDiskManager()
{
  return (VirtualDiskManager) createMO(getServiceContent()
      .getVirtualDiskManager());
}

public OptionManager getOptionManager()
{
  return (OptionManager) createMO(getServiceContent()
      .getSetting());
}

public OvfManager getOvfManager()
{
  return (OvfManager) createMO(getServiceContent()
      .getOvfManager());
}

private ManagedObject createMO(ManagedObjectReference mor)
{
```

```
    return MorUtil.createExactManagedObject(
        getServerConnection(), mor);
  }
}
```

ExtensibleManagedObject

This class is the base for many managed objects that can define customized fields. You can use these fields to tag the managed objects as needed.

ExtensibleManagedObject has two properties defined; therefore, two getter methods are provided to access them, respectively. It also has one method defined to set the value to a predefined field.

Overall ExtensibleManagedObject is a simple class. Listing 5-5 shows the source code of the class.

Listing 5-5
ExtensibleManagedObject.java

```java
package com.vmware.vim25.mo;
import java.rmi.RemoteException;

import com.vmware.vim25.*;

/**
 * The managed object class corresponding to the one defined in
 * the VI SDK API reference.
 *
 * @author Steve JIN (sjin@vmware.com)
 */

abstract public class ExtensibleManagedObject extends
    ManagedObject
{
  public CustomFieldDef[] getAvailableField()
      throws InvalidProperty, RuntimeFault, RemoteException
  {
    return (CustomFieldDef[]) getCurrentProperty("availableField");
```

```
}

public CustomFieldValue[] getValues() throws InvalidProperty,
    RuntimeFault, RemoteException
{
  return (CustomFieldValue[]) getCurrentProperty("value");
}

public ExtensibleManagedObject(
    ServerConnection serverConnection,
    ManagedObjectReference mor)
{
  super(serverConnection, mor);
}

public void setCustomValue(String key, String value)
    throws RuntimeFault, RemoteException
{
  getVimService().setCustomValue(getMOR(), key, value);
}
}
```

ManagedEntity

ManagedEntity is a subtype of ExtensibleManagedObject. It is the immediate super-class for all the types you can find in the inventory tree. It encapsulates all the common properties and behaviors of these types.

Besides the name and parent properties, one important property is permission. In the VI SDK, only subtypes of ManagedEntity can be controlled and protected. Chapter 15, "User and License Administration," discusses more details about the VI SDK security model.

Like all the other managed objects in the API, ManagedEntity doesn't define properties but the getter methods for all the corresponding properties. It has 15 methods, 12 of which are getters and 3 of which are normal methods. Chapter 6 discusses more on how to use these methods.

Listing 5-6 presents the source code of the ManagedEntity class.

Listing 5-6

ManagedEntity.java

```java
package com.vmware.vim25.mo;
import java.rmi.RemoteException;
import com.vmware.vim25.*;
import com.vmware.vim25.mo.util.*;


/**
 * ManagedEntity represents the managed objects that can be
 * listed in the inventory tree.
 *
 * @author Steve JIN (sjin@vmware.com)
 */

public class ManagedEntity extends ExtensibleManagedObject
{
  public ManagedEntity(ServerConnection sc,
      ManagedObjectReference mor)
  {
    super(sc, mor);
  }

  /** @since SDK4.0 */
  public boolean getAlarmActionEabled()
  {
    return ((Boolean) getCurrentProperty("alarmActionsEnabled"))
        .booleanValue();
  }

  public Event[] getConfigIssue()
  {
    return (Event[]) getCurrentProperty("configIssue");
  }

  public ManagedEntityStatus getConfigStatus()
  {
    return (ManagedEntityStatus)
      getCurrentProperty("configStatus");
```

```
}

public CustomFieldValue[] getCustomValue()
{
  return (CustomFieldValue[])
    getCurrentProperty("customValue");
}

public AlarmState[] getDeclaredAlarmState()
{
  return (AlarmState[])
    getCurrentProperty("declaredAlarmState");
}

public String[] getDisabledMethod()
{
  return (String[]) getCurrentProperty("disabledMethod");
}

public int[] getEffectiveRole()
{
  return (int[]) getCurrentProperty("effectiveRole");
}

public String getName()
{
  return (String) getCurrentProperty("name");
}

public ManagedEntityStatus getOverallStatus()
{
  return (ManagedEntityStatus)
    getCurrentProperty("overallStatus");
}

public ManagedEntity getParent()
{
  return (ManagedEntity) this.getManagedObject("parent");
}
```

```java
public Permission[] getPermission()
{
  return (Permission[]) getCurrentProperty("permission");
}


public Task[] getRecentTasks()
{
  return getTasks("recentTask");
}


/** @since SDK4.0 */
public Tag[] getTag()
{
  return (Tag[]) getCurrentProperty("tag");
}


public AlarmState[] getTriggeredAlarmState()
{
  return (AlarmState[])
    getCurrentProperty("triggeredAlarmState");
}


public Task destroy_Task() throws VimFault, RuntimeFault,
    RemoteException
{
  ManagedObjectReference taskMor = getVimService()
      .destroy_Task(getMOR());
  return new Task(getServerConnection(), taskMor);
}


public void reload() throws RuntimeFault, RemoteException
{
  getVimService().reload(getMOR());
}


public Task rename_Task(String name) throws InvalidName,
    DuplicateName, RuntimeFault, RemoteException
{
  ManagedObjectReference taskMor = getVimService()
```

```
        .rename_Task(getMOR(), name);
    return new Task(getServerConnection(), taskMor);
  }
}
```

Utility Classes

Besides the core managed object API are several utility classes in the API: MorUtil, InventoryNavigator, PropertyCollectorUtil, and so on.

MorUtil

The most often-used utility class is MorUtil.java, which is a group of methods for working work with ManagedObjectReference and related managed object types. Listing 5-7 shows the source code of the class.

Listing 5-7
MorUtil.java

```java
package com.vmware.vim25.mo.util;
import java.lang.reflect.Constructor;
import com.vmware.vim25.*;
import com.vmware.vim25.mo.*;

/**
 * Utility class for the managed object and
 * ManagedObjectReference.
 *
 * @author Steve JIN (sjin@vmware.com)
 */

public class MorUtil
{
    final public static String moPackageName =
      "com.vmware.vim25.mo";

    public static ManagedObjectReference[] createMORs(
```

```java
    ManagedObject[] mos)
{
  if (mos == null)
  {
    throw new IllegalArgumentException();
  }
  ManagedObjectReference[] mors =
    new ManagedObjectReference[mos.length];
  for (int i = 0; i < mos.length; i++)
  {
    mors[i] = mos[i].getMOR();
  }
  return mors;
}


public static ManagedObject createExactManagedObject(
    ServerConnection sc, ManagedObjectReference mor)
{
  if (mor == null)
  {
    return null;
  }

  String moType = mor.getType();

  try
  {
    Class moClass = Class
        .forName(moPackageName + "." + moType);
    Constructor constructor = moClass
        .getConstructor(new Class[] { ServerConnection.class,
            ManagedObjectReference.class });
    return (ManagedObject) constructor
        .newInstance(new Object[] { sc, mor });
  }
  catch (Exception e)
  {
    e.printStackTrace();
    return null;
  }
```

```
}

public static ManagedEntity createExactManagedEntity(
    ServerConnection sc, ManagedObjectReference mor)
{
  return (ManagedEntity) createExactManagedObject(sc, mor);
}

public static ManagedEntity[] createManagedEntities(
    ServerConnection sc, ManagedObjectReference[] mors)
{
  ManagedEntity[] mes = new ManagedEntity[mors.length];

  for (int i = 0; i < mors.length; i++)
  {
    mes[i] = createExactManagedEntity(sc, mors[i]);
  }

  return mes;
}
}
```

The methods createExactManagedObject() and createExactManagedEntity() are useful. The first one uses the Java reflection API to create a real managed object from a ManagedObjectReference object. The latter is just a helper method that calls into the first one and casts the return to ManagedEntity instead of ManagedObject.

Both methods take in two parameters: the ServerConnection object, which you can get from any managed object residing on the same server, and the ManagedObjectReference object. Whenever you're getting a MOR object from a data object, you can use one of the two methods to perform conversion.

The following code is an example extracted from the HostSystem class. Inside the method, createExactManagedObject() is used to create a managed object with the MOR as returned from getConfigManager().getHealthStatusSystem(). Because the HostHealthStatusSystem is on the same server as the HostSystem, getServerConnection() can easily get the ServerConnection object as the first parameter.

```
public HostHealthStatusSystem getHealthStatusSystem() throws
             InvalidProperty, RuntimeFault, RemoteException
```

```
{
  return (HostHealthStatusSystem)
MorUtil.createExactManagedObject(getServerConnection(),
        getConfigManager().getHealthStatusSystem());
}
```

Although best efforts have been made to convert the MORs to corresponding types, the Java API cannot do much with those scattered in the various data objects, especially ones nested inside other data objects. When you get a MOR, you can always convert it using the methods in the MorUtil class.

InventoryNavigator

The InventoryNavigator class is the helper to find managed entities inside the inventory. Currently, four methods are defined, representing four ways to obtain one or a set of managed objects.

Instead of working on the TraversalSpec, you can have one line of code get all the subnodes with a specified type of managed entities, or you can get a managed entity by its name.

Listing 5-8 lists the source code of the InventoryNavigator class.

Listing 5-8
InventoryNavigator.java

```
package com.vmware.vim25.mo;
import java.rmi.RemoteException;

import com.vmware.vim25.*;
import com.vmware.vim25.mo.util.*;
import com.vmware.vim25.mo.util.PropertyCollectorUtil;

public class InventoryNavigator
{
  private ManagedEntity rootEntity = null;

  public InventoryNavigator(ManagedEntity rootEntity)
```

```
{
  this.rootEntity = rootEntity;
}


/**
 * Retrieve container contents from specified parent
 * recursively if requested.
 *
 * @param recurse whether recursively from the root down
 * @throws RemoteException
 * @throws RuntimeFault
 * @throws InvalidProperty
 */
public ManagedEntity[] searchManagedEntities(boolean recurse)
    throws InvalidProperty, RuntimeFault, RemoteException
{
  String[][] typeinfo = new String[][] {
      new String[] { "ManagedEntity", } };
  return searchManagedEntities(typeinfo, recurse);
}


/**
 * Get the first ManagedObjectReference from the current node
 * for the specified type
 */
public ManagedEntity[] searchManagedEntities(String type)
    throws InvalidProperty, RuntimeFault, RemoteException
{
  String[][] typeinfo = new String[][] { new String[] { type,
      "name", }, };
  return searchManagedEntities(typeinfo, true);
}


/**
 * Retrieve content recursively with multiple properties. The
 * typeinfo array contains typename + properties to retrieve.
 *
 * @param typeinfo
 *           2D array of properties for each typename
```

```
 * @param recurse
 *           retrieve contents recursively from the root down
 * @return retrieved object contents
 * @throws RemoteException
 * @throws RuntimeFault
 * @throws InvalidProperty
 */
public ManagedEntity[] searchManagedEntities(
    String[][] typeinfo, boolean recurse)
    throws InvalidProperty, RuntimeFault, RemoteException
{
  ObjectContent[] ocs = retrieveObjectContents(typeinfo,
      recurse);
  return createManagedEntities(ocs);
}


private ObjectContent[] retrieveObjectContents(
    String[][] typeinfo, boolean recurse)
    throws InvalidProperty, RuntimeFault, RemoteException
{
  if (typeinfo == null || typeinfo.length == 0)
  {
    return null;
  }

  PropertyCollector pc = rootEntity.getServerConnection()
      .getServiceInstance().getPropertyCollector();

  SelectionSpec[] selectionSpecs = null;
  if (recurse)
  {
    selectionSpecs = PropertyCollectorUtil
        .buildFullTraversal();
  }

  PropertySpec[] propspecary = PropertyCollectorUtil
      .buildPropertySpecArray(typeinfo);

  ObjectSpec os = new ObjectSpec();
```

```java
    os.setObj(rootEntity.getMOR());
    os.setSkip(Boolean.FALSE);
    os.setSelectSet(selectionSpecs);

    PropertyFilterSpec spec = new PropertyFilterSpec();
    spec.setObjectSet(new ObjectSpec[] { os });
    spec.setPropSet(propspecary);

    return pc
        .retrieveProperties(new PropertyFilterSpec[] { spec });
}


private ManagedEntity[] createManagedEntities(
    ObjectContent[] ocs)
{
  if (ocs == null)
  {
    return new ManagedEntity[] {};
  }
  ManagedEntity[] mes = new ManagedEntity[ocs.length];

  for (int i = 0; i < mes.length; i++)
  {
    ManagedObjectReference mor = ocs[i].getObj();
    mes[i] = MorUtil.createExactManagedEntity(rootEntity
        .getServerConnection(), mor);
  }
  return mes;
}


/**
 * Get the ManagedObjectReference for an item under the
 * specified parent node that has the type and name specified.
 *
 * @param type
 *           type of the managed object
 * @param name
 *           name to match
 * @return First ManagedEntity object of the type / name pair
```

147

```
 *          found
 * @throws RemoteException
 * @throws RuntimeFault
 * @throws InvalidProperty
 */
public ManagedEntity searchManagedEntity(String type,
    String name) throws InvalidProperty, RuntimeFault,
    RemoteException
{
  if (name == null || name.length() == 0)
  {
    return null;
  }

  if (type == null)
  {
    type = "ManagedEntity";
  }

  String[][] typeinfo = new String[][] { new String[] { type,
      "name", }, };

  ObjectContent[] ocs = retrieveObjectContents(typeinfo, true);

  if (ocs == null || ocs.length == 0)
  {
    return null;
  }

  for (int i = 0; i < ocs.length; i++)
  {
    DynamicProperty[] propSet = ocs[i].getPropSet();

    if (propSet.length > 0)
    {
      String nameInPropSet = (String) propSet[0].getVal();
      if (name.equalsIgnoreCase(nameInPropSet))
      {
        ManagedObjectReference mor = ocs[i].getObj();
```

```
      return MorUtil.createExactManagedEntity(rootEntity
          .getServerConnection(), mor);
    }
   }
  }
  return null;
 }
}
```

Other Classes

`PropertyCollectorUtil.java` groups some frequently used methods to create `PropertyCollector`-related data objects (for example, the `buildFullTraversal()` method as listed in Listing 4-2 in Chapter 4). It's often used in the backend by other classes. As an API user, you don't need it and don't see it much, simply because you don't necessarily use `PropertyCollector` in the Java API.

As one of its design goals, the Java API provides a better abstraction than Web Services API but does not remove or hide anything. As such, `PropertyCollector` is available for use. You can also take advantage of the `PropertyCollectorUtil` class while using the `PropertyCollector` class.

Last, but not least, two classes parse command-line commands. They are not a core part of the API, but an optional helper. You can use whatever command-line parsers you like or just use a simple fixed command-line syntax.

For more details, download the latest JAR file from the project home. All the binary and source code and some sample code are available.

High-Performance Web Services Engine

In VI Java API 2.0, a new Web Services engine was introduced. It's significantly faster and smaller than AXIS for VI SDK. The new engine is not a generic Web Services engine, but a Just Enough Web Service Engine (JEWSE). The principle can be applied with other Web Services APIs where performance is a critical concern.

Because the new engine replaces AXIS only, the upper-level APIs are still the same. The applications built on top of the VI Java API run much faster (4X) and use less memory.

Motivation

The biggest advantage of the new JEWSE is better performance. The VI SDK application using the AXIS engine takes from 3 to 6 seconds in initial loading. It's not acceptable for utility-type applications. After loading, the serialization and deserialization are also pretty slow. The new engine takes only 0.2 to 0.4 second in loading and runs 4 times faster than AXIS after loading.

A second advantage of JEWSE is that it's more compatible. The VI SDK has two incompatible versions: VI SDK 2.0 and 2.5. Besides of the additional properties and methods in 2.5, they in fact share most types. But due to different namespaces, these types are generated to different packages, thus causing coding trouble. For example, `com.vmware.vim.ManagedObjectReference` and `com.vmware.vim25.ManagedObjectReference` are pretty much the same except they are defined in different packages. When you have an application talking to two versions of servers, you may need to have two sets of libraries and fully qualify the type definition everywhere.

A third advantage is that the data objects generated with JEWSE are cleaner and smaller than those generated with AXIS. Even a data object with no property defined can be 50+ lines long in AXIS. With everything together, including the `dom4j` library, the VI Java API runtime is 1.3M versus 5M (AXIS 1.4) and 40M (AXIS 2). You don't need to work with many JAR files from AXIS. All you need in VI Java API 2.0 are two jar files.

A fourth advantage is that the JEWSE architecture is simpler to debug through the calling stack than AXIS. It's also more flexible to get the XML request and XML response.

Last but not least, JEWSE doesn't have all the legal concerns of AXIS. AXIS has dependencies on libraries that ISV cannot freely redistribute, which creates complications for end users. Everything in and referenced by VI Java API is under BSD license.

Architecture

The JEWSE is designed to replace AXIS. The fewest changes are to the upper-layer APIs. So it's best to keep interfaces similar to what AXIS provides.

Figure 5-3 shows how the new engine is related to others.

During development, a code generator reads the latest WSDL file and generates new VIM stubs including all the new POJO data object types. This code generation is needed only once for creating the API and totally invisible from API users.

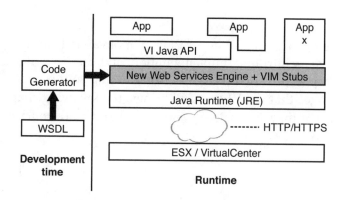

Figure 5-3 The architecture of new JEWSE engine

In the runtime stack, the VIM stubs and the engine run on the Java runtime and provide services to the VI Java API. It's also possible for applications to talk to the VIM stubs directly. Given the small overhead of the VI Java API, there is little reason to do so.

Figure 5-4 provides a detailed view of the box "New Web Services Engine + VIM Stubs" in Figure 5-3. There are three layers:

- **Web Services Client**—It's responsible for creating the connections and maintaining the session with the server side.

- **Serialization and deserialization engine**—It converts the data objects to the XML requests and the XML responses to the corresponding data objects. This is the most challenging part in the engine.

- **VIM stubs and data object types**—It provides all the programming interfaces that are defined in the WSDL.

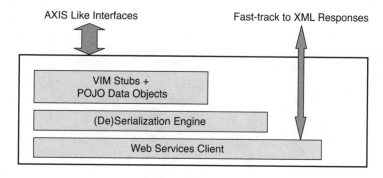

Figure 5-4 The layers of the new high-performance JEWSE engine

Summary

This chapter discussed the open source VI Java API from motivations, design objectives, and guidelines to architecture, implementation, and use. To better illustrate how it works, this chapter provided the UML diagrams and source code.

Given all these advantages that the VI Java API brings, the following chapters use it to build samples so that they are easier to understand and more concise.

Chapter 6

Managing Inventory

This chapter discusses the VI inventory structure in detail and how to manage the managed entities in the inventory. The inventory tree is important because it reflects how different managed entities are structured and organized, and it provides a unified mechanism for navigation. You learn how to create a new managed entity, move an existing managed entity, and delete a managed entity you no longer need.

This chapter also introduces you to the View and its five related managed objects. These six managed objects are useful to develop a GUI application that closely monitors the changes in the inventory and reflects them visually in your application in real time.

Managed Objects: ManagedEntity, Folder, Datacenter, CustomFieldsManager; View, ManagedObjectView, ViewManager, ContainerView, InventoryView, ListView

Inventory Hierarchical Structure

Chapter 2, "VI SDK Basics," briefly introduced the inventory structure and VI SDK basics. This section revisits it and examines the structure in greater detail.

Figure 6-1 illustrates the hierarchy of the inventory tree for both ESX and VC server from a ServiceInstance object. From the ServiceInstance object, you can get hold of the rootFolder, which is a Folder managed object. Note that in the VI SDK, you first get the

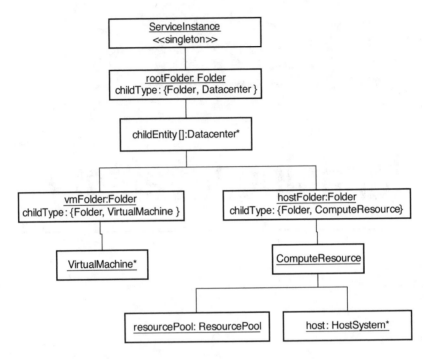

Figure 6-1 Unified inventory tree structure

ServiceContent object and then the rootFolder; you can get hold of the rootFolder directly in the VI Java API.

The Folder object is a container type. What it can have as its children depends on its property childType, which is an array of strings. This property is set by the system, and you cannot change it. As you can tell from the figure, the rootFolder can have two types of children: Folder and Datacenter. The real values stores are actually vim.Folder and vim.Datacenter. To save space, vim is ignored in Figure 6-1.

Because rootfolder can have Folder objects as its children, you can have a recursive structure in which Folder objects are nested to an unlimited number of levels (not shown in Figure 6-1). The nested structure is not only possible, but necessary in a big computing infrastructure where you want to organize the computing resources into a meaningful structure for easy management. For example, you can have folders for different locations, for different departments, for different categories, or a mixture of these.

From the rootfolder, there can be many Datacenter and Folder objects as children. No matter how the structure looks, the Folder/Datacenter recursion has to end up with a Datacenter object, which is the basic unit of the whole computing structure.

The Datacenter managed object doesn't necessarily reflect a typical data center in a physical world, which refers to a facility where a lot of servers are hosted. In VMware Infrastructure, the Datacenter is more conceptual than physical. It is where the physical server and virtual machines are aggregated into a single management unit.

The Datacenter has two Folder objects attached to it. One contains VirtualMachine objects or nested Folder objects. Any sub Folder objects created beneath the top vmFolder have the same restriction on the childType, meaning you can only find either Folder or VirtualMachine objects there.

The other Folder object contains the ComputeResource object or Folder objects. The folder name hostFolder can cause confusion because you would expect it to contain HostSystem directly based on its name.

Any sub Folder object created there can only have Folder or ComputerResource objects as its children. Although only ComputeResource is listed as the type, its subtype ClusterComputeResource can also show up anywhere ComputeResource does. So you can find a mixture of ComputeResource, ClusterComputeResource, and Folder objects under a hostFolder.

ComputeResource is an aggregation of many computing resources from HostSystem, Datastore, and Network to ResourcePool. Because Datastore and Network are not managed entities in 2.5, they are omitted in the diagram. It's easy to understand the HostSystem as part of the ComputeResource. How about ResourcePool?

The ResourcePool represents a set of physical resources: either a single host machine or aggregation from multiple hosts. These resources can be further divided into small chunks in different ways such as ratio and absolute value. Each ComputeResource has only one root ResourcePool, and the root has a recursive structure of ResourcePool objects underneath it.

Now that the overall structure is clear, let's look at the difference of the inventory in ESX and VC servers. The main difference is that the quantities of different managed entities can show up in the inventory tree. Overall, the ESX server inventory tree is simpler than that of the VC server, which can manage hundreds of ESX servers at a time. An ESX server inventory tree always has one Datacenter and one HostSystem, and the structure is pretty fixed. Many of the sample code listings in the following sections work only with the VC server, not the ESX server.

Managed Entities

ManagedEntity has seven subtypes, including Folder, Datacenter, VirtualMachine, ComputeResource, ClusterComputeResource, ResourcePool, and HostSystem (see Figure 6-2). These managed entity objects make up the entire inventory tree.

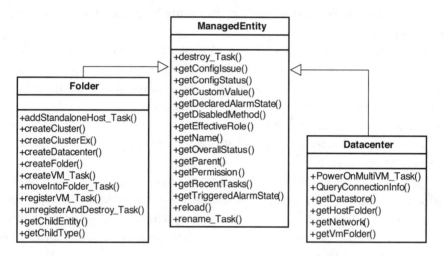

Figure 6-2   The UML diagram of ManagedEntity and its subtypes Folder and Datacenter

Of all these managed entities, this chapter focuses on the three managed objects that are most related to inventory management: ManagedEntity, Folder, and Datacenter. The remaining five managed objects are covered in detail in the following chapters.

ManagedEntity

ManagedEntity is the base type for all the possible object types that can be included in an inventory. It captures all the common properties and common behaviors of all the inventory items. The UML diagram ignores the 12 properties, but it includes their getter methods. As a subtype of ExtensibleManagedObject, ManagedEntity inherits the two properties availableField and value, as well as the method setCustomValue().

To help you understand ManagedEntity, Table 6-1 lists all the properties. Those properties whose names suffix with * are not required. The corresponding getter methods might return a null pointer. Check the return value before using it.

Table 6-1

Properties Defined on ManagedEntity

Name	Type	Explanation
name	xsd:string	Name of this entity. Must be unique relative to its parent. Special characters are escaped: / (slash) ➔ %2F or %2f; \ (backslash) ➔ %5C or %5c; % (percent) ➔ %25 When you read the name, your client needs to reverse it back.
parent*	ManagedEntity	Parent of this entity. Null for the root Folder.
overallStatus	ManagedEntityStatus	General health of this managed entity. The value is calculated based on the status of all the alarms attached to this managed entity; pick the highest value in an order from green, yellow, red, and gray. If any of the alarms has a gray status, the overall status of the managed entity is red. The overall status is green only when all the alarm statuses are green.
permission*	Permission[]	List of permissions defined for this entity.
effectiveRole*	xsd:int[]	Access rights the current user has to this entity. Note: This is an array of integers representing the role IDs.
disabledMethod*	xsd:string[]	List of methods that are disabled based on the current runtime state of this entity. For example, if a VirtualMachine is up and running, the powerOn method is in this list. The method names are in the format of vim.VirtualMachine.powerOn or vim.ExtensibleManagedObject.setCustomValue. You can use this list to determine whether to enable or disable an operation in the GUI. Note: This list does not consider the permissions and the different support on either ESX or the VC server. The unimplemented methods don't show up in this list.
customValue*	CustomFieldValue[]	Custom field values. Custom fields are not supported on the ESX server.

continues...

Table 6-1   continued

Properties Defined on `ManagedEntity`		
Name	**Type**	**Explanation**
`configIssue*`	`Event[]`	Current configuration issues associated with this entity. Typically, these issues have already been logged as events. The entity stores these events as long as they are still current. The `configStatus` property provides an overall status based on these events.
`configStatus`	`ManagedEntityStatus`	Indicates whether the system has detected a configuration issue involving this entity. For example, a duplicated IP address or MAC address or a host in a cluster might be out of compliance.
		The meanings of the `configStatus` values are as follows:
		red: A problem has been detected involving the entity.
		yellow: A problem is about to occur, or a transient condition has occurred (for example, reconfigure fail-over policy).
		green: No configuration issues have been detected.
		gray: The configuration status of the entity is not being monitored.
		A green status means only that a problem has not been detected; it is not a guarantee that the entity is problem-free.
`triggeredAlarmState`	`AlarmState[]`	A set of alarm states for alarms triggered by this entity or by its descendants. Triggered alarms are propagated up the inventory hierarchy so that a user can readily tell when a descendant has triggered an alarm.
`recentTask*`	`Task[]` (`ManagedObjectReference[]`)	The set of recent tasks operating on this managed entity. This is a subset of `recentTask` belonging to this entity. A task in this list can be in one of the four states: pending, running, success, or error.
		This property can deduce intermediate power states for a virtual machine entity. For example, if the current `powerState` is `poweredOn` and there is a running task performing the `suspend` operation, the virtual machine's intermediate state might be described as "suspending."
		Most tasks (such as power operations) obtain exclusive access to the virtual machine, so it is unusual for this list to contain more than one running task. One exception is the task of cloning a virtual machine.

Table 6-1   continued

Properties Defined on ManagedEntity		
Name	**Type**	**Explanation**
declaredAlarmState*	AlarmState[]	A set of alarm states for alarms that apply to this managed entity. The set includes alarms defined on this entity and alarms inherited from the parent entity or above in the inventory hierarchy.
		Alarms are inherited if they can be triggered by this entity or its descendants. This set does not include alarms that are defined on descendants of this entity.

The ManagedEntity already captures the common properties, ranging from tree structure (name, parent), status (overallStatus, configStatus, configIssue, disabledMethod), alarm (declaredAlarmState, triggeredAlarmState), security (effectiveRole, permission), task (recentTask), to customization (customValue, availableField(inherited), and value(inherited)).

Only three methods are defined with ManagedEntity:

- destroy_Task() destroys this managed entity, just as its name suggests. It also deletes the managed entity's contents and removes itself from its parent. For example, when called on the virtual machine, the method not only removes it from the inventory but also deletes related files permanently.[1] If the managed entity is a container like Folder, all the child inventory items will be deleted as well. Given the impact and possible consequence, be cautious while calling this method, especially when you log in as a super user with all privileges.

  The caller must have appropriate privileges on the entity and its parent entity. The required privileges vary from subtype to subtype. Table 6-2 lists the privileges required for each subtype.

- rename_Task() just changes the entity's name to a new one as specified in the parameter. Just as described in the name property, you should escape any special characters, such as slash, backslash, and percent. A new name /SuSe_server10%\ is saved as %2fSuSe_server10%25%5c. When reading it out for display, you need to reverse the encoding.

---

[1] You can remove the virtual machine from the inventory without deleting the related files on the disk by calling the unregisterVM() method of the VirtualMachine managed object.

Table 6-2

Privileges Required for Different Managed Entities	
Type	Privilege
VirtualMachine	VirtualMachine.Inventory.Delete
Datacenter	Datacenter.Delete
Folder	Folder.Delete
HostSystem	Host.Inventory.RemoveHostFromCluster
ResourcePool	Resource.DeletePool
ComputeResource	Host.Inventory.RemoveHostFromCluster
ClusterComputeResource	Host.Inventory.DeleteCluster

- reload() reloads the managed entity. It is only necessary when the managed entity is changed without using the Web Services API. For example, a VirtualMachine's configuration .vmx file can be changed manually in the Console OS. In this case, the application should invoke reload() to update the entity with the latest changes.

Folder

Folder is a subtype of ManagedEntity, so whatever holds true of ManagedEntity is applicable on it as well.

Beyond that, the Folder defines two more properties:

- **childEntity**—This is an array of ManagedEntity. In theory, these managed entities could be any subtypes, such as Folder itself, VirtualMachine, HostSystem, and so on. In reality, the types can be added as childEntity is decided by the childType.

- **childType**—This is an array of strings. Only those types included in the array can be added to the childEntity. For example, in Figure 6-1, the rootFolder has only two types included: Folder and Datacenter. Therefore you can only create Folder and Datacenter objects underneath. The childType is read only, and you cannot change it directly or indirectly. It's reserved by the system to control the structure of inventory hierarchy.

You can read childEntity to get all the immediate children of the current Folder object. To dig down the possible hierarchy, you can design your own recursive algorithm to grab all the children, including immediate or nonimmediate ones. Alternatively, you can use the TraversalSpec discussed in Chapter 4, "Using PropertyCollector and SearchIndex," to get managed entities recursively.

Nine methods are defined directly on Folder: addStandaloneHost_Task(), createCluster(), createClusterEx(), createDatacenter(), createFolder(), createVM_Task(), moveIntoFolder_Task(), registerVM_Task(), and unregisterAndDestroy_Task(). The createCluster() method is deprecated in favor of createClusterEx() as of version 2.5.

These methods are discussed in detail in the next several sections, which include samples.

Datacenter

Datacenter is a subtype of ManagedEntity; whatever is applicable for ManagedEntity works for Datacenter. Beyond that, Datacenter defines four properties: datastore, hostFolder, network, and vmFolder, whose types and meaning are detailed in Table 6-3.

Table 6-3

Properties Defined in **Datacenter** Managed Object		
Property	**Type**	**Explanation**
datastore*	ManagedObjectReference[] to a Datastore[]	The datastore objects available in this datacenter
network*	ManagedObjectReference[] to a Network[]	The network objects available in this datacenter
hostFolder	ManagedObjectReference to a Folder	The folder that contains the compute resources, including hosts and clusters, for this datacenter
vmFolder	ManagedObjectReference to a Folder	The folder hierarchy that contains all the virtual machines and templates for this datacenter

The Datacenter defines only two methods by itself:

- powerOnMultiVM_Task() powers on multiple virtual machines in this Datacenter at a time. It takes a list of VirtualMachine objects to be powered on. These virtual machines can be distributed in different clusters and hosts. If any of these virtual machines is suspended, it resumes execution at its point of suspension.

  If any virtual machine in the list is managed by VMware DRS in manual mode, a DRS recommendation is generated and the users have to approve it before the virtual machine can really power on. By default, the virtual machine is powered on the current host. If DRS is running in automatic mode, the virtual machine is powered on the recommended hosts, which might cause a migration of the virtual machine to another host.

- queryConnectionInfo() gets a HostConnectInfo from a HostSystem before the HostSystem is added to the datacenter. Therefore, all the information about the host and login credentials is needed as a parameter to this method:

  - **Hostname**—The target HostSystem's DNS name or IP address.
  - **Port**—The port number for the connection. For ESX 2.x, this is the authd daemon port (902 by default). For ESX 3.x and above and for VMware Server hosts, this is the https port (443 by default). You can specify –1 to have the VirtualCenter server try the default ports.
  - **Username**—The user's login name.
  - **Password**—The user's password.
  - **sslThumbprint**—The expected SSL thumbprint of the target host's certificate.

  Given its purpose, queryConnectionInfo() is a VC-only method and is not available on the ESX server. Because the stub is there, you can still call it but get NotImplement fault upon the call.

Basic Inventory Operations

This section mainly focuses on the folder and datacenter and leaves the operations of the virtual machine and physical host to the following chapters.

Like many other methods, these inventory manipulation methods require some privileges. Check the API reference for the detailed privilege requirement for each method of interest. Also, make sure to test your applications using the credentials of your targeted users before you deliver them because users are assigned with unique roles and privileges that can lead to different results while invoking these methods.

Adding a Folder or a Datacenter

You can add a new `Folder` or a `Datacenter` object as a child of a `Folder`. Listing 6-1 is a sample to add several folders and datacenters. Because the inventory structure of an ESX server is pretty much fixed, creating a new folder under the root folder or a new datacenter is not supported. Try the sample with a VirtualCenter server.

Running the sample creates a hierarchy, with each folder representing a location. From one of the location folders, the sample creates another subfolder. Under these folders, the sample creates several datacenters. Datacenters and subfolders can coexist in the same parent folder as long as they have different names.

Listing 6-1
`CreateFolderDatacenter.java`

```
package vim25.samples.mo;
import java.net.URL;
import com.vmware.vim25.mo.Folder;
import com.vmware.vim25.mo.ServiceInstance;

public class CreateFolderDatacenter
{
  public static void main(String[] args) throws Exception
  {
    if(args.length != 3)
    {
      System.out.println("Usage: java CreateFolderDatacenter" +
        " <url> <username> <password>");
      return;
    }

    ServiceInstance si = new ServiceInstance(new URL(args[0]),
      args[1], args[2], true);
```

```
Folder rootFolder = si.getRootFolder();

rootFolder.createDatacenter("HeadQuarter");

Folder paFolder = rootFolder.createFolder("Palo Alto");
Folder engFolder = paFolder.createFolder("Engineering");
engFolder.createDatacenter("Dev");
engFolder.createDatacenter("QA");
paFolder.createDatacenter("Sales");
paFolder.createDatacenter("Corporate");

Folder bFolder = rootFolder.createFolder("Boston");
bFolder.createDatacenter("Engineering");

Folder lFolder = rootFolder.createFolder("London");
lFolder.createDatacenter("Engineering");

si.getServerConnection().logout();
  }
}
```

Deleting an Existing Entity

Deleting an existing item is relatively easy because destroy_Task is already defined
on ManagedEntity. You can call this method on any managed entity in the inventory. Upon this call, the managed entity is removed from its parent; so are all its
children, if any.

Listing 6-2 shows a sample to delete one folder and all its contents and one
datacenter from the entities created in Listing 6-1.

Listing 6-2
DeleteFolderDatacenter.java

```
package vim25.samples.mo;
import java.net.URL;
```

```java
import com.vmware.vim25.mo.*;

public class DeleteFolderDatacenter
{
  public static void main(String[] args) throws Exception
  {
    if(args.length != 3)
    {
      System.out.println("Usage: java DeleteFolderDatacenter " +
        "<url> <username> <password>");
      return;
    }

    ServiceInstance si = new ServiceInstance(new URL(args[0]),
      args[1], args[2], true);

    Folder rootFolder = si.getRootFolder();

    ManagedEntity[] mes = rootFolder.getChildEntity();

    for(int i=0; mes!=null && i<mes.length; i++)
    {
      String name = mes[i].getName();
      if("Palo Alto".equals(name) || "HeadQuarter".equals(name))
      {
        mes[i].destroy_Task();
      }
    }

    si.getServerConnection().logout();
  }
}
```

Renaming an Existing Entity

It's easy to rename a managed entity in the inventory given because a
rename_Task() method is already defined on the ManagedEntity type. You can apply
this method on any managed entity in the inventory. Listing 6-3 shows a sample to
change a virtual machine's name and verify its success by tracing the Task object
that is returned.

Listing 6-3

VmRename.java

```java
package vim25.samples.mo;
import java.net.URL;
import com.vmware.vim25.mo.*;


public class VmRename
{
  public static void main(String[] args) throws Exception
  {
    if(args.length != 3)
    {
      System.out.println("Usage: java SearchIndexSample <url> "
          + "<username> <password>");
      return;
    }

    ServiceInstance si = new ServiceInstance(
            new URL(args[0]), args[1], args[2], true);

    Folder rootFolder = si.getRootFolder();
    VirtualMachine vm = (VirtualMachine) new InventoryNavigator(
        rootFolder).searchManagedEntities("VirtualMachine")[0];

    Task task = vm.rename_Task("myvm");
    String result = task.waitForMe();

    if(result == Task.SUCCESS)
    {
      System.out.println("The name has been changed.");
    }
    else
    {
      System.out.println("The name cannot be changed.");
    }
    si.getServerConnection().logout();
  }
}
```

Moving Existing Entities

You can move managed entities like folders and datacenters into a new folder with the `moveIntoFolder_Task()` method. Listing 6-4 shows an example of moving a data center from the `Boston` folder up to the root folder. This moving is subject to the restriction of child types of the destination folder. For example, you cannot move a virtual machine to a folder allowing only `Folder` and `Datacenter` as its children.

The method can move multiple entities at a time. If an exception is raised during the process, the method terminates with the rest of the managed entities in their original location and processed entities in their new location.

Listing 6-4
`MoveDatacenter.java`

```
package vim25.samples.mo;
import java.net.URL;
import com.vmware.vim25.mo.*;


public class MoveDatacenter
{
  public static void main(String[] args) throws Exception
  {
    if(args.length != 3)
    {
      System.out.println("Usage: java MoveDatacenter <url> "
          + "<username> <password>");
      return;
    }

    ServiceInstance si = new ServiceInstance(new URL(args[0]),
        args[1], args[2], true);

    Folder rootFolder = si.getRootFolder();
    SearchIndex searchIndex = si.getSearchIndex();
    ManagedEntity me = searchIndex.findByInventoryPath(
        "Boston/Engineering");
    rootFolder.moveIntoFolder_Task(new ManagedEntity[] {me});
```

```
    si.getServerConnection().logout();
  }
}
```

Managing Custom Fields

The CustomFieldsManager adds and removes the custom fields to managed objects that are extended from ExtensibleManagedObject. These custom fields are extensions to the predefined properties and represent a standard mechanism to extend the managed objects. The typical use of custom fields is to tag the managed objects for management purposes.

> Custom fields are supported only on the VirtualCenter server, not the ESX server. The custom fields and their values of HostSystem and VirtualMachine are displayed in the "Annotations" sections in the VI Client.
>
> To tag a virtual machine with ESX only, you can use its config.annotation property, which you can change with the reconfigVM_Task() method. The limitation is that you can have only one string. To support multiple tags, you can use key/value pairs with delimiters, or just XML.

The CustomFieldsManager has one property field that holds an array of CustomFieldDef data objects, each of which describes a custom field. The CustomFieldDef type defines six properties, as shown in Figure 6-3. Two properties are related to privileges; one is for the field definition and the other for the instances of the field. The property key is an integer as primary key. The managedObjectType is new in SDK 2.5 to specify the target managed objects that are applicable. When not specified, it's valid for all the managed objects. The name is a string as the name of the field. The type is the data type of the field, such as string.

When a new field is added, it shows up in the availableField property of the managed object where it's applicable. From the managed object, you can call the setCustomValue() method to assign a value to the custom field. Upon successful invocation, the new value shows up in the property value.

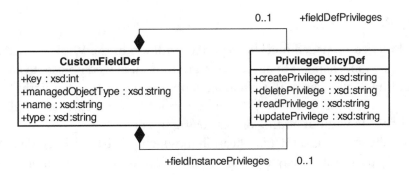

Figure 6-3 The CustomFieldDef data object

> In the managed objects extended from ManagedEntity, there is a duplicated property called customValue holding the same CustomFieldValue object array.

Although you use the name of the custom field for the parameter key when you call setCustomValue(), the saved CustomFieldValue actually does not keep the name but the integer key of the CustomFieldDef. So don't be confused with the name and key in different places.

Four methods are defined with CustomFieldsManager:

- addCustomFieldDef() adds a new custom field. It takes in the name, managed object type, field privileges, and instance privileges as parameters. You don't specify the key; the system assigns an integer for you. You must not add a new field whose name already exists.

- removeCustomFieldDef() removes an existing custom field. It takes in the unique key of the custom field definition. Note: Removing the definition also removes all the instance values of the definition.

- renameCustomFieldDef() renames a custom field. You provide the unique key to locate the custom field definition and new name as arguments.

- setField() assigns a value to a managed object. You provide the managed object, the unique key of the custom field, and a string value.

  This method is equivalent to the setCustomValue() method defined with ExtensibleManagedObject. Although they both require a parameter called key, setField() stands for something different. With setField(), the key is the unique integer value; with the setCustomValue(), the key is the name of the custom field, which is a unique string.

Using Views

View and related managed objects are a new addition to the VI SDK since 2.5. They provide a mechanism to aggregate a group of managed objects to ease the access and track changes of these managed objects. Used together with PropertyCollector, these View objects can dynamically change the set of observed managed objects without adding or destroying filters.

A typical use case is a GUI application in which you have a large inventory tree but only part of it is visible at a given time. You don't want to monitor all the changes in the inventory tree since that could be a performance killer and also not necessary. Instead, you monitor only those that are visible in the GUI. Any update on those invisible managed objects can be ignored.

There are six managed objects included: ViewManager, View, ManagedObjectView, ContainerView, ListView, and InventoryView, as shown in Figure 6-4.

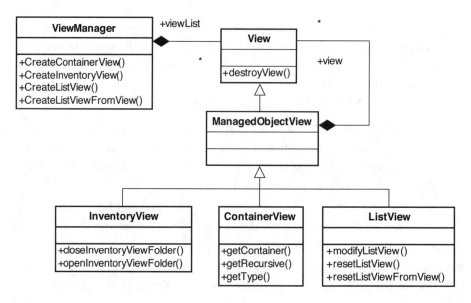

Figure 6-4 The ViewManager and all types of View managed objects

ViewManager

ViewManager is a singleton managed object that you can access from the ServiceInstance. It has one property defined as viewList as an array of View objects, including those subtype objects. Four methods are defined in ViewManager, all for creating different View objects. Depending on the subtypes of the Views, the parameters needed are different. The createListViewFromView() method is special because it creates a ListView from an existing View object: either ContainerView or InventoryView.

After a create*() method finishes, it returns the just-created View managed object. On the server side, the newly created View object is also added to the viewList array property. There is no explicit limitation on how many views you can create. You can find out the number of View objects and what they are by retrieving the viewList property.

View and ManagedObjectView

Now let's look at these two View managed objects. Their ManagedObjectReference values are like the following format:

```
session[52d748ff-865f-443a-9a91-5f0389a225d6]5273c93c-bd55-2a9e-1d94-d0b68070ac88
```

The string inside [] is the current user's session ID, and the string after] is the View ID. This format implies that the View is closely related to a session and cannot be shared across sessions. If you have multiple GUI clients running under different users, each GUI client can track the View separately and doesn't interfere with the other.

View is the supertype for all View objects. It has only one method defined, which is destroy(). When it's called, the View object is deleted on the server side and removed from the viewList property in the ViewManager.

Just below the View is the ManagedObjectView, which has one property defined as an array of View objects. This makes the ManagedObjectView and its subtypes capable of aggregating multiple View objects and potentially creating a tree-like hierarchy in each.

Under the ManagedObjectView are three subtypes: ContainerView, InventoryView, and ListView.

ContainerView

ContainerView groups the contents of a single container managed object. When creating a ContainerView from ViewManager, you need to provide the following:

- A container managed entity, such as a Folder, Datacenter, ComputeResource, or ResourcePool object

- An optional filter type list. If you don't provide a list, all the types are included by default.
- A Boolean whether to include the objects from subcontainers or just immediate children.

These parameters are saved into the `ContainerView` as properties. The `ContainerView` doesn't define normal methods other than the inherited `destroyView()` method from the `View` type.

InventoryView

This reflects the server inventory as a whole. Therefore, the `createInventoryView()` doesn't require additional parameters; neither does it have properties defined directly other than the inherited view property from `ManagedObjectView`.

It defines two methods:

- `openInventoryViewFolder()` takes in an array of `ManagedEntity` objects, which are to expand in the inventory. It tells the `InventoryView` object to include these child managed entities under any of the `ManagedEntity` in the arrays. It's possible that not every entity in the array can be resolved. Those entities that cannot be resolved are sent back as the return of this method.
- `closeInventoryViewFolder()` does the opposite of `openInventoryViewFolder()`. It tells the `InventoryView` that one or more managed entities in the inventory are collapsed visually and excludes them accordingly. The return of this method is also a list of entities that cannot be resolved. Therefore, you would hope to get an empty array of entities as a return of both methods.

ListView

Unlike `InventoryView` and `ContainView`, `ListView` groups an arbitrary set of managed objects. When creating a `ListView` from `ViewManager` by invoking the `createListView()` method, just provide a list of managed objects to be included in this `View` initially. Alternatively, you can create a `ListView` from an existing `View` object using the `createListViewFromView()` method.

After you create a `ListView` object, you can change the managed objects included. You can invoke any of the three methods as follows:

- `modifyListView()` takes in the managed objects to be added or to be removed. Even if some of the managed objects cannot be resolved, the call still succeeds. The list of the managed objects that cannot be added is sent back as return of the method.

- `resetListView()` replaces all the existing managed objects with these in an array parameter. Similar to the previous method, it returns a list of managed objects that cannot be resolved.

- `resetListViewFromView()` functions similarly. Instead of getting the new managed objects from parameters, it gets them from a `View` object specified as a parameter. Unlike the previous two methods, it doesn't return anything.

Sample Code

Listing 6-5 is sample code based on the use case described in the API reference. In the use case, a client wants not only updates on a subset of the objects under a container entity, but notifications whenever objects are added or removed from the container. The flow of the application is as follows:

1. Create a `ContainerView` on the container.
2. Create a filter on the `ContainerView`'s view property, retrieving only the list of managed objects but not their properties.
3. Create a `ListView` from the container using the `createListFromView()` method.
4. Create a filter on the `ListView` that returns the desired managed object's properties.
5. After the first update from this filter, modify the `ListView` to contain only the desired subset of objects.

This sample can be used to monitor the power status change of the virtual machines included in the list. To show how to remove/add managed objects in the `ListView`, the first machine (not necessarily the first you see from a VI Client) is removed. Therefore, the power status change of that particular virtual machine is no longer monitored by the property filter.

Because the `waitForUpdate()` is in an infinite loop, the sample continues until you stop it manually.

Listing 6-5
ViewSample.java

```java
package vim25.samples.mo;
import java.net.URL;
import com.vmware.vim25.ManagedObjectReference;
import com.vmware.vim25.ObjectSpec;
import com.vmware.vim25.ObjectUpdate;
import com.vmware.vim25.PropertyChange;
import com.vmware.vim25.PropertyFilterSpec;
import com.vmware.vim25.PropertyFilterUpdate;
import com.vmware.vim25.PropertySpec;
import com.vmware.vim25.SelectionSpec;
import com.vmware.vim25.TraversalSpec;
import com.vmware.vim25.UpdateSet;
import com.vmware.vim25.mo.ContainerView;
import com.vmware.vim25.mo.Folder;
import com.vmware.vim25.mo.ListView;
import com.vmware.vim25.mo.PropertyCollector;
import com.vmware.vim25.mo.PropertyFilter;
import com.vmware.vim25.mo.ServiceInstance;
import com.vmware.vim25.mo.View;
import com.vmware.vim25.mo.ViewManager;

public class ViewSample
{
  public static void main(String[] args) throws Exception
  {
    if(args.length != 3)
    {
      System.out.println("Usage: java ViewSample <url> "
          + "<username> <password>");
      return;
    }
```

```
ServiceInstance si = new ServiceInstance(new URL(args[0]),
  args[1], args[2], true);

Folder rootFolder = si.getRootFolder();
ViewManager vm = si.getViewManager();
PropertyCollector pc = si.getPropertyCollector();

//create a ContainerView with all VirtualMachine objects
//covered recursively
ContainerView cv = vm.createContainerView(rootFolder,
  new String[]{"VirtualMachine"}, true);

PropertyFilterSpec pfs = new PropertyFilterSpec();
pfs.setObjectSet(new ObjectSpec[]{createObjSpec(cv)});
pfs.setPropSet(new PropertySpec[]{
    createPropSpec("VirtualMachine", new String[]{})});

//create a Property with partialUpdate as true
PropertyFilter pf = pc.createFilter(pfs, true);

//wait for initial update with empty version string
UpdateSet uSet = pc.waitForUpdates("");
String ver = uSet.getVersion();

//print out all the VirtualMachine objects
printUpdateSet(uSet);

//create a ListView from a ContainerView
ListView lv = vm.createListViewFromView(cv);

lv.getServerConnection().getVimService().modifyListView(
    lv.getMOR(),
    new ManagedObjectReference[]{},
    //remove the first VirtualMachine in the list
    new ManagedObjectReference[]{
      uSet.getFilterSet()[0].getObjectSet()[0].getObj()});
```

```java
PropertyFilterSpec pfs1 = new PropertyFilterSpec();

pfs1.setObjectSet(new ObjectSpec[]{createObjSpec(lv)});
pfs1.setPropSet(new PropertySpec[]{
    createPropSpec("VirtualMachine",
        new String[]{"runtime.powerState"})});

pf.destroyPropertyFilter();
PropertyFilter pf1 = pc.createFilter(pfs1, true);

while(true)
{
  System.out.println("Waiting update from version: " + ver);
  try{
    uSet = pc.waitForUpdates(ver);
  }catch(Exception e)
  {
    System.out.println("exception:" + e);
    continue;
  }
  ver = uSet.getVersion();
  printUpdateSet(uSet);
}
}

private static ObjectSpec createObjSpec(View view)
{
  ObjectSpec oSpec = new ObjectSpec();
  oSpec.setSkip(true); //skip this ContainerView object
  oSpec.setObj(view.getMOR());

  TraversalSpec tSpec = new TraversalSpec();
  tSpec.setType(view.getMOR().getType());
  tSpec.setPath("view");
  oSpec.setSelectSet(new SelectionSpec[] {tSpec});

  return oSpec;
}
```

```java
private static PropertySpec createPropSpec(String type,
    String[] props)
{
  PropertySpec pSpec = new PropertySpec();
  pSpec.setType(type);
  pSpec.setAll(Boolean.FALSE);
  pSpec.setPathSet(props);
  return pSpec;
}

private static void printUpdateSet(UpdateSet uSet)
{
  PropertyFilterUpdate[] pfu = uSet.getFilterSet();

  for(int i=0; i<pfu.length; i++)
  {
    ObjectUpdate[] ous = pfu[i].getObjectSet();
    for(int j=0; ous!=null && j<ous.length; j++)
    {
      System.out.println(ous[j].getObj().getType() + ":"
        + ous[j].getObj().get_value());
      PropertyChange[] pcs = ous[j].getChangeSet();
      for(int k=0; pcs!=null && k<pcs.length; k++)
      {
        System.out.println(pcs[k].getName() + " —>"
            + pcs[k].getVal());
      }
    }
  }
}
```

Summary

This chapter discussed how to manage the inventory using the VI SDK. It introduced the inventory structure and told how it differs from ESX to VirtualCenter. It then examined the ManagedEntity and its subtypes—Folder and Datacenter—which manipulate the inventory structure by adding, deleting, renaming, and moving managed entities.

Finally, this chapter introduced the six View-related managed objects that are mainly used to monitor the changes in GUI-intensive applications. They were originally designed for the VI Client, but they can be leveraged in your application as well. Using them effectively reduces the scope of the monitored managed objects and thus the workload on the server.

Chapter 7

Managing Host Systems

The HostSystem is the managed object that models the physical host and ESX. It provides management interfaces to the platform where the virtual machines run. This chapter first introduces the HostSystem with its properties and methods. It then covers host power management, memory management, connection management, configuration management, patch management, time management, diagnostic partition management, and so on.

This chapter covers all the aspects of host management except networking and storage management, which are discussed in later chapters.

Managed Objects: HostSystem, HostDateTimeSystem, HostBootDeviceSystem, HostDiagnosticSystem, HostCpuSchedulerSystem, HostFirmwareSystem, HostHealthStatusSystem, HostAutoStartManager, HostMemorySystem, HostPatchManager

HostSystem Managed Object

HostSystem is a subtype of ManagedEntity; therefore, it inherits all of ManagedEntity's properties and methods. Besides the inherited properties and methods, HostSystem directly defines 11 properties and 15 methods. Table 7-1 lists the 11 properties and their types with a brief explanation.

Table 7-1

Properties of HostSystem Managed Object

Name	Type	Explanation
Capability*	HostCapability	Host capabilities (see Figure 7-1)
config*	HostConfigInfo	Host configuration information
configManager[1]	HostConfigManager	A data object holding all the managed objects attached to the HostSystem, such as HostFirewallSystem
datastore*	ManagedObjectReference[] to a Datastore[]	The datastore objects that are available in this HostSystem
datastoreBrowser	ManagedObjectReference to a HostDatastoreBrowser	DatastoreBrowser to browse datastores for this host
hardware*	HostHardwareInfo	Hardware configuration of the host
network*	ManagedObjectReference[] to a Network[]	The network objects that are available to this HostSystem
runtime	HostRuntimeInfo	Runtime state information about the host, such as connection state
summary	HostListSummary	Basic information about the host, including connection state
systemResources*	HostSystemResourceInfo	The system resource hierarchy, used for configuring the set of resources reserved to the system and unavailable to virtual machines
vm*	ManagedObjectReference[] to a VirtualMachine[]	List of virtual machines associated with this host

[1]In the VI Java API, you don't see a getter method for configManager, which holds ManagedObjectReference objects to different managed objects, such as HostFirewallSystem, attached to the host. Instead of returning back the configManager, the API skips this intermediate data object and provides getter methods to all the managed objects referred to in the configManager.

Some properties are optional and might not be available on VirtualCenter when the host is disconnected or powered off.

Fifteen methods are defined in HostSystem, as follows.

- **acquireCimServicesTicket()** creates and returns a one-time credential that establishes a remote connection to the host's CIM interface. The port to connect to is the standard well-known port for the service. (See Chapter 18, "Advanced Topics," for more details.)

- **disconnectHost_Task()** disconnects from a host and instructs the server to stop sending heartbeats to VirtualCenter.

- **enterMaintenanceMode_Task()** puts the host into maintenance mode.

- **exitMaintenanceMode_Task()** takes the host out of maintenance mode.

- **powerDownHostToStandBy_Task()** puts the host in a standby state in which the host can be powered up remotely.

- **powerUpHostFromStandBy_Task()** takes the host out of standby mode.

- **queryHostConnectionInfo()** gets connection information about a host.

- **queryMemoryOverhead()** is deprecated as of 2.5. Use QueryMemoryOverheadEx() instead.

- **queryMemoryOverheadEx()** determines the amount of memory overhead necessary to power on a virtual machine with the specified characteristics.

- **rebootHost_Task()** reboots a host.

- **reconfigureHostForDAS_Task()** reconfigures the host for the VMware High Availability (HA) cluster. If the host is part of an HA cluster, this operation reconfigures the host for HA. For example, this operation may be used if a host is added to an HA-enabled cluster and the automatic HA configuration system task fails. Automatic HA configuration may fail for a variety of reasons. For example, the host may be configured incorrectly.

- **reconnectHost_Task()** reconnects to a host. This method is supported only in VirtualCenter.

- **shutdownHost_Task()** shuts down a host. This method is not supported on all hosts. Check the host capability shutdownSupported.

- **updateFlags()** updates flags that are part of the HostFlagInfo Object.

- **updateSystemResources()** updates the configuration of the system resource hierarchy.

As you might have noticed, there aren't many methods defined to change the configurations of the host. Perhaps you are wondering: Is it because you cannot change the host as you like to?

Definitely not. Because you can change so many things about the host, instead of defining methods directly on the HostSystem, the designers came up with 17 singleton managed objects that manage different aspects of a host. For example, HostCpuSchedulerSystem retrieves and configures the host CPU scheduler policies that affect the performance of running virtual machines; and HostStorageSystem manages the storage subsystem of a host. The design pattern is the same as with ServiceInstance, which has many singleton managed objects attached, each of which is responsible for one aspect of global management.

Retrieving Information

As shown in Table 7-1, many properties are defined with the HostSystem. Retrieving these properties provides useful information about the host, including its capabilities, configuration, hardware information, running status, and quick summary.

Host Capabilities

A host's capabilities are captured in its property capability (type: HostCapability). The HostCapability is a data object type whose 28 properties are either Boolean or integer type. Some of them are new additions as of version 2.5. Figure 7-1 lists all of them in the UML diagram.

Most of the property names are self-explanatory, and you don't need to check the API reference. For example, iscsiSupported is a Boolean variable standing for whether the access to iSCSI devices is supported or not. When in doubt, check the API reference for details.

Not all the capabilities are captured in this data object. Three capabilities (HostNetCapabilities, HostDatastoreSystemCapabilities, and HostNetOffloadCapabilities) are somehow held in the HostConfigInfo data object.

HostCapability
+backgroundSnapshotsSupported : xsd:boolean
+cpuMemoryResourceConfigurationSupported: xsd:boolean
+datastorePrincipalSupported : xsd:boolean
+highGuestMemSupported : xsd:boolean
+iscsiSupported : xsd:boolean
+localSwapDatastoreSupported : xsd:boolean
+maintenanceModeSupported : xsd:boolean
+maxRunningVMs : xsd:int
+maxSupportedVcpus : xsd:int
+maxSupportedVMs : xsd:int
+nfsSupported : xsd:boolean
+nicTeamingSupported : xsd:boolean
+perVmSwapFiles : xsd:boolean
+preAssignedPCIUnitNumbersSupported : xsd:boolean
+rebootSupported : xsd:boolean
+recursiveResourcePoolsSupported : xsd:boolean
+restrictedSnapshotRelocateSupported : xsd:boolean
+sanSupported : xsd:boolean
+scaledScreenshotSupported : xsd:boolean
+screenshotSupported : xsd:boolean
+shutdownSupported : xsd:boolean
+standbySupported : xsd:boolean
+suspendedRelocateSupported : xsd:boolean
+unsharedSwapVMotionSupported : xsd:boolean
+vlanTaggingSupported : xsd:boolean
+vmotionSupported : xsd:boolean

Figure 7-1   `HostCapability` data object

Runtime Information

All the runtime-related information is captured in the `runtime` property of the `HostRuntimeInfo` type. `HostRuntimeInfo` is a complicated data object. Its UML diagram is shown in Figure 7-2.

As with any other complicated data object, you can obtain any subproperty and nested data object down to the primitive data types or enumerations. The UML diagram shows the relationships among different data objects. The most often-used information pieces, like connection status and power status, are direct children of `HostRuntimeInfo` for convenient retrievals.

Configuration

The configuration of a host is complicated. Figure 7-3 shows the UML diagram of the `HostConfigInfo` data object. As mentioned earlier, it includes three capability-

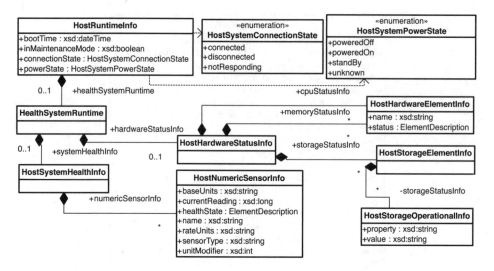

Figure 7-2   The `HostRuntimeInfo` data object

related data objects: `HostNetCapabilities`, `HostNetOffloadCapabilities`, and `HostDatastoreSystemCapabilities`. (Given the page limit, not all the data objects are expanded to primitive data types.)

Some of the properties in the configuration can also be retrieved from attached managed objects. For example, the `HostAutoStartManagerConfig` data object is also defined in the `HostAutoStartManager` managed object as a property. You have two options for retrieving this configuration: either from the `HostConfigInfo` or from the related managed object. To change the configuration, you have to obtain the related managed objects.

Given the size of configuration, avoid retrieving the entire data object at one time, and get only those parts that you are interested in with property path notation.

Hardware Information

You can find any hardware-related information in the `hardware` property. Figure 7-4 illustrates the structure of the `HostHardwareInfo` data object. As in the UML diagram, you can find all the information about the system BIOS, CPU, memory, NUMA, PCI devices, hardware model, vendor, BIOS ID, and so on.

This hardware-related information helps you figure out the underlying hardware configuration. For an asset management system, this information is a must-have to build the asset inventory database.

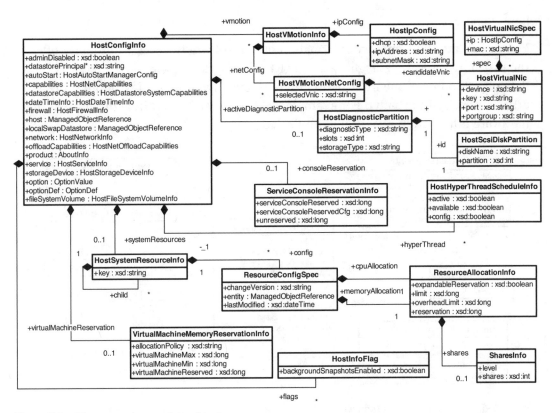

Figure 7-3   The `HostConfigInfo` data object

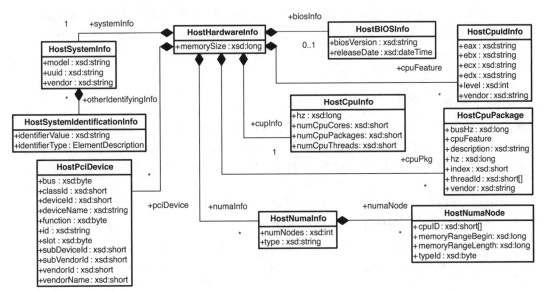

Figure 7-4   `HostHardwareInfo` data object

Quick Summary

You can obtain the summary information of a host from the summary property of the HostListSummary type. Figure 7-5 is the UML diagram of the HostListSummary data object. Some of the information there is actually duplicated with other properties (entirely or partially). For example, HostRuntimeInfo is entirely duplicated; the hardware information is partially duplicated.

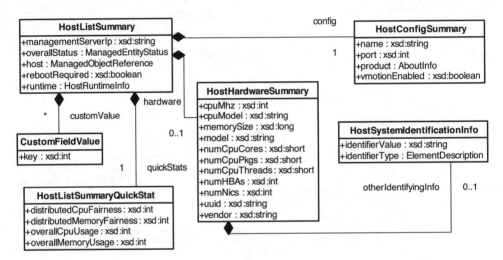

Figure 7-5 HostListSummary data object

Because the summary property captures the most often-used information displayed in summary pages in the VI Client, you might find this property useful. If you find what you need in summary, use it instead of the other properties.

Power Management

A physical host can have several states in terms of power management: maintenance mode, standby mode, powered on, and powered off. It's critical to understand these different power states and their implications to the virtual machine operations. Figure 7-6 shows the four different power states and how they transition from one to the other. (Note that not all the transitions can be done programmatically.)

Here are brief descriptions of each power mode:

- **PoweredOn**—Basic mode in which the host is up and running and good to power on virtual machines and provision system resources.

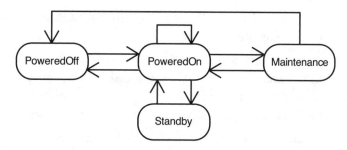

Figure 7-6 The different power states of the ESX host

The `rebootHost_Task()` method allows the host to temporarily get into `PoweredOff` mode and return quickly to the `PoweredOn` state.

No method is defined to power on the host from the `PoweredOff` state because the VI SDK cannot control a powered-off host. You can manually turn it on, or use features like "Wake on LAN" (WOL). Most new motherboards and NICs support WOL these days. Just enable it from BIOS. These are not part of the VI SDK.

- **Maintenance**—A power state in which no virtual machine can be powered on, and no provisioning can be done. Once a host is in this state, you can go ahead with maintenance work or power off the host without corrupting any virtual machine.

  To get into this mode from powered on mode, call the `enterMaintenanceMode_Task()` method. It takes in an integer timeout and a Boolean flag to evacuate the powered-off virtual machines. If the timeout is set to 0 or less, there is no timeout. If the Boolean flag is `true`, this method won't succeed until all the powered-off virtual machines are reregistered with other hosts (either manually or automatically depending on whether DRS is active or not). This flag is only supported by VirtualCenter server.

  The call returns whether it succeeds or the timeout expires. When the latter happens, the returned task contains a `Timeout` fault.

  The method completes after there are no powered-on virtual machines and no provisioning operations in progress on the host. The operation does not directly initiate operations to evacuate or power down powered-on virtual machines. However, if the host is part of a cluster with VMware DRS enabled, the DRS provides migration recommendations to evacuate the powered-on virtual machines. If the DRS is in fully automatic mode, these are automatically executed.

If the host is part of a cluster and the task is issued through VirtualCenter with `evacuatePoweredOffVms` set to `true`, the task will not succeed unless all the powered-off virtual machines are reregistered to other hosts. If VMware DRS is enabled, VC automatically evacuates powered-off virtual machines.

To get out of `maintenance` mode, call `exitMaintenanceMode_Task()`, which takes in an integer timeout. This call is blocked if maintenance operations are ongoing (such as upgrading VMFS volumes). If timeout is set to 0 or less, there is no timeout. The method is cancelable.

- **Standby**—Similar to `Maintenance` mode. The host stops responding and is ready to be turned on remotely. If the DPM feature is turned on, a host may be put into `standby` mode to save energy.

  To get into `standby` mode, call `powerDownHostToStandBy_Task()`. While this method is running, no virtual machines can be powered on, and no provisioning operations can be performed on the host. The task completes only if there are no powered-on virtual machines, no provisioning operations in progress on the host, and the host stops responding.

  The operation does not directly initiate operations to evacuate or power down powered-on virtual machines. If the host is part of a cluster and the method is called through VirtualCenter with `evacuatePoweredOffVms` set to `true`, the task will not succeed unless all the powered-off virtual machines are reregistered to other hosts. If VMware DRS is enabled in automatic mode, VC automatically evacuates powered-off virtual machines.

  To exit, call `powerUpHostFromStandBy_Task()`. If the method is successful, the host wakes up and starts sending heartbeats. This method may be called automatically by DRS (DPM) to add capacity to a cluster. The method is cancelable.

  The parameters to these two methods are the same as that of `enterMaintenanceMode_Task()` and `exitMaintenanceMode_Task()`; therefore, they are not repeated here.

- **PoweredOff.** Similar to the `standby` mode, but it's a complete shutdown and you normally cannot return to the powered-on state easily without remote power control system on the server.

To get into poweredOff mode, call shutdownHost_Task() method with a Boolean parameter indicating whether you want to force it to shut down regardless of whether or not it's in a maintenance mode.

> If this method is successful, the host is shut down. Thus, the caller never gets an indicator of success in the returned task if it's connecting directly to the host. The same goes for rebootHost_Task().

Querying the Memory Requirement for Virtual Machines

A virtual machine cannot be powered on if there is not sufficient memory. It's not as simple as adding up the memory requirement from the virtual machine point of view. There is also memory overhead for running a virtual machine. queryMemoryOverhead() and queryMemoryOverheadEx() are the two methods to calculate the memory overhead. As its name indicates, queryMemoryOverhead() is deprecated in favor of the new queryMemoryOverheadEx() method.

The old queryMemoryOverhead() method is straightforward, with three parameters for system memory size, video RAM size, and number of virtual CPUs. The return is a long integer that stands for the amount of overhead memory in bytes required to power on such a virtual machine.

The new queryMemoryOverheadEx() takes in the VirtualMachineConfigInfo object with more information included. VirtualMachineConfigInfo is the same type of the config property defined on VirtualMachine. Of course, most of the properties in VirtualMachineConfigInfo are optional; therefore, you can safely ignore them.

Before you power a virtual machine, check out the memory overhead to see whether the host has sufficient memory to run it.

Managing Connections

Three methods are defined for connection-related management, mainly for the VC server to manage the connections to the hosts:

- queryHostConnectionInfo() returns HostConnectionInfo, which includes information about a host that the Connection Wizard can use to add a host into the VC server. The information includes the cluster support indicator, a list of datastores, `HostListSummary`, networks configured, VC server IP (if any), a list of virtual machines, and whether the host requires a `vimAccountName` in the `ConnectionSpec`. The returned `HostConnectionInfo` type is the same as what the `Datacenter.queryConnectionInfo()` method returns.

- `reconnectHost_Task()` reinstalls agents and reconfigures the host, if it is out of sync with VirtualCenter. The reconnection process goes through many of the same steps as the `addHost_Task()` method: ensuring the correct set of licenses for the number of CPUs on the host, ensuring the correct set of agents is installed, and ensuring that networks and datastores are discovered and registered with VirtualCenter.

  `reconnectHost_Task()` takes in a `HostConnectionSpec` object, which includes username, password, port, and so on. It returns a `Task`, with which you can track the progress. The `HostConnectionSpec` is the same parameter type for `addHost_Task` defined on `ClusterComputeResource` and `addStandaloneHost_Task()` on `Folder`.

The client can change the IP address and port of the host when reconnecting. This can be useful if the client wants to preserve existing metadata, even though the host is changing its IP address. For example, clients can preserve existing statistics, alarms, and privileges.

- `disconnectHost_Task()` disconnects a host from a VC server and instructs the server to stop sending heartbeats. Upon the success of this method, the VC server no longer manages the host.

An ESX server can be managed by only one VC server at a time. Disconnect the host before adding it to another VirtualCenter inventory.

Configuring the Host

As mentioned earlier, the `HostSystem` managed object does not define many methods for changing system configuration. The majority of configuration change is done by the different singleton managed objects attached to the HostSystem object. (For example, HostAutoStartManager changes the automatic start or stop of virtual machines on the host.) These singleton managed objects are covered in the rest of the chapter, except the networking and storage related managed object. Both the networking and storage management are so broad that each deserves its own chapter.

The three methods defined directly on HostSystem for configuration are as follows:

- reconfigureHostForDAS_Task() works only if the host is part of an HA cluster. It takes in no parameter and returns a Task for tracking progress. This method is normally used after an automatic HA configuration failure caused by a variety of reasons, such as the host being misconfigured. It has to be invoked on VirtualCenter server; a NotSupported fault is thrown if on an ESX host.

- updateFlags() sets the flags property inside HostSystem's config property. It takes a HostFlagInfo object and returns none. The HostFlagInfo is indeed a simple data object that has only one Boolean property defined directly. That flag is to specify whether background snapshots are enabled. With the HostFlagInfo structure in place, it can always be expanded to include more flags in the future.

- updateSystemResources() is much like a setter method that takes in a HostSystemResourceInfo object and assigns it to the systemResources property.

Configuring Auto Start/Stop of Virtual Machines

You can use HostAutoStartManager to configure the automatic start/stop of virtual machines on a host. When a virtual machine is configured to use this feature, it can be started or stopped when the host is powered on or shut down. This feature works while connecting to either a VC server or ESX server.

Figure 7-7 is a UML diagram of the HostAutoStartManager and its related data object types. The HostAutoStartManager has one property config, typed as HostAutoStartManagerConfig. The HostAutoStartManagerConfig includes two properties typed as AutoStartPowerInfo and AutoStartDefaults, respectively. These two data objects are similar in content, but one is for host scope default setting and the other for per-virtual-machine setting. The latter, when specified, always overwrites the former.

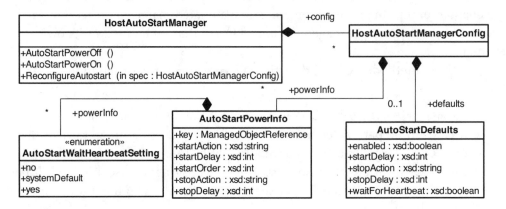

Figure 7-7   `HostAutoStartManager` and related data object types

The property `key` in the `AutoStartPowerInfo` refers to a virtual machine. If no `AutoStartPowerInfo` object is defined for a virtual machine, it takes the system default from `AutoStartDefaults`.

The `startOrder` in the `AutoStartPowerInfo` can be useful when you have multiple virtual machines whose order to start up is critical. An example is if you have a three-tier system in which the database server, application server, and client applications are in different virtual machines and should start up in that sequence. The virtual machine with the lower `startOrder` number is powered on before the one with higher number. When powering off, it takes the opposite order.

To change the configuration, simply call the `reconfigureAutoStart()` method. It's similar to a `setter` method except that the `HostAutoStartManagerConfig` is an incremental change to the current configuration.

The other two methods, `autoStartPowerOff()` and `autoStartPowerOn()`, power off and power on virtual machines according to the current auto start configuration. It provides auto start/stop management on a group of virtual machines.

Managing the Time of the Host

To manage the time of a host, use the `HostDateTimeSystem` managed object (shown in Figure 7-8), which is associated with the `HostSystem`. You can get the `dateTimeInfo` property of the `HostDataTimeSystem` and further drill down to the time zone information and the Network Time Protocol (NTP) servers.

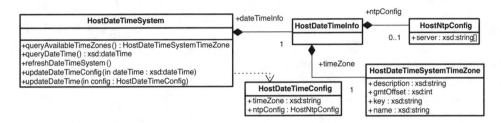

Figure 7-8 `HostDateTimeSystem` and related data object types

You can also call the `queryAvailableTimeZones()` methods to get a list of all the available time zones that the server supports. The return is a big array of `HostDateTimeSystemTimeZone` objects, each of which represents a time zone. When you set a time zone, make sure it's in the array of available time zones.

The `queryDateTime()` method takes in no parameter and just returns the time of the host. The `refreshDateTimeSystem()` refreshes the `DateTime` related settings.

The `updateDateTime()` method allows you to update the date and time on the host. This method doesn't consider network delay. If there is a big delay, it can lead to time skew on the host.

The last method, `updateDateTimeConfig()`, updates the date/time configuration on the host.[2] The parameter type `HostDateTimeConfig` is very much like `HostDateTimeInfo` except that `HostDateTimeConfig` has only one string for the time zone. As mentioned just now, the `timeZone` string must be one of the names of the available time zones returned from `queryAvailableTimeZones()`.

Listing 7-1 is a sample that prints out the NTP servers and current time zone information and then rolls back the ESX time by one hour. At the end, it recovers the original time by calling the `updateDateTime()` method again.

---

[2] The timezone cannot be set on ESXi 3.5.

Listing 7-1
SetHostTime.java

```java
package vim25.samples.mo.host;
import java.net.URL;
import java.util.Calendar;

import com.vmware.vim25.HostDateTimeInfo;
import com.vmware.vim25.HostDateTimeSystemTimeZone;
import com.vmware.vim25.HostNtpConfig;
import com.vmware.vim25.mo.Folder;
import com.vmware.vim25.mo.HostDateTimeSystem;
import com.vmware.vim25.mo.HostSystem;
import com.vmware.vim25.mo.InventoryNavigator;
import com.vmware.vim25.mo.ServiceInstance;

public class SetHostTime
{
  public static void main(String[] args) throws Exception
  {
    if(args.length != 4)
    {
      System.out.println("Usage: java SetHostTime " +
            "<url> <username> <password> <hostname>");
      return;
    }

    ServiceInstance si = new ServiceInstance(
        new URL(args[0]), args[1], args[2], true);

    String hostname = args[3];
    Folder rootFolder = si.getRootFolder();
    HostSystem host = null;
    host = (HostSystem) new InventoryNavigator(
        rootFolder).searchManagedEntity("HostSystem", hostname);

    if(host==null)
    {
      System.out.println("Cannot find the host:" + hostname);
      si.getServerConnection().logout();
      return;
```

```
    }
    HostDateTimeSystem hdts = host.getHostDateTimeSystem();

    HostDateTimeInfo info = hdts.getDateTimeInfo();

    System.out.println("The NTP Servers:");
    HostNtpConfig cfg = info.getNtpConfig();
    String[] svrs = cfg.getServer();
    for(int i=0; svrs!=null && i<svrs.length; i++)
    {
      System.out.println("Server["+i+"]:" + svrs[i]);
    }

    System.out.println("\nCurrent Time Zone:");
    HostDateTimeSystemTimeZone tz = info.getTimeZone();
    System.out.println("Key:" + tz.getKey());
    System.out.println("Name:" + tz.getName());
    // the GMT offset is in seconds.
    // for example, America/Los_Angeles, -28800
    System.out.println("GmtOffset:" + tz.getGmtOffset());
    System.out.println("Description:" + tz.getDescription());

    Calendar curTime = si.currentTime();
    System.out.println("\nCurrent time:" + curTime.getTime());
    //roll back one hour
    curTime.roll(Calendar.HOUR, false);
    hdts.updateDateTime(curTime);

    curTime = si.currentTime();
    System.out.println("Current time (after):"
        + curTime.getTime());

    // reset the time
    curTime.roll(Calendar.HOUR, true);
    hdts.updateDateTime(curTime);

    si.getServerConnection().logout();
  }
}
```

Configuring the Booting Device

You can manage the host booting device by using the HostBootDeviceSystem managed object. Figure 7-9 shows the UML diagram of the HostBootDeviceSystem and related data objects. It has no property but two methods defined:

- queryBootDevices() returns a HostBootDevice data object, which includes the key of the current boot device and an array of HostBootDevice data objects. Each HostBootDevice object has two string typed properties: one is the key and the other is a brief description. The currentBootDeviceKey has to be in one of the HostBootDevice objects in the array.

- updateBootDevice() changes the boot device. Once the method is successful, the currentBootDeviceKey reflects the change in the next queryBootDevice() call. Of course, you have to wait for the next booting (rebooting) to see the real effects.

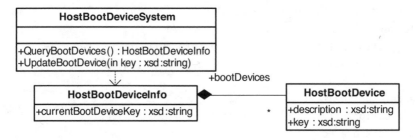

Figure 7-9 The HostBootDeviceSystem and related data objects

Configure the Diagnostic Partition

The HostDiagnosticSystem is the managed object with which you can manage the diagnostic partition for the VMKernel to dump its memory in case of Purple Screen of Death (PSOD). Figure 7-10 shows the UML diagram of the HostDiagnosticSystem and related data object types.

The property activePartition represents the active partition used for diagnostic purposes. Within it are four properties:

- **diagnosticType**—Either singleHost or multiHost
- **slots**—1 for singleHost and larger for multiHost

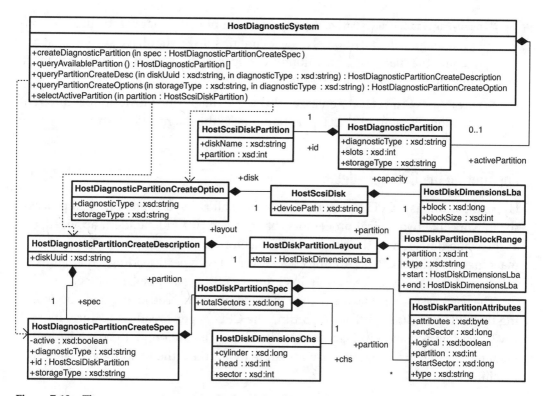# Configure the Diagnostic Partition

Figure 7-10 The HostDiagnosticSystem and related data objects

- **storageType**—Either directAttached or networkAttached
- **id**—The HostScsiDiskPartition object

Five methods are defined with HostDiagnosticSystem.

- **createDiagnosticPartition()** creates a diagnostic partition according to the specification. You can specify whether you want the newly created disk to be the active partition.

- **queryAvailablePartition()** returns a list of available diagnostic partitions in order of preference. In general, local diagnostic partitions are better than shared diagnostic partitions simply because it's impossible for multiple servers to share the same partition.

- **queryPartitionCreateDesc()** retrieves the diagnostic partition creation description for a given disk. The description details how the diagnostic partition is created on the disk and provides a creation specification that is needed to invoke the creation operation.

- `queryPartitionCreateOptions()` returns a list of disks that can be used to contain a diagnostic partition. This list contains disks that have sufficient space to contain a diagnostic partition of the specific type in an order that is most preferable as determined by the system.

- `selectActivePartition()` changes the active diagnostic partition to a different partition. Passing in a NULL partition unsets the diagnostic partition.

Configuring the CPU Scheduler

Hyperthreading is a CPU technology from Intel allowing a single physical processor to work like two logical processors that can run two independent applications at the same time. Given the demand of the computing power, many of the machines with Intel CPUs running ESX server have hyperthreading capabilities. Effectively managing the feature helps improve ESX system performance.

The `HostCpuSchedulerSystem` is the managed object for retrieving and configuring the CPU scheduler policies regarding the CPU hyperthreading feature. Its UML diagram is shown in Figure 7-11. This is only useful on platforms where resource management controls are available to optimize the running virtual machines.

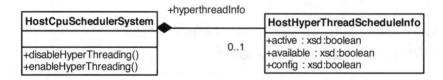

Figure 7-11 The `HostCpuSchedulerSystem` and related data object

Compared to other similar singleton managed objects, the `HostCpuSchedulerSystem` is simple. It has one property and two methods defined. The property `hyperthreadInfo` is of type `HostHyperThreadScheduleInfo` data object. It might be set only when the CPU scheduler is capable of scheduling hyperthreads as resources.

The `HostHyperThreadSheduleInfo` has three direct properties defined, all Boolean types:

- **active**—A flag indicating whether or not the CPU scheduler is currently treating hyperthreads as schedulable resources. It can be turned on or off with the two methods.

- **available**—A flag whether hyperthreading optimization is available on the system. This flag is preset by VMware before installation.

- **config**—A flag whether or not the CPU scheduler should treat hyperthreads as schedulable resources the next time the CPU scheduler starts.

The two methods turn the hyperthreading feature on or off. They take in no parameters. Upon successful invocation, the active property is updated.

Managing Firmware[3]

Managing Firmware is an experimental feature with ESXi that is subject to change in future releases. The `HostFirmwareSystem` managed object type can be used to back up/restore/reset the configuration of an embedded ESX host. As shown in Figure 7-12, it has four methods defined:

```
┌────────────────────────────────────────────────────────────┐
│                    HostFirmwareSystem                        │
├────────────────────────────────────────────────────────────┤
│                                                              │
├────────────────────────────────────────────────────────────┤
│ +backupFirmwareConfiguration() : xsd :string                 │
│ +queryFirmwareConfigUploadURL() : xsd :string                │
│ +resetFirmwareToFactoryDefaults() : xsd :string              │
│ +restoreFirmwareConfiguration(in force : xsd:boolean)        │
└────────────────────────────────────────────────────────────┘
```

Figure 7-12 `HostFirmwareSystem`

- `backupFirmwareConfiguration()` backs up the configuration of a host and creates a bundle. It takes in no parameter and returns a URL string pointing to the bundle. You can download it using an HTTP protocol.

- `queryFirmwareConfigUploadURL()` returns a URL string to which a configuration bundle must be uploaded before the `restoreFirmwareConfiguration()` method is invoked.

---

[3] Firmware refers to the ESXi, not any other firmware in other system devices.

- `resetFirmwareToFactoryDefaults()` resets all the configuration options, including the root password to the factory defaults. The host needs to be in maintenance mode; otherwise, an `InvalidState` fault is thrown. If successful, the host reboots itself immediately.

- `restoreFirmwareConfiguration()` restores the configuration of the host from the bundle uploaded. It takes in one parameter whether it should force the restoration even if the bundle is mismatched.

Managing the Health Status

`HostHealthStatusSystem` is the managed object for managing the health status of the hardware of a host. It has one property called `runtime`, which is defined as a type of `HealthSystemRuntime` in Figure 7-2. Figure 7-13 omits its detailed structure.

HostHealthStatusSystem
+runtime : HealthSystemRuntime
+resetSystemHealthInfo() +refreshHealthStatusSystem()

Figure 7-13 `HostHealthStatusSystem`

Two methods are defined on `HostHealthStatusSystem`:

- `refreshHealthStatusSystem()` refreshes the available runtime hardware health information. It takes no parameter and returns nothing.

- `resetSystemHealthInfo()` resets the state of the sensors of the IPMI subsystem. It is needed because IPMI sensors on certain types of hardware remain in an unhealthy state until you reset them explicitly using this method.

You can also get the health information of a host from the CIM interface. VMware and hardware vendors ship CIM providers for you to query hardware statuses. Chapter 18 has a sample showing how to gain access to CIM and retrieve information from it.

Managing the Host Memory

On an ESX host, the memory is allocated to VMKernel, Console OS, and virtual machines. The VMKernel takes at least 50MB, plus additional memory for device drivers. By default, the COS gets 272MB (285,212,672 bytes) and can be adjusted. The virtual machines, when powered on, have memory overhead anywhere from 79 to 350MB. For example, the 79MB overhead would be for a 32-bit single CPU virtual machine with 256 to 512MB maximum memory. See the Resource Management Guide[4] for a table of memory overhead values for both 32- and 64-bit virtual machines.

The `HostMemorySystem` can configure the reserved memory for both virtual machines and the console OS. As shown in Figure 7-14, it has two properties and two methods defined. The details of `ServiceConsoleReservationInfo` and `VirtualMachineMemoryReservationInfo` are illustrated in Figure 7-3. You can retrieve the information from the `config` property defined in `HostSystem`.

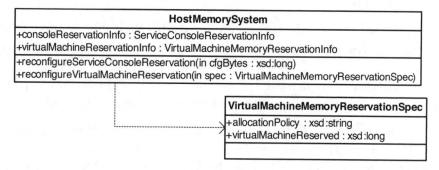

Figure 7-14 `HostMemorySystem` and related data object

The `reconfigureServiceConsoleReservation()` method takes in a parameter of long integer type for the new amount of memory reserved for the console OS. This change only takes effect on the next booting.

The `reconfigureVirtualMachineReservation()` method is doing similar things for the virtual machines. It takes in a parameter-typed `VirtualMachineMemory ReservationSpec` data object, which defines only two properties: `allocationPolicy` and `virtualMachineReserved`. The first stands for allocation policy that has one value from the `VirtualMachineMemoryAllocationPolicy` enumeration type; the second is a long integer for the amount of memory to be reserved for all running virtual

---

[4] http://www.vmware.com/pdf/vi3_35/esx_3/r35/vi3_35_25_resource_mgmt.pdf

machines in bytes. The allocation policies can be any one of the three values as follows:

- **swapMost**—Allows most virtual machine memory to be swapped.
- **swapSome**—Allows some virtual machine memory to be swapped.
- **swapNone**—Fits all virtual machine memory into reserved host memory.

Note that the change you make affects the memory reservation, not the real memory a virtual machine or COS really uses. It does affect the performance of the COS and virtual machines, especially when there is contention for memory resulting in too frequent swapping.

Patch Management

VMware publishes patch updates through its external Web site.[5] An update may contain many individual patch binaries, but its installation and uninstallation are atomic.

HostPatchManager is the managed object for scanning and installing patches. As shown in Figure 7-15, it has no property, and two methods are defined:

- scanHostPath_Task() scans the host for the patch status. It takes in repository as the scan target and updateID strings, which can include wildcards. It returns a Task that can be further checked on progress and even be cancelled. Furthermore, the info.result of the Task managed object contains the HostPatchManagerStatus data object upon success. It can determine whether the patch is applicable to the host, the integrity of the metadata, and so on. The integrity checking is performed on the metadata only. This is an interesting way of returning results on an asynchronous method via the Task managed object.

- installHostPath_Task() actually patches the host. It takes the repository info, update ID, and a flag for forcing reinstallation of the update. By default, trying to install an already installed patch fails with the PatchAlreadyInstalled fault. If forced, the patch manager reinstalls the patch and overwrites the existing installation anyway.

---

[5] http://support.vmware.com/selfsupport/download/

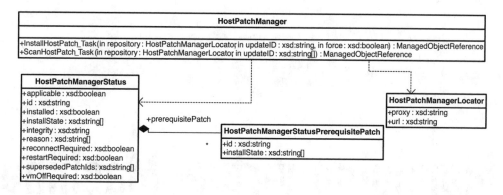

Figure 7-15   HostPatchManager and related data object types

Summary

The host is the virtualization platform on which virtual machines are running. This chapter introduced the HostSystem, the managed object that models the host and exposes many information and management interfaces ranging from configuration management and power management to time management and patch management.

Seventeen singleton managed object types are closely associated to the HostSystem in a similar pattern to the 21 singleton managed object types to the ServiceInstance. Each of the 17 managed object types is responsible for one aspect of host management. All the managed objects were discussed except those related to networking and storage, which have their own dedicated chapters.

Chapter 8

Managing Virtual Machines, Snapshots, and VMotion

This chapter goes virtual by introducing the virtual machine and its management. It first discusses the `VirtualMachine` managed object itself and then moves onto different aspects of the management, including life cycle management, configuration management, power management, guest operating system management and customization, VMware Tools installation, and upgrading.

The second part introduces the virtual machine snapshot, snapshot hierarchy, and creating/deleting/reverting a snapshot from the hierarchy.

Finally, this chapter discusses the advanced features VMotion and storage VMotion, which require VirtualCenter and corresponding licenses.

Managed Objects: `VirtualMachine`, `CustomizationSpecManager`, `VirtualMachineSnapshot`

Virtual Machine

A virtual machine functions just like its counterpart in the physical world. It can be powered on and off and run operating systems and applications. From the guest operating system running on a virtual machine, you can hardly tell the difference.

Unlike a physical machine, a virtual machine doesn't have its own physical components like CPU, memory, disk, and network card. All the virtual machines share the resources of the physical machine managed by the hypervisor underneath.

Files of a Virtual Machine

A virtual machine consists of several files, each of which represents one aspect of the virtual machine. Table 8-1 lists all the file types that make up a virtual machine in ESX. You can specify the extension type while doing a targeted search using HostDatastoreBrowser (to be covered in Chapter 11, "Managing Storage and Datastores").

Table 8-1

Files That Make Up a Virtual Machine in ESX	
Extension	**Description**
*.vmx	VM configuration file in ASCII format.
*.vmxf	Supplemental configuration information for teamed VMs.
*.vmdk	Virtual disk description file in ASCII format.
*-flat.vmdk	Virtual disk image in binary format.
*.vswp	Per-VM swap files.
*.nvram	Non-volatile RAM, which stores VM BIOS information.
*.vmsd	Virtual machine snapshot metadata.
*-00000#-delta.vmdk	Snapshot difference file. You can get double or even triple digits if you have enough snapshots.
*-00000#.vmdk	Metadata about a snapshot.
*-Snapshot#.vmsn	A snapshot of virtual machine memory. Its size equals the size of your virtual machine's maximum memory.
*.log	Virtual machine log files.

The most important of these files is the VMX file, which includes many key/value pairs, including configuration version, virtual hardware version, and virtual devices. It's the high-level description of a virtual machine, and it's normally regarded as the virtual machine. In the VI Client, the configuration file carries the virtual machine icon.

The following snippet shows a small part of a typical configuration file.

```
#!/usr/bin/vmware
config.version = "8"
virtualHW.version = "4"
floppy0.present = "true"
nvram = "sdk_prim.nvram"
deploymentPlatform = "windows"
virtualHW.productCompatibility = "hosted"
tools.upgrade.policy = "manual"
powerType.powerOff = "default"
powerType.powerOn = "default"
powerType.suspend = "default"
powerType.reset = "default"

displayName = "sdk_prim"
......
checkpoint.vmState = ""
```

All the operations with a virtual machine affect these files directly or indirectly. For example, when you power on a virtual machine, the related files are locked. Most of the time, you don't need to, and shouldn't, touch the files associated with a virtual machine. Just use the VI SDK interfaces as follows.

`VirtualMachine` Managed Object

The `VirtualMachine` managed object typically represents a virtual machine, but it may also represent a virtual machine template that can be deployed repeatedly. It is a subtype of `ManagedEntity`, which is the immediate supertype for all items in the inventory; therefore, it inherits all the properties and behaviors of `ManagedEntity`. Inside the inventory, a `VirtualMachine` instance must be included in a `Folder` object, either directly attached to a datacenter or a nested `Folder` underneath the direct `Folder`.

In addition to the inherited properties and methods, the `VirtualMachine` type defines 13 properties and 28 methods that are unique to virtual machines. Table 8-2 lists the 13 properties with name, type, and a brief explanation. You can find similar design pattern and naming convention to the `HostSystem` discussed earlier.

Table 8-2

Properties Defined in `VirtualMachine` Managed Object

Name	Type	Explanation
capability	VirtualMachineCapability	Information about the capabilities of this virtual machine.
config*	VirtualMachineConfigInfo	Configuration of this virtual machine, including the name and UUID.
datastore*	ManagedObjectReference[] to Datastore[]	A collection of `Datastore` objects that this virtual machine uses.
environmentBrowser	ManagedObjectReference to an EnvironmentBrowser	The current virtual machine's environment browser object. This contains information on all the configurations that can be used on the virtual machine. It is identical to the environment browser on the `ComputeResource` to which this virtual machine belongs.
guest*	GuestInfo	All the information about VMware Tools and the guest OS. Guest operating system information reflects the last known state of the virtual machine. For powered-on machines, this is current information. For powered-off machines, this is the last recorded state before the virtual machine was powered off.
guestHeartbeatStatus	ManagedEntityStatus	The guest OS heartbeat status.

continues...

Table 8-2   continued

Properties Defined in `VirtualMachine` Managed Object		
Name	**Type**	**Explanation**
`layout*`	`VirtualMachineFileLayout`	Detailed information about the files that comprise this virtual machine.
`network*`	`ManagedObjectReference[]` `to Network[]`	A collection of references to the subset of network objects in the datacenter that is used by this virtual machine.
`resourceConfig*`	`ResourceConfigSpec`	The resource configuration for a virtual machine. The shares in this specification are evaluated relative to the resource pool to which it is assigned. It is null if the infrastructure that the virtual machine is registered on does not support resource configuration.
`resourcePool*`	`ManagedObjectReference` `to a ResourcePool`	The current resource pool that specifies resource allocation for this virtual machine. This property is set when a virtual machine is created or associated with a different resource pool, and it is null if the virtual machine is a template or the current session has no access to the resource pool.
`runtime`	`VirtualMachineRuntimeInfo`	Runtime information of the virtual machine, including power state and memory/CPU usage.
`snapshot*`	`VirtualMachineSnapshotInfo`	Current snapshot and tree. The property is valid if snapshots have been created for this virtual machine.

Table 8-2   continued

Properties Defined in `VirtualMachine` Managed Object		
Name	Type	Explanation
summary	VirtualMachineSummary	Basic information about this virtual machine, including `runtimeInfo`, guest OS, basic configuration, alarms, and performance information.

Retrieving Information

The `VirtualMachine` has many defined properties. Retrieving these properties can reveal much information about the virtual machine, including capabilities, runtime status, configuration, guest OS information, and summary.

Virtual Machine Capabilities

The virtual machine's capabilities are inside the `capability` property of type `VirtualMachineCapability`. Inside the `VirtualMachineCapability` data object, 22 boolean variables are defined to indicate whether the specific capabilities are supported. For example, `toolAutoUpdateSupported` indicates whether it supports the automatic updating of the VMware Tools installed in the guest OS running on the virtual machine.

As shown in the UML diagram of the `VirtualMachineCapability` data object in Figure 8-1, the names of these variables are self-explanatory, so they are not discussed further here. When in doubt for a specific capability, just check out the API reference.

Virtual Machine Configuration

The configuration is captured in the `config` property of the `VirtualMachine`. The property is set when a virtual machine is created or when the `reconfigVM()` method is called.

The configuration property is optional, and as usual it is not guaranteed to be available. For example, the configuration would not be available if the server was unable to access the corresponding virtual machine files on disk, and it's often unavailable during the initial phases of virtual machine creation.

VirtualMachineCapability
+bootOptionsSupported: xsd:boolean
+consolePreferencesSupported: xsd:boolean
+cpuFeatureMaskSupported: xsd:boolean
+disableSnapshotsSupported: xsd:boolean
+diskSharesSupported: xsd:boolean
+lockSnapshotsSupported: xsd:boolean
+memorySnapshotsSupported: xsd:boolean
+multipleSnapshotsSupported: xsd:boolean
+npivWwnOnNonRdmVmSupported: xsd:boolean
+poweredOffSnapshotsSupported: xsd:boolean
+quiescedSnapshotsSupported: xsd:boolean
+revertToSnapshotSupported: xsd:boolean
+s1AcpiManagementSupported: xsd:boolean
+settingScreenResolutionSupported: xsd:boolean
+settingVideoRamSizeSupported: xsd:boolean
+snapshotConfigSupported: xsd:boolean
+snapshotOperationsSupported: xsd:boolean
+swapPlacementSupported: xsd:boolean
+toolsAutoUpdateSupported: xsd:boolean
+toolsSyncTimeSupported: xsd:boolean
+virtualMmuUsageSupported: xsd:boolean
+vmNpivWwnSupported: xsd:boolean

Figure 8-1 The `VirtualMachineCapability` data object

The type of the `config` is `VirtualMachineConfigInfo`, which is shown in Figure 8-2. It is indeed a complicated data object with many data objects nested inside. It covers all the configuration related information. From the UML diagram, you can find how different types are related to each other and how to navigate from a parent object to a nested child object. You can also use the UML diagram for a property path to get only that specific piece of information without retrieving all the parent data objects.

Runtime Information

You can retrieve the runtime information from the `runtime` property of the `VirtualMachine` managed object. The `runtime` property is typed as `VirtualMachineRuntimeInfo`, and the structure is shown in Figure 8-3.

From the `runtime` property, you can find the connection state, power state, booting time of this run, and CPU and memory usage. The `VirtualMachineRuntimeInfo` data object is also included in the `VirtualMachineSummary` data object, so you can get the same information from there.

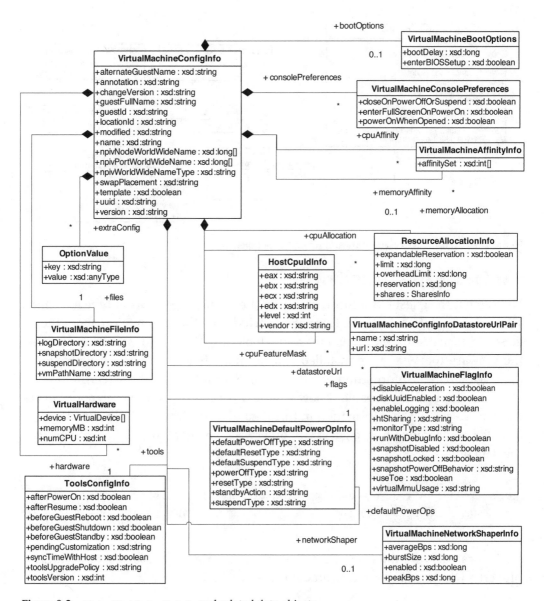

Figure 8-2 `VirtualMachineConfigInfo` and related data objects

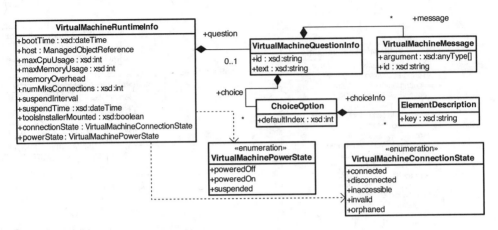

Figure 8-3 `VirtualMachineRuntimeInfo` and related data objects

Guest Operating System Information

You can get the guest OS information from the `guest` property as of type `GuestInfo`. The `GuestInfo` data object (see Figure 8-4) includes all the information about the guest OS installed on the virtual machine, including the type of guest OS, whether the VMware Tools has been installed and running, the virtual disks available to the guest OS, NIC information, IP addresses,[1] and the size of the screen.

A virtual machine does not know what OS is running on top of it, and it doesn't care. To get all the information in this data object, VMware Tools must be installed and running in the guest OS; otherwise, you get few valid properties in the data object.

> A powered-off VM returns the last-known values for VMware Tool configuration. To make sure the value is up-to-date, check the VM running state.

You can also get the guest OS heartbeat status from the `guestHeartbeatStatus` property, which is an enumeration data type with the following options.

---

[1] The IP address could be 0:0:0:0 if there is a network issue, such as an IP address conflict. To clear OS information that can be cached, call the `resetGuestInfomation()` method. It works only when the VMware Tools is not running. You can call it on a powered-off virtual machine so that the cached information does not affect the others. Looking from another perspective, however, the cached information can help reserve the IP, which is a good feature in some cases. Use your judgment here.

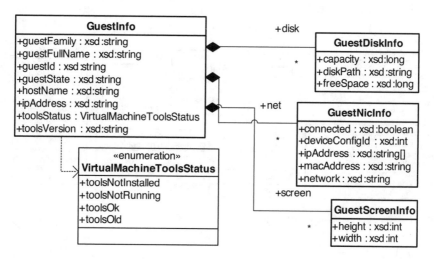

Figure 8-4 GuestInfo data object

- **Gray**—VMware Tools is not installed or not running.
- **Red**—No heartbeat. The guest operating system may have stopped responding.
- **Yellow**—Intermittent heartbeat, possibly due to a heavy load at the guest OS.
- **Green**—Guest operating system is responding normally.

The guest heartbeat status is a statistics metric on which alarms can be configured to monitor the changes and trigger e-mails or other actions accordingly.

Quick Summary

The property summary defines basic information about the virtual machine, including runtime info, guest OS, basic configuration, and alarms and performance statistics. It includes all the information you find in the Summary tab of a virtual machine.

Similar to the summary of HostSystem, the included information might be duplicated with other properties directly or indirectly. The runtime, for example, is an exact duplication of the runtime property of VirtualMachine; therefore, it's not expanded further in Figure 8-5. The VirtualMachineConfigSummary is a miniature version of the VirtualMachineConfigInfo.

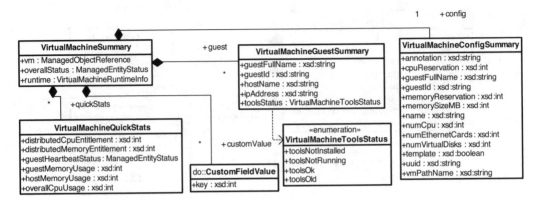

Figure 8-5 `VirtualMachineSummary` data object

Virtual Machine File Layout

The `layout` property of the `VirtualMachine`, whose type is shown in Figure 8-6, describes all the files that make up a virtual machine on disk. The file layout is broken into five sections:

- **Configuration**—A list of configuration files including `.vmsd`, `.vmss`, `.vmxf`, and `.nvram`, but excluding `.vmx`
- **Log**—The log files with a `.log` extension
- **Disk**—All the virtual disks mounted to the virtual machine
- **Snapshot**—The snapshot files for all different snapshots that have been taken on the virtual machine
- **Swapping**—The `.vswp` file for the virtual machine

The swap file and snapshot files are in an absolute path format with the datastore name in it, whereas all the others are in a relative path from the `.vmx` file.

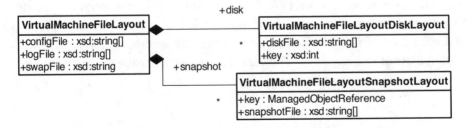

Figure 8-6 `VirtualMachineFileLayout` data object

214

Resource Allocation

In VI, a VM can be given specific allocations of CPU and memory. These resources can be allotted in several ways. For example, the reservation makes sure a VM never receives less than that amount of the resource; the limit makes sure the VM does not receive more than its limit. As of VI 3.5, other shared resources, such as network and storage bandwidth, cannot be controlled in these ways.

To find out the resource allocation policy on the virtual machine, you can use the resourceConfig property typed as ResourceConfigSpec data object. The same data object is used by the methods to create and configure ResourcePool managed objects. Its UML diagram is shown in Figure 8-7.

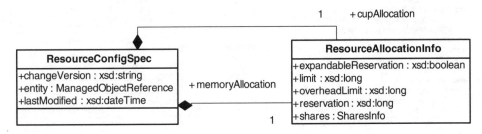

Figure 8-7 ResourceConfigSpec data object

To change the resource allocation, just get the ResourcePool managed object and call its updateConfig() method.

Reconfiguring Virtual Machine

The reconfigVM_Task() method changes the configuration of a virtual machine. The method signature is simple in that it takes in only parameters typed as VirtualMachineConfigSpec, which encapsulates all the configuration settings. However, the complexity is hidden inside the VirtualMachineConfigSpec data object.

Figure 8-8 shows the structure of the data object. The same type is also used during creation of a new virtual machine by invoking the createVM_Task() method on the Folder managed object. As you can see from the diagram, it's a pretty sophisticated data structure that covers all different aspects of the configuration from virtual hardware to the guest OS.

Some configurations, such as virtual device configurations, are persisted into the .vmx file in the virtual machine home directory on the datastore.

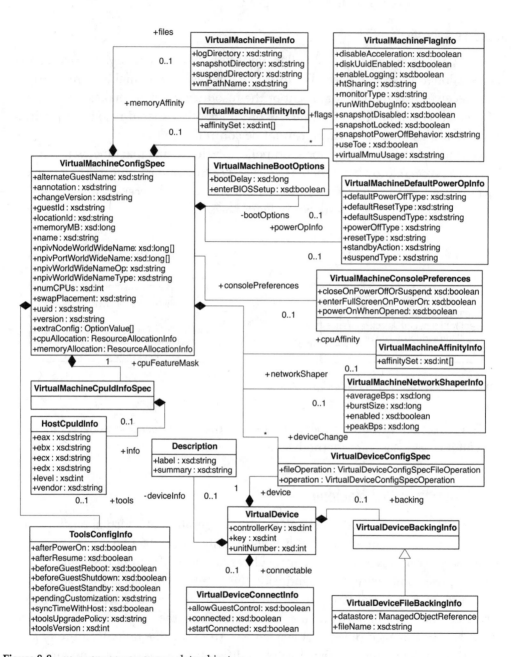

Figure 8-8 `VirtualMachineConfigSpec` data object

You can add new entries into the `.vmx` file programmatically. Notice the `extraConfig` in the `VirtualMachineConfigSpec`, which is an array of `OptionValue` objects. For every one of your key/value entries, create a new `OptionValue` object and add it to the array to be assigned to the `extraConfig` property. Make sure your new keys are not the same as any existing ones.

To support incremental changes, all the properties of `VirtualMachineConfigSpec` are designed optionally. This is, of course, not the case when creating a new virtual machine. To clear an existing configuration, such as the `config.annotation`, you must explicitly set it to an empty string in the parameter to the `reconfigVM_Task()` method.

Changing the configuration of a virtual machine can result in many actions behind the scenes. For example, you can change the virtual devices (network card, virtual disk, and so on) settings so that they can be added or removed as a result.

Depending on what needs to be reconfigured, the privileges required are different. Table 8-3 lists the privileges required for changing specific parts of the configuration.

Table 8-3

Possible Privileges Required for Reconfiguring a Virtual Machine

If You Want To...	You Need...
Change the runtime connection state of a device as embodied by the `Connectable` property	`VirtualMachine.Interact.DeviceConnection`
Change the backing of a CD-ROM device	`VirtualMachine.Interact.SetCDMedia`
Change the backing of a floppy device	`VirtualMachine.Interact.SetFloppyMedia`
Rename the virtual machine	`VirtualMachine.Config.Rename`
Add a virtual disk device that is backed by an existing virtual disk file	`VirtualMachine.Config.AddExistingDisk`
Add a virtual disk device for which the backing virtual disk file is to be created	`VirtualMachine.Config.AddNewDisk`

continues...

Table 8-3   continued

Possible Privileges Required for Reconfiguring a Virtual Machine

If You Want To...	You Need...
Remove a virtual disk device that refers to a virtual disk file	`VirtualMachine.Config.RemoveDisk`
Change the number of CPUs	`VirtualMachine.Config.CPUCount`
Set the amount of memory	`VirtualMachine.Config.Memory`
Add, remove, or edit a raw device mapping (RDM) or SCSI passthrough device	`VirtualMachine.Config.RawDevice`
Add or remove any device other than disk, raw, or USB	`VirtualMachine.Config.AddRemoveDevice`
Change the settings of any device	`VirtualMachine.Config.EditDevice`
Change any basic settings such as those in `ToolsConfigInfo`, `FlagInfo`, or `DefaultPowerOpInfo`	`VirtualMachine.Config.Settings`
Change resource allocations, affinities, or setting network traffic shaping or virtual disk shares	`VirtualMachine.Config.Resource`
Change values in `extraConfig`	`VirtualMachine.Config.AdvancedConfig`
Change `swapPlacement`	`VirtualMachine.Config.SwapPlacement`
Add, remove, or edit a `VirtualUSB` device backed by the host USB device	`VirtualMachine.Config.HostUSBDevice`
Extend an existing `VirtualDisk` device	`VirtualMachine.Config.DiskExtend`

Listing 8-1 shows a sample that uses the `reconfigVM_Task()` method to remove a virtual disk. You can change the code to remove other devices as well. Note that the virtual disks can be destroyed upon removal. You can keep the disk file in the datastore while removing it from the particular virtual machine (see comments in code). The disk can be remounted or used by other virtual machines.

Listing 8-1

`RemoveVmDisk.java`

```java
package vim25.samples.mo.vm;
import java.net.URL;

import com.vmware.vim25.VirtualDevice;
import com.vmware.vim25.VirtualDeviceConfigSpec;
import com.vmware.vim25.VirtualDeviceConfigSpecFileOperation;
import com.vmware.vim25.VirtualDeviceConfigSpecOperation;
import com.vmware.vim25.VirtualDisk;
import com.vmware.vim25.VirtualMachineConfigInfo;
import com.vmware.vim25.VirtualMachineConfigSpec;
import com.vmware.vim25.mo.Folder;
import com.vmware.vim25.mo.InventoryNavigator;
import com.vmware.vim25.mo.ServiceInstance;
import com.vmware.vim25.mo.Task;
import com.vmware.vim25.mo.VirtualMachine;

public class RemoveVmDisk
{
  public static void main(String[] args) throws Exception
  {
    if(args.length!=5)
    {
      System.out.println("Usage: java RemoveVmDisk <url> " +
            "<username> <password> <vmname> <diskname>");
      System.exit(0);
    }
    String vmname = args[3];
    String diskName = args[4];
```

```
ServiceInstance si = new ServiceInstance(
    new URL(args[0]), args[1], args[2], true);

Folder rootFolder = si.getRootFolder();
VirtualMachine vm = (VirtualMachine) new InventoryNavigator(
  rootFolder).searchManagedEntity("VirtualMachine", vmname);

if(vm==null)
{
  System.out.println("No VM " + vmname + " found");
  si.getServerConnection().logout();
  return;
}

VirtualMachineConfigSpec vmConfigSpec =
    new VirtualMachineConfigSpec();

VirtualDeviceConfigSpec vdiskSpec =
    createRemoveDiskConfigSpec(vm.getConfig(), diskName);
vmConfigSpec.setDeviceChange(
    new VirtualDeviceConfigSpec[]{vdiskSpec} );
Task task = vm.reconfigVM_Task(vmConfigSpec);

if(task.waitForMe()==Task.SUCCESS)
{
  System.out.println("Disk removed.");
}
else
{
  System.out.println("Error while removing disk");
}

si.getServerConnection().logout();
}

static VirtualDeviceConfigSpec createRemoveDiskConfigSpec(
    VirtualMachineConfigInfo vmConfig, String diskName)
        throws Exception
```

```
  {
    VirtualDeviceConfigSpec diskSpec =
        new VirtualDeviceConfigSpec();
    VirtualDisk disk = (VirtualDisk) findVirtualDevice(
        vmConfig, diskName);

    if(disk != null)
    {
      diskSpec.setOperation(
          VirtualDeviceConfigSpecOperation.remove);
// removing the following line can keep the disk file
      diskSpec.setFileOperation(
          VirtualDeviceConfigSpecFileOperation.destroy);
      diskSpec.setDevice(disk);
      return diskSpec;
    }
    else
    {
      throw new Exception("No device found: " + diskName);
    }
  }

  private static VirtualDevice findVirtualDevice(
      VirtualMachineConfigInfo cfg, String name)
  {
    VirtualDevice [] devices = cfg.getHardware().getDevice();
    for(int i=0;devices!=null && i<devices.length; i++)
    {
      if(devices[i].getDeviceInfo().getLabel().equals(name))
      {
        return devices[i];
      }
    }
    return null;
  }
}
```

Power Operations

Similar to its physical counterpart, a virtual machine can have power states. It can be in one of these three power states:

- **Powered on**—The virtual machine is up and running. You can install the OS and run it as on a physical machine.

- **Powered off**—The virtual machine shuts down and you cannot run anything. The management system can still work on the virtual disks to update software, which is not possible for a physical system.

- **Suspended**—The virtual machine is paused and can be resumed. This is like the hibernate state in the physical world.

Accordingly, four methods are available to manipulate the virtual machine power states as follows, all returning Task for monitoring the progress.

- **powerOnVM_Task()** powers on the virtual machine. It takes in an optional parameter representing the host on which the virtual machine is to be powered. If the parameter is not specified, the currently associated host is used. If the parameter is specified, it should be a host in the same ComputeResource; otherwise, use the currently associated host.

  If the method is called when a virtual machine is suspended, it resumes execution from the suspended point. If the virtual machine is part of a cluster, the system might implicitly or according to the host argument relocate the virtual machine to another host. The errors related to this relocation can be thrown. The power on operation may also fail if it does not pass the cluster's admission control checks.

- **suspendVM_Task()** suspends the execution of the virtual machine. The suspended state is unique to virtual machines. At this stage, the virtual machine can be resumed with powerOnVM_Task(), but it cannot be further powered off using powerOffVM_Task(). suspendVM_Task() suspends the execution of the virtual machine with no parameter. The state of the virtual machine is still kept after suspension.

- **powerOffVM_Task()** is relatively simple. It powers off the virtual machine, takes no parameter, and returns a Task. It is a hard shutdown of the virtual machine regardless of the running state of the guest OS.

Before powering off a virtual machine, shut down the guest OS; otherwise, it might corrupt the guest OS or cause data loss.

■ **resetVM_Task**() resets the power on this virtual machine, just like pushing the reset button on the physical machine. It first powers off the virtual machine and then powers it on. Even though two steps are involved, the operation is atomic, meaning that no other power operation can happen before the two steps are finished. resetVM_Task() takes in no parameter.

All these power methods are sensitive to the current power state. If the virtual machine is already powered on, for example, you cannot simply call powerOnVM_Task(); otherwise, an InvalidePowerState fault is thrown.

To avoid the fault, you can check the power state from the runtime information, or you can find out whether the method shows up in the disabledMethod property.

The method names in the disabledMethod property are not the same as the method names you use in code. For example, powerOnVM_Task() is represented as vim.VirtualMachine.powerOn there. You have to keep a mapping table yourself.

There is an interesting method related to the power on operation: answerVM(). It answers virtual machine questions that are blocking a virtual machine from being powered on or getting into the BIOS boot. This method is not used frequently.

The virtual machine questions (represented by VirtualMachineQuestionInfo) are special conditions in the platform that must be answered before the virtual machine can resume. For example, if the configured hard disk is marked as being formatted on a virtual machine that used a BusLogic SCSI controller but the current virtual machine has an LSI Logic controller, the VMKernel wants to verify that it is okay to change the disk marking and continue booting.

Virtual machine questions are not intended for or available to guest software. They are a low-level intrusive solution for special closed-ended problems, as an alternative to simply refusing to boot until the problem is fixed.

The answerVM() method takes two parameters: one string as the question ID, and the other string as the answer. The VirtualMachineQuestionInfo embedded inside the VirtualMachineRuntimeInfo has the question ID, as well as the ChoiceOption from which the answer must be chosen.

Listing 8-2 shows how to manage the power state of the virtual machine or reset/standby guest OS. When you run the sample, just select a virtual machine with the name and change the operation you want to take.[2]

Listing 8-2
VMPowerOps

```
package vim25.samples.mo.vm;
import java.net.URL;

import com.vmware.vim25.mo.Folder;
import com.vmware.vim25.mo.InventoryNavigator;
import com.vmware.vim25.mo.ServiceInstance;
import com.vmware.vim25.mo.Task;
import com.vmware.vim25.mo.VirtualMachine;

public class VMpowerOps
{
  public static void main(String[] args) throws Exception
  {
    if(args.length!=5)
    {
      System.out.println("Usage: java VMpowerOps <url> " +
            "<username> <password> <vmname> <op>");
      System.out.println("op - reboot¦poweron¦poweroff" +
         "¦reset¦standby¦suspend¦shutdown");
      System.exit(0);
    }

    String vmname = args[3];
    String op = args[4];

    ServiceInstance si = new ServiceInstance(
        new URL(args[0]), args[1], args[2], true);
```

---

[2] As mentioned earlier, the operation must be appropriate to the current power state, or a fault is thrown. You can check the state from the VI Client, or you can enhance this sample by incorporating the logic for checking the power state before calling any method.

```
Folder rootFolder = si.getRootFolder();
VirtualMachine vm = (VirtualMachine) new InventoryNavigator(
  rootFolder).searchManagedEntity("VirtualMachine", vmname);

if(vm==null)
{
  System.out.println("No VM " + vmname + " found");
  si.getServerConnection().logout();
  return;
}

if("reboot".equalsIgnoreCase(op))
{
  vm.rebootGuest();
  System.out.println(vmname + " guest OS rebooted");
}
else if("poweron".equalsIgnoreCase(op))
{
  Task task = vm.powerOnVM_Task(null);
  if(task.waitForMe()==Task.SUCCESS)
  {
    System.out.println(vmname + " powered on");
  }
}
else if("poweroff".equalsIgnoreCase(op))
{
  Task task = vm.powerOffVM_Task();
  if(task.waitForMe()==Task.SUCCESS)
  {
    System.out.println(vmname + " powered off");
  }
}
else if("reset".equalsIgnoreCase(op))
{
  Task task = vm.resetVM_Task();
  if(task.waitForMe()==Task.SUCCESS)
  {
    System.out.println(vmname + " reset");
  }
```

```
    }
    else if("standby".equalsIgnoreCase(op))
    {
      vm.standbyGuest();
      System.out.println(vmname + " guest OS stoodby");
    }
    else if("suspend".equalsIgnoreCase(op))
    {
      Task task = vm.suspendVM_Task();
      if(task.waitForMe()==Task.SUCCESS)
      {
        System.out.println(vmname + " suspended");
      }
    }
    else if("shutdown".equalsIgnoreCase(op))
    {
      Task task = vm.suspendVM_Task();
      if(task.waitForMe()==Task.SUCCESS)
      {
        System.out.println(vmname + " suspended");
      }
    }
    else
    {
      System.out.println("Invalid operation. Exiting...");
    }
    si.getServerConnection().logout();
  }
}
```

Managing the Virtual Machine Life Cycle

A virtual machine has its life cycle, from creation to final removal. The following section goes over the typical scenarios in life cycle management.

Creating a New Virtual Machine

The method to create a new virtual machine is not defined on the `VirtualMachine` type, but on the `Folder` object that can be parent to a virtual machine in the inventory tree. The `createVM_Task()` takes in three parameters and returns a `Task`.

The first parameter is a `VirtualMachineConfigSpec` object, the same type as that of `reconfigVM_Task()`. The second is the resource pool to which the virtual machine will be attached. The last one is `HostSystem`, on which the virtual machine will be running. The host and resource pool have to be in the same `ComputeResource`. For a standalone host or a DRS-enabled cluster, the host can be `null` and the system can then select a default host for you.

Listing 8-3 shows a sample that creates a new virtual machine with one SCSI controller, one virtual disk, and one NIC card. You can achieve the same result as you would with the New Virtual Machine Wizard in the VI Client. With the API, you can actually do more than with the wizard. For example, you can add more than one virtual disk at the same time with the API.

To run this code in your environment, you should change the datacenter name, datastore name, network name, and so on accordingly.

Listing 8-3
CreateVM.java

```java
package vim25.samples.mo.vm;
import java.net.URL;

import com.vmware.vim25.Description;
import com.vmware.vim25.VirtualDeviceConfigSpec;
import com.vmware.vim25.VirtualDeviceConfigSpecFileOperation;
import com.vmware.vim25.VirtualDeviceConfigSpecOperation;
import com.vmware.vim25.VirtualDisk;
import com.vmware.vim25.VirtualDiskFlatVer2BackingInfo;
import com.vmware.vim25.VirtualEthernetCard;
import com.vmware.vim25.VirtualEthernetCardNetworkBackingInfo;
import com.vmware.vim25.VirtualLsiLogicController;
import com.vmware.vim25.VirtualMachineConfigSpec;
import com.vmware.vim25.VirtualMachineFileInfo;
import com.vmware.vim25.VirtualPCNet32;
import com.vmware.vim25.VirtualSCSISharing;
import com.vmware.vim25.mo.Datacenter;
import com.vmware.vim25.mo.Folder;
import com.vmware.vim25.mo.InventoryNavigator;
import com.vmware.vim25.mo.ResourcePool;
import com.vmware.vim25.mo.ServiceInstance;
import com.vmware.vim25.mo.Task;
```

```java
public class CreateVM
{
  public static void main(String[] args) throws Exception
  {
    if(args.length!=3)
    {
      System.out.println("Usage: java CreateVM <url> " +
            "<username> <password>");
      System.exit(0);
    }

    String dcName = "ha-datacenter";
    String vmName = "vimasterVM";
    long memorySizeMB = 500;
    int cupCount = 1;
    String guestOsId = "sles10Guest";
    long diskSizeKB = 1000000;
    // mode: persistent¦independent_persistent,
    // independent_nonpersistent
    String diskMode = "persistent";
    String datastoreName = "storage1 (2)";
    String netName = "VM Network";
    String nicName = "Network Adapter 1";

    ServiceInstance si = new ServiceInstance(
        new URL(args[0]), args[1], args[2], true);

    Folder rootFolder = si.getRootFolder();

    Datacenter dc = (Datacenter) new InventoryNavigator(
        rootFolder).searchManagedEntity("Datacenter", dcName);
    ResourcePool rp = (ResourcePool) new InventoryNavigator(
        dc).searchManagedEntities("ResourcePool")[0];

    Folder vmFolder = dc.getVmFolder();

    // create vm config spec
    VirtualMachineConfigSpec vmSpec =
```

```
        new VirtualMachineConfigSpec();
    vmSpec.setName(vmName);
    vmSpec.setAnnotation("VirtualMachine Annotation");
    vmSpec.setMemoryMB(memorySizeMB);
    vmSpec.setNumCPUs(cupCount);
    vmSpec.setGuestId(guestOsId);

    // create virtual devices
    int cKey = 1000;
    VirtualDeviceConfigSpec scsiSpec = createScsiSpec(cKey);
    VirtualDeviceConfigSpec diskSpec = createDiskSpec(
        datastoreName, cKey, diskSizeKB, diskMode);
    VirtualDeviceConfigSpec nicSpec = createNicSpec(
        netName, nicName);

    vmSpec.setDeviceChange(new VirtualDeviceConfigSpec[]
        {scsiSpec, diskSpec, nicSpec});

    // create file info for the vmx file
    VirtualMachineFileInfo vmfi = new VirtualMachineFileInfo();
    vmfi.setVmPathName("["+ datastoreName +"]");
    vmSpec.setFiles(vmfi);

    // call the createVM_Task method on the vm folder
    Task task = vmFolder.createVM_Task(vmSpec, rp, null);
    String result = task.waitForMe();
    if(result == Task.SUCCESS)
    {
      System.out.println("VM Created Sucessfully");
    }
    else
    {
      System.out.println("VM could not be created. ");
    }
}


static VirtualDeviceConfigSpec createScsiSpec(int cKey)
{
  VirtualDeviceConfigSpec scsiSpec =
    new VirtualDeviceConfigSpec();
```

```
  scsiSpec.setOperation(VirtualDeviceConfigSpecOperation.add);
  VirtualLsiLogicController scsiCtrl =
      new VirtualLsiLogicController();
  scsiCtrl.setKey(cKey);
  scsiCtrl.setBusNumber(0);
  scsiCtrl.setSharedBus(VirtualSCSISharing.noSharing);
  scsiSpec.setDevice(scsiCtrl);
  return scsiSpec;
}


static VirtualDeviceConfigSpec createDiskSpec(String dsName,
    int cKey, long diskSizeKB, String diskMode)
{
  VirtualDeviceConfigSpec diskSpec =
      new VirtualDeviceConfigSpec();
  diskSpec.setOperation(VirtualDeviceConfigSpecOperation.add);
  diskSpec.setFileOperation(
      VirtualDeviceConfigSpecFileOperation.create);

  VirtualDisk vd = new VirtualDisk();
  vd.setCapacityInKB(diskSizeKB);
  diskSpec.setDevice(vd);
  vd.setKey(0);
  vd.setUnitNumber(0);
  vd.setControllerKey(cKey);

  VirtualDiskFlatVer2BackingInfo diskfileBacking =
      new VirtualDiskFlatVer2BackingInfo();
  String fileName = "["+ dsName +"]";
  diskfileBacking.setFileName(fileName);
  diskfileBacking.setDiskMode(diskMode);
  diskfileBacking.setThinProvisioned(true);
  vd.setBacking(diskfileBacking);
  return diskSpec;
}


static VirtualDeviceConfigSpec createNicSpec(String netName,
    String nicName) throws Exception
{
  VirtualDeviceConfigSpec nicSpec =
```

```
    new VirtualDeviceConfigSpec();
nicSpec.setOperation(VirtualDeviceConfigSpecOperation.add);

VirtualEthernetCard nic =  new VirtualPCNet32();
VirtualEthernetCardNetworkBackingInfo nicBacking =
    new VirtualEthernetCardNetworkBackingInfo();
nicBacking.setDeviceName(netName);

Description info = new Description();
info.setLabel(nicName);
info.setSummary(netName);
nic.setDeviceInfo(info);

// type: "generated", "manual", "assigned" by VC
nic.setAddressType("generated");
nic.setBacking(nicBacking);
nic.setKey(0);

nicSpec.setDevice(nic);
return nicSpec;
    }
}
```

Registering a Virtual Machine

Datastores in your VI may contain virtual machine files that are not registered as VMs. This can happen if you copy the VM files from another system or if you remove them from inventory using the VI Client. The VI cannot effectively manage them before it is registered into the inventory. Before registration finishes, no VirtualMachine object is available to work with. So the registerVM_Task() is defined with the Folder managed object, which allows VirtualMachine as its child type.

The registerVM_Task() takes in five parameters.

- **path**—The datastore path to the virtual machine.
- **name**—The name to be assigned to the virtual machine. It should not be duplicated with any other VirtualMachine in the same folder.
- **asTemplate**—A boolean flag to specify whether the virtual machine is to be marked as a virtual machine template.

- **pool**—The resource pool to which the virtual machine should be attached. If asTemplate is set to true, it's not needed.

- **host**—The target host on which the virtual machine will be running. The host must be in the same ComputeResource as the pool.

Upon invocation, the method returns immediately with a Task managed object. You can not only monitor the operation, but also obtain the newly registered VirtualMachine via the info.result property of the Task if it is successful.

Cloning a Virtual Machine

The cloneVM_Task() defined on VirtualMachine creates a clone of this virtual machine. The source could be a virtual machine or virtual machine template. Depending on the source and destination type and the clone spec parameter, the privileges required could be different. Check out the API reference for more details.

> Cloning a virtual machine is regarded as an advanced feature; therefore, it is supported only on VirtualCenter, not ESX.

The method takes in three parameters.

- **Name of the newly cloned virtual machine**—The name is just a string. Any % (percent) character used in this name parameter must be escaped, unless it is used to start an escape sequence. Clients may also escape any other character.

- **The newly folder location**—The folder must be a VirtualMachine folder whose childType property includes VirtualMachine. It has to exist before this invocation. If not, you should create one as discussed in Chapter 6, "Managing Inventory."

- **The clone specification**—The spec is typed as VirtualMachineCloneSpec, which is a complicated data object type that specifies how to clone the virtual machine. It embeds VirtualMachineConfigSpec, CustomizationSpec, and VirtualMachineRelocateSpec data objects. With these data objects, you can further define the configuration, customization, and relocation details.

Listing 8-4 shows a sample that clones a virtual machine to a new one in the same vm folder. Note that the cloning method is sensitive to the power state. It throws a fault when the source virtual machine is still powered on. To run this sample, power off the virtual machine before it is cloned.

Listing 8-4

CloneVM.java

```java
package vim25.samples.mo.vm;
import java.net.URL;

import com.vmware.vim25.VirtualMachineCloneSpec;
import com.vmware.vim25.VirtualMachineRelocateSpec;
import com.vmware.vim25.mo.Folder;
import com.vmware.vim25.mo.InventoryNavigator;
import com.vmware.vim25.mo.ServiceInstance;
import com.vmware.vim25.mo.Task;
import com.vmware.vim25.mo.VirtualMachine;

public class CloneVM
{
  public static void main(String[] args) throws Exception
  {
    if(args.length!=5)
    {
      System.out.println("Usage: java CloneVM <url> " +
      "<username> <password> <vmname> <clonename>");
      System.exit(0);
    }

    String vmname = args[3];
    String cloneName = args[4];

    ServiceInstance si = new ServiceInstance(
        new URL(args[0]), args[1], args[2], true);

    Folder rootFolder = si.getRootFolder();
    VirtualMachine vm = (VirtualMachine) new InventoryNavigator(
        rootFolder).searchManagedEntity(
            "VirtualMachine", vmname);
```

```
if(vm==null)
{
  System.out.println("No VM " + vmname + " found");
  si.getServerConnection().logout();
  return;
}

VirtualMachineCloneSpec cloneSpec =
  new VirtualMachineCloneSpec();
cloneSpec.setLocation(new VirtualMachineRelocateSpec());
cloneSpec.setPowerOn(false);
cloneSpec.setTemplate(false);

Task task = vm.cloneVM_Task((Folder) vm.getParent(),
    cloneName, cloneSpec);
System.out.println("Launching the VM clone task. " +
  "Please wait ...");

String status = task.waitForMe();
if(status==Task.SUCCESS)
{
  System.out.println("VM got cloned successfully.");
}
else
{
  System.out.println("Failure -: VM cannot be cloned");
}
  }
}
```

Destroying a Virtual Machine

Because `VirtualMachine` is a subtype of `ManagedEntity`, it inherits the `destroy_Task()` method from `ManagedEntity`. Destroying a virtual machine disposes not only itself, but all associated storage, including the virtual disks. Again, you should be extremely cautious while calling this method.

To remove a virtual machine while retaining its virtual disk storage, a client must remove the virtual disks from the virtual machine before destroying it. You can use the `reconfigVM_Task()` to remove any of the virtual disks.

Optionally, you can remove the virtual machine from inventory while keeping everything intact by unregistering it.

Converting To/From Templates

A virtual machine template is a virtual machine that cannot be powered on and is not associated with a resource pool. It's used to quickly and repeatedly deploy new virtual machines. You can convert a virtual machine to a template and vice versa when a virtual machine is powered off. This feature is supported only on the VC Server.

> To tell whether a virtual machine is a template, just check the `config.template` property (type: `boolean`) of the `VirtualMachine` object.

To convert to a template, you can call the `markAsTemplate()` method. It takes in no parameter and returns nothing. Upon the success of this method, the `template` flag in the `VirtualMachineConfigInfo` is set to `true`.

The reversed direction is a little bit complicated. You can call `markAsVirtualMachine()` to turn a template back to a normal virtual machine. You have to provide the resource pool and optionally the host to which the new virtual machine will be associated. Again, the resource pool and the host must be under the same `ComputeResource`. For a standalone host or a DRS cluster, the system selects a default when the host is not specified.

Upgrading a Virtual Machine

The `upgradeVM_Task()` upgrades the virtual machine's virtual hardware to the latest revision that is supported by the virtual machine's current host. It takes an option string parameter as the version number. If the parameter is not set, it is upgraded to the latest virtual hardware supported on the host. If the virtual hardware is already up-to-date, an `AlreadyUpgraded` fault is thrown.

The virtual hardware supported in ESX3.5 is version 4. This method is only useful when you want to run your virtual machine on a newer hypervisor that supports newer version of virtual hardware. The virtual hardware definition is relatively stable and only changes with major releases.

Unregistering a Virtual Machine

The `unregisterVM()` method removes this virtual machine from the inventory without deleting any of the virtual machine's files on disk. All the high-level information stored with the ESX server or VC server (for example, statistics, resource pool association, permissions, alarms) is removed. The related disk and configuration are still in the datastore, so you can always register the virtual machine back to inventory later on.

This method takes in no parameter and returns `none` or a fault thrown. Before the invocation, the virtual machine should be powered off; otherwise, an `InvalidPowerState` fault is thrown.

There is another alternative to unregister a virtual machine. You can call the `unregisterAndDestroy_Task()` method defined in the `Folder` managed object. Upon being invoked, the method recursively unregisters all virtual machines and destroys all child virtual machine folders. This is a group of actions happening to a virtual machine folder. Given its potential consequences, you should be extremely careful while using this method.

Managing the Guest Operating System

The guest OS is running on top of the virtual machine and, just like the virtual machine, it has several states: `running`, `shutting down`, `resetting`, `standby`, and `not running`. From the VI SDK point of view, there is one more state that is `unknown`, meaning it cannot tell the exact state.

As mentioned earlier, a virtual machine doesn't know the guest OS unless the VMware Tools is installed. The guest OS–related info is mainly held in the property `guest`, which is typed as `GuestInfo`, as shown in Figure 8-4. For the methods discussed in this section, you must have the VMware Tools installed and running already. Refer to the next section for installing and upgrading the VMware Tools.

Six methods are defined on `VirtualMachine` to manage the guest OS:

- `shutdownGuest()` sends a command to the guest OS for it to perform a clean shutdown. It closes all the services, saves the system setting and unsaved data in memory, and brings down the OS. The method takes in no parameter and returns immediately with nothing. A fault might be thrown if the method fails. For example, you can get a `ToolsUnavailable` fault if the VMware Tools is not installed; `InvalidPowerState` if the virtual machine is not powered on; and so on.

- **`rebootGuest()`** issues a command to the guest OS to be rebooted. It brings the guest OS down and then back up running again. The method takes in no parameter and returns immediately with nothing or one of the possible faults.

- **`standbyGuest()`** issues a command to suspend the guest OS to standby mode. It's different from the `suspendVM_Task()` that puts the virtual machine to suspended mode. It takes in a parameter and returns nothing or with a fault.

- **`resetGuestInfomation()`** clears the cached guest information. It can only be done when the VMware Tools is not running because the virtual machine is powered off, suspended, or the guest OS is running without VMware Tools. It's useful when you want to clear the stale information that prevents an IP or MAC address from being reused.

- **`customizeVM_Task()`** customizes a virtual machine when deploying or migrating with the parameter typed as `CustomizationSpec`. The `CustomizationSpec` data object, as shown in Figure 8-9, is a complicated data object that includes the public encryption key, IP, NIC, and guest OS setting for customization needs.

- **`setScreenResolution()`** sets the console screen size of the guest OS. It takes two integer parameters representing the width and height in pixels. Upon invocation, it returns immediately with `none` or a fault thrown. The screen size change is immediately reflected in the virtual machine console in the VI Client. This is one of the features that the VI Client doesn't touch because you cannot change the guest OS screen size from there.

Upgrading VMware Tools

Just like a physical machine, a virtual machine doesn't know what operating system is to be installed on it, and it doesn't care. To better manage the virtual environment, you may want to find out basic information about the guest OS and possibly control it to some extent. To achieve this, you need to install a small software agent into the guest OS.

The VMware Tools is such an agent. From the VI Client, you can choose to install the VMware Tools when a virtual machine is selected and the target guest OS is running. The VMware Tools has five subcomponents: toolbox, VMware device drivers, shared folders, guest SDK, and Wyse Multimedia Support. The device drivers include SCSI, SVGA, mouse, VMXnet NIC, memory control, and file-system sync drivers. They are intended to improve the related performance of

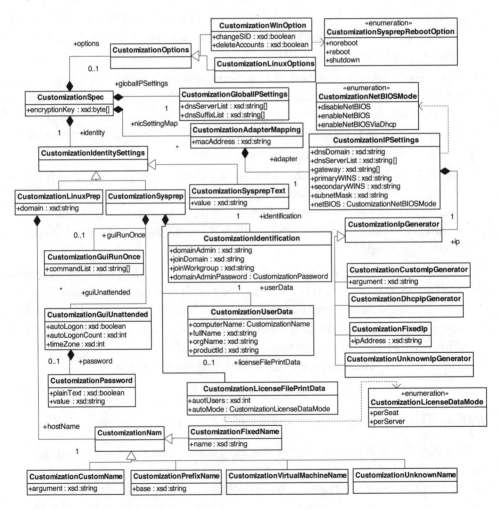

Figure 8-9   The CustomizationSpec data object

the virtual machine. The shared folders allow files to be shared between the virtual machine and the host computer. The guest SDK provides interfaces for the applications running in the guest OS to read information about the virtual machine state and performance. You can decide what subcomponents to install with the installer. Note that the shared folders feature of the VMware Tools is only enabled on some of the hosted products—Workstation, Player, and Fusion—not on the VMware Server, and not on the ESX Server.

The information that the VMware Tools collects is stored in the `GuestInfo` data object, which is shown in Figure 8-4. The tool also helps with guest OS–related operations like `shutdownGuest()`, `rebootGuest()`, and `standbyGuest()`.

`VirtualMachine` provides three methods to automate the tool installation and upgrade:

- `mountToolInstaller()` mounts the VMware Tools CD as a CD-ROM for the guest OS. To verify the progress of the tool installation, you can check the `toolStatus` in the `GuestInfo` data object.

- `unmountToolsInstaller()` unmounts the VMware Tools installer CD.

- `upgradeTools_Task()` starts upgrading the VMware tools. It takes in one string parameter as command-line options to the installer to customize the installation procedure. As its name suggest, the method assumes VMware Tools has been installed and running before invocation.

> Although these methods are provided, the VMware Tools installation still requires human interaction. To avoid the interaction, you can install once on one virtual machine and clone from it or from a template converted from the virtual machine.

Customizing the Guest OS

You can customize the identity and network settings of a guest operating system so that it can start to work immediately in your target environment after deploying it from template or cloning it from an existing virtual machine. In the `VirtualMachineCloneSpec` to the `cloneVM_Task()` method, `CustomizationSpec` is included. You can also customize an existing virtual machine's guest OS using the `customizeVM_Task()` method, which has the `CustomizationSpec` as parameter as well.

For the customization to work, you must install VMware Tools on the source virtual machine or template. In addition, you should make sure the virtual machine has SCSI disk(s). You should read carefully the related contents in the Basic System Administration.[3]

If it's a Windows guest OS, you should also install the Microsoft Sysprep tools on the same machine where the VirtualCenter server is installed.[4] If your guest OS is not a volume-licensed version of Windows, you might have to reactivate your OS on the new virtual machine.

For Linux or other OSes,[5] VMware has provided several Perl scripts under the VirtualCenter installation directory.[6] These scripts are copied over to the ESX host's /etc directory when VirtualCenter customizes a target. VMware Tools then runs them.

Managing the Customization Spec

On the VI Client connecting to a VirtualCenter, you can create/modify customization specifications in the Customization Specification Manager dialog box, which can be brought up from the Edit, Customization Specification menu. If you choose New, you will see the VMware Infrastructure Client Guest Customization Wizard. Going through these steps definitely helps to understand the data objects to be discussed in the following.

You can create multiple customization specifications for deployment. When you clone a virtual machine, you can reference one of these existing specifications, which can save you much time. The VI SDK also provides you interfaces to manage these specifications and export them to, or import from, XML. You can edit the XML file(s) offline and import them back again.

The CustomizationSpecManager is the managed object to manage the customization specifications. It is a singleton managed object attached to ServiceInstance, and it is only available when you connect to the VirtualCenter server.

---

[3] http://www.vmware.com/pdf/vi3_35/esx_3/r35/vi3_35_25_admin_guide.pdf, see page 216.
[4] Basic System Administration (http://www.vmware.com/pdf/vi3_35/esx_3/r35/vi3_35_25_admin_guide.pdf); see Appendix B, "Installing the Microsoft Sysprep Tools."
[5] By default, RedHat, OpenSUSE, and SunOS are supported. You need to develop your own customization scripts for other OSes. Reading the existing scripts is a good starting point.
[6] C:\Program Files\VMware\Infrastructure\VirtualCenter Server\imgcust-scripts

CustomizationSpecManager has two properties:

- **encryptionKey**—An array of bytes that is the public key for encrypting the passwords of administrators stored in the specification
- **info**—An array of CustomizationSpecInfo objects, each of which lists the name, type of the guest OS to customize, change version, description, and last updated time.

Ten methods are defined in CustomizationSpecManager:

- **checkCustomizationResources()** validates whether required resources exist to customize a specific guest OS whose name is input as an argument. Even though you have specifications for a guest OS, it doesn't mean you can customize it if Sysprep tools are not installed, for example. If everything works fine, it returns nothing; otherwise CustomizationFault or its subtype can be thrown. It's always a good idea to call this method to check before you customize a guest OS.

- **createCustomizationSpec()** creates a new specification. It takes in the CustomizationSpecItem data object, whose UML diagram is shown in Figure 8-10. The CustomizationSpecItem includes CustomizationSpecInfo and CusomizationSpec. After they have been created successfully, the CustomizationSpecInfo is added into the array of property Info. The name of the specification must be unique within the VirtualCenter. The method returns none, meaning successful, or a fault like AlreadyExists, CannotDecryptPasswords, or CustomizationFault.

- **customizationSpecItemToXml()** converts a CustomizationSpecItem to an XML string. It returns a string of XML content. Used with getCustomizationSpec(), this method can export a specification into an XML string, which can be saved to a file or database. Your application can modify it and then import it back with the xmlToCustomizationSpecItem() method.

- **deleteCustomizationSpec()** removes an existing specification and takes in a name for the specification. It returns None if successful, or the NotFound fault for a nonexisting spec.

- **doesCustomizationSpecExist()** checks whether a customization spec exists. It takes name as the argument and returns a boolean as the result.

- **duplicateCustomizationSpec()** copies an existing specification to a new name. It takes in names of source and destination specifications. It returns none or throws a NotFound, AlreadyExist, or RuntimeFault fault.

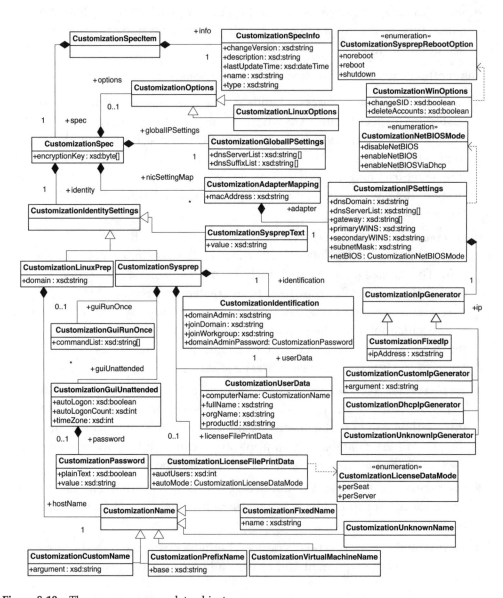

Figure 8-10 The CustomizationSpec data object

- `getCustomizationSpec()` retrieves the specification by a given name. It returns a `CustomizationSpecItem` object.

- `overwriteCustomizationSpec()` modifies an existing specification. Based on the item's `changeVersion` value, if the overwrite process detects that the specification has changed since its retrieval, a `ConcurrentAccess` fault can be thrown to warn the client that it might overwrite another client's change.

- `renameCustomizationSpec()` renames a specification from an old name to a new one.

- `xmlToCustomizationSpecItem()` converts an XML string to specification. It takes an XML string and returns a `CustomizationSpecItem` object. If something goes wrong with the conversation, a `CustomizationFault` can be thrown. Used with `createCustomizationSpec()`, this method can import an existing specification in XML.

Managing Virtual Machine Snapshots

A virtual machine snapshot is a full capture of the whole virtual machine, including the configuration, disks, and memory image (optional) at a specific point in time. With a snapshot, you can restore the virtual machine to the exact state when the snapshot was taken.

Snapshot Hierarchy

One virtual machine can have multiple snapshots, and these snapshots can be structured into a tree hierarchy in which the parent snapshot represents the starting point from which the child snapshot was taken. This potentially complicated structure allows you to track multiple parallel execution paths of a virtual machine. It is useful for testing and development purposes.

Figure 8-11 shows the `VirtualMachineSnapshotInfo`, which is the type for the snapshot property. It holds a reference to the current (or latest) snapshot and an array of `VirtualMachineSnapshotTree` objects. As you find in the UML diagram, `VirtualMachineSnapshotTree` includes an array of the same type, allowing infinite nesting. Of course, the snapshot takes a large amount of system resource–like storage; you don't want to keep too many snapshots. When you no longer need a snapshot, you should remove it. The next section discusses how to manage individual snapshots.

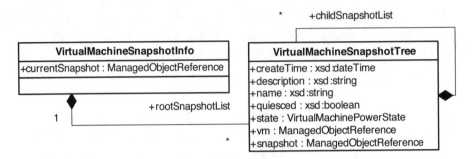

Figure 8-11 `VirtualMachineSnapshotInfo` data object

Creating, Restoring, and Removing Snapshots

When you take a snapshot, a corresponding delta disk file is created in the datastore. Any new change from that point is written to the delta disk, and the existing disk file remains the same. If you take a snapshot Y from another snapshot X, the delta disk for X remains the same.

Deleting the current snapshot does two things simultaneously. First, it commits the changes in the corresponding delta disk back to the parent disk (either the disk or the delta disk). Second, it removes the delta disk. It's different from reverting to a snapshot, in which the delta disk is then removed without committing back.

Three snapshot-related methods are defined in the `VirtualMachine` type.

- `createSnapshot_Task()` creates a new snapshot of the virtual machine and updates the `currentSnapshot` property in the `VirtualMachineSnapshotInfo` object. As expected, it takes the information needed for the `VirtualMachineSnapshotTree`, including name, description, quiesced flag, plus the memory flag specifying whether to create a dump of the internal states of the virtual machine, mainly a memory dump.

- `revertToCurrentSnapshot_Task()` reverts the virtual machine to the current snapshot as held in the `currentSnapshot` property in

VirtualMachineSnapshotInfo. This method is essentially a shorthand method equivalent to invoking the revertToSnapshot_Task() method on the currentSnapshot object.

- **removeAllSnapshots_Task(),** as its name suggests, removes all the snapshots attached to this virtual machine and resets the related data. It there is no snapshot, it just returns success. Alternatively, you can call the removeSnapshot_Task() method on all the VirtualMachineSnapshot managed objects, as discussed next.

VirtualMachineSnapshot Managed Object

This managed object type specifies the interface to the individual virtual machine snapshot. Because snapshots are closely attached to a virtual machine, they're useless without the virtual machine from which they're taken.

The VirtualMachineSnapshot defines one property of type VirtualMachineConfigInfo. It's a copy of the virtual machine configuration when the snapshot was taken. Retrieving the property there gives you the old configuration. It also defines three methods:

- **removeSnapshot_Task()** just removes itself and deletes any associated storage. It takes one boolean parameter specifying whether to remove the sub snapshot tree underneath it. When only the current snapshot is removed, the sub snapshots move up one level to the parent.

- **renameSnapshot()** updates the snapshot with a new name, a new description, or both. The change is reflected in the corresponding properties in the VirtualMachineSnapshotTree data object shown in Figure 8-11.

- **revertToSnapshot_Task()** restores the current virtual machine to the exact state when the snapshot was taken. It has one optional parameter for the host to run the virtual machine in case the operation causes the virtual machine to power on. If you apply a snapshot of a running virtual machine when it's powered off, the method causes the virtual machine to power on. When it happens, the host parameter is needed to identify your choice of host.

If the host parameter is not specified and the DRS is enabled in automatic mode, a host is automatically selected. Otherwise, the virtual machine just uses the current host.

With all the methods just discussed, you can manage the snapshot tree easily. Note that the virtual machine snapshot is closely related to the virtual machine from which it's taken. If the virtual machine is no longer there, the snapshot is useless. You basically cannot apply a snapshot of one virtual machine to another.

Listing 8-5 shows how to list all the snapshots, create a new snapshot, remove one snapshot or all the snapshots, and revert to an existing snapshot for a given virtual machine. To run the code, you specify the virtual machine and operation you want to take. Depending on the operations, you may need to change the extra variables as commented in the source code.

Listing 8-5
VMSnapshot.java

```java
package vim25.samples.mo.vm;
import java.net.URL;

import com.vmware.vim25.ManagedObjectReference;
import com.vmware.vim25.VirtualMachineSnapshotInfo;
import com.vmware.vim25.VirtualMachineSnapshotTree;
import com.vmware.vim25.mo.Folder;
import com.vmware.vim25.mo.InventoryNavigator;
import com.vmware.vim25.mo.ServiceInstance;
import com.vmware.vim25.mo.Task;
import com.vmware.vim25.mo.VirtualMachine;
import com.vmware.vim25.mo.VirtualMachineSnapshot;

public class VMSnapshot
{
  public static void main(String[] args) throws Exception
  {
    if(args.length!=5)
    {
      System.out.println("Usage: java VMSnapshot <url> " +
        "<username> <password> <vmname> <op>");
      System.out.println("op - list, create, remove, " +
```

```
    "removeall, revert");
  System.exit(0);
}

String vmname = args[3];
String op = args[4];
//please change the following three depending on your op
String snapshotname = "test";
String desc = "A description for sample snapshot";
boolean removechild = true;

ServiceInstance si = new ServiceInstance(
    new URL(args[0]), args[1], args[2], true);

Folder rootFolder = si.getRootFolder();
VirtualMachine vm = (VirtualMachine) new InventoryNavigator(
  rootFolder).searchManagedEntity("VirtualMachine", vmname);

if(vm==null)
{
  System.out.println("No VM " + vmname + " found");
  si.getServerConnection().logout();
  return;
}

if("create".equalsIgnoreCase(op))
{
  Task task = vm.createSnapshot_Task(
      snapshotname, desc, false, false);
  if(task.waitForMe()==Task.SUCCESS)
  {
    System.out.println("Snapshot was created.");
  }
}
else if("list".equalsIgnoreCase(op))
{
  listSnapshots(vm);
}
else if(op.equalsIgnoreCase("revert"))
```

```
{
  VirtualMachineSnapshot vmsnap = getSnapshotInTree(
      vm, snapshotname);
  if(vmsnap!=null)
  {
    Task task = vmsnap.revertToSnapshot_Task(null);
    if(task.waitForMe()==Task.SUCCESS)
    {
      System.out.println("Reverted to snapshot:"
          + snapshotname);
    }
  }
}
else if(op.equalsIgnoreCase("removeall"))
{
  Task task = vm.removeAllSnapshots_Task();
  if(task.waitForMe()== Task.SUCCESS)
  {
    System.out.println("Removed all snapshots");
  }
}
else if(op.equalsIgnoreCase("remove"))
{
  VirtualMachineSnapshot vmsnap = getSnapshotInTree(
      vm, snapshotname);
  if(vmsnap!=null)
  {
    Task task = vmsnap.removeSnapshot_Task(removechild);
    if(task.waitForMe()==Task.SUCCESS)
    {
      System.out.println("Removed snapshot:" + snapshotname);
    }
  }
}
else
{
  System.out.println("Invalid operation");
  return;
}
```

```
  si.getServerConnection().logout();
}

static VirtualMachineSnapshot getSnapshotInTree(
    VirtualMachine vm, String snapName)
{
  if (vm == null || snapName == null)
  {
    return null;
  }

  VirtualMachineSnapshotTree[] snapTree =
      vm.getSnapshot().getRootSnapshotList();
  if(snapTree!=null)
  {
    ManagedObjectReference mor = findSnapshotInTree(
        snapTree, snapName);
    if(mor!=null)
    {
      return new VirtualMachineSnapshot(
          vm.getServerConnection(), mor);
    }
  }
  return null;
}

static ManagedObjectReference findSnapshotInTree(
    VirtualMachineSnapshotTree[] snapTree, String snapName)
{
  for(int i=0; i <snapTree.length; i++)
  {
    VirtualMachineSnapshotTree node = snapTree[i];
    if(snapName.equals(node.getName()))
    {
      return node.getSnapshot();
    }
    else
    {
      VirtualMachineSnapshotTree[] childTree =
          node.getChildSnapshotList();
```

```java
    if(childTree!=null)
    {
      ManagedObjectReference mor = findSnapshotInTree(
          childTree, snapName);
      if(mor!=null)
      {
        return mor;
      }
    }
  }
}
return null;
}


static void listSnapshots(VirtualMachine vm)
{
  if(vm==null)
  {
    return;
  }
  VirtualMachineSnapshotInfo snapInfo = vm.getSnapshot();
  VirtualMachineSnapshotTree[] snapTree =
    snapInfo.getRootSnapshotList();
  printSnapshots(snapTree);
}


static void printSnapshots(
    VirtualMachineSnapshotTree[] snapTree)
{
  for (int i = 0; snapTree!=null && i < snapTree.length; i++)
  {
    VirtualMachineSnapshotTree node = snapTree[i];
    System.out.println("Snapshot Name : " + node.getName());
    VirtualMachineSnapshotTree[] childTree =
      node.getChildSnapshotList();
    if(childTree!=null)
    {
      printSnapshots(childTree);
    }
```

```
        }
      }
  }
```

Migrating Live Virtual Machines (VMotion)

VMotion is an advanced feature that allows running virtual machine to continue throughout a live migration from one physical host to another. After the virtual machine is migrated to the new host, it runs on the new host. From outside, you don't observe much noticeable disruption of services on the virtual machine. This feature is only available from VirtualCenter, not a single ESX(i) server.

When VMotion happens, the entire state of the virtual machine and its configuration file, if necessary, are moved to the new host. The associated virtual disk remains in the same location on the storage that is shared between the two hosts. Shared storage is a fundamental prerequisite for VMotion.

The state information includes the current memory content and all the information that defines and identifies the virtual machine. The memory content includes transaction data and whatever bits of the operating system and applications are in the memory. The defining and identification information stored in the state include all the data that maps to the virtual machine hardware elements, such as BIOS, devices, CPU, MAC addresses for the Ethernet cards, chip set states, registers, and so forth.

Migration with VMotion happens in three steps.

1. Upon VMotion request, VirtualCenter or the ESX Server host verifies that the existing virtual machine is in a stable state with its current host.

2. The virtual machine state information, such as memory, registers, and network connections, is copied to the target host. The virtual machine is "stunned" before the move begins. VM execution halts briefly.

3. The virtual machine resumes its activities on the new host. If any error occurs during VMotion, the process stops and virtual machines return to their original states and locations.

To have a successful VMotion, make sure certain requirements are satisfied. The requirements are for both the virtual machine and hosts, as shown in Table 8-4. In fact, many things can fail a VMotion. You can check out the `MigrationFault` and its subtypes in the API reference.

Table 8-4

VMotion Requirements	
For the Virtual Machine	**For the Hosts (Source and Destination)**
Has no active connection to an internal virtual switch	Access to all the SAN (either Fibre Channel or iSCSI) and NAS devices used by the virtual machine
Has no active connection to a CD-ROM or floppy device with a local image mounted	VMKernel port with VMotion enabled[8] (for better VMotion experience, a Gigabit Ethernet backplane is highly recommended)
Has its CPU affinity set to run on one or more specific physical CPUs	Access to the same physical network
Is not in a cluster relationship with another VM	Consistently labeled virtual switch port groups
	Compatible CPUs

[8]HostVMotionSystem, *to be discussed in Chapter 10, "Managing Networking," can help with the configuration.*

VMotion can be performed only between hosts in the same datacenter. To move a virtual machine from one datacenter to another, you must power it off before migration.

In the VI SDK, the method for VMotion is `migrateVM_Task()`,[7] which can handle migration of powered-off VMs as well. It takes parameters such as target resource pool, target host, migration priority, and state. The first two are pretty easy to understand. The migration priority is an enumeration type with three levels: `defaultPriority`, `highPriority`, `lowPriority`. The state is an enumeration as well with three predefined states: `powerOn`, `powerOff`, and `suspended`. The system only migrates the VM when its state matches the specified. When the state is not specified, it defaults to all states, meaning it migrates the virtual machine despite its running state. When the virtual machine is powered off, it has fewer requirements for migration than when it is powered on.

Listing 8-6 shows a sample that migrates a running virtual machine to a new host. As you can tell from the code, it only checks the CPU and software compatibility. You can add more checks in your own application code.

---

[7] The relocate `VM_Task` method is mainly for storage VMotion, but it also can optionally migrate a virtual machine from host to host.

Listing 8-6
MigrateVM.java

```java
package vim25.samples.mo.vm;
import java.net.URL;
import com.vmware.vim25.HostVMotionCompatibility;
import com.vmware.vim25.TaskInfo;
import com.vmware.vim25.VirtualMachineMovePriority;
import com.vmware.vim25.VirtualMachinePowerState;
import com.vmware.vim25.mo.ComputeResource;
import com.vmware.vim25.mo.Folder;
import com.vmware.vim25.mo.HostSystem;
import com.vmware.vim25.mo.InventoryNavigator;
import com.vmware.vim25.mo.ServiceInstance;
import com.vmware.vim25.mo.Task;
import com.vmware.vim25.mo.VirtualMachine;

public class MigrateVM
{
  public static void main(String[] args) throws Exception
  {
    if(args.length!=5)
    {
      System.out.println("Usage: java MigrateVM <url> " +
      "<username> <password> <vmname> <newhost>");
      System.exit(0);
    }

    String vmname = args[3];
    String newHostName = args[4];

    ServiceInstance si = new ServiceInstance(
        new URL(args[0]), args[1], args[2], true);

    Folder rootFolder = si.getRootFolder();
    VirtualMachine vm = (VirtualMachine) new InventoryNavigator(
        rootFolder).searchManagedEntity(
            "VirtualMachine", vmname);
    HostSystem newHost = (HostSystem) new InventoryNavigator(
        rootFolder).searchManagedEntity(
```

```
                "HostSystem", newHostName);
    ComputeResource cr = (ComputeResource) newHost.getParent();


    String[] checks = new String[] {"cpu", "software"};
    HostVMotionCompatibility[] vmcs =
        si.queryVMotionCompatibility(vm, new HostSystem[]
          {newHost},checks );


    String[] comps = vmcs[0].getCompatibility();
    if(checks.length != comps.length)
    {
      System.out.println("CPU/software NOT compatible. Exit.");
      si.getServerConnection().logout();
      return;
    }


    Task task = vm.migrateVM_Task(cr.getResourcePool(), newHost,
        VirtualMachineMovePriority.highPriority,
        VirtualMachinePowerState.poweredOn);


    if(task.waitForMe()==Task.SUCCESS)
    {
      System.out.println("VMotioned!");
    }
    else
    {
      System.out.println("VMotion failed!");
      TaskInfo info = task.getTaskInfo();
      System.out.println(info.getError().getFault());
    }
    si.getServerConnection().logout();
  }
}
```

Storage VMotion

VMware storage VMotion is an advanced feature that moves the virtual disks and
other files related to a running virtual machine to another location with zero
downtime. After the storage VMotion, the virtual machine still runs on the same

host. It allows the users to perform storage maintenance, consolidate storage, balance storage workload, and many other works. It also helps to upgrade VMFS nondisruptively.

This is an experimental feature as of 2.5 and only available with VirtualCenter. The VI Client has no GUI support as of VI 3.5, but you can use it either via the svmotion command line in the Remote CLI or through the VI SDK.

VMotion and storage VMotion cannot be executed at the same time. You can, however, execute them sequentially. You should check the preconditions for each of them.

Storage VMotion takes place in six steps:

1. Copy the virtual machine home to a new location.
2. Self-VMotion to a new virtual machine home.
3. Create a child disk by taking a disk-only snapshot.
4. Copy virtual machine disks to their destination.
5. Consolidate the child disk into copied disks.
6. Delete the original virtual machine home and disks.

Similar to VMotion, Storage VMotion has many prerequisites. Because during the process self-VMotion is used, it includes the VMotion prerequisites,[9] including a valid VMotion license. Beyond that, it has the following.

- Virtual machines with snapshots cannot be migrated.
- The virtual machine's disks must be eligible for snapshots. RDM disks, if used, must be in virtual compatibility mode.
- The host on which the virtual machine is running must have sufficient resources. To be exact, it must accommodate another virtual machine of the same resource allocation running at the same time.
- The ESX host must have access to both source and target datastores.
- Only one migration can happen per datastore at any given time.
- No cluster relationship can exist with another virtual machine.

To perform a storage VMotion, you need to use the relocateVM_Task() method, which takes in the VirtualMachineRelocateSpec (see Figure 8-12) parameter and

---

[9] Because the storage VMotion involves only self-VMotion, the requirement for the host can be easily satisfied.

returns a `Task` object. Just as `migrateVM_Task()` can migrate powered-off virtual machines, storage VMotion can move storages for powered-off virtual machines. When the virtual machine is powered on, it requires the `Resource.HotMigrate` privilege. If the pool property is specified in the spec, the `Resource.AssignVMToPool` privilege is required on the pool.

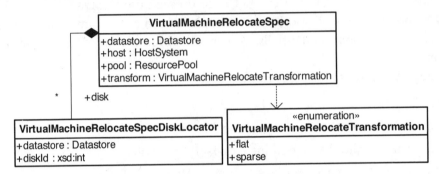

Figure 8-12   The `VirtualMachineRelocateSpec` data object

Summary

A virtual machine functions much like its equivalent physical machine, which you can turn on and off, and install various guest operating systems. This chapter discussed the virtual machine and related functions. It introduced how to retrieve information and manage different aspects of the virtual machine, including life cycle management, power management, VMware Tools management, guest OS management, and customization.

Better than its physical counterpart, a virtual machine can preserve, and recover exactly, to its running state at a specific point in time with snapshots. This chapter introduced the snapshot hierarchy and how to create, restore, and remove snapshots.

Finally, this chapter discussed the advanced features—VMotion and storage VMotion—by which virtual machines can migrate across the host or relocate their files to different storage locations. These advanced features require VirtualCenter and corresponding licenses.

Chapter 9

Managing Clusters and Resource Pools

This chapter first introduces the basics of resource management and how to use the related managed object `ResourcePool` to effectively manage the resources with shares, reservations, limits, and affinity/anti-affinity rules.

The second part shows you how to create, configure, and manage the advanced Distributed Resource Scheduler (DRS) and High Availability (HA) clusters. It provides the basic concepts of VMware clustering, and then it moves on to the `ComputeResource` and its subtype `ClusterComputeResource` managed objects. It covers how to achieve various management tasks via these two managed objects.

Managed Objects: `ResourcePool`, `ComputeResource`, `ClusterComputeResource`

Managing Resources with `ResourcePool`

One of the technical advantages of virtualization is that virtual machines can more efficiently share computing resources on the same physical hardware and across the cluster, datacenter, and even computing clouds. To effectively manage the resources, you need to understand how the resource management works in the VMware Infrastructure (VI) and how to take advantage of it.

Virtual Resource Management Basics

The VI can aggregate all the resources, CPU, and memory only as of VI 3.5, to manage them effectively across the cluster. It's a good way for you to set up systems to meet Service Level Agreement (SLA).

All the physical resources are grouped to the root resource pool, which can be divided recursively in a tree-like hierarchy. Within the hierarchy, you can manage the resource allocation for the resource pools and virtual machines by specifying the shares, reservations, limits, or affinity/anti-affinity rules.

The shares are integer numbers representing the relative entitlement of resource pools. The values are only meaningful relative to their peers; you should not compare the shares with those of the upper or lower levels of resource pools. They come into play only when contending for an overcommitted resource.

Figure 9-1 shows a hierarchy of resource pools and their shares. The HQ is the root resource pool that is divided by Eng and D1 with 300 and 200 shares, respectively. Underneath Eng are two virtual machines, VM1 and VM2, both of which have 80 shares. Underneath D1 is the virtual machine VM3, which has 400 shares. When all the virtual machines are competing for resources, VM1, VM2, and VM3 get 30%, 30%, and 40% of all the system resources, respectively.

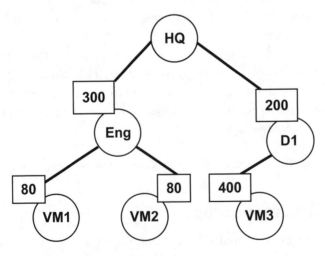

Figure 9-1   The hierarchy of resource pool with shares

The reservation specifies the minimum number of resources in absolute units, such as XXX GHz for CPU resource, YYY M for memory. These resources are guaranteed to be available whenever needed. When not used, they are available for others to use. A child resource pool's reservation cannot exceed that of its parent's available reservation. The total amount of the reserved resources from all the sub-resource pools cannot exceed the total of the root, which is ultimately limited by the physical resources. A reservation can be configured as expandable toward its parent for available capacity.

With reservation, you can guarantee the resources. Overusing it, however, limits the flexibility of resource sharing and can cause problems. For example, specifying too big a reservation for a virtual machine may prevent it from powering on.

The limit specifies the maximum resource allowed in absolute units. It's an effective way to restrict certain virtual machines from abusing system resources.

The affinity/anti-affinity rules limit what virtual machines should or should not be on the same physical machine for various considerations like performance or availability. For example, you don't want your backup Web server running on the same physical host as the primary one, just to make sure your Web servers are immune to single host hardware failure. The anti-affinity rule does not prevent one from manually migrating virtual machines onto the same physical host.

For more details on resource management, check out the Resource Management Guide.[1]

`ResourcePool` Managed Object

`ResourcePool` is the managed object that represents a set of physical resources, including a single host, a subset of a host's resources, or resources spanning multiple hosts. To run a virtual machine, it must be associated with a resource pool as a child.

A resource pool can be divided by creating child resource pools, which can in turn be divided recursively into their own child resource pools. The top of the tree hierarchy is known as the root resource pool. In the `ResourcePool` managed object, the child `ResourcePool` objects are stored in the `resourcePool` property.

The `ResourcePool` managed object is a subtype of `ManagedEntity`. Besides the inherited properties, it defines seven properties (listed in Table 9-1).

---

[1] http://vmware.com/pdf/vi3_35/esx_3/r35u2/vi3_35_25_u2_resource_mgmt.pdf

Table 9-1

The Properties of `ResourcePool`

Name	Type	Explanation
childConfiguration	ResourceConfigSpec[]	The resource configuration of all direct children (VirtualMachine and ResourcePool) of this resource group.
config	ResourceConfigSpec	Configuration of this resource pool.
owner	ManagedObjectReference to ComputeResource	The ComputeResource that owns the resource pool.
resourcePool	ManagedObjectReference[] to ResourcePool[]	The child resource pools. See Figure 9-2.
runtime	ResourcePoolRuntimeInfo	Runtime information of a resource pool.
summary	ResourcePoolSummary	Basic information of a resource pool.
vm	ManagedObjectReference[] to VirtualMachine[]	The virtual machines associated with this resource pool.

Five methods are defined on the `ResourcePool`:

- **`createResourcePool()`** creates a new child resource pool. It requires a name and a `ResourceConfigSpec` as parameters, and it returns the newly created `ResoucePool`.

You don't need to create the root resource pools. They are created implicitly when `ComputeResource` or `ClusterResourcePool` is created.

- **`destroyChildren()`** deletes the child resource pools recursively. The virtual machines associated with these deleted resource pools are moved up with this resource pool. The `Resource.DeletePool` and `Resource.AssignVMToPool` privileges are needed for this operation. The method returns `none`.

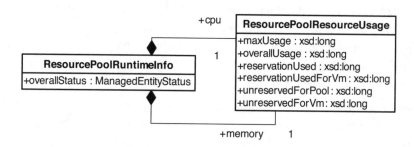

Figure 9-2 The `ResourcePoolRuntimeInfo` data object

- **`moveIntoResourcePool()`** moves a list of resource pools or virtual machines into this pool. The resource pools and virtual machines must be part of the cluster or standalone host that contains this pool.

  The method is subject to different privilege checks depending on the managed entity to be moved. If the object is a `ResourcePool`, then `Resource.MovePool` must be there on the pool being moved, its former parent pool, and the target pool. If the object is a `VirtualMachine`, then the `Resource.AssignVMToPool` privilege must be granted to the login user on the target pool and the virtual machine.

  This operation is transactional only for movement of each entity. The entities are moved one by one in the same order as they are placed in the list parameter, and they are committed one at a time. If a failure is detected, the method terminates with an exception, with the rest of the entities remaining in their original places.

  You can use this method to implement drag-and-drop functionality in a GUI application where a group of virtual machines or resource pools can be moved with a mouse.

The root resource pools are special in that they cannot be moved or deleted.

- `updateChildResourceConfiguration()` changes the configuration of the child resource pool. It takes in an array of `ResourceConfigSpec` objects and returns `none`. The operation is not transactional for all the configuration changes, but is for each one in the array. When a failure happens in the middle, the remaining configurations remain unchanged.

- `updateConfig()` updates the current resource pool's configuration. It is a little interesting because it includes not only a `ResourceConfigSpec` object but also a string to be the new name for the resource pool as parameters. Given that the ResourcePool is a subtype of `ManagedEntity`, the name can be changed with the `rename_Task()` method as well.

DRS and HA Clustering

In the VI, a group of physical servers can be grouped into a cluster for advanced features, such as DRS and HA. Both of them require VirtualCenter.

The HA and DRS are complementary and can be enabled in the same cluster at the same time to create a reliable and efficient computing environment. In fact, most enterprises use them together in a production environment.

High Availability

VMware HA protects the infrastructure against physical host failure. In case of server failure, the affected virtual machines[2] are restarted on other physical servers that have spare capacity. VMware HA is not fault tolerant, which means that the downtime could be minimal but not zero, and data loss is possible. It does not use VMotion technology, but it does require that each host in a cluster can access the same storage resources.

When configuring a cluster for VMware HA, you need to specify the number of host failures from which you would like to be able to recover. If you specify the number of host failures allowed as 1, VMware HA keeps enough capacity across the cluster to handle the failure of one host so that all running virtual machines on that host can be restarted on the remaining hosts.

---

[2] Only those powered-on virtual machines will be restarted. The virtual machine with higher priority will be started first.

When a host is added into the HA cluster, several HA components are pushed down to the host and are installed there. These components monitor heartbeats every 5 seconds and take the necessary action if problems are detected. The heartbeat timeout value defaults to 15 seconds. The timeout value can be configured, but the longer the timeout, the less sensitive the host is to the failure.

To prevent false alarms caused by network issues, set up redundant network connections. It's also important to set up Domain Name Service (DNS) correctly on every host involved.

Although you need the VirtualCenter server to create and configure VMware HA, it continues to work even when the VirtualCenter server is down. The ESX servers in the cluster have special components to coordinate among themselves to respond to any host failure.

Distributed Resource Scheduler

VMware DRS is a feature that helps balance resource allocation and reduces power consumption across a cluster. It collects resource usage information for all hosts and virtual machines in the cluster, provides recommendations on initial placements for powering on virtual machines, and balances workloads by migrating virtual machines across the cluster. As of VI 3.5, DRS covers only memory and CPU.

You can set up various policies for the DRS to make decision or recommendations. These policies include shares, reservations, limits, and affinity/anti-affinity rules.

The new DRS includes the Distributed Power Management (DPM) feature (experimental as of VI 3.5). When DPM is enabled, VirtualCenter analyzes cluster and host-level capacity to the demands of virtual machines running in a cluster. Based on the analysis result, DRS recommends (or automatically implements) actions that reduce the cluster's overall power consumption.

Because DRS relies on VMotion, the hosts in the cluster need to have access to the shared storage and other prerequisites for VMotion.

The management interfaces of all these features are exposed via the `ClusterComputeResource` and its superclass `ComputeResource`. Let's start with the superclass.

ComputeResource Managed Object

The ComputeResource managed object is extended from ManagedEntity. It represents a set of physical compute resources for a set of virtual machines. Besides its inherited properties, it has seven properties defined in Table 9-2.

Table 9-2

The Properties of ComputeResource

Name	Type	Explanation
configurationEx	ComputeResourceConfigInfo	Configuration of the compute resource; applies to both standalone hosts and clusters. For a cluster, this property returns a ClusterConfigInfoEx object, which is a subtype.
datastore	ManagedObjectReference[] to Datastore[]	The datastore objects available to this ComputeResource. It is computed as the aggregation of datastores available to all the hosts that are part of this compute resource.
environmentBrowser	ManagedObjectReference to EnvironmentBrowser	The environment browser object that identifies the environments that are supported on this compute resource.
Host	ManagedObjectReference[] to HostSystem[]	List of hosts that are part of this compute resource. If the compute resource is a standalone type, this list contains just one element.
network	ManagedObjectReference[] to Network[]	The network objects available to this ComputeResource in the datacenter. It is computed as the aggregation of all the networks available to all the hosts that are part of this compute resource.
resourcePool	ManagedObjectReference to ResourcePool	Root resource pool.

Table 9-2   continued

The Properties of ComputeResource		
Name	**Type**	**Explanation**
summary	ComputeResourceSummary	Basic information about a compute resource. It is used on summary screens and in list views. See Figure 9-3.

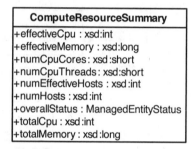

ComputeResourceSummary
+effectiveCpu : xsd:int
+effectiveMemory : xsd:long
+numCpuCores : xsd:short
+numCpuThreads : xsd:short
+numEffectiveHosts : xsd:int
+numHosts : xsd:int
+overallStatus : ManagedEntityStatus
+totalCpu : xsd:int
+totalMemory : xsd:long

Figure 9-3   The ComputeResourceSummary data object

ComputeResourceConfigInfo is a simple data object (see Figure 9-4). It has one property, vmSwapPlacement, with string values only from the enumeration type, VirtualMachineConfigInfoSwapPlacementType, with three possible choices:

- **hostLocal**—Storing the swap file in the datastore specified by the localSwapDatastore property of the virtual machine's host, if that property is set and indicates a datastore with sufficient free space; otherwise, storing the swap file in the same directory as the virtual machine. This setting may degrade VMotion performance.

- **inherit**—Honoring the swap file placement policy of the compute resource that contains this virtual machine.

- **vmDirectory**—Storing the swap file in the same directory as the virtual machine.

The subtype `ClusterConfigInfoEx` is fairly complicated and is also shown in Figure 9-4. It contains seven sub data objects, among which are three pairs of data objects for HA, DRS, and DPM. Each pair of data objects contains one object for system defaults and one object for an array of specific settings for each virtual machine.

The seventh data object is the `ClusterRuleInfo`, which defines the rules for affinity and anti-affinity policies. The affinity rules specify virtual machines that

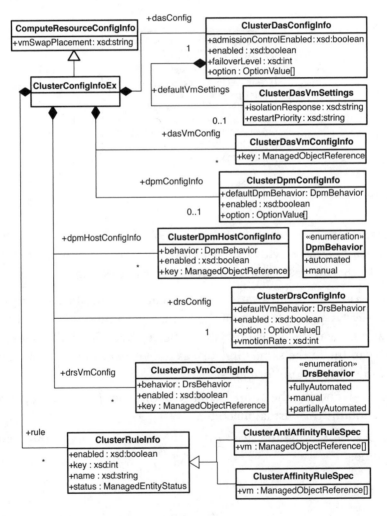

Figure 9-4   The `ComputeResourceConfigInfo` data object

must always be on the same host, whereas the anti-affinity rules specify virtual machines that must never be on the same host. These policies can be used for performance and reliability. For example, you may want a virtual machine running an application server to stay on the same host as the one running a database server in a system. Two virtual machines running a DNS server must not run on the same host; this ensures that they aren't affected at the same time by one host's hardware failure.

The configuration property of type `ClusterConfigInfo` of the `ClusterComputeResource` has been deprecated in VI SDK 2.5 in favor of the `configurationEx` property in `ComputeResource`. To retrieve this property from a `ClusterComputeResource` object, just cast it explicitly to the `ClusterConfigEx` type to access the various cluster-related setting.

`ComputeResource` has one direct method, `reconfigureComputeResource_Task`, which reconfigures the compute resource. It takes in two parameters: the `ComputeResourceConfigSpec`, and a boolean to modify the configuration incrementally or overwrite totally. If set to `false`, the configuration of the cluster matches the specification exactly. In this case, any unset portions of the specification result in unset or default portions of the configuration.

`ComputeResourceConfigSpec`, shown in Figure 9-5, is much like `ComputeResourceConfig`. Therefore, the data types illustrated in Figure 9-4 are not expanded.

Like the `configuration` property of the `ClusterComputeResource`, the related method `reconfigureCluster_Task()` is also deprecated in favor of `reconfigureComputeResource_Task` defined in `ComputeResource`. While calling on the `ClusterConfigSpecEx` managed object, you should pass in a `ClusterConfigSpecEx` object as a parameter. However, the interface cannot enforce this. You can pass in a `ComputeResourceConfigSpec`, and the code still compiles well. You have to pay extra attention to this.

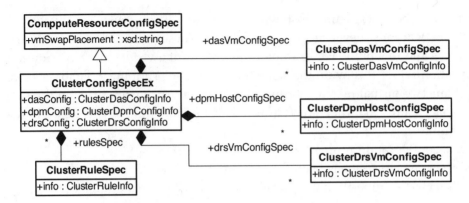

Figure 9-5 The `ComputeResourceConfigSpec` data object

ClusterComputeResource Managed Object

The `ClusterComputeResource` managed object is a subtype of the `ComputeResource` managed object. It represents a cluster of computing resources, normally consisting of a group of physical hosts. In addition to inherited properties, Table 9-3 lists all its direct properties. Figures 9-6 and 9-7 show the data structure of the types used as property types.

Table 9-3

Properties of `ClusterComputeResource`		
Name	**Type**	**Explanation**
actionHistory	ClusterActionHistory[]	The set of actions that have been performed recently. See Figure 9-4.
configuration	ClusterConfigInfo	Deprecated as of VI API 2.5, use `configurationEx` defined in its parent type.
drsRecommendation*	ClusterDrsRecommendation[]	Deprecated. As of VI API 2.5, use `recommendation` instead.
migrationHistory*	ClusterDrsMigration[]	The migrations that have recently been performed. This list is populated only when DRS is in automatic mode. See Figure 9-4.

Table 9-3   continued

Properties of **ClusterComputeResource**

Name	Type	Explanation
recommendation	ClusterRecommendation[]	Holds the list of recommended actions for the cluster. It is possible that the current set of recommendations is empty, either because there are no recommended actions at this time or because DRS is not enabled. See Figure 9-5.

Figure 9-6 shows the UML diagram of ClusterActionHistory. As you can see, the ClusterAction is included in the history object and extended by three subtypes. Each subtype represents one specific action (for example, the initial placement of virtual machines to a specific host and the migration of a virtual machine). The ClusterMigrationAction is the most complicated one; it includes ClusterDrsMigration, which is where you can find the source and destination host system. The ClusterDrsMigration is also the type for the migrationHistory property of ClusterComputeResource.

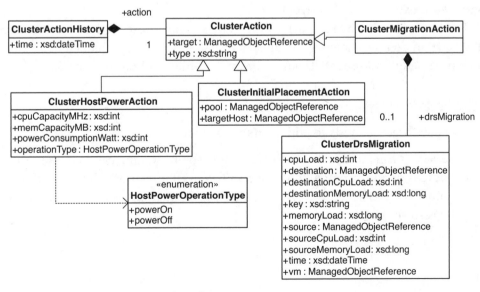

Figure 9-6   The **ClusterActionHistory** data object

Seven methods are defined with the `ClusterComputeResource`: `addHost_Task()`, `applyRecommendation()`, `moveHostInto_Task()`, `moveInto_Task()`, `recommendHostsForVm()`, `reconfigureCluster_Task()`, and `refreshRecommendation()`. The `recommendHostsForVm()` and `reconfigureCluster_Task()` methods have been deprecated in 2.5, in favor of the `powerOnMultiVM_Task` method in the datacenter and the `reconfigureComputeResource_Task()` method in its supertype, respectively. Therefore, they are not discussed in the following section.

Managing Clusters

With the VI SDK, you can do many things to a cluster, including creating and removing it, reconfiguring it, and adding and removing hosts in it.

Creating a New Cluster

Creating a new cluster is defined outside the `ClusterComputeResource` managed object. The `Folder` managed object has two methods for this job: `createCluster()` and `createClusterEx()`. Because `createCluster()` is deprecated in VI SDK 2.5, it is not discussed here.

The `createClusterEx()` method takes in a name string and a spec defined as the `ClusterConfigSpec` type, which is the same as the type for reconfiguration method. Figure 9-5 illustrated its data structure.

The name should have a special `%` (percent) character escaped unless it is needed to start an escape sequence. A caller may also escape other characters in this name parameter and process them accordingly while reading them back.

Adding Hosts to a Cluster

You can use three methods to add host(s) to a cluster.

- **`addHost_Task()`** adds a host to the cluster. The hostname can be either an IP address or a host name. If a host name is used, it can be a fully qualified name, such as `host1.xyz.com`, or a short name such as `host1` (as long as it can be resolved).

If the cluster supports nested resource pools and the user specifies the optional `ResourcePool` parameter, the host's root resource pool becomes the specified resource pool. The standalone host resource hierarchy is imported into the new nested resource pool. If the cluster does not support nested resource pools, the standalone host resource hierarchy is discarded and all virtual machines on the host are put under the cluster's root resource pool.

- `moveHostInto_Task()` moves an existing host into a cluster. The host must be part of the same datacenter, and if the host is part of a cluster, the host must be in maintenance mode. If the host is standalone, its parent `ComputeResource` is removed as part of this operation. All virtual machines associated with the host, either running or not, are moved with the host into the cluster. If you don't want specific virtual machines to be moved into the cluster, migrate them away from the host before calling this method.

  If the host is standalone, the cluster supports nested resource pools, and the user specifies the optional `resourcePool` argument, the standalone host's root resource pool becomes the specified resource pool and the standalone host resource hierarchy is imported into the new nested resource pool. If the cluster does not support nested resource pools or the `resourcePool` argument is not specified, the standalone host resource hierarchy is ignored.

- `moveInto_Task()` works like `MoveHostInto_Task()`, except that it takes in an array of the hosts at a time, and you cannot preserve the resource pool hierarchy from a standalone host. The operation is transactional only with each host in the array. If a failure occurs in the process, the moved hosts are in the cluster and the rest of the hosts remain with their original locations.

Reconfiguring a Cluster

To reconfigure a cluster, use the `reconfigureComputeResource_Task()` method defined in the `ComputeResource` managed object type. (The `reconfigureCluster_Task()` method is deprecated in 2.5.) When the method is used with a `ClusterComputerResource`, pass in a `ClusterConfigSpecEx` data object as the parameter. As shown in Figure 9-5, the `ClusterConfigSpecEx` data object is complicated. Understanding it is critical to reconfiguring a cluster.

Removing a Host from a Cluster

There is no explicit way to remove a host from an existing cluster. You can use the moveIntoFolder_Task() defined in the Folder managed object. However, you must do the following:

1. Power off or suspend all the virtual machines running on the host and put the host into maintenance mode.

2. Find the destination host folder of a datacenter and call the moveIntoFolder_Task() method with the host as a parameter.

When you are done with the move, you can call the exitMaintenanceMode_Task() method so that the host exits the maintenance mode.

Removing a Cluster

Because ClusterComputeResource is a subtype (indirect) of ManagedEntity, use the inherited destroy_Task() method to destroy a cluster. The login user must have the Host.Inventory.DeleteCluster privilege to perform this operation.

Interacting with the DRS Cluster

The DRS can be running in three different modes, as defined in the DrsBehavior enumeration type.

- **fullyAutomated**—VirtualCenter automates both the migration of virtual machines and their initial placement upon powering on.
- **manual**—VirtualCenter generates recommendations for virtual machine migration and for initial placement with a host, and it waits for users' approval before implementing them.
- **partiallyAutomated**—VirtualCenter generates recommendations for virtual machine migration and for initial placement with a host, but it only automatically implements the placement upon powering on.

You can define the behavior at both the cluster level and the virtual machine level. The virtual machine level setting always overwrites that of the cluster.

The DRS can generate three types of recommendations while running in manual and partially automated mode:

- **Initial placement**—When a virtual machine is powered on in the cluster, the DRS can generate a recommendation on which host is appropriate to place it.

- **Migration**—While the cluster is running, the DRS tries to fix rule violations, improve resource utilization across the cluster, and provide recommendations as to which virtual machines should be migrated from the current host to which new host.

- **Power management**—When the DPM feature is turned on, the DRS compares cluster- and host-level capacity to the demands of running virtual machines in the cluster. It makes recommendations for placing hosts into standby power mode to save energy if excess capacity is found or powering on hosts if capacity is needed. Depending on the host power state recommendations, virtual machines might need to be migrated to and from the hosts. Again, this is an experimental feature as of VI 3.5.

These recommendations are stored in the `recommendation` property of the cluster. You can retrieve them as an array of `ClusterRecommendation`. As shown in Figure 9-7, a `ClusterRecommendation` object has several properties including the `key`, `rating`, `reason`, and `target`. It also might include a prerequisite specifying another recommendation it depends on that must be applied before itself. In addition, it includes an array of `ClusterAction` objects, which could be any of the three subtypes that were shown in Figure 9-6. That means it might involve several actions to implement a recommendation.

Once examining the recommendations retrieved from the property, you can implement any of them by invoking the `applyRecommendation()` of `ClusterComputeResource`. All you need is the property `key` from the `ClusterRecommendation`. If the recommendation is DRS migration or power management, the `Resource.ApplyRecommendation` privilege is required.

Each recommendation is only valid for about 5 minutes and can be applied only once, or an `InvalidArgument` fault is thrown. So you should act quickly if you want to apply it. If the time window is over, you should retrieve the recommendation property again.

ClusterRecommendation
+action : ClusterAction []
+key : xsd:string
+prerequisite : xsd:string[]
+rating : xsd:int
+reason : xsd:string
+reasonText : xsd:string
+target : ManagedObjectReference
+time : xsd:dateTime
+type : xsd:string

Figure 9-7 The ClusterRecommendation data object

The refreshRecommendation() method requests DRS to recalculate and return a new list of recommendations. Concurrent refreshRecommendation() requests may be combined and trigger only one DRS recalculation. Therefore, it's more like suggestion than a strict command. The newly calculated recommendations are stored at the recommendation property that you can retrieve.

Now you know the basics of the DRS and how to use the API to retrieve the recommendations. Look at Listings 9-1 and 9-2. These listings have two files:

- **DrsApp.java**—The main class; it gets the first DRS cluster[3] and then retrieves the recommendations every minute. If a recommendation is available, DrsApp.java sends an e-mail to a prespecified account or mailing list. The e-mail includes basic information about the recommendation, including the rating, reason, target host, key, and more importantly a hyperlink allowing you to apply that recommendation from a Web browser.

---

[3] The cluster should be preconfigured in manual mode before running this sample.
[4] The mail.jar and activation.jar of JavaMail 1.2 or higher are needed. For more information on JavaMail, see http://java.sun.com/products/javamail/FAQ.html.

■ **EmailMessenger.java**—A helper class; it connects to the SMTP server to send the e-mail with the JavaMail APIs. You have to include the two JAR files[4] needed to run this sample.

Listing 9-1

DrsApp.java

```java
package vim25.samples.mo.cluster;
import java.net.URL;
import java.util.Date;

import com.vmware.vim25.ClusterRecommendation;
import com.vmware.vim25.mo.ClusterComputeResource;
import com.vmware.vim25.mo.Folder;
import com.vmware.vim25.mo.InventoryNavigator;
import com.vmware.vim25.mo.ManagedEntity;
import com.vmware.vim25.mo.ManagedObject;
import com.vmware.vim25.mo.ServiceInstance;

public class DrsApp
{
  public static void main(String[] args) throws Exception
  {
    if(args.length!=3)
    {
      System.out.println("Usage: java DrsApp " +
                "<url> <username> <password>");
      System.exit(0);
    }

    ServiceInstance si = new ServiceInstance(
        new URL(args[0]), args[1], args[2], true);
    Folder root = si.getRootFolder();
    ManagedEntity[] mes = new InventoryNavigator(
        root).searchManagedEntities("ClusterComputeResource");
    if(mes==null || mes.length == 0)
```

```java
{
  System.out.println("There is no DRS cluster. Exiting.");
  si.getServerConnection().logout();
  return;
}


ClusterComputeResource ccr =
    ((ClusterComputeResource)mes[0]);
EmailMessenger em = new EmailMessenger(
    "mail.acme.com", "username", "password");

for(;;)
{
  StringBuffer sb = new StringBuffer();
  ClusterRecommendation[] recs = ccr.getRecommendation();
  if(recs!=null)
  {
    for(int i=0; i< recs.length; i++)
    {
      sb.append("\n\nRecommendation #" + (i+1));
      sb.append(recommendationToString(recs[i]));
      sb.append("\nPlease click the following URL " +
            "and enter " + recs[i].getKey()
            + " as key to apply this recommendation:");
      sb.append(createMobUrl(args[0], ccr)
          + "&method=applyRecommendation");
      sb.append("\nThe time window for applying " +
            "recommendations is 5 mins. Please act ASAP!");
    }


    // the receiver's e-mail address
    String recvEmail = "admin@acme.com";
    System.out.println("Sending DRS recommendation email to:"
        + recvEmail);
    em.sendEmailTo(recvEmail, "DRS Messenger — "
        + recs.length + " recommendation(s)", sb.toString());
  }
  Thread.sleep(1*60*1000); //wait for 1 minute
}
```

```
}

    static String recommendationToString(
        ClusterRecommendation rec)
    {
      StringBuffer sb = new StringBuffer();
      sb.append("\nRating:" + rec.getRating());
      sb.append("\nReasonText:" + rec.getReasonText());
      sb.append("\nKey:" + rec.getKey());
      sb.append("\nTarget:" + rec.getTarget());
      sb.append("\nTime:" + new Date(
          rec.getTime().getTimeInMillis()));
      return sb.toString();
    }

    static String createMobUrl(String serviceUrl, ManagedObject mo)
    {
      int sdkLoc = serviceUrl.indexOf("/sdk");
      String baseUrl = serviceUrl.substring(0, sdkLoc);
      return baseUrl + "/mob/?moid=" + mo.getMOR().get_value();
    }
}
```

Listing 9-2
`EmailMessenger.java`

```
import java.util.Properties;
import javax.mail.Message;
import javax.mail.Session;
import javax.mail.Transport;
import javax.mail.internet.InternetAddress;
import javax.mail.internet.MimeMessage;

public class EmailMessenger
{
  Properties props = null;

  public EmailMessenger(String host, String username,
```

```
      String password)
{
  props = new Properties();
  props.setProperty("mail.transport.protocol", "smtp");
  props.setProperty("mail.host", host);
  props.setProperty("mail.user", username);
  props.setProperty("mail.password", password);
}

public void sendEmailTo(String receiver, String subject,
    String body) throws Exception
{
  Session mailSession = Session.getDefaultInstance(
      props, null);
  Transport transport = mailSession.getTransport();

  MimeMessage message = new MimeMessage(mailSession);

  message.setSubject(subject);
  message.setContent(body, "text/plain");
  message.addRecipient(Message.RecipientType.TO,
      new InternetAddress(receiver));

  transport.connect();
  transport.sendMessage(message,
      message.getRecipients(Message.RecipientType.TO));
  transport.close();
  }
}
```

Querying the Environment for Virtual Machines

The EnvironmentBrowser provides access to the environment that a ComputeResource presents for creating and configuring a virtual machine. The environment has three main components:

- **Virtual machine configuration options**—Each `VirtualMachineConfigOption` data object describes the execution environment for a virtual machine and the particular set of virtual hardware that is supported. A `ComputeResource` might support multiple sets, each of which is identified by key in the `VirtualMachineConfigOptionDescriptor` returned by the `queryConfigOptionDescriptor()` method.

- **Supported device targets**—Each virtual device specified in the virtual machine needs to be mapped to a "physical" counterpart. For networks, this means choosing a network name; for a virtual CD, this might be an ISO image. The `EnvironmentBrowser` provides access to the device targets through the `queryConfigTarget()` method.

- **Storage locations and files**—A selection of locations where the virtual machine files can be stored, and the possibility to browse for existing virtual disks and ISO images. The datastore browser, by the `datastoreBrowser` property, provides access to the contents of one or more datastores. The items in a datastore are files that contain configuration, virtual disks, and the other data associated with a virtual machine.

The `EnvironmentBrowser` has one property, `datastoreBrowser`, that points to a `HostDataStoreBrowser` object that can be used to browse the datastores available. It defines three methods.

- **`queryConfigOption()`**—Retrieves the `VirtualMachineConfigOption` (see Figure 9-8). The `VirtualMachineConfigOption` is a complicated data object that includes various aspects of virtual machine configuration options, such as capabilities, guest OS options, and virtual hardware options.

  The method takes in two optional parameters. One is the key to identify the option, and the other is the host as the target for the option. If the `EnvironmentBrowser` object is from a virtual machine, you don't need either of these two parameters.

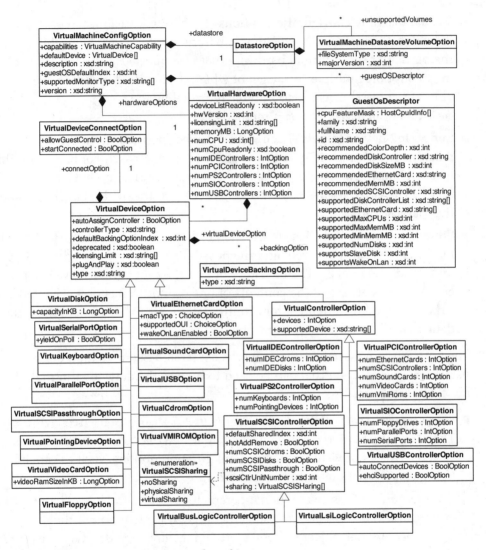

Figure 9-8 The `VirtualMachineConfigOption` data object

However, if `EnvironmentBrowser` is from a `ComputeResource` or `ClusterComputeResource`, different argument combinations can get you different results. If a key is specified, the `VirtualMachineConfigOption` corresponding to that key value is returned. If a host is specified, the default

VirtualMachineConfigOption for that host is returned. If both key and host are specified, the VirtualMachineConfigOption corresponding to the given key for that host is returned. If neither is specified, the default VirtualMachineConfigOption for this environment browser is returned. Typically, the default contains the options for the most recent virtual hardware supported.

- **queryConfigOptionDescription()**—Returns the full list of ConfigOption keys available on this entity. It takes no parameter. Each returned VirtualMachineConfigOptionDescriptor object includes a key as the identifier that can be used as a parameter to the queryConfigOption() method, a string description for the option, and a list of HostSystems, which this option applies.

- **queryConfigTarget()**—Queries for information about a specific target, a "physical" device that can be used to back virtual devices. It takes in an optional parameter that specifies the HostSystem from which you want to retrieve information. The method returns a ConfigTarget that indicates the "physical" devices that can support the virtual machine. If the EnvironmentBrowser is from a VirtualMachine, a host should not be specified.

  If the EnvironmentBrowser is from a ComputeResource or ClusterComputeResource, the host argument can return the ConfigTarget provided by a particular host in the compute resource or cluster. If host is specified and the EnvironmentBrowser is from a ComputeResource or ClusterComputeResource, the union of all the devices is returned and the configurationTag of various properties indicates how widely the device is available across the compute resource or cluster.

Summary

This chapter introduced the advanced features of VMware Infrastructure: HA and DRS clustering (including DPM). It started with the basics of the two cluster features and then discussed the related ComputeResource and ClusterComputeResource managed objects and how to manage a cluster with the related interfaces. A sample showed how to interact with and control DRS while in manual mode.

Resource management was also introduced with the `ResourcePool` managed object. You can specify resource allocation using shares, reservations, limits, and affinity/anti-affinity rules. `ResourcePool` objects can be grouped in a tree-like hierarchy for broader resource sharing and allocation. With `ResourcePool` managed object, you can create, configure, move, and delete resource pools.

Chapter 10

Managing Networking

This chapter introduces the networking aspect of the HostSystem. It first introduces several key concepts, including the virtual switch, port group, and virtual network interface card (NIC), which are the virtual counterparts to the equivalent physical gears. It then examines the HostNetworkSystem, which is the key managed object for various management tasks, such as adding new virtual switches, defining network policies, changing different configuration parameters, and so on.

After that, this chapter discusses the management of the SNMP system, firewall, network services, and VMotion networks.

Managed Objects: HostNetworkSystem, Network, HostFirewallSystem, HostSnmpSystem, HostServiceSystem, HostVMotionSystem

Key Concepts

Virtual networking emulates what the physical world already has; therefore, many concepts are similar to physical networking. Given that many virtual machines run on an ESX server, they are networked like they would be in a physical LAN. To communicate with an external network, the virtual LAN must connect with the ESX host's physical adapter. This section briefly introduces several key concepts before discussing the programming interfaces.

Virtual Switch

A virtual switch (vSwitch) is a network switch (Layer 2) that connects virtual machines. It models a physical Ethernet switch. It can send network traffic internally between virtual machines or link to an external network by connecting to physical Ethernet adapters, also known as uplink adapters.

The default number of logical ports for a vSwitch is 56, and it can have as many as 1,016 ports in an ESX Server (as of version 3.5). The number 1,016 is the 10th power of 2 minus 8, which is the number of ports reserved for uplinks. You can connect one network adapter of a virtual machine to each port. Each uplink adapter that connects to outside the ESX server uses one port in vSwitch as well.

Port Group

A port group aggregates multiple ports under a common configuration and provides a stable anchor point for virtual machines connecting to the labeled networks. It is identified by a label, which must be unique to the current host. The optional VLAN ID restricts port group traffic to a logical Ethernet segment within the network.

> Although the port group names must be unique to the host, they should be the same across hosts for the vMotion to work smoothly.

Each vSwitch can also have one or more port groups assigned to it. Each logical port on the vSwitch can be a member of a single port group.

Connections are one of three types: virtual machine (to handle virtual machine network traffic), VMKernel (to handle the system-critical traffic like VMotion, iSCSI, and NFS), and Service Console (to handle host management traffic).

Virtual NIC

A virtual NIC is attached to a virtual machine just like a physical NIC attaches to a host. Depending on the version of the virtual machine and guest operating system, several types of NICs could be available: Vlance, vmxnet, Flexible, e1000, and enhanced vmxnet. More information on NICs can be found in the VMware Knowledge Base article 1001805.[1]

In general, use the vmxnet driver, which is tuned to work with the VMKernel and shares a ring buffer between the virtual machine and the VMKernel. It has important advantages, such as ZeroCopy operations, possible offloading of TCP checksum calculation to the hardware, batching packets and issuing a single interrupt, and so on.

A physical NIC managed by ESX does not have an IP address directly associated. There could be IP addresses with either console operating system (COS) virtual NIC or the VMKernel virtual NIC.

The config.network.pnic (type: PhysicalNic) of HostSystem does define spec.ip.ipAddress (type: String) for holding IP addresses. But this is really for VMware Server, not for ESX(i) where spec.ip is NULL.

HostNetworkSystem Managed Object

The HostNetworkSystem managed object type describes the host networking configuration and serves as the top-level container for relevant networking data objects. It's a singleton managed object that is closely attached to the HostSystem managed object.

Properties

HostNetworkSystem extends ExtensibleManagedObject and defines 7 properties and 20 methods. Table 10-1 lists the 7 properties with their types and brief descriptions.

---

[1] http://kb.vmware.com/selfservice/documentLink.do?externalID=1001805

Table 10-1

Properties Defined on HostNetworkSystem		
Name	**Type**	**Explanation**
capabilities	HostNetCapabilities	Holding a set of subproperties indicating the networking capabilities of the host.
consoleIpRouteConfig	HostIpRouteConfig	IP route configuration for the service console, including the default gateway IP address and the device.
dnsConfig	HostDnsConfig	The client-side DNS configuration for the host. This DNS configuration is global to the entire host.
ipRouteConfig	HostIpRouteConfig	The IP route configuration for the host.
networkConfig	HostNetworkConfig	Network configuration information. The information is a strict subset of the information available in HostNetworkInfo.
networkInfo	HostNetworkInfo	The network configuration and runtime information.
offloadCapabilities	HostNetOffloadCapabilities	The offload capabilities for better virtual machine networking performance, including whether to offload checksum, TCP segmentation, and zero copy transmit from virtual machine to either the host or physical hardware.

The following discusses three data objects used as property types.

- **HostNetCapabilites**—Shown in Figure 10-1, this data object is a vector of boolean, integer, or string[] variables, each of which indicates one aspect of the host networking capabilities. For example, the supportVlan is a boolean flag, whether VLAN is supported or not by this host. The variable names are pretty self-explanatory and don't require much more detail here. By retrieving the property, you can get a good idea of what is supported and what the limits are.

HostNetCapabilities
+canSetPhysicalNicLinkSpeed : xsd:boolean
+dhcpOnVnicSupported : xsd:boolean
+dnsConfigSupported : xsd:boolean
+ipRouteConfigSupported : xsd:boolean
+maxPortGroupsPerVswitch : xsd:int
+nicTeamingPolicy : xsd:string[]
+supportsNetworkHints : xsd:boolean
+supportsNicTeaming : xsd:boolean
+supportsVlan : xsd:boolean
+usesServiceConsoleNic : xsd:boolean
+vnicConfigSupported : xsd:boolean
+vswitchConfigSupported : xsd:boolean

Figure 10-1   The HostNetCapabilities data object

- **HostNetworkInfo**—One of the most complicated data objects in the entire VI SDK. It covers all the basic aspects of networking on a host, including NAT service, IP routing configuration, DHCP configuration, physical NIC information, virtual switches, and port groups. To represent all this information, another 25 data objects are illustrated in Figure 10-2.

  The UML diagram does not intend to give you every detail, but an overview of what information is there and how these different data objects are grouped and linked. Therefore, you can easily find the path to navigate to the desired information as needed from a HostNetworkInfo object.

- **HostNetworkConfig**—As shown in Figure 10-3, HostNetworkConfig is another complicated data object. The types in this data object are a subset of what are in HostNetworkInfo; to save space, those data objects whose structures have been included in HostNetworkInfo are not further expanded. This data object is also a parameter to the updateNetworkConfig() method.

Overview of Methods

As mentioned earlier, 20 methods are defined with HostNetworkSystem, 12 of which are related to the managing virtual components such as virtual NIC, virtual switch, port group, and serviceConsoleNIC, as Table 10-2 shows.

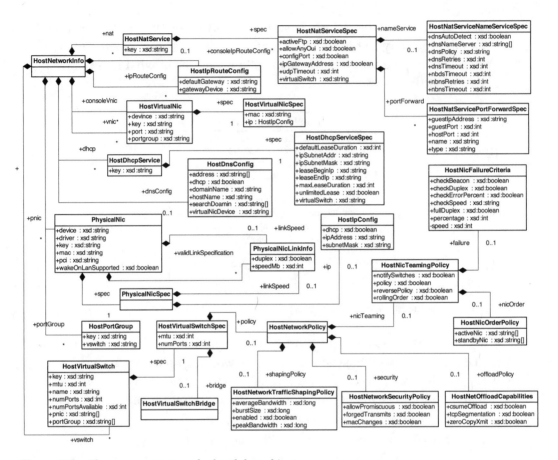

Figure 10-2 The `HostNetworkInfo` and related data objects

Table 10-2

Twelve Methods to Manage Virtual Components

	VirtualSwitch	VirtualNic	PortGroup	ServiceConsoleVirtualNic
Add	addVirtualSwitch	addVirtualNic	addPortGroup	addServiceConsoleVirtualNic
Remove	removeVirtualSwitch	removeVirtualNic	removePortGroup	removeServiceConsoleVirtualNic
Update	updateVirtualSwitch	updateVirtualNic	updatePortGroup	updateServiceConsoleVirtualNic

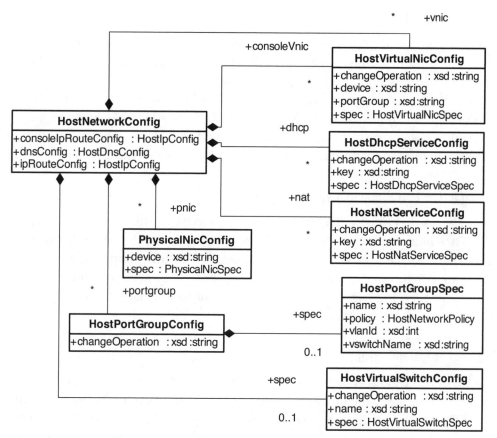

Figure 10-3 The HostNetworkConfig and related data objects

The four updateXXX() methods are used like setter methods to change the properties: updateConsoleIpRouteConfig(), updateDnsConfig(), updateIpRouteConfig(), and updateNetworkConfig(). These methods update the related properties in an incremental way, not simply replace as a typical setter method does.

The remaining four methods are restartServiceConsoleVirtualNic(), queryNetworkHint(), refreshNetworkSystem(), and updatePhysicalNicLinkSpeed().

These methods are covered in the following discussion of the samples.

Managing Virtual Network Components

Table 10-2 listed the 12 methods that are related to managing the virtual switches, virtual NIC, port group, and service console NIC. Now it's time to look at how to add the virtual switches, port group, and virtual NIC. Listing 10-1 illustrates the sample code to perform all these tasks.

Adding a Virtual Switch

The `addVirtualSwitch()` method adds a new virtual switch with the specified name. The name must be different from any other virtual switch on the same host, and it cannot exceed 32 characters in length.

Besides the name parameter, the `HostVirtualSwitchSpec` parameter provides detailed specifications. As shown in Figure 10-2, the `HostVirtualSwitchSpec` has four properties covering the bridge specification, the maximum transmission unit (MTU) in bytes, the total number of ports, and the network policy.

Adding a New Port Group to a Virtual Switch

The `addPortGroup()` method adds a new port group based on the `HostPortGroupSpec`, which has four properties, including the port group name, the network policy, the virtual LAN ID, and the virtual switch name to which the group is attached.

As expected, you can also specify the network policy here. Whatever policy you specify with the port group overwrites that of the virtual switch and sets the default for all the ports in this group.

Adding a Virtual NIC (VNIC)

The `addVirtualNic()` method adds a virtual network adapter based on the `HostVirtualNicSpec`, which includes both the MAC address of the adapter and the IP configuration specified in the `HostIpConfig` data object. The `HostIpConfig` further includes a boolean flag specifying whether to use DHCP, IP address, and subnet mask. When DHCP is enabled, you can safely ignore the last two.

> This method works for both `VMKernel` and the console OS, but not the virtual machine. To add a virtual NIC to a virtual machine, use `reconfigVM_Task()`.

Listing 10-1 shows how to add a virtual switch, a port group, and a virtual NIC.

Listing 10-1
`AddNIC.java`

```
package vim25.samples.mo.net;
import java.net.URL;
import com.vmware.vim25.HostIpConfig;
```

```
import com.vmware.vim25.HostNetworkPolicy;
import com.vmware.vim25.HostPortGroupSpec;
import com.vmware.vim25.HostVirtualNicSpec;
import com.vmware.vim25.HostVirtualSwitchSpec;
import com.vmware.vim25.mo.Folder;
import com.vmware.vim25.mo.HostNetworkSystem;
import com.vmware.vim25.mo.HostSystem;
import com.vmware.vim25.mo.InventoryNavigator;
import com.vmware.vim25.mo.ServiceInstance;

public class AddNIC
{
  public static void main(String[] args) throws Exception
  {
    if(args.length != 3)
    {
      System.out.println("Usage: java AddNIC <url> "
          + "<username> <password>");
      return;
    }

    ServiceInstance si = new ServiceInstance(
        new URL(args[0]), args[1], args[2], true);

    String hostname = "dev.acme.com";
    String portGroupName = "ViMaster PortGroup";
    String switchName = "ViMaster Switch";

    Folder rootFolder = si.getRootFolder();
    HostSystem host = null;
    host = (HostSystem) new InventoryNavigator(
        rootFolder).searchManagedEntity("HostSystem", hostname);

    HostNetworkSystem hns = host.getHostNetworkSystem();

    // add a virtual switch
    HostVirtualSwitchSpec spec = new HostVirtualSwitchSpec();
    spec.setNumPorts(8);
    hns.addVirtualSwitch(switchName, spec);
```

```
// add a port group
HostPortGroupSpec hpgs = new HostPortGroupSpec();
hpgs.setName(portGroupName);
hpgs.setVlanId(0); // not associated with a VLAN
hpgs.setVswitchName(switchName);
hpgs.setPolicy(new HostNetworkPolicy());
hns.addPortGroup(hpgs);

// add a virtual NIC to VMKernel
HostVirtualNicSpec hvns = new HostVirtualNicSpec();
hvns.setMac("00:50:56:7d:5e:0b");
HostIpConfig hic = new HostIpConfig();
hic.setDhcp(false);
hic.setIpAddress("10.20.143.204");
hic.setSubnetMask("255.255.252.0");
hvns.setIp(hic);
String result = hns.addVirtualNic("VMKernel", hvns);
System.out.println(result);

si.getServerConnection().logout();
  }
}
```

Managing Service Console Networking

The classic ESX has a COS for managing the ESX server. It's much like a typical OS, but it's treated differently in ESX. In the new architecture of ESXi, the console OS is no longer there, so the following discussion related to the service console is not applicable.

Although DHCP can be used for COS, it's highly recommended that you use a static IP. If the DHCP server is down, ESX won't be able to connect to the network, impacting the operation. Also, the change of IP may fail VI SDK clients who use an IP address for connection.

VI SDK clients talk to the software agent running in the console OS. Any change of configuration for COS networking could cause disconnection from your

SDK client to the server. For example, you could change the IP address of the COS and drop your SOAP connection thereafter. Because of this potential risk, you should be extremely cautious while reconfiguring anything with COS networking.

Configuring the Host Networking

You can change many aspects of networking through the VI SDK. This section discusses how to change IP routing, network configuration, and so on.

Changing the IP Routing Configuration

`updateIpRouteConfig()` changes the IP routing configuration based on the `HostIpRouteConfig` data object, which further includes the default gateway address.

Another method, `updateConsoleIpRouteConfig()`, does pretty much the same thing, but just for the console OS.

Changing the DNS Configuration

`updateDnsConfig()` changes the DNS configuration as specified in the `HostDnsConfig` data object. The `HostDnsConfig` includes a list of the strings for the DNS IP address, whether DHCP is enabled, the domain name, the host name, a list of domain IP addresses, and the virtual NIC name of the service console when DHCP is enabled.

Changing the Network Configuration

`updateNetworkConfig()` changes the network configuration. It takes in `HostNetworkConfig` (see Figure 10-3) and a string as parameters. The string parameter specifies the change mode and can either be `modify` or `replace`.

When in replace mode, the `HostNetworkConfig` is fully applied upon success. As a result, objects can be created or destroyed to match exactly the elements in the array of configurations. When in modify mode, the changes are incremental, and only these specified changes are made. For these array elements, the property `changeOperation` can be `add`, `edit`, or `remove`, specifying the corresponding actions. While specified as `edit` or `remove`, the element must exist or a fault is thrown. If `add` is specified, the full specification should be provided.

Defining the Host Network Policy

You can specify five types of policies for a port group or a virtual switch.

- **VLAN policy**—The VLAN technology allows creation of multiple logical LANs within or across physical segments, resulting in improved security and performance and lower cost. The ESX server includes support for IEEE 802.1Q VLAN tagging. You can assign an integer as VLAN ID to a port group as in `HostPortGroupSpec`, and the `VMKernel` takes care of all the tagging and untagging as the packets pass through the virtual switch.

- **Security policy**—This includes settings such as whether to allow all traffic seen on the port, whether a virtual NIC should be allowed to send network traffic with a different MAC address than that of the virtual NIC, and whether to allow MAC address changes. These three aspects are captured in the `HostNetworkPolicy` data object with the three boolean properties `allowPromiscuous`, `forgedTransmits`, and `macChanges`.

- **Traffic shaping**—This controls the outbound traffic pattern by specifying the average and peak bandwidth in bits per second and the maximum burst size allowed in bytes. They are captured in the `HostNetworkTrafficShappingPolicy` data object.

  The traffic shaping can be specified at the virtual switch or port group level, but it's applied on a per-virtual-machine basis. For example, if you set the average bandwidth on a port group to be 100Mbps, any virtual machine connecting to the port group can use an average bandwidth of 100Mbps. The real bandwidth it can achieve is limited by the physical NIC as well.

> The traffic shaping does *not* work for the inbound traffic. To control the incoming traffic, use a load balancing system, or turn on the rate limiting feature of your router.

- **NIC teaming**—This allows you to group physical NICs for load balancing and failover protection. The specification is captured in the `HostNicTeamingPolicy` data object, which includes the criteria to detect the physical NIC failure, the failover order, and the load balancing and failover algorithm (MAC-based, IP-based, originating port–based, and so on).

- **Offloading setting**—This can offload some operations from the virtual machine to the host or to physical hardware. It is captured in the

`HostNetOffloadCapabilites`, which includes three properties specifying whether to offload the checksum calculation, whether to offload TCP segmentation, and whether to use zero-copy transmits.

A port group inherits the policies from the virtual switch it belongs to. It can overwrite any of the policies by specifying a new one.

To define a new network policy, you can specify it when a new virtual switch or port group is first created, or you can update it on an existing one. Table 10-3 shows what methods to use and when.

Table 10-3

Methods to Define Network Policies		
	While Creating New	**Update Existing**
Virtual switch	`addVirtualSwitch()`	`updateVirtualSwitch()`
Port group	`addPortGroup()`	`updatePortGroup()`

Network Managed Object

The `Network` object represents a network that is accessible by either hosts or virtual machines. This can be physical or logical network, such as a VLAN.

The `Network` object is a subtype of `ExtensibleManagedObject`, but not `ManagedEntity` as of version 2.5. So you don't see it in the inventory tree, and you cannot have permission control over it.

Table 10-4 lists all the properties defined in the `Network` type. As you can see, a `network` can be shared by several hosts and virtual machines. At the same time, a host or a virtual machine can connect to multiple networks at the same time. They have a many-to-many relationship.

Table 10-4

Properties of the `Network` Managed Object		
Name	**Type**	**Explanation**
host	ManagedObjectReference[] to HostSystem[]	Hosts attached to this network

continues...

Table 10-4   continued

Properties of the Network Managed Object		
Name	**Type**	**Explanation**
name	xsd:string	Name of this network
summary	NetworkSummary	Properties of this network, such as name
vm	ManagedObjectReference[] to VirtualMachine[]	Virtual machines using this network

The Network objects are created in these ways:

- Implicitly when configuring a host by a new switch with a nonexisting network
- Automatically when adding a host to VirtualCenter
- Automatically when adding a new virtual machine to a host or to VirtualCenter

Network has only one method defined: destroyNetwork(). As of version 2.5, it's deprecated. If invoked, it throws a ResourceInUse fault. A Network object is like an object in Java. When it's no longer in use, the system removes it (garbage collects it) automatically.

Managing SNMP with HostSnmpSystem

SNMP is an ISO standard for managing networks. The SNMP agent running a host is Version 1, 2c compliant. All the MIB definition files are stored in the /usr/lib/vmware/snmp/mibs directory. Browsing these MIB files identifies what information is exposed, what can be configured, and what traps can be sent out as notification to registered listeners.

The path to the root of VMware is

```
iso.org.dod.internet.private.enterprises.vmware
```

or

```
1.3.6.1.4.1.6876
```

Under the root are subtrees, such as `vmwSystem(1)`, `vmwVirtMachines(2)`, `vmwResources (3)`, `vmwProductSpecific(4)`, `vmwTraps(50)`, `vmwOID(60)`, and `vmwExperimental(70)`.

The `HostSnmpSystem` is the singleton managed object that manages the SNMP agent on an ESX server. It has two properties defined, as shown in Figure 10-4.

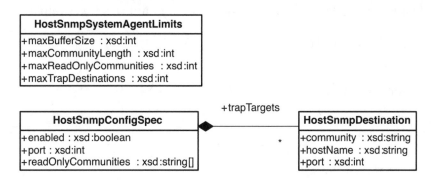

Figure 10-4 The `HostSnmpSystemAgentLimit` and `HostSnmpConfigSpec` data object

- **configuration (type: `HostSnmpConfigSpec`)**—HostSnmpSystemAgentLimits describes the limits of the SNMP agent (for example, the maximum trap destinations). You can read them, but there is no public interface to change them. By default, the maximum trap destination is 3, maxReadOnlyCommunites is 10, maxCommunityLength is 64, and maximum buffer size is 1500.

- **limits (type: `HostSnmpSystemAgentLimits`)**—HostSnmpConfigSpec holds the information of enabling status, port number, SNMP trap targets, and so on. `HostSnmpDestination` holds the host name, port number, and the community string. The community string acts like a password and is sent with each SNMP trap. If the trap receiver does not have the same trap community string configured, the trap is probably dropped. Make sure you configure the right community string with the trap targets.

Two methods are defined with `HostSnmpSystem`.

- **reconfigureSnmpAgent()**—Takes in a `HostSnmpConfigSpec` object as the new configuration. Upon success, it changes the configuration property of `HostSnmpSystem`.

■ **sendTestNotification()**—Sends out a testing notification message to all the trapTargets defined in HostSnmpDestination data objects. This method is helpful if you want to test whether the SNMP agent is configured as expected.

Listing 10-2 shows a sample that uses the reconfigureSnmpAgent() method to configure the SNMP system. Because the configManager.snmpSystem property is not set with a HostSystem object in VirtualCenter, you should run this sample only with ESX.

Listing 10-2
ConfigureSnmpSystem.java

```
package vim25.samples.mo.net;
import java.net.URL;

import com.vmware.vim25.HostSnmpConfigSpec;
import com.vmware.vim25.HostSnmpDestination;
import com.vmware.vim25.mo.Folder;
import com.vmware.vim25.mo.HostSnmpSystem;
import com.vmware.vim25.mo.HostSystem;
import com.vmware.vim25.mo.InventoryNavigator;
import com.vmware.vim25.mo.ServiceInstance;

public class ConfigureSnmpSystem
{
  public static void main(String[] args) throws Exception
  {
    if(args.length != 4)
    {
      System.out.println("Usage: java ConfigureSnmpSystem " +
        "<url> <username> <password> <hostname>");
      return;
    }

    ServiceInstance si = new ServiceInstance(
        new URL(args[0]), args[1], args[2], true);

    String hostname = args[3];
    Folder rootFolder = si.getRootFolder();
```

```
HostSystem host = null;
host = (HostSystem) new InventoryNavigator(
    rootFolder).searchManagedEntity("HostSystem", hostname);

if(host==null)
{
  System.out.println("Cannot find the host:" + hostname);
  si.getServerConnection().logout();
  return;
}
HostSnmpSystem hss = host.getHostSnmpSystem();

HostSnmpConfigSpec spec = new HostSnmpConfigSpec();
spec.setEnabled(true);
spec.setReadOnlyCommunities(new String[] {"visdk"});
HostSnmpDestination dest = new HostSnmpDestination();
dest.setCommunity("visdk");
dest.setHostName("192.168.8.8");
dest.setPort(162);
spec.setTrapTargets(new HostSnmpDestination[] {dest});

hss.reconfigureSnmpAgent(spec);

si.getServerConnection().logout();
  }
}
```

Managing the Firewall with `HostFirewallSystem`

`HostFirewallSystem` is the singleton managed object attached to a `HostSystem` object to manage its firewall. It's extended from `ExtensibleManagedObject` and has one new property—`firewallInfo`—whose type `HostFirewallInfo` is shown in Figure 10-5.

The `HostFirewallInfo` has two properties for the default policy and rule set, respectively. When configuring the firewall, you should first set the default policy and then make exception cases to the default policy to get the openness you want.

Table 10-5 lists all the common firewall rules on ESX with detailed information such as key, protocol, port, and direction.

Table 10-5

Common Firewall Rules on ESX

Key	Label	Protocol	Port	Direction	Required	Enabled[2]
ftpClient	FTP Client	TCP	21	Outbound	False	False
ftpServer	FTP Server	TCP	21	Inbound	False	True
kerberos	Kerberos	TCP	749	Outbound	False	False
legatoNetWorker	EMC NetWorker Agent	TCP	7937	Inbound	False	False
nfsClient	NFS Client	UDP	111	Outbound	False	False
nisClient	NIS Client	UDP	111	Outbound	False	False
ntpClient	NTP Client	UDP	123	Outbound	False	False
smbClient	SMB Client	TCP	137	Outbound	False	False
snmpd	SNMP Server	UDP	161	Inbound	False	False
sshClient	SSH Client	TCP	22	Outbound	False	False
sshServer	SSH Server	TCP	22	Inbound	False	True
swISCSIClient	Software iSCSI Client	TCP	3260	Outbound	False	True
symantecBackupExec	Symantec Backup Exec Agent	TCP	10000	Inbound	False	False
symantecNetBackup	Symantec Net Backup Agent	TCP	13724	Inbound	False	False
telnetClient	Telnet Client	TCP	23	Outbound	False	False

Table 10-5   continued

Common Firewall Rules on ESX

Key	Label	Protocol	Port	Direction	Required	Enabled[2]
updateManager	update Manager	TCP	80	Outbound	False	False
vncServer	VNC Server	TCP	5900	Inbound	False	False
vpxHeartbeats	VMware VirtualCenter Agent	UDP	902	Outbound	False	True

[2]The default setting after the system is installed. You can always change the effectiveness using the `enableRuleset()` and `disableRuleset()`

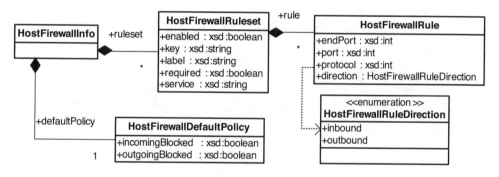

Figure 10-5   The `HostFirewallInfo` data object

Four methods are defined with the `HostFirewallSystem`:

- **`enableRuleset()`**—This turns on a specific rule set, which affects the enabled property in the corresponding `HostFirewallRuleset` object in the `HostFirewallInfo` data object. It takes in a parameter that identifies the rule set. The rule set ID must be one of the property keys of the `HostFireallRuleset` objects; otherwise, a `NotFound` fault is thrown.

- **`disableRuleset()`**—This turns off a specific rule set. The enabled property in the corresponding `HostFirewallRuleset` object in `HostFirewallInfo` data object changes accordingly. It takes the same parameter as the `enableRuleset` and is bound to the same requirement on the parameter.

Like many other VI SDK methods, enableRuleset() and disableRuleset() are sensitive to the rule set's current state. For example, if you call the enabling method on an already-enabled rule set, a fault is thrown. You should either check the enabling status before the call or try/catch the fault while calling the method.

- **refreshFirewall()**—The firewall settings can be modified directly in the console OS without the knowledge of the VI SDK. To pick up these changes, call refreshFirewall() to refresh the firewall information and settings. It takes in no parameter.

- **updateDefaultPolicy()**—This updates the default policy and takes in a simple HostFirewallDefaultPolicy data object as the new default policy. As shown in Figure 10-5, HostFirewallDefaultPolicy is a simple data object with only two properties specifying whether to block incoming or outgoing network traffic. Upon the success of this method, the new default policy is saved in the firewallInfo.defaultPolicy property.

Notice that no method is defined to change the rule set. You can directly configure it in the ESX console OS using the esxcfg-firewall command line and then call refreshFirewall() to pick it up. The firewall API by no means gives you complete control over the firewall.

Listing 10-3 is a sample that prints out the current policies and turns them on.

Listing 10-3
TurnOnFirewallPolicy.java

```java
package vim25.samples.mo.net;
import java.net.URL;

import com.vmware.vim25.HostFirewallDefaultPolicy;
import com.vmware.vim25.HostFirewallInfo;
import com.vmware.vim25.HostFirewallRule;
import com.vmware.vim25.HostFirewallRuleset;
import com.vmware.vim25.mo.Folder;
import com.vmware.vim25.mo.HostFirewallSystem;
import com.vmware.vim25.mo.HostSystem;
import com.vmware.vim25.mo.InventoryNavigator;
import com.vmware.vim25.mo.ServiceInstance;
```

```java
public class TurnOnFirewallPolicy
{
  public static void main(String[] args) throws Exception
  {
    if(args.length != 4)
    {
      System.out.println("Usage: java TurnOnFirewallPolicy " +
        "<url> <username> <password> <hostname>");
      return;
    }

    ServiceInstance si = new ServiceInstance(
        new URL(args[0]), args[1], args[2], true);

    String hostname = args[3];
    Folder rootFolder = si.getRootFolder();
    HostSystem host = null;
    host = (HostSystem) new InventoryNavigator(
        rootFolder).searchManagedEntity("HostSystem", hostname);

    if(host==null)
    {
      System.out.println("Cannot find the host:" + hostname);
      si.getServerConnection().logout();
      return;
    }

    HostFirewallSystem hss = host.getHostFirewallSystem();

    HostFirewallInfo hsi = hss.getFirewallInfo();

    System.out.println("Default Firewall Policy:");
    HostFirewallDefaultPolicy defPolicy = hsi.getDefaultPolicy();
    System.out.println("IncomingBlocked:"
        + defPolicy.getIncomingBlocked());
    System.out.println("OutgoingBlocked:"
        + defPolicy.getOutgoingBlocked());

    HostFirewallRuleset[] rs = hsi.getRuleset();
    for(int i=0; rs!=null && i<rs.length; i++)
```

```
  {
    printRuleSet(rs[i]);
    if(!rs[i].isEnabled())
    {
      hss.enableRuleset(rs[i].getKey());
    }
  }
  si.getServerConnection().logout();
}
static void printRuleSet(HostFirewallRuleset rule)
{
  System.out.println("\nKey:" + rule.getKey());
  System.out.println("Label:" + rule.getLabel());
  System.out.println("Required:" + rule.isRequired());
  System.out.println("Service:" + rule.getService());

  System.out.print("Rules:");
  HostFirewallRule[] rules = rule.getRule();
  for(int j=0; rules!=null && j<rules.length; j++)
  {
    System.out.println("Protocol:" + rules[j].getProtocol());
    System.out.println("Port:" + rules[j].getPort());
    System.out.println("Direction:" + rules[j].getDirection());
    System.out.println("EndPort:" + rules[j].getEndPort());
  }
  System.out.println("Enabled:" + rule.isEnabled());
 }
}
```

Managing Network Services with `HostServiceSystem`

There could be many network services, such as NTP and SSH, running on an ESX host. `HostServiceSystem` manages these services. It extends from `ExtensibleManagedObject` with one direct property, `serviceInfo`, defined.

The type for the property is `HostServiceInfo`, as shown in Figure 10-6. Notice the rule set in `HostService`; the strings must be valid keys from valid `HostFirewallRuleset` objects defined in the `HostFirewallSystem`.

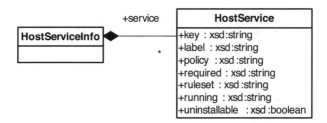

Figure 10-6 The `HostServiceInfo` data object

The `HostServiceSystem` object has six methods to manage the network services on an ESX server.

- **`refreshServices()`** forces the system to refresh service information and settings to pick up all the changes made directly on the host. It does not take in a parameter. Upon success, the `serviceInfo` property is updated to reflect the latest changes on the ESX system.

- **`startService()`** starts a specific network service whose key is the parameter.

- **`restartService()`** restarts a specific network service whose key is the parameter.

- **`stopService()`** stops a specific network service whose key is the parameter.

> To call any of the preceding methods, make sure the service is in a proper state; otherwise, an `InvalidState` fault is thrown. For example, calling `stopService()` while the service is not running results in the fault.
>
> Also, the `key` argument must be a valid one from `HostServiceInfo`.

- **`uninstallService()`** uninstalls the specific service from the host. If the service is running, it is stopped before being uninstalled.

- **`updateServicePolicy()`** updates the activation policy for a service. It takes in two string parameters: one to identify the service, and the other to identify the new activation policy with options defined in the `HostServicePolicy` enumeration type. The three options are `automatic` (should run if and only if it has open firewall ports), `off` (should not be started when the host starts up), and `on` (should be started when the host starts up).

Listing 10-4 is a sample that prints each network service and flips its running states by calling startService() and stopService() accordingly.

Listing 10-4
`FlipNetworkService.java`

```java
package vim25.samples.mo.net;
import java.net.URL;

import com.vmware.vim25.HostService;
import com.vmware.vim25.HostServiceInfo;
import com.vmware.vim25.mo.Folder;
import com.vmware.vim25.mo.HostServiceSystem;
import com.vmware.vim25.mo.HostSystem;
import com.vmware.vim25.mo.InventoryNavigator;
import com.vmware.vim25.mo.ServiceInstance;

public class FlipNetworkService
{
  public static void main(String[] args) throws Exception
  {
    if(args.length != 3)
    {
      System.out.println("Usage: java FlipNetworkService " +
        "<url> <username> <password>");
      return;
    }

    ServiceInstance si = new ServiceInstance(
        new URL(args[0]), args[1], args[2], true);

    String hostname = "dev.acme.com";
    Folder rootFolder = si.getRootFolder();
    HostSystem host = null;
    host = (HostSystem) new InventoryNavigator(
        rootFolder).searchManagedEntity("HostSystem", hostname);

    if(host==null)
```

```
    {
      System.out.println("Cannot find the host:" + hostname);
      si.getServerConnection().logout();
      return;
    }

    HostServiceSystem hss = host.getHostServiceSystem();

    HostServiceInfo hsi = hss.getServiceInfo();
    HostService[] ss = hsi.getService();
    for(int i=0; ss!=null && i<ss.length; i++)
    {
      printService(ss[i]);
      if(ss[i].isRunning())
      {
        hss.stopService(ss[i].getKey());
        System.out.println("Service stopped.");
      }
      else
      {
        hss.startService(ss[i].getKey());
        System.out.println("Service started.");
      }
    }

    si.getServerConnection().logout();
}

static void printService(HostService si)
{
  System.out.println("\nKey:" + si.getKey());
  System.out.println("Label:" + si.getLabel());
  System.out.println("Policy:" + si.getPolicy());
  System.out.println("Required:" + si.isRequired());
  System.out.print("RuleSet:");
  String[] rules = si.getRuleset();
  for(int j=0; rules!=null && j<rules.length; j++)
  {
    System.out.print(rules[j] + " ");
```

```
    }
    System.out.println("\nRunning:" + si.isRunning());
    System.out.println("Uninstallable:" + si.isUninstallable());
  }
}
```

Configuring VMotion Network Using `HostVMotionSystem`

`HostVMotionSystem` describes the VMotion configuration of a host. It is extended from the `ExtensibleManagedObject`. Besides the inherited properties, it defines two properties:

- **`ipConfig`** (type: `HostIpConfig`) for the IP configuration of the VMotion virtual NIC

- **`netConfig`** (type: `HostVMotionNetConfig`) containing the networking configuration for VMotion operations

`HostIpConfig` includes three properties for the IP address, the subnet mask, and a flag whether DHCP is enabled. `HostVMotionNetConfig` includes an array of virtual NICs that can be used for VMotion and the currently selected virtual NIC.

The managed object defines three methods.

- **`deselectVnic()`**—Instructs that no virtual NIC should be used for VMotion. It does not take extra parameters and returns `none` when successful. `HostConfigFault` or `RuntimeFault` can be thrown if anything goes wrong.

- **`selectVnic()`**—Specifies a virtual NIC used for VMotion. It takes a string that uniquely identifies the virtual NIC. It returns `none` when successful. If the virtual NIC does not exist, an `InvalidArgument` is thrown.

- **`updateIpConfig()`**—Updates the IP configuration of the VMotion virtual NIC. It takes in a parameter of `HostIpConfig` type, as was shown in Figure 10-2.

Summary

Networking is a key aspect of managing the VMware Infrastructure. This chapter first introduced the key concepts and then introduced HostNetworkSystem, which is the major managed object closely attached to a host for you to manage its networking configuration and manipulate virtual network components such as virtual switches, virtual NIC, and port groups.

Finally, this chapter covered how to manage the firewall, SNMP, network services, and VMotion network using the corresponding singleton managed objects attached to the HostSystem.

Chapter 11

Managing Storage and Datastores

This chapter discusses the storage subsystem of a host, which is an important part of virtualization management and happens to be one of the most confusing areas of the entire VI SDK. The confusion mostly comes from the complexity of storage system in enterprise computing. Before moving on the formal discussion, this chapter briefly covers some basics of storage virtualization and how it's layered.

The focus then moves to the HostStorageSystem, which manages low-level storage components, such as Host Bus Adapter (HBA), SCSI disks/logical unit numbers (LUNs), iSCSI configuration, file system volume, and so on; HostDatastoreSystem, which manages datastores; HostDatastoreBrowser, which provides access to the files in one or more datastores; and Datastore, which represents a storage abstraction for virtual machine files backed by the VMware File System (VMFS) volume, network attached storage (NAS), or a local file system.

Finally, this chapter introduces the FileManager, which manages and transfers files; and VirtualDiskManager, which provides management interfaces on virtual disks.

To represent the different entities and concepts in a storage subsystem, many complicated data object types are involved. The difficulty of this chapter does not come from the programming, but the domain knowledge of storage systems and the way ESX manages the storage system in general.

Managed Objects: HostStorageSystem, HostDatastoreSystem, Datastore, HostDatastoreBrowser, FileManager

Key Concepts

Storage virtualization, especially when associated with an enterprise-level storage system, is complicated because it closely relates to how the host virtualizes the storage system and abstracts it as a higher-level storage service.

In general, the ESX server has four layers of storage abstraction, as shown in Figure 11-1. At the bottom are the different physical storage drivers for either the local Small Computer Systems Interface (SCSI) disk or storage area network (SAN) (FC or iSCSI). On top of these, a VMFS can be built. Together with the NAS, VMFS is abstracted to a datastore on which all the virtual machine–related files are stored, including the virtual disk files that can be used by a virtual machine just like a physical disk by a physical machine.

vmx, VMDK, and other files		
Datastore		
Local FS	VMFS	NAS
Local SCSI	SAN (FC) / SAN (iSCSI)	

Figure 11-1 The four layers of storage system

SCSI

SCSI is a set of American National Standards Institute (ANSI) electronic interfaces that allow personal computers to communicate with peripheral hardware, such as disk drives, CD-ROM drives, tape drives, printers, and scanners—faster and more flexibly than previous interfaces. The current set of SCSIs are parallel interfaces.

ESX servers mainly use SCSI disks because they perform better than predecessor Integrated Development Environment (IDE) disks.

To identify the two ends of the storage communication, an initiator and target are used. A SCSI initiator is the endpoint that initiates a SCSI session and sends a SCSI command. A SCSI target is the endpoint that does not start sessions but instead waits for initiators' commands and provides required input/output data transfers. Typically, a computer is an initiator and a data storage device is a target.

Storage devices assign the LUNs to a storage unit, such as a logical volume. The LUN provides a unique address or identifier for the logical volume.

SAN

A SAN is a special network that connects remote computer storage devices (such as disk arrays, tape libraries, and optical jukeboxes) to servers. To the operating system (OS), these devices appear as if they are locally attached. This allows organizations to consolidate storage into datacenter storage arrays while providing hosts (such as database and Web servers) with the illusion of locally attached disks.

Unlike NAS, which uses file-based protocols (such as NFS or SMB/CIFS), SAN access is disk-block-based and therefore allows faster random access.

Most SANs use the Fibre Channel because it was developed first, and costs have started to drop recently.

iSCSI

Internet SCSI (iSCSI) is a protocol that allows clients (initiators) to send SCSI commands to SCSI storage devices (targets) on remote servers over IP networks. It is a popular SAN protocol these days.

Better than Fibre Channel, iSCSI doesn't require special-purpose cabling and can be run over long distances using existing Internet Protocol (IP)-based network infrastructure. To make sure it performs up to the expectation, use Gigabit network as the underlying network infrastructure.

HBA

HBA is a physical board that is inserted into a host computer and initiates all communication between the host and the external devices.

VMFS

VMFS is designed specifically for virtualization. One of the most notable features of VMFS is the big block size that optimizes the access of virtual disk files. The default block size in version 3 is 1MB and can go up to 8MB. It also has cluster computing in mind and can be shared in a cluster.

NAS

The underlying protocol for NAS could be Network File System (NFS) or Common Internet File System (CIFS). As of VI 3.5, only NFS is officially supported.[1] The file access is per-file based, meaning that you can read the whole file but cannot directly access specific blocks of the file. It is not as efficient as SAN/iSCSI when it comes to big files for random access.

HostStorageSystem Managed Object

The HostStorageSystem is a singleton managed object closely attached to the HostSystem managed object, responsible for managing the storage subsystem of the ESX server. It has 2 properties and 24 methods.

Table 11-1 shows the two property names, types, and brief descriptions.

Table 11-1

Properties of the HostStorageSystem Managed Object		
Name	**Type**	**Explanation**
fileSystemVolumeInfo	HostFileSystemVolumeInfo	All the file system volume information of the host
storageDeviceInfo	HostStorageDeviceInfo	All the information about storage devices on the host

The two properties are the critical parts of the HostStorageSystem managed object. All the methods directly or indirectly affect these two properties and their

---

[1] CIFS support is experimental as of ESX 3.5.

nested data objects. Therefore, understanding these two data object types is critical to understanding the ESX storage system and the related methods. The following two sections detail each property.

The properties can be out of sync with the real system because of changes by ESX commands from the service console. To pick up the latest changes, call the `refreshStorageSystem()` method before retrieving the properties.

HostStorageDeviceInfo

The `HostStorageDeviceInfo` data object is yet another one of a few complicated data objects in the entire VI SDK. As you can see from Figure 11-2, it's related to more than 29 other data object types or enumerations.

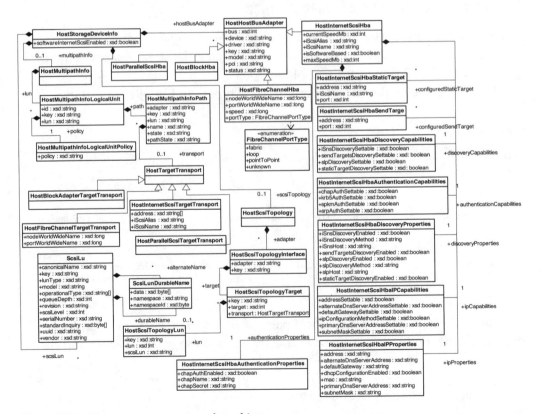

Figure 11-2 The `HostStorageDeviceInfo` data object

`HostStorageDeviceInfo` has six subproperties representing the list of available HBAs, the SCSI LUN multipath configuration, the list of SCSI LUNs available on the host, the storage topology view of SCSI storage, and a flag indicating whether the software iSCSI initiator is enabled.

In the nesting structure, `HostHostBusAdapter` includes four different subtypes: `HostInternetScsiHba`, `HostFibreChannelHba`, `HostBlockHba`, and `HostParallelScsiHba`. So even though the parent type is used as the property type for `hostBusAdapter`, you get one of the four subtypes while retrieving the property. The last two subtypes do not have an extra property defined, so it's okay to use the parent type. For the first two subtypes, check the type and cast it before using the respective extra properties.

The same pattern repeats with `HostTargetTransport` and its four subtypes. The four subtypes closely relate to the four subtypes of `HostHostBusAdapter`. That is understandable in that the multipath configuration should really be adapter-type specific.

The HBA provides the hardware facilitation. The `ScsiLu` is the data object representing the SCSI logical unit available on the ESX host.

With the SCSI logical units in place, you have the `HostScsiTopology` data object to describe the topology in a tree-like structure. It lists SCSI interfaces, each of which contains targets and in turn contains logical units. So you can find out which adapter supports which targets and which SCSI LUNs.

HostFileSystemVolumeInfo

Compared to its peer data object type, the `HostFileSystemVolumeInfo` is much simpler (see Figure 11-3). This data type describes the file system volume information for the host.

A file system volume refers to a storage abstraction that allows files to be created and organized. It is backed by disk storage. It can span one or more disks or use part of an entire disk.

A host can have multiple file system volumes. The file system volumes are typically mounted into a file namespace to allow all the files in mounted file systems to be accessible from the host. A file system volume must be mounted on the file system to be present in the data structure.

`HostFileSystemVolumeInfo` has two properties: `volumeTypeList`, which is an array of support file system types (VMFS, NFS, or CIFS); and an array of

`HostFileSystemMountInfo`. Each `HostFileSystemMountInfo` has both volume description by `HostFileSystemVolume` and mount information by `HostMountInfo`. Because a volume has to be one of the concrete subtypes of `HostFileSystemVolume`, the real type of volume would be `HostVmfsVolume`, `HostNasVolume`, or `HostLocalFileSystemVolume`. Again, you have to do casting after obtaining the `volume` property.

Listing 11-1 shows a sample that retrieves the direct properties of the `HostStorageSystem` and prints them out. It doesn't include every one of the embedded properties given the large number of these properties. Running this sample should give you good information about the storage attached to an ESX host.

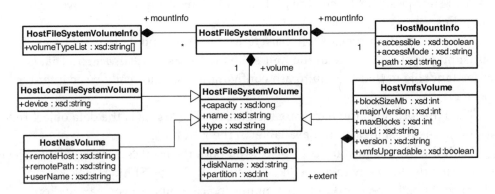

Figure 11-3 `HostFileSystemVolumeInfo` data object

Listing 11-1
PrintStorageSystem.java

```java
package vim25.samples.mo.storage;
import java.net.URL;

import com.vmware.vim25.HostFileSystemMountInfo;
import com.vmware.vim25.HostFileSystemVolume;
import com.vmware.vim25.HostFileSystemVolumeInfo;
import com.vmware.vim25.HostHostBusAdapter;
import com.vmware.vim25.HostMountInfo;
import com.vmware.vim25.HostMultipathInfo;
import com.vmware.vim25.HostMultipathInfoLogicalUnit;
import com.vmware.vim25.HostMultipathInfoLogicalUnitPolicy;
import com.vmware.vim25.HostMultipathInfoPath;
```

```java
import com.vmware.vim25.HostScsiTopology;
import com.vmware.vim25.HostScsiTopologyInterface;
import com.vmware.vim25.HostScsiTopologyLun;
import com.vmware.vim25.HostScsiTopologyTarget;
import com.vmware.vim25.HostStorageDeviceInfo;
import com.vmware.vim25.ScsiLun;
import com.vmware.vim25.mo.Folder;
import com.vmware.vim25.mo.HostStorageSystem;
import com.vmware.vim25.mo.HostSystem;
import com.vmware.vim25.mo.InventoryNavigator;
import com.vmware.vim25.mo.ServiceInstance;

public class PrintStorageSystem
{
  public static void main(String[] args) throws Exception
  {
    if(args.length != 3)
    {
      System.out.println("Usage: java PrintStorageSystem "
        + "<url> <username> <password>");
      return;
    }

    ServiceInstance si = new ServiceInstance(
      new URL(args[0]), args[1], args[2], true);

    String hostname = "dev.acme.com";

    Folder rootFolder = si.getRootFolder();
    HostSystem host = null;

    host = (HostSystem) new InventoryNavigator(
        rootFolder).searchManagedEntity("HostSystem", hostname);

    if(host==null)
    {
      System.out.println("Host not found");
      si.getServerConnection().logout();
      return;
```

```
  }

  HostStorageSystem hds = host.getHostStorageSystem();

  System.out.println("Supported file system volume types:");
  HostFileSystemVolumeInfo vi = hds.getFileSystemVolumeInfo();
  printFileVolumeInfo(vi);

  System.out.println("\nStorage device information:");
  HostStorageDeviceInfo hsdi = hds.getStorageDeviceInfo();
  printStorageDeviceInfo(hsdi);

  si.getServerConnection().logout();
}

static void printStorageDeviceInfo(HostStorageDeviceInfo hsdi)
{
  System.out.println("\nHost bus adapters");
  printHBAs(hsdi.getHostBusAdapter());

  System.out.println("\nMultipath information");
  HostMultipathInfo hmi = hsdi.getMultipathInfo();
  printMultiPathInfo(hmi);

  System.out.println("\nSCSI LUNs");
  printScsiLuns(hsdi.getScsiLun());

  HostScsiTopology hst = hsdi.getScsiTopology();
  printScsiTopology(hst);

  System.out.println("\nSoftware iSCSI enabled:"
      + hsdi.isSoftwareInternetScsiEnabled());
}

static void printHBAs(HostHostBusAdapter[] hbas)
{
  for(int i=0; hbas!=null && i<hbas.length; i++)
  {
    System.out.println("Device:" + hbas[i].getDevice());
```

```
      System.out.println("Bus:" + hbas[i].getBus());
      System.out.println("Driver:" + hbas[i].getDriver());
      System.out.println("Key:" + hbas[i].getKey());
      System.out.println("Model:" + hbas[i].getModel());
      System.out.println("PCI:" + hbas[i].getPci());
      System.out.println("Status:" + hbas[i].getStatus());
    }
}


static void printScsiTopology(HostScsiTopology hst)
{
  HostScsiTopologyInterface[] hstis = hst.getAdapter();

  for(int i=0; hstis!=null && i<hstis.length; i++)
  {
    System.out.println("Adapter:" + hstis[i].getAdapter());
    System.out.println("Key:" + hstis[i].getKey());
    HostScsiTopologyTarget[] hstts = hstis[i].getTarget();

    for(int j=0; hstts!=null && j<hstts.length; j++)
    {
      System.out.println("Key:" + hstts[j].getKey());
      System.out.println("Target:" + hstts[j].getTarget());
      System.out.println("Transport:"
          + hstts[j].getTransport().getClass().getName());
      HostScsiTopologyLun[] luns = hstts[j].getLun();
      for(int k=0; luns!=null && k<luns.length; k++)
      {
        System.out.println("Key:" + luns[k].getKey());
        System.out.println("LUN:" + luns[k].getLun());
        System.out.println("ScsiLun:" + luns[k].getScsiLun());
      }
    }
  }
}


static void printScsiLuns(ScsiLun[] sls)
{
  for(int i=0; sls!=null && i<sls.length; i++)
```

```
  {
    System.out.println("UUID:" + sls[i].getUuid());
    System.out.println("CanonicalName:"
        + sls[i].getCanonicalName());
    System.out.println("LunType:" + sls[i].getLunType());
    System.out.print("OperationalState:");
    String[] states = sls[i].getOperationalState();
    for(int j=0; states!=null && j<states.length; j++)
    {
      System.out.print(states[j] + " ");
    }
    System.out.println("\nSCSI Level:"
        + sls[i].getScsiLevel());
    System.out.println("Vendor:" + sls[i].getVendor());
  }
}


static void printMultiPathInfo(HostMultipathInfo hmi)
{
  HostMultipathInfoLogicalUnit[] lus = hmi.getLun();
  for(int i=0; lus!=null && i<lus.length; i++)
  {
    System.out.println("ID:" + lus[i].getId());
    System.out.println("Key:" + lus[i].getKey());
    System.out.println("LUN:" + lus[i].getLun());

    HostMultipathInfoPath[] hmips = lus[i].getPath();
    for(int j=0; hmips!=null && j<hmips.length; j++)
    {
      System.out.println("Adpator:" + hmips[j].getAdapter());
      System.out.println("Key:" + hmips[j].getLun());
      System.out.println("Name:" + hmips[j].getName());
      System.out.println("PathState:"
          + hmips[j].getPathState());
      System.out.println("Transport:"
          + hmips[j].getTransport().getClass().getName());
    }
    HostMultipathInfoLogicalUnitPolicy policy =
        lus[i].getPolicy();
```

```
     System.out.println("Policy:" + policy.getPolicy());
   }
 }


  static void printFileVolumeInfo(HostFileSystemVolumeInfo info)
  {
    String[] volTypes = info.getVolumeTypeList();
    for(int i=0; volTypes!=null && i<volTypes.length; i++)
    {
      System.out.println(volTypes[i]);
    }


    System.out.println("\nThe file system volumes mounted:");
    HostFileSystemMountInfo[] mis = info.getMountInfo();
    for(int i=0; mis!=null && i<mis.length; i++)
    {
      HostMountInfo hmi = mis[i].getMountInfo();
      System.out.println("\nAccessible:" + hmi.getAccessible());
      System.out.println("AccessMode:" + hmi.getAccessMode());
      System.out.println("Path:" + hmi.getPath());

      HostFileSystemVolume hfsv = mis[i].getVolume();
      System.out.println("Capacity:" + hfsv.getCapacity());
      System.out.println("Name:" + hfsv.getName());
      System.out.println("Type:" + hfsv.getType());
    }
  }
}
```

Discovering HBAs

HBAs represent the physical adapters on the ESX server and have to have corresponding physical adapters in place. So there is no creation of the HBAs via the application programming interface (API), just the discovery of existing HBAs.

Two methods (both defined in HostStorageSystem) are involved:

- **rescanAllHba()** rescans for possible new storage devices. It does not require a parameter and returns none. The properties are updated as a result. If the rescanning fails, a HostConfigFault fault is thrown.

> The rescanAllHba() method call can be expensive and should be used judiciously. But do rescan whenever your storage changes.

- **rescanHba()** rescans a specific HBA for new storage devices. It takes in the device name of an existing HBA device and returns none. The device name has to be a HostHostBusAdapter.device, in a format such as vmhba*, where * is a decimal number to identify the adapter. If you give a nonexisting device, a NotFound fault is thrown.

Managing iSCSI

With the iSCSI storage, you change the static and dynamic discovery list and update various configurations.

Manipulating Discovery List

To find out what storage resource on the network is available for access, the iSCSI initiators may use either of two approaches: dynamic discovery or static discovery.

In dynamic discovery, the initiator sends a SendTargets request to a specified target address and port number for a discovery session with this target. The target device responds with a list of additional targets that the initiator is allowed to access.

In static discovery, you use a fixed target list, which may be returned from dynamic discovery and adjusted manually. This approach is available only with hardware-initiated storage.

Four methods handle these two cases with adding/removing functions, respectively: addInternetScsiSendTargets(), removeInternetScsiSendTargets(), addInternetScsiStaticTargets(), and removeInternetScsiStaticTargets(). The names of these four methods are self-explanatory. Check out the API reference for more details.

To use the `addInternetScsiSendTargets()` and `removeInternetScsiSendTargets()` methods, you must turn on the `HostInternetScsiHbaDiscoveryProperties.sendTargetsDiscoveryEnabled` flag by calling the `updateInternetScsiDiscoveryProperties()` method. Similarly for the static target discovery, you have to turn on the `HostInternetScsiHbaDiscoveryProperty.staticTargetDiscoveryEnabled` using the same update method.

Configuring iSCSI

iSCSI is an emerging technology that enables SAN over an IP network. Even though it's a type of storage HBA, it's by far the most complicated one to manage and configure.

You can change several aspects of the iSCSI settings, from the alias to different properties. Each of the following six methods changes one of these aspects and most likely changes the `HostInternetSisiHba` data object representing the HBA:

- **updateInternetScsiAlias()**—An iSCSI alias is a UTF-8 text string as an additional descriptive name for an initiator and target. It does not have to be unique or comply with other requirements of the iSCSI name. The alias strings are communicated between the initiator and target at login and can be displayed by a user interface on either end, helping the user easily tell whether the initiators or targets at the other end appear to be correct. It is not used to identify, address, or authenticate initiators and targets.

  The method takes in two parameters: the iSCSI HBA device string and the new alias name. When the iSCSI is being used, you cannot change the alias name; otherwise, a `HostConfigFault` is thrown.

- **updateInternetScsiAuthenticationProperties()**—This method changes the `HostInternetScsiHbaAuthenticationProperties` data object nested in `HostInternetScsiHba`. It takes in two parameters: the iSCSI device string and a new `HostInternetScsiHbaAuthenticationProperties` data object with authentication information such as whether Challenge-Handshake Authentication Protocol (CHAP) authentication is enabled, the CHAP name, and the secret string.

- **updateInternetScsiDiscoveryProperties()**—This method updates the `HostInternetScsiHbaDiscoveryProperties` data object nested in

`HostInternetScsiHba`. It takes in two parameters: the iSCSI device string and a new `HostInternetScsiHbaDiscoveryProperties` object including `sendTargetsDiscoveryEnable` and `staticTargetDiscoveryEnabled` discussed earlier.

- **updateInternetScsiIPProperties()**—This method updates the `HostInternetScsiHbaIPProperties` data object nested in `HostInternetScsiHba`. It takes in two parameters: the iSCSI device string and a new `HostInternetScsiHbaIPProperties` object that encapsulates the IP address, gateway, MAC address, and subnet masking.

- **updateInternetScsiName()**—This method changes the iSCSI name. It takes two string parameters: the iSCSI device string and a new name for the iSCSI name. Although you can use an arbitrary string for the name, there is an industry standard–based naming convention[2] like this:

```
<Type>.<Date>.<Organizational Naming Authority>[:<Subgroup Naming
Authority>]
```

An example is as follows:

```
iqn.1998-01.com.xyz:host1-0a62b676
```

- **updateSoftwareInternetScsiEnabled()**—This method enables or disables the software iSCSI. It takes one boolean flag to specify whether to enable software iSCSI. When true, it's enabled; otherwise, it's disabled.

Managing Disk Partitioning

When you have a disk, you can find out its partitioning information. The following part discusses three methods that are related to partition management.

With all these methods, the device path identifies a disk. The device path is not the canonical name of the disk, such as `vmhba0:0:0`, but a string in the format like the following:

```
/vmfs/devices/disks/vml.0100000000334b5335474c31363030303039373039525237583453543
3313436
```

---

[2] http://tools.ietf.org/html/rfc3721

where the string after vml. is the universally unique identifier (UUID) of the disk.

- **computeDiskPartitionInfo()**—This method computes the disk partition information based on the specified HostDiskPartitionLayout object and returns a HostDiskPartitionInfo object.

  As shown in Figure 11-4, the HostDiskPartitionLayout provides a total number of blocks on the disk and an array of block ranges in disks. The possible types for a range in the partition are extended, linuxNative, LinuxSwap, none, ntfs, vmfs, and vmkDiagnostic.

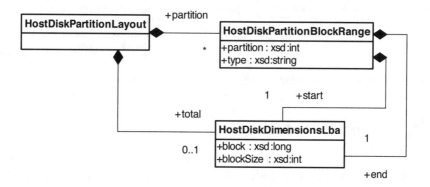

Figure 11-4 HostDiskPartitionLayout data object

The returned HostDiskPartitionInfo data object is shown in Figure 11-5. It includes a copy of the input parameter typed as HostDiskPartitionLayout and a HostDiskPartitionSpec object, which includes a HostDiskDimentionsChs object and an array of HostDiskPartitionAttributes. The HostDiskPartitionAttributes describes a contiguous set of blocks on the disk, including the starting and ending sector number.

- **retrieveDiskPartitionInfo()**—This method gets the disk partition information from a group of disks specified by their device paths. Accordingly, the return is an array of HostDiskPartitionInfo data objects, each of which corresponds to a disk from the input.

- **updateDiskPartitions()**—This method changes the partitions on a disk with the specified HostDiskPartitionSpec object, as shown in Figure 11-3. It returns none, or a fault is thrown for exceptional cases like invalid HostDiskPartitionSpec input, invalid device path for a disk, and so on.

Unlike the `retrieveDiskPartition()` method, this method only works on one disk at a time.

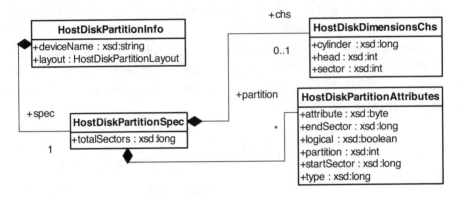

Figure 11-5 `HostDiskPartitionInfo` data object

Managing the VMFS File System

VMFS is the VMware proprietary file system designed specifically for virtualization and clustering. By default, ESX creates VMFS file systems on the attached local storage.

To manage the VMFS file system, four methods are defined with `HostStorageSystem`:

- **`rescanVmfs()`** instructs the hypervisor to rescan for any new VMFS that might have been added. It takes in no parameter, and returns `none` upon completion or a fault is thrown. The result is reflected in the corresponding properties.

- **`formatVmfs()`** formats a new VMFS partition on a disk. It takes in one `HostVmfsSpec` data object, as shown in Figure 11-6. The data object specifies the block size, version number and volume label, as well as the head extent.

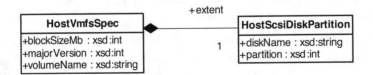

Figure 11-6 The `HostVmfsSpec`

- **upgradeVmfs()** upgrades the VMFS to the current version supported by the host. It takes one string parameter pointing to the VMFS. The format of the VMFS path is like the following:

```
/vmfs/volumes/4731c49c-692a1ec0-ae98-0030485cd2c8
```

When the VMFS is being used, you cannot upgrade it, or an InvalidState fault is thrown.

- **attachVmfsExtent()** extends an existing VMFS by attaching a new disk partition. It takes two parameters: a vmfs path string pointing to a VMFS system, and a HostScsiDiskPartition data object. The definition of the HostScsiDiskPartition data object is shown in Figure 11-3.

Managing Storage Multipath

Multipathing is a feature in which there is more than one data path between one host and one disk array. When one path fails, the rest of the paths continue to work, and the communication between the two ends does not stop. It provides better reliability for the storage system. In the meantime, multiple data paths can provide more bandwidth for the communication of the two ends, resulting in faster data access and better system response.[3]

Three methods manage the multipathing feature in the VI SDK: enableMultipathPath(), disableMultipathPath(), and setMultipathLunPolicy.

The first two methods are straightforward. They take one string parameter for the path to be enabled or disabled. Upon success, they return none; otherwise, a fault is thrown. The string path should be in the format vmhba32:3:0.

setMultipathLunPolicy() takes two parameters. The first is the logical unit ID string, and the second is a HostMultipathInfoLogicalUnitPolicy data object. Inside the data object is one string property with three possible values: fixed (use a preferred path whenever possible), rr (round robin for load balancing), and mru (use the most recently used path). The logical unit ID is in the format vmhba0:0:0.

---

[3] For better performance, increase the queue depth, which can be done via the storage driver.

Managing Datastores Using `HostDatastoreSystem`

The past several sections have discussed low-level storage management. With the file system ready and mounted, it's time to move forward with datastore management. The corresponding managed object is `HostDatastoreSystem`.

A datastore is an abstraction that stores virtual machine files. It can be on top of the three types of storage volumes: VMFS, local file system, or NAS volume.

The local file system–backed datastore uses a local file system volume, such as `ext3` on Linux. You can provide a path to a directory to create such a datastore.

The NAS-backed datastore can be created by specifying where to connect the volume over the network.

The VMFS-backed datastore uses the VMFS volume, which can be created on a disk with unpartitioned space or on an existing VMFS by rescanning the HBA. The datastore label is the same as the VMFS volume label, or it's extended by appending a suffix when a name is in conflict with another (for example, `storage1 (2)`).

Defined on the `HostDatastoreSystem` type are two properties and ten methods, with no extra property or method inherited. The two properties are capabilities of the `HostDatastoreSystemCapabilities` type and datastore, which is an array of the `Datastore` managed object.

`HostDatastoreSystemCapabilities` has only three boolean properties, indicating whether local datastores are supported; whether mounting the NFS volume is required to create a NAS datastore; and whether mounting the NFS volume is supported when a NAS datastore is created.

The `datastore` property holds the same set of `Datastores` as the `datastore` property in the parent `HostSystem` managed object, listing all the `Datastore` objects available to the host.

Creating a New Datastore

Depending on the type of datastore, you can use one of these three methods to create a new datastore:

- `createLocalDatastore()`—This creates a new datastore on a local host. It takes in two string parameters: one for the name of a datastore and the other for the path of a directory in which virtual machine files to be stored. Upon success, it returns a `Datastore` object; otherwise, a fault of `DuplicateName`, `HostConfigFault`, or `RuntimeFault` is thrown.

- **`createNasDatastore()`**—This creates a new datastore on a NAS. It requires one parameter typed as `HostNasVolumeSpec`, which includes information such as remote server, type of NAS volume, username, and password. It returns a `Datastore` object as well. When type is not specified, NFS is presumed.

- **`createVmfsDatastore()`**—This creates a new VMFS datastore. It requires one parameter whose type is `VmfsDatastoreCreateSpec`, as shown in Figure 11-7. Like the other two methods, it returns a `Datastore` object.

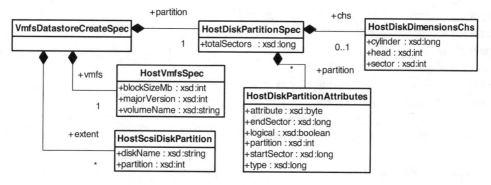

Figure 11-7 `VmfsDatastoreCreateSpec` data object

For the VMFS datastore, there is a `queryVmfsDatastoreCreateOptions()` method to query the options with which a VMFS datastore was created. The returned data object is shown in Figure 11-8. `VmfsDatastoreSpec` is extended by `VmfsDatastoreCreateSpec`. You might find it helpful to reference the creation spec of an existing datastore.

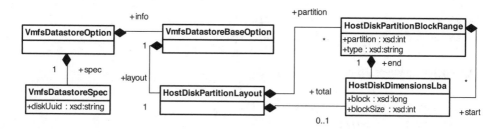

Figure 11-8 `VmfsDatastoreOption` data object

Listing 11-2 shows a sample that adds an NFS datastore. You can create a datastore with CIFS (experimental feature), which requires slightly more parameters in the `HostNasVolumeSpec` (for example, the username and password).

Listing 11-2

`AddDatastore.java`

```
package vim25.samples.mo.storage;
import java.net.URL;

import com.vmware.vim25.DatastoreInfo;
import com.vmware.vim25.HostNasVolumeSpec;
import com.vmware.vim25.mo.Datastore;
import com.vmware.vim25.mo.Folder;
import com.vmware.vim25.mo.HostDatastoreSystem;
import com.vmware.vim25.mo.HostSystem;
import com.vmware.vim25.mo.InventoryNavigator;
import com.vmware.vim25.mo.ServiceInstance;

public class AddDatastore
{
  public static void main(String[] args) throws Exception
  {
    if(args.length != 3)
    {
      System.out.println("Usage: java AddDatastore "
        + "<url> <username> <password>");
      return;
    }

    ServiceInstance si = new ServiceInstance(
      new URL(args[0]), args[1], args[2], true);

    String hostname = "dev.acme.com";

    Folder rootFolder = si.getRootFolder();
    HostSystem host = null;
```

```
host = (HostSystem) new InventoryNavigator(
    rootFolder).searchManagedEntity("HostSystem", hostname);

if(host==null)
{
  System.out.println("Host not found");
  si.getServerConnection().logout();
  return;
}

HostDatastoreSystem hds = host.getHostDatastoreSystem();

HostNasVolumeSpec hnvs = new HostNasVolumeSpec();
hnvs.setRemoteHost("10.20.140.25");
hnvs.setRemotePath("/home/vm_share");
hnvs.setLocalPath("VM_Share");
hnvs.setAccessMode("readWrite"); // or, "readOnly"

Datastore ds = hds.createNasDatastore(hnvs);
DatastoreInfo di = ds.getInfo();

System.out.println("Name:" + di.getName());
System.out.println("FreeSpace:" + di.getFreeSpace());

si.getServerConnection().logout();
  }
}
```

Extending a VMFS Datastore

An existing VMFS file system can be extended by attaching more partitions to it. Three methods are related to extending the VMFS datastore, the first two of which are to query information:

- **`queryAvailableDisksForVmfs()`** returns a list of `HostScsiDisk` objects that can contain VMFS datastore extents. It takes in an optional parameter as a `Datastore` managed object. If specified, the list of disks is particular to the `Datastore`; otherwise, the list is for containing new VMFS datastores. The parameter must point to a VMFS datastore; otherwise, an `InvalidArgument` fault is thrown.

- **queryVmfsDatastoreExtendOptions()** queries the options to extend an existing VMFS datastore for a disk. It returns an array of VMFS datastore–provisioning options that can be applied on the disk as specified as the second parameter. The first parameter is the `Datastore`.

- **extendVmfsDatastore()** extends an existing `Datastore` based on the `VmfsDatastoreExtendSpec` data object, which is similar to `VmfsDatastoreCreateSpec` (refer to Figure 11-5) but does not include the `HostVmfsSpec` data object.

Removing an Existing Datastore

The `removeDatastore()` method removes an existing datastore specified by the parameter. It returns `none` if successful or a fault when an exception happens.

Another alternative method, `destroyDatastore()`, is defined on the `Datastore` type doing a similar action, but it was deprecated as of SDK 2.5. A `Datastore` object is removed automatically when it's no longer in use by any host or virtual machine. This works like the Java garbage collection mechanism.

Managing the Swap Datastore

`updateLocalSwapDatastore()` changes the `localSwapDatastore` property defined on `HostSystem`. It takes in the new swap `Datastore` as its parameter and returns `none` when successful.

The change affects virtual machines that subsequently power on or resume from a suspended state at this parent host. It also works for a running virtual machine that migrates to this machine.

Configuring the `Datastore` Principal

`configureDatastorePrincipal()` configures the datastore principal user for the host. Once configured, all the virtual machine–related file input/output (I/O) is performed under this user. As a result, all virtual machine files are checked for proper access. If a virtual machine file is not read/writable by this user, the virtual machine–related operations such as power on and configuration change may fail.

This change must be performed in maintenance mode and requires a host reboot after invocation.

The method itself is simple, with two string parameters for username and password, respectively. It returns none, or a fault is thrown for an exceptional case.

Datastore Managed Object

A Datastore object represents a storage location for virtual machine files. The storage location can be a VMFS volume, a directory on NAS, or a local file system path.

A datastore is platform-independent and host-independent. It therefore allows the virtual machines they contain to move between hosts. The scope of a datastore is a datacenter; the datastore must be uniquely named within the datacenter.

Any reference to a virtual machine or file accessed by any host within the datacenter must use a datastore path in the format as follows:

```
[<datastore>] <path>
```

<datastore> is the datastore name, and <path> is a forward-slash-delimited path from the root of the datastore. Note: There is a space between the two elements. A sample datastore path is like the following:

```
[storage 1] winxp/winxp.vmx
```

It's important to become familiar with this naming scheme because all files are referenced implicitly using a datastore path in the VI SDK API.

When a client application creates a virtual machine, it may specify only the name of the datastore and omit the path. The VirtualCenter or the ESX can automatically assign filenames and create directories on the given datastore. For example, specifying My_Datastore as a location for a virtual machine called MyVm results in a datastore location:

```
[My_Datastore] MyVm/MyVm.vmx
```

Datastores are configured per host. As part of host configuration, a HostSystem can be configured to mount several network drives, and multiple hosts can be configured to point to the same storage location. Each datacenter can have only one Datastore, for each such shared location. Each Datastore object stores references to the set of hosts that have mounted the datastore. A Datastore object can be removed only if no hosts currently have the datastore mounted.

Thus, datastores are managed at both the host level and the datacenter level. Each host is configured explicitly with the set of datastores it can access. So is the Datacenter.

Table 11-2 lists six properties defined on the Datastore object. From a Datastore object, you can easily find the list of hosts attached, the datastore capabilities/info/summary, a list of virtual machines whose files are stored on the datastore, as well as the link to the HostDatastoreBrowser managed object. Figure 11-9 shows the structures of the data objects that are related.

Table 11-2

Properties Defined on the Datastore Managed Object

Name	Type	Explanation
browser	HostDatastoreBrowser	The DatastoreBrowser object used to browse this datastore
capability	DatastoreCapability	Capabilities of this datastore
host	DatastoreHostMount[]	All hosts attached to this datastore
Info	DatastoreInfo	Information about the datastore, including free space, maximum file size, name, and URL representation of this datastore
summary	DatastoreSummary	Basic properties of the datastore
vm	ManagedObjectReference[] to VirtualMachine[]	Virtual machines stored on this datastore

Three methods are defined on the Datastore managed object:

- **renameDatastore()** renames a datastore. It takes in one parameter as a new name string for the datastore. As stated earlier, the name must be unique within the whole datacenter.

DatastoreCapability
+directoryHierarchySupported : xsd:boolean
+perFileThinProvisioningSupported : xsd:boolean
+rawDiskMappingsSupported : xsd:boolean

DatastoreHostMount
+key : ManagedObjectReference
+mountInfo : HostMountInfo

DatastoreInfo
+freeSpace : xsd:long
+maxFileSize : xsd:long
+name : xsd:string
+url : xsd:string

DatastoreSummary
+accessible : xsd:boolean
+capacity : xsd:long
+datastore : ManagedObjectReference
+freeSpace : xsd:long
+multiHostAccess : xsd:boolean
+name : xsd:string
+type : xsd:string
+url : xsd:string

Figure 11-9 Several data objects related to `Datastore`

- **`refreshDatastore()`** refreshes a datastore. It updates both `freeSpace` (in both `DatastoreInfo` and `DatastoreSummary`) and `capacity` (only in `DatastoreSummary`) values. It's a good idea to call this method before you access either of the two nested properties affected for their current values. The method takes no parameter and returns `none`.

- **`destroyDatastore()`** removes a datastore. As mentioned earlier, it is deprecated as of VI SDK 2.5 because it's not really needed. When a datastore is no longer in use, it's removed automatically. If it's still in use, you cannot remove it. To remove a datastore, make sure you delete everything in it.

Search Datastore with `HostDatastoreBrowser`

`HostDatastoreBrowser` provides search capabilities within one or more datastores. The typical use case of this managed object is to provide functionality similar to a file chooser in a user interface.

`HostDatastoreBrowser` has two properties: `datastore`, which is an array of `Datastore` objects that can be searched with this `HostDatastoreBrowser`; and `supportedType`, which is an array of `FileQuery` objects listing supported file types. As shown in Figure 11-10, the `FileQuery` has eight subtypes, each of which represents a file type or a folder that could be in the datastore. The `VmConfigFileQuery` has a little extra that allows searching based on virtual machine versions.

Three methods are defined: `deleteFile()`, `searchDatastore_Task()`, and `searchDatastoreSubFolders_Task()`. The first method is deprecated as VI SDK 2.5; therefore, it's not covered here. You can use the `FileManager` to delete files, but be cautious.

With all the other two methods, the client must have at least `Datastore.Browse` privilege to the given datastore path.

The `searchDatastore_Task()` takes in a datastore path string and a
`HostDatastoreBrowserSearchSpec` object, which specifies a set of search criteria. The
data structure of `HostDatastoreBrowserSearchSpec` is shown in Figure 11-10. It
includes not only the file types but also the match pattern,[4] whether it is case sensitive, and so on.

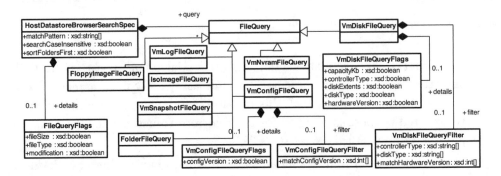

Figure 11-10   The `HostDatastoreBrowserSearchSpec` data object

The return from `searchDatastore_Task()` is a `Task` object. When the task is complete, you can access its `info.result` property to get the
`HostDatastoreBrowserSearchResults` data object, which includes the folder path and
a list of `FileInfo` objects representing the files that satisfy the search specification.

> The `fileSize` you get might be different from what you see in the datastore browser
> from the VI Client. In the ESX console, you can find a pair of `.vmdk` files for one `.vmdk`
> file that is visible in the datastore browser GUI. For example, if you find `sdk101.vmdk` in
> the GUI, there is actually another `sdk101-flat.vmdk` file in the same directory but invis-
> ible in the GUI. If you use `VmDiskFileQuery` in your filter spec, you only get the
> `sdk101.vmdk`, which is normally several hundred bytes. This can cause confusion. Do
> not rely on this file size as your virtual disk size. If you do need the actual disk size, you
> should use a search pattern of `*.vmdk`, which gets you both files of the pair.

The types of the elements in the list are `FileInfo` or either one of its subtypes, meaning you might need to do casting before accessing them. However,

---

[4] The match pattern does not support regular expressions as of 2.5.

Figure 11-11 shows that if you search the .vmdk file, the returned FileInfo object is not really VmDiskFileInfo, which has extra information.

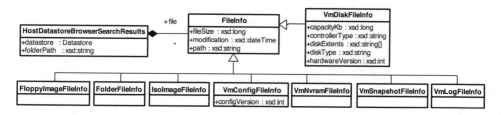

Figure 11-11   The `HostDatastoreBrowserSearchResult` data object

The searchDatastoreSubFolders_Task() method takes in the same parameters as searchDatastore_Task(), but it gets back a list of subfolders as a result of the returned Task object.

Listing 11-3 shows how to use this managed object to search all the .vmdk files prefixed with sdk in a datastore attached to a specified host. Note: The printExtraDiskFileInfo() method isn't really used because of the reason just mentioned.

This sample works with ESX and VirtualCenter, but you need to change some of the variables accordingly.

Listing 11-3
`SearchDatastore.java`

```java
package vim25.samples.mo.storage;
import java.net.URL;

import com.vmware.vim25.ArrayOfHostDatastoreBrowserSearchResults;
import com.vmware.vim25.DatastoreInfo;
import com.vmware.vim25.FileInfo;
import com.vmware.vim25.FileQuery;
import com.vmware.vim25.FileQueryFlags;
import com.vmware.vim25.HostDatastoreBrowserSearchResults;
import com.vmware.vim25.HostDatastoreBrowserSearchSpec;
import com.vmware.vim25.VmDiskFileInfo;
import com.vmware.vim25.VmDiskFileQuery;
```

```java
import com.vmware.vim25.mo.Datastore;
import com.vmware.vim25.mo.Folder;
import com.vmware.vim25.mo.HostDatastoreBrowser;
import com.vmware.vim25.mo.HostSystem;
import com.vmware.vim25.mo.InventoryNavigator;
import com.vmware.vim25.mo.ServiceInstance;
import com.vmware.vim25.mo.Task;

public class SearchDatastore
{
  public static void main(String[] args) throws Exception
  {
    if(args.length != 3)
    {
      System.out.println("Usage: java SearchDatastore <url> "
        + "<username> <password>");
      return;
    }

    ServiceInstance si = new ServiceInstance(
        new URL(args[0]), args[1], args[2], true);

    String hostname = "10.20.8.8";
    String datastorePath = "[storage1 (2)]";

    Folder rootFolder = si.getRootFolder();
    HostSystem host = null;

    host = (HostSystem) new InventoryNavigator(
        rootFolder).searchManagedEntity("HostSystem", hostname);

    if(host==null)
    {
      System.out.println("Host not found");
      si.getServerConnection().logout();
      return;
    }

    HostDatastoreBrowser hdb = host.getDatastoreBrowser();
```

```
System.out.println("print out the names of the datastores");
Datastore[] ds = hdb.getDatastores();
for(int i=0; ds!=null && i<ds.length; i++)
{
  System.out.println("datastore["+i+"]:");
  DatastoreInfo di = ds[i].getInfo();
  System.out.println("Name:" + di.getName());
  System.out.println("FreeSpace:" + di.getFreeSpace());
  System.out.println("MaxFileSize:" + di.getMaxFileSize());
}


System.out.println("print out supported query types");
FileQuery[] fqs = hdb.getSupportedType();
for(int i=0; fqs!=null && i<fqs.length; i++)
{
  System.out.println("FileQuery["+i+"]="
      + fqs[i].getClass().getName());
}


HostDatastoreBrowserSearchSpec hdbss =
  new HostDatastoreBrowserSearchSpec();
hdbss.setQuery(new FileQuery[] { new VmDiskFileQuery()});
FileQueryFlags fqf = new FileQueryFlags();
fqf.setFileSize(true);
fqf.setModification(true);
hdbss.setDetails(fqf);
hdbss.setSearchCaseInsensitive(false);
hdbss.setMatchPattern(new String[] {"sdk*.*"});


Task task = hdb.searchDatastoreSubFolders_Task(
    datastorePath, hdbss);
if(task.waitForMe()==Task.SUCCESS)
{
  Object obj = task.getTaskInfo().getResult();
  if(obj instanceof ArrayOfHostDatastoreBrowserSearchResults)
  {
    HostDatastoreBrowserSearchResults[] results =
      ((ArrayOfHostDatastoreBrowserSearchResults)
```

```java
        obj).getHostDatastoreBrowserSearchResults();

    for(int i=0; i<results.length; i++)
    {
      HostDatastoreBrowserSearchResults result = results[i];
      System.out.println("\nFolder:"
          + result.getFolderPath());
      FileInfo[] fis = result.getFile();
      for(int j=0; fis!=null && j<fis.length; j++)
      {
        System.out.println("Path:" + fis[j].getPath());
        System.out.println("FileSize:"
            + fis[j].getFileSize());
        System.out.println("Modified:"
            + fis[j].getModification().getTime());
        if(fis[j] instanceof VmDiskFileInfo)
        {
          printExtraDiskFileInfo((VmDiskFileInfo)fis[j]);
        }
      }
    }
  }
  si.getServerConnection().logout();
  }
}


static void printExtraDiskFileInfo(VmDiskFileInfo info)
{
  System.out.println("CapacityKB:" + info.getCapacityKb());
  System.out.println("ControllerType:"
      + info.getControllerType());
  System.out.println("DiskType:" + info.getDiskType());
  System.out.println("DiskExtents:");
  String[] exts = info.getDiskExtents();
  for(int i =0; i<exts.length; i++)
  {
    System.out.print(exts[i] + " ");
  }
}
}
```

Managing Datastores with `FileManager`

Managing datastores with `FileManager` is an experimental feature, so it's subject to change in future releases. With this managed object, you can manage and manipulate files and folders on datastores. The files and folders can be represented with a URL or datastore path.

The URL is in a format similar to the following:

```
scheme://authority/folder/path?dcPath=dcPath&dsName=dsName
```

`scheme` is either http or https; `authority` specifies the hostname or IP address of the VirtualCenter or ESX server and optionally the port; `dcPath` is the inventory path to the datacenter containing the datastore; `dsName` is the name of the datastore; `path` is a slash-delimited path from the root of the datastore. If you are not sure about a path, just try the Web-based datastore browser discussed in Chapter 2, "VI SDK Basics."

The `FileManager` is purely a utility class with no property defined. It has four methods defined: `makeDirectory()`, `copyDatastoreFile_Task()`, `moveDatastoreFile_Task()`, and `deleteDatastoreFile_Task()`. All take in either primitive data or managed objects.

> The `FileManager` doesn't provide you the service to list all the files or directories in a specified directory. For this functionality, you can use `HostDatastoreBrowser`, introduced earlier.

`makeDirectory()` creates a new folder with the specified name in the specified datacenter. If the boolean `createParentDirectories` parameter is `true`, it can create all the intermediate-level folders if they don't exist yet; otherwise, a `FileNotFound` fault is thrown. When you connect to ESX, the datacenter argument can be `null`.

`copyDatastoreFile_Task()` copies a file to a new location. It has the following parameters:

- **sourceName**—The name of the source, either a URL or a datastore path referring to the file.

- **sourceDatacenter**—The datacenter with which the source datastore is associated. It's a must when the sourceName is a datastore path; otherwise, it's not needed.

- **destinationName**—The name of the destination, either a URL or a datastore path referring to the file.

- **destinationDatacenter**—The datacenter with which the destination datastore is associated. It's a must when the sourceName is a datastore path; otherwise, it's not needed.

- **force**—If true, overwrite the existing file at the destination.

moveDatastoreFile_Task() copies a file from its source to a new location. It takes the same parameters as copyDatastoreFile_Task().

deleteDatastoreFile_Task() deletes the specified file or folder from a datastore. It takes in both a name and a Datacenter object. If the name is a URL, the Datacenter object is not needed. Before you delete a folder, you should delete the files in it first.

This deleteDatastoreFile_Task() method treats everything to be deleted as a normal file. If you accidentally delete a virtual machine file, you may corrupt the virtual machine.

Listing 11-4 shows a sample that first creates a directory and then copies a file into it. In the end, it cleans things up by deleting both the copied file and a new directory after a 30-second delay. When you run this sample, change the related datacenter name, source file path, and so on to your own environment. The program logic works for both ESX and VirtualCenter.

Listing 11-4
CopyFile.java

```
package vim25.samples.mo.storage;
import java.net.URL;

import com.vmware.vim25.mo.Datacenter;
import com.vmware.vim25.mo.FileManager;
```

```java
import com.vmware.vim25.mo.InventoryNavigator;
import com.vmware.vim25.mo.ServiceInstance;
import com.vmware.vim25.mo.Task;

public class CopyFile
{
  public static void main(String[] args) throws Exception
  {
    if(args.length != 3)
    {
      System.out.println("Usage: java CopyFile "
        + "<url> <username> <password>");
      return;
    }

    ServiceInstance si = new ServiceInstance(
      new URL(args[0]), args[1], args[2], true);

    Datacenter dc = (Datacenter)new InventoryNavigator(
        si.getRootFolder()).searchManagedEntity(
          "Datacenter", "ha-datacenter");
    FileManager fileMgr = si.getFileManager();
    if(fileMgr==null)
    {
      System.out.println("FileManager not available.");
      si.getServerConnection().logout();
      return;
    }

    String basePath = "[storage1 (2)] Nostalgia011";
    String dirPath = basePath + "/" + "testDir";
    // create parent directories if needed - true
    fileMgr.makeDirectory(dirPath, dc, true);

    String srcPath = basePath + "/Nostalgia011.vmdk";
    String dstPath = dirPath + "/copy of Nostalgia011.vmdk";
    Task cTask = fileMgr.copyDatastoreFile_Task(srcPath, dc,
        dstPath, dc, true);
```

```
if(cTask.waitForMe()==Task.SUCCESS)
{
  System.out.println("File copied successfully!");
}
else
{
  System.out.println("File copy failed!");
  return;
}
Thread.sleep(30*1000);

fileMgr.deleteDatastoreFile_Task(dstPath, dc);
fileMgr.deleteDatastoreFile_Task(dirPath, dc);
si.getServerConnection().logout();
  }
}
```

Managing Virtual Disks with `VirtualDiskManager`

`VirtualDiskManager` is the managed object type that manages and manipulates the virtual disks in datastores. It's an experimental feature as of SDK 2.5, and it's only supported on ESX, not VirtualCenter.

`VirtualDiskManager` is closely attached to `ServiceInstance`, like many other singleton managed objects. You can obtain this object with one call in the VI Java API. It's a pure utility type of managed object, so no property is defined. It does have 13 methods defined, as listed in Table 11-3.

Table 11-3

Methods Defined in `VirtualDiskManager`	
Name	**Description**
`copyVirtualDisk_Task()`	Copy a virtual disk, performing conversions as specified in the spec.
`createVirtualDisk_Task()`	Create a new virtual disk

Table 11-3   continued

Methods Defined in `VirtualDiskManager`

Name	Description
`defragmentVirtualDisk_Task()`	Defragment a sparse virtual disk. Note that this defragments the virtual disk file(s) in the host operating system, not the guest operating system file system inside the virtual disk.
`deleteVirtualDisk_Task()`	Delete a virtual disk. All files relating to the disk are deleted. You should be careful not to delete a disk file accidentally.
`extendVirtualDisk_Task()`	Expand the capacity of a virtual disk to the new capacity in kilobytes.
`inflateVirtualDisk_Task()`	Inflate a sparse virtual disk up to the full size.
`moveVirtualDisk_Task()`	Move a virtual disk and all related files from the source location specified by `sourceName` and `sourceDatacenter` to the destination location specified by `destName` and `destDatacenter`.
`queryVirtualDiskFragmentation()`	Return the percentage of fragmentation of the sparse virtual disk. This is the fragmentation of virtual disk file(s) in the host operating system, not the fragmentation of the guest operating system's file system inside the virtual disk.
`queryVirtualDiskGeometry()`	Get the disk geometry information for the virtual disk, including the number of cylinders, the number of heads per cylinder, and the number of sectors per head.
`queryVirtualDiskUuid()`	Get the UUID of the virtual disk.
`setVirtualDiskUuid()`	Set the UUID of the virtual disk.
`shrinkVirtualDisk_Task()`	Deflate a sparse virtual disk. This feature is useful because it can significantly reduce the disk size, meaning the same physical storage can provision much more virtual machines than otherwise.
`zeroFillVirtualDisk_Task()`	Overwrite all blocks of the virtual disk with zeros. All data will be lost. Be extremely careful while calling this method.

Most methods need to locate the virtual disk before they can work. To achieve this, a combination of two parameters is used: <name and datacenter>. The name could be a full URL or a datastore path. In the first case, the datacenter can be null.

The VirtualDiskSpec is important to understand some of the APIs. The data object has two properties. One is the adapterType, which can be busLogic, ide, or lsiLogic. The other is diskType, which can be eagerZeroedThick, preallocated, raw, rdm, rdmp, sparse2Gb, thick, thick2Gb, or thin. To find out more details about the disk type, check out the VirtualDiskType in the API reference.

Listing 11-5 shows a sample that queries and prints a virtual disk's fragmentation percentage, UUID, and disk geometry (cylinder, head, sector). Because VirtualDiskManager is not supported in VirtualCenter, run the sample on ESX only.

When trying this sample, replace the vmdkPath with a VMDK path to your virtual machine, either powered on or powered off. You can even provide a path to a virtual machine disk that is not registered into the system inventory yet.

Listing 11-5
QueryVirtualDisk.java

```
package vim25.samples.mo.storage;
import java.net.URL;

import com.vmware.vim25.HostDiskDimensionsChs;
import com.vmware.vim25.mo.ServiceInstance;
import com.vmware.vim25.mo.VirtualDiskManager;

public class QueryVirtualDisk
{
  public static void main(String[] args) throws Exception
  {
    if(args.length != 3)
    {
      System.out.println("Usage: java QueryVirtualDisk "
        + "<url> <username> <password>");
      return;
    }

    ServiceInstance si = new ServiceInstance(
```

```
    new URL(args[0]), args[1], args[2], true);

  VirtualDiskManager vdMgr = si.getVirtualDiskManager();
  if(vdMgr==null)
  {
    System.out.println("VirtualDiskManager not available.");
    si.getServerConnection().logout();
    return;
  }

  String vmdkPath =
    "[storage1 (2)] Nostalgia011/Nostalgia011.vmdk";

  int fragPerfent = vdMgr.queryVirtualDiskFragmentation(
      vmdkPath, null);
  System.out.println("Defragmentation:" + fragPerfent + "%");

  String uuid = vdMgr.queryVirtualDiskUuid(vmdkPath, null);
  System.out.println("Disk UUID:" + uuid);

  HostDiskDimensionsChs hddc = vdMgr.queryVirtualDiskGeometry(
      vmdkPath, null);
  System.out.println("Cylinder:" + hddc.getCylinder());
  System.out.println("Head:" + hddc.getHead());
  System.out.println("Sector:" + hddc.getSector());

  si.getServerConnection().logout();
  }
}
```

After the sample runs, the console has printouts that look like the following:

```
Defragmentation:0%
Disk UUID:60 00 C2 97 0e 1c 27 59-f3 b0 60 d7 2f ff 65 e4
Cylinder:1044
Head:255
Sector:63
```

Summary

This chapter introduced how to manage the storage system and datastores and how to use the services for file management and virtual disk management. To get you started, it provided a brief overview of storage virtualization. After reading this chapter, you should be able to manage the storage subsystems, including the datastores and files, using the SDK.

Chapter 12

Events and Alarms

This chapter discusses events and alarms, which are useful in system management.

`Event` and `EventManager` establish the foundation for signaling events of different natures happening in the system and allowing interested parties to handle these events accordingly. With the `EventHistoryCollector` managed object, you can retrieve the historical events on the given ESX or vCenter server during a certain period.

The alarm system provides a mechanism to monitor the system with predefined conditions and then trigger follow-up actions. You can create and manage alarms to automate the VMware Infrastructure. `Alarm` and `AlarmManager` are examined in detail in the second half of this chapter.

Managed Objects: EventManager, EventHistoryCollector, Alarm, AlarmManager

Event Data Object

Each type of `Event` represents a specific thing happening or having happened in the system. For example, `DrsEnabledEvent` represents that Distributed Resource Scheduler (DRS) was enabled on a cluster.

`Events` are logged after they happen. For some important processes, two separate `Events` are logged to represent both the starting and ending points of the process. You can, therefore, have a chance to respond to the process upon its starting. For example, VmSuspendingEvent indicates that a virtual machine has started to suspend, whereas VmSuspendedEvent indicates that the virtual machine has finished suspending.

VI SDK 2.5 has at least 276 types of defined Events. Figure 12-1 shows the hierarchy of the Event family. Clearly, Figure 12-1 does not include all Event types simply because there are too many. The figure shows only the immediate subtypes of Event. Each subtype can have many subtypes underneath it. Check out the API reference for all the details.

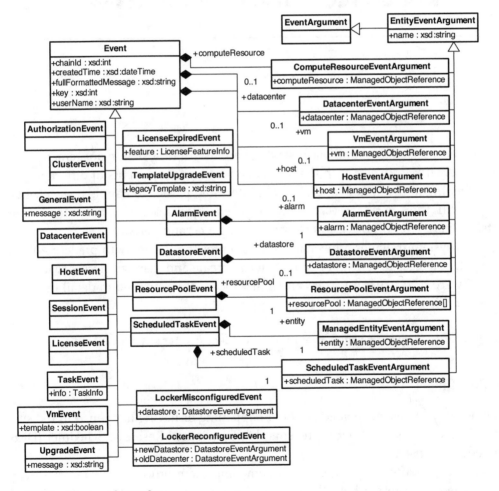

Figure 12-1 The Event hierarchy

Unlike the Task (discussed in Chapter 14, "Task and ScheduledTask") and Alarm, the Event is a data object. As you can see from Figure 12-1, the top Event defines nine properties, including when, who, and what. Most of the subtypes do not define new properties, because the Event itself has provided enough information.

Closely related to the Event are the EventArgument and its subtypes.[1] They are included as part of the Event or its subtypes to provide extra information specific to the Event type.

EventManager Managed Object

The EventManager provides services for managing events. It's a singleton object that is closely attached to the ServiceInstance object. It has three properties: description, latestEvent, and maxCollector (see Table 12-1).

Table 12-1

Properties Defined in EventManager

Name	Type	Description
description	EventDescription	Static descriptive strings used in events[2] like event categories, mainly for display in a user interface. There are four categories: info, warning, error, and user.
latestEvent	Event	The latest event that happened on the server.
maxCollector	xsd:int	For each client, the maximum number of event collectors that can exist simultaneously. It's 1,000 on ESX and 32 on VirtualCenter. You cannot change it via the API.

[2]The eventInfo property is not set on ESX or VirtualCenter. In theory, it should provide several format strings for each type of event. These strings can be used to format the display message in different scenarios. For example, the formatOnDatacenter string for VmRenamedEvent can be Renamed {vm.name} from {oldName} to {newName}. You can then replace the real value of the event in the string for display. These strings are subject to localization.

---

[1] The subtypes of the EventArgument are really not necessary in design because they have the same data structure with one extra property of type ManagedObjectReference even though they are named differently.

Although the latestEvent property is a type of Event, the real object from your retrieval is one of the concrete subtypes, such as UserLoginSessionEvent, which might have more properties defined. You can use the Event type to get useful information, but to access the additional properties, you must cast it to the concrete type. For example, the UserLoginSessionEvent has three extra properties—ipAddress, sessionId, and locale—and you must cast the object before you can access any of these properties in a compiling language like Java.

Given the hundreds of subtypes of the Event, this can be a lot of work. But the good news is that you watch only those types you are interested in and leave the rest to other interested parties to process.

There are four methods in EventManager.

- **createCollectorForEvent()** creates a collector for retrieving historical events.

- **logUserEvent()** creates a user-defined event represented by GeneralUserEvent on a managed entity. The entity must be a root Folder, a Datacenter, a VirtualMachine, a HostSystem, or a ComputeResource. The message property of the GeneralUserEvent is assigned with the value of the msg parameter to the method.

- **postEvent()** posts a specified event and optionally associates with a Task. It takes in two parameters: one is the fully specified event to post, and the other is the optional associated Task.

logUserEvent and postEvent seem a little strange for client application developers. They are for server applications designed to be integrated with the VirtualCenter server and want to take advantage of the infrastructure of the VirtualCenter server. For normal applications, you can safely ignore their existence.

- **queryEvents()** retrieves the events based on the specified EventFilterSpec, the same type of parameter to the createCollectorForEvents(). The difference is that the queryEvents() method returns a one-time result—an array of Event objects—whereas the latter returns a collector-managed object.

The array is a mixture of real events. Don't assume that all event types are the same and cast them according to the first event. More often than not, you get a ClassCastException if you are coding in this way. Instead, you should check each element's type and cast accordingly if you want extra information defined in subtypes.

queryEvents() returns up to 1,000 events at a time. If you get 1,000 events from the call,[3] you cannot tell whether there are exactly 1,000 events that satisfy your filter spec, or more. If you need to retrieve more than 1,000 events, use the history collector, to be discussed shortly.

Now let's look at the EventFilterSpec object shown in Figure 12-2. As you can see, the spec defines a vector of criteria, such as under which username, with what managed object, during what time frame, whether or not to disable the full formatted message, and so on. Just like most of the spec data objects, all the properties in the EventFilterSpec are optional, which allows arbitrary combination of criteria.

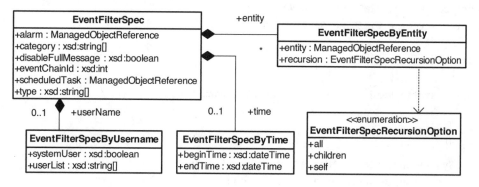

Figure 12-2   The EventFilterSpec and related data objects

Listing 12-1 shows how to create an EventFilterSpect object. The filter spec gets error and warning events that the Administrator user caused during the past month. The entity filter doesn't really limit anything, but I wanted to show how to use the data object for scoping managed entities.

This sample works on VirtualCenter only because the queryEvents() method doesn't work well against ESX.

---

[3] You can easily get 1,000 events returned with an empty filter with VirtualCenter.

Listing 12-1

QueryEvents.java

```java
package vim25.samples.mo.event;
import java.net.URL;
import java.util.Calendar;

import com.vmware.vim25.Event;
import com.vmware.vim25.EventFilterSpec;
import com.vmware.vim25.EventFilterSpecByEntity;
import com.vmware.vim25.EventFilterSpecByTime;
import com.vmware.vim25.EventFilterSpecByUsername;
import com.vmware.vim25.EventFilterSpecRecursionOption;
import com.vmware.vim25.mo.EventManager;
import com.vmware.vim25.mo.ServiceInstance;

public class QueryEvents
{
  public static void main(String[] args) throws Exception
  {
    if(args.length != 3)
    {
      System.out.println("Usage: java QueryEvents "
          + "<url> <username> <password>");
      return;
    }

    ServiceInstance si = new ServiceInstance(
        new URL(args[0]), args[1], args[2], true);

    // get the latest event and print it
    EventManager evtMgr = si.getEventManager();
    Event latestEvent = evtMgr.getLatestEvent();
    printEvent(latestEvent);

    // create a filter spec for querying events
    EventFilterSpec efs = new EventFilterSpec();
    // limit to only error and warning
    efs.setType(new String[] {"VmFailedToPowerOnEvent",
```

```
            "HostConnectionLostEvent"});
      // limit to error and warning only
      efs.setCategory(new String[] {"error", "warning"});

      // limit to the children of the root folder
      EventFilterSpecByEntity eFilter =
        new EventFilterSpecByEntity();
      eFilter.setEntity(si.getRootFolder().getMOR());
      eFilter.setRecursion(
          EventFilterSpecRecursionOption.children);

      // limit to events from the past month
      EventFilterSpecByTime tFilter = new EventFilterSpecByTime();
      Calendar startTime = si.currentTime();
      startTime.roll(Calendar.MONTH, false);
      tFilter.setBeginTime(startTime);
      efs.setTime(tFilter);
      // limit to the user of "administrator"
      EventFilterSpecByUsername uFilter =
          new EventFilterSpecByUsername();
      uFilter.setSystemUser(false);
      uFilter.setUserList(new String[] {"administrator"});

      Event[] events = evtMgr.queryEvents(efs);

      // print each of the events
      for(int i=0; events!=null && i<events.length; i++)
      {
        System.out.println("\nEvent #" + i);
        printEvent(events[i]);
      }

    si.getServerConnection().logout();
}

/**
 * Only print an event as Event type.
 * More info can be printed if it's casted to a subtype.
 */
static void printEvent(Event evt)
{
```

```
String typeName = evt.getClass().getName();
int lastDot = typeName.lastIndexOf('.');
if(lastDot != -1)
{
  typeName = typeName.substring(lastDot+1);
}
System.out.println("Type:" + typeName);
System.out.println("Key:" + evt.getKey());
System.out.println("ChainId:" + evt.getChainId());
System.out.println("User:" + evt.getUserName());
System.out.println("Time:" + evt.getCreatedTime().getTime());
System.out.println("FormattedMessage:"
    + evt.getFullFormattedMessage());
if(evt.getDatacenter()!= null)
{
  System.out.println("Datacenter:"
      + evt.getDatacenter().getDatacenter());
}
if(evt.getComputeResource()!=null)
{
  System.out.println("ComputeResource:"
      + evt.getComputeResource().getComputeResource());
}
if(evt.getHost()!=null)
{
  System.out.println("Host:" + evt.getHost().getHost());
}
if(evt.getVm()!=null)
{
  System.out.println("VM:" + evt.getVm().getVm());
}
 }
}
```

Retrieving Historical Events with `EventHistoryCollector`

As mentioned in the previous section, `createCollectorForEvents()` returns an `EventHistoryCollector` managed object. It takes in an `EventFilterSpec` object as its parameter and returns `EventHistoryCollector`. Because `EventFilterSpec` has already been introduced, refer to Figure 12-2 for more details.

The `EventHistoryCollector` is a subtype of `HistoryCollector`. Let's take a little time to introduce this supertype. It's also helpful to understand the `TaskHistoryCollector`, which is discussed in Chapter 14.

`HistoryCollector` Managed Object

Figure 12-3 shows the UML diagram of the three collector types.[4] As you can see, the `EventHistoryCollector` and `TaskHistoryCollector` are two subtypes of `HistoryCollector` that define similar properties and methods.

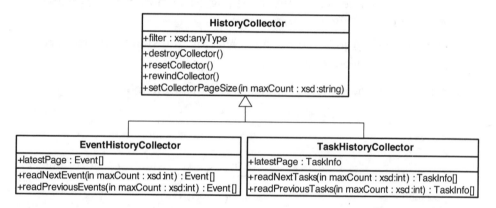

Figure 12-3   The `HistoryCollector` and its two subtypes

The collector objects are closely related to a session, and not persistent across different sessions. If you log in again even with the same credential, you have to re-create the collector objects as needed.

The `HistoryCollector` has one property `filter` that is defined as `xsd:anyType`, meaning it can hold anything, including `EventFilterSpec` and `TaskFilterSpec`.

---

[4] The properties are shown as public, which is not the same as you will see in the VI Java API. It just reflects the API reference, which doesn't clearly define the publicity of the managed object. For the properties in the managed object, we have public getter methods in the VI Java API.

Four simple and self-explanatory methods are defined in the `HistoryCollector`:

- **`resetCollector()`** moves the "scrollable view" to the item immediately preceding the "viewable latest page." If you use `readPreviousTasks` or `readPreviousEvents`, all items are retrieved from the newest item to the oldest item.

- **`rewindCollector()`** moves the "scrollable view" to the oldest item. If you use `readNextTasks()` or `readNextEvents()`, all items are retrieved from the oldest item to the newest item. This is the default setting when the collector is created.

- **`setCollectorPageSize()`** sets the size of the viewable latest page. It limits how many results can be held in the latest page. The more results you specify, the slower it would be to retrieve the `lastestPage`.

- **`destroyCollector()`** just removes the collector. You should destroy a collector when you don't need it anymore.

Figure 12-4 shows how these methods affect the scrollable view.

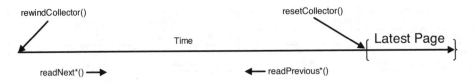

Figure 12-4   The effects of method calls on the "scrollable view"

`EventHistoryCollector` Managed Object

In addition to the properties and methods inherited from the parent type just discussed, the `EventHistoryCollector` defines a new property `latestPage`, typed as an array of `Event` objects. Again, depending on how the collector is created, the array is most likely a mixture of subtyped `Event` objects; therefore, you should be cautious while using and casting the elements.

The two methods `readPreviousEvents()` and `readNextEvents()` get `Event` objects back and forth. They take in one integer parameter as the maximum number of returned `Event` objects.

Now let's look at Listing 12-2. The sample code retrieves all the events from the target. It can work against both ESX and VirtualCenter. Because ESX doesn't keep too many events, you don't normally see many events there. But VirtualCenter keeps a lot more events, and it might take a while before getting all of them.

Listing 12-2
QueryHistoricalEvents.java

```
package vim25.samples.mo.event;
import java.net.URL;

import com.vmware.vim25.Event;
import com.vmware.vim25.EventFilterSpec;
import com.vmware.vim25.mo.EventHistoryCollector;
import com.vmware.vim25.mo.EventManager;
import com.vmware.vim25.mo.ServiceInstance;

public class QueryHistoricalEvents
{
  public static void main(String[] args) throws Exception
  {
    if(args.length != 3)
    {
      System.out.println("Usage: java QueryHistoricalEvents "
        + "<url> <username> <password>");
      return;
    }

    ServiceInstance si = new ServiceInstance(
      new URL(args[0]), args[1], args[2], true);

    EventManager evtMgr = si.getEventManager();

    if(evtMgr!=null)
    {
      EventFilterSpec eventFilter = new EventFilterSpec();
      EventHistoryCollector ehc =
        evtMgr.createCollectorForEvents(eventFilter);

      int total = 0;
```

```
   Event[] latestEvts = ehc.getLatestPage();
   printEvents(latestEvts, 0);
   total += latestEvts==null? 0 : latestEvts.length;


   System.out.println("\nBefore Latest Page:");
   ehc.resetCollector();
   while(true)
   {
     Event[] events = ehc.readPreviousEvents(50);
     if(events==null)
     {
       break;
     }
     printEvents(events, total);
     total += events.length;
   }
 }
 si.getServerConnection().logout();
}

static void printEvents(Event[] events, int total)
{
  for(int i=0; i<events.length; i++)
  {
    System.out.println("Event[" + (total+i) + "]=" +
events[i].getClass().getName());
    System.out.println("Event: " + events[i].getCreatedTime().getTime());
  }
}
}
```

Alarm Managed Object

In VI, an alarm can be triggered under predefined conditions and cause an action in response. Note that `Alarm` and `AlarmManager` are not supported in ESX, but in the VirtualCenter. So the following introductions and code samples are applicable only on VirtualCenter.

The `Alarm` is the managed object type representing such an alarm. It's extended from `ExtensibleManagedObject`. It has a property called `info` of type `AlarmInfo` whose UML diagram is shown in Figure 12-5.

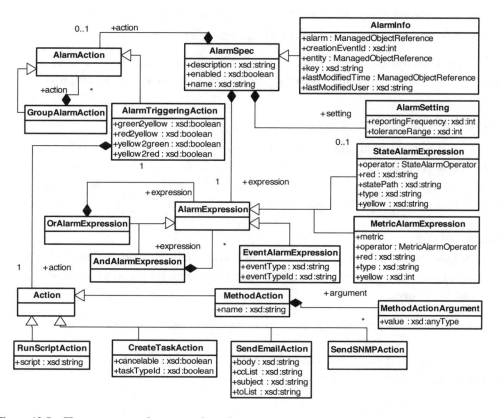

Figure 12-5   The `AlarmInfo` and `AlarmSpec` data objects

The `AlarmInfo` data object is inherited from `AlarmSpec`, which is a complicated data object. Besides the inherited properties, it holds the managed entity with which it's associated, the creation time, the creator, and the ID that identifies the event (`AlarmCreatedEvent`) indicating the creation of this alarm.

The main parts of the `AlarmSpec` are the conditions to trigger an alarm and the actions that should be taken once triggered. The `AlarmSpec` definition does not relate to an entity; therefore, the same `AlarmSpec` can potentially be reused with different managed entities to create different `Alarm` objects.

Triggering Conditions

Triggering conditions are defined by the `AlarmExpression` and its subtypes.

- `EventAlarmExpression` watches specific events.
- `StateAlarmExpression` watches the change of system state.
- `MetricAlarmExpression` watches performance metrics.

These conditions can be combined logically with `AndAlarmExpression` and `OrAlarmExpression`. This allows you to express fairly complicated conditions.

Follow-Up Actions

The action to react to an alarm is represented by `AlarmAction`, which is extended by `GroupAlarmAction` and `AlarmTriggeringAction`. The latter type contains an `Action` whose subtypes represent the concrete actions. The former type allows you to define several actions in a single one.

Sending an E-Mail

`SendEmailAction` represents an action to send an e-mail with predefined templates and cc a group of accounts. You can use predefined variables in your subject and content as follows:

```
"Alarm - {alarmName} \nDescription: {eventDescription}"
```

The predefined variables, listed in Table 12-2, are included in the `ActionParameter` enumeration type.

Table 12-2

Predefined Variables	
Name	**Description**
`Alarm`	The object of the triggering alarm
`alarmName`	The name of the triggering alarm
`declaringSummary`	A summary of declarations made during the triggering of the alarm
`eventDescription`	The event description

Table 12-2   continued

Predefined Variables

Name	Description
newStatus	The status after the alarm is triggered
oldStatus	The status prior to the alarm being triggered
Target	The object of the entity where the alarm is associated
targetName	The name of the entity where the alarm is triggered
triggeringSummary	A summary of information involved in triggering the alarm

You must configure the SMTP server before VirtualCenter can send an e-mail. You have two options:

- **Use the VI Client**—Just click the Administration, VirtualCenter Management Server Configuration, which brings up a dialog box. After selecting Mail from the left pane, check the required parameters on the right pane. Fill in the SMTP server and sender account, and you are done.

- **Configure it using the OptionManager API**—The related, self-explanatory keys are as follows. The default port number is always 25; that is why, in VI Client, you don't see the field at all:

```
mail.sender
mail.smtp.server
mail.smtp.port
```

Running a Script

RunScriptAction specifies a script to run on the VC server. The property script should hold a fully qualified path to a shell script. You can include any variables shown previously in the path to provide additional parameters to the script. Refer to Table 12-1 for all the variables.

For example, the following script has targetName and alarmName as variables. When the script is executed, these two variables are replaced with a real target name and alarm name.

```
c:\TrackProcess.bat {targetName} {alarmName}
```

Given the flexibilities of a shell script on the server side, this action actually gives you the ultimate freedom to do anything you want. Note that the VirtualCenter runs on Windows or in Linux virtual appliance, so your scripts must be able to run on the underlying platform.

Creating a New Task

`CreateTaskAction` allows you to create a new `Task` object in the system so that administrators or other applications can track the task or even cancel it if necessary. The `Task` is specified by the `taskTypeId` as registered by a server extension. Given the limited nature of the server extension, it's not a commonly used action.

Sending a SNMP Trap

`SendSNMPAction` sends a Simple Network Management Protocol (SNMP) trap as a triggered action. You have to configure 1 to 4 SNMP trap receivers before the VirtualCenter server can send a trap. The management information base (MIB) for traps can be found at

```
<VirtualCenter_Home>\MIBS\VMWARE-TRAPS-MIB.mib
```

where the home is normally

```
C:\Program Files\VMware\Infrastructure\VirtualCenter Server
```

Just like configuring a mail server, you have two options. First, you can go to the same dialog box as when you're configuring a mail server and select SNMP from the left pane. Change all the required and optional parameters on the right pane.

The second option is to use the `OptionManager`. Just specify the name, port, community, and whether it's enabled for each receiver. For example, the following are four keys for the primary SNMP trap receiver that you provide values for. The default port is 162.

```
snmp.receiver.1.name
snmp.receiver.1.port
snmp.receiver.1.community
snmp.receiver.1.enabled
```

You can specify up to four receivers. The remaining three trap receivers have a similar set of keys but different numbers in place of 1. For example, the second trap receiver has the following keys:

```
snmp.receiver.2.name
snmp.receiver.2.port
snmp.receiver.2.community
snmp.receiver.2.enabled
```

Invoking a Method

`MethodAction` allows you to invoke a method as you would from a VI SDK client. The property name holds the name of the method, and the property argument holds a list of arguments for the method. The `MethodActionArgument` type has one property defined as `xsd:anyType`; therefore, you can pass in any parameter as required by the method. As you might have wondered, it works similarly to the reflection API in Java.

> The method name to be invoked must be the WSDL method name; it is case sensitive. Given the naming convention of Java in which all methods start with lowercase, you should double-check when you type the method names. Also, the VI Java API has more methods than WSDL methods, so avoid the additional VI Java API methods while creating a `MethodAction`.

Although `MethodAction` doesn't include a managed entity, it's clear that the method invocation works only with appropriate managed entities that have the method defined. That doesn't mean you must create an alarm on an entity that has the method defined. You can define it on an entity that has appropriate descendant entities because alarms can be inherited down the inventory hierarchy. For example, you can define an alarm on a datacenter entity that powers off a virtual machine as action. It can apply to all the virtual machines in the datacenter.

Reconfiguring an Alarm

You can reconfigure an existing alarm using the `reconfigureAlarm()` method with the `AlarmSpec` parameter. Because `AlarmSpec` does not have information associated with a managed entity, you cannot change it with this method. You have to use the `AlarmManager` to create a new `Alarm`. Still, you can change the `Alarm` quite a bit with a new `AlarmSpec` object, including name, condition, and actions.

One more thing you can change with `AlarmSpec` is the `AlarmSetting`. This specifies how often the alarm is triggered (measured in seconds) and what the tolerance range is (`MetricAlarmExpression`, measured in one hundredth percentage). A zero tolerance value means that the alarm triggers right away after the metric value is above or below the specified value. A non-zero value means that the alarm triggers only after reaching a certain percentage above or below the nominal trigger value.

Removing an Alarm

The `removeAlarm()` method removes an existing `Alarm` managed object. It takes in no additional information and returns `none` when it's done. When you no longer need an `Alarm`, it's recommended that you remove it because it uses system resources to monitor and take corresponding actions.

As you might find out, there is no method to create a new `Alarm` object with an `Alarm` type. It's actually the functionality of the `AlarmManager`.

AlarmManager Managed Object

The `AlarmManager` manages the `Alarm` objects in the system scope. It's a global singleton managed object closely attached to the starting `ServiceInstance` managed object.

`AlarmManager` has two properties and three methods defined. Table 12-3 lists the two properties with types and brief descriptions.

Table 12-3

Properties of `AlarmManager`		
Name	**Type**	**Description**
defaultExpression	AlarmExpression[]	The default setting for each alarm expression, used to populate the initial client wizard screen.
description	AlarmDescription	The static descriptive strings used in alarm displays. It doesn't change, so you need to retrieve it once and only once in your application.

Listing 12-3 is a sample that retrieves these properties and prints them. Because an alarm feature is available only on VirtualCenter, you can run the sample only against VirtualCenter.

To display any description included in `AlarmManager`, retrieve it from the server instead of reinventing a new description. `AlarmManager` description strings are in a localized version of the server product. You can cache these descriptions for reuse during the same session. It's not recommended that you use the descriptions across the server or persist them for later sessions.

Listing 12-3

PrintAlarmManager.java

```
package vim25.samples.mo.alarm;
import java.net.URL;

import com.vmware.vim25.AlarmDescription;
import com.vmware.vim25.AlarmExpression;
import com.vmware.vim25.ElementDescription;
import com.vmware.vim25.MetricAlarmExpression;
import com.vmware.vim25.ScheduledTaskDetail;
import com.vmware.vim25.StateAlarmExpression;
import com.vmware.vim25.TypeDescription;
import com.vmware.vim25.mo.AlarmManager;
import com.vmware.vim25.mo.ServiceInstance;

public class PrintAlarmManager
{
  public static void main(String[] args) throws Exception
  {
    if(args.length != 3)
    {
      System.out.println("Usage: java PrintAlarmManager "
        + "<url> <username> <password>");
      return;
    }

    ServiceInstance si = new ServiceInstance(
      new URL(args[0]), args[1], args[2], true);

    AlarmManager alarmMgr = si.getAlarmManager();
```

```
  System.out.println("Alarm expressions:");
  AlarmExpression[] defaultExps = alarmMgr.getDefaultExpression();
  printAlarmExpressions(defaultExps);

  System.out.println("\n\nAlarm descriptions:");
  AlarmDescription ad = alarmMgr.getDescription();
  printAlarmDescription(ad);

  si.getServerConnection().logout();
}

static void printAlarmDescription(AlarmDescription ad)
{
  System.out.println("Entity statuses:");
  printElementDescriptions(ad.getEntityStatus());

  System.out.println("\nHostSystem connection states:");
  printElementDescriptions(ad.getHostSystemConnectionState());

  System.out.println("\nMetric operators:");
  printElementDescriptions(ad.getMetricOperator());

  System.out.println("\nState operators:");
  printElementDescriptions(ad.getStateOperator());

  System.out.println("\nVirtual machine power states:");
  printElementDescriptions(ad.getVirtualMachinePowerState());

  System.out.println("\nAction class descriptions:");
  printTypeDescriptions(ad.getAction());

  System.out.println("\nDescriptions of expressioin type " +
     "for triggers:");
  printTypeDescriptions(ad.getExpr());
}

static void printAlarmExpressions(AlarmExpression[] exps)
{
  for(int i=0; exps!=null && i<exps.length; i++)
```

```java
  {
    System.out.println("\nAlarm expression #" + i);
    if(exps[i] instanceof MetricAlarmExpression)
    {
      MetricAlarmExpression mae =
        (MetricAlarmExpression) exps[i];
      System.out.println("metric:"
          + mae.getMetric().getCounterId());
      System.out.println("red:" + mae.getRed());
      System.out.println("type:" + mae.getType());
      System.out.println("yellow:" + mae.getYellow());
    }
    else if(exps[i] instanceof StateAlarmExpression)
    {
      StateAlarmExpression sae =
        (StateAlarmExpression) exps[i];
      System.out.println("operator:" + sae.getOperator());
      System.out.println("red:" + sae.getRed());
      System.out.println("statePath:" + sae.getStatePath());
      System.out.println("type:" + sae.getType());
      System.out.println("yellow:" + sae.getYellow());
    }
  }
}


static void printTypeDescriptions(TypeDescription[] tds)
{
  for(int i=0; tds!=null && i<tds.length; i++)
  {
    printTypeDescription(tds[i]);
  }
}


static void printTypeDescription(TypeDescription td)
{
  System.out.println("\nKey:" + td.getKey());
  System.out.println("Label:" + td.getLabel());
  System.out.println("Summary:" + td.getSummary());
  if(td instanceof ScheduledTaskDetail)
```

```
    {
      System.out.println("Frequency:" +
((ScheduledTaskDetail)td).getFrequency());
    }
  }


  static void printElementDescriptions(ElementDescription[] eds)
  {
    for(int i=0; eds!=null && i<eds.length; i++)
    {
      printElementDescription(eds[i]);
    }
  }


  static void printElementDescription(ElementDescription ed)
  {
    System.out.println("\nKey:" + ed.getKey());
    System.out.println("Label:" + ed.getLabel());
    System.out.println("Summary:" + ed.getSummary());
  }
}
```

The following is the printout of the sample against a VirtualCenter. To save space, several alarm expressions are omitted.

```
Alarm expressions:
Alarm expression #0
operator:isEqual
red:notResponding
statePath:runtime.connectionState
type:HostSystem
yellow:null


...


Alarm expression #10
metric:89
red:9000
```

```
type:VirtualMachine
yellow:7500
```

```
Alarm descriptions:
Entity statuses:
```

```
Key:gray
Label:Gray
Summary:No status available
```

```
Key:green
Label:Green
Summary:Green indicates normal operation
```

```
Key:yellow
Label:Yellow
Summary:Yellow indicates an error
```

```
Key:red
Label:Red
Summary:Red indicates an error
```

```
HostSystem connection states:
```

```
Key:connected
Label:Connected
Summary:Host is connected
```

```
Key:notResponding
Label:Not responding
Summary:VirtualCenter is not receiving heartbeats from the host
```

```
Key:disconnected
Label:Disconnected
Summary:The user has explicitly taken the host down
```

Metric operators:

Key:isAbove
Label:Is Above
Summary:Test if the target metric item is above a given value

Key:isBelow
Label:Is Below
Summary:Test if the target metric item is below a given value

State operators:

Key:isEqual
Label:Is Equal To
Summary:Test if the target state is a given state

Key:isUnequal
Label:Not Equal To
Summary:Test if the target state is not a given state

Virtual machine power states:

Key:poweredOff
Label:Powered Off
Summary:Virtual Machine is powered off

Key:poweredOn
Label:Powered On
Summary:Virtual Machine is powered on

Key:suspended
Label:Suspended
Summary:Virtual Machine is suspended

Action class descriptions:

Key:SendEmailAction
Label:Send E-mail
Summary:Action to send an e-mail

Key:RunScriptAction
Label:Run a Script
Summary:Action to run a server script

Key:CreateTaskAction
Label:Create a Task
Summary:Action to create a task

Key:MethodAction
Label:Method Action
Summary:Action invoked by standard entity APIs

Key:SendSNMPAction
Label:Send SNMP
Summary:Action to send a SNMP trap

Descriptions of expressioin type for triggers:

Key:OrAlarmExpression
Label:OR
Summary:Alarm expression describes united alarm expressions

Key:AndAlarmExpression
Label:AND
Summary:Alarm expression describes combined alarm expressions

Key:StateAlarmExpression
Label:Entity State
Summary:Alarm expression defined on the connection state of the host or the power state of a virtual machine

Key:EventAlarmExpression
Label:Event
Summary:Event alarm expression

Key:MetricAlarmExpression
Label:Entity Metric
Summary:Alarm expression defined on the metric data of an entity

The three methods of `AlarmManager` are `createAlarm()`, `getAlarm()`, and `getAlarmState()`. The following sections discuss each of them exclusively.

Creating a New Alarm

As mentioned earlier, the creation of a new alarm is the job of `AlarmManager`. It is supported with the `createAlarm()` method.

The method takes in two parameters: the managed entity on which a new alarm is to be created, and the `AlarmSpec`, which was discussed earlier in this chapter. The return of the method is an `Alarm`, on which you can perform several operations and from which you can retrieve properties.

Listing 12-4 shows a sample that sets up an alarm on a virtual machine whose name is provided from the command line. It monitors the virtual machine power state. When it's powered off, the system does two things: sends an e-mail about this alarm with details, and powers on the virtual machine again.

Listing 12-4
`CreateVmAlarm.java`

```
package vim25.samples.mo.alarm;
import java.net.URL;

import com.vmware.vim25.Action;
import com.vmware.vim25.AlarmAction;
import com.vmware.vim25.AlarmSetting;
import com.vmware.vim25.AlarmSpec;
import com.vmware.vim25.AlarmTriggeringAction;
import com.vmware.vim25.GroupAlarmAction;
import com.vmware.vim25.MethodAction;
import com.vmware.vim25.MethodActionArgument;
import com.vmware.vim25.SendEmailAction;
import com.vmware.vim25.StateAlarmExpression;
import com.vmware.vim25.StateAlarmOperator;
import com.vmware.vim25.mo.AlarmManager;
import com.vmware.vim25.mo.InventoryNavigator;
import com.vmware.vim25.mo.ServiceInstance;
import com.vmware.vim25.mo.VirtualMachine;
```

```java
public class CreateVmAlarm
{
  public static void main(String[] args) throws Exception
  {
    if(args.length != 4)
    {
      System.out.println("Usage: java CreateVmAlarm "
          + "<url> <username> <password> <vmname>");
      return;
    }

    ServiceInstance si = new ServiceInstance(
        new URL(args[0]), args[1], args[2], true);

    String vmname = args[3];
    InventoryNavigator inv = new InventoryNavigator(
        si.getRootFolder());
    VirtualMachine vm = (VirtualMachine)inv.searchManagedEntity(
          "VirtualMachine", vmname);
    if(vm==null)
    {
      System.out.println("Cannot find the VM " + vmname
        + "\nExisting...");
      si.getServerConnection().logout();
      return;
    }

    AlarmManager alarmMgr = si.getAlarmManager();

    AlarmSpec spec = new AlarmSpec();

    StateAlarmExpression expression =
      createStateAlarmExpression();
    AlarmAction emailAction = createAlarmTriggerAction(
        createEmailAction());
    AlarmAction methodAction = createAlarmTriggerAction(
        createPowerOnAction());
    GroupAlarmAction gaa = new GroupAlarmAction();
```

```
  gaa.setAction(new AlarmAction[]{emailAction, methodAction});
  spec.setAction(gaa);
  spec.setExpression(expression);
  spec.setName("VmPowerStateAlarm");
  spec.setDescription("Monitor VM state and send email " +
    "and power it on if VM powers off");
  spec.setEnabled(true);

  AlarmSetting as = new AlarmSetting();
  as.setReportingFrequency(0); //as often as possible
  as.setToleranceRange(0);

  spec.setSetting(as);

  alarmMgr.createAlarm(vm, spec);

  si.getServerConnection().logout();
}


static StateAlarmExpression createStateAlarmExpression()
{
  StateAlarmExpression expression =
    new StateAlarmExpression();
  expression.setType("VirtualMachine");
  expression.setStatePath("runtime.powerState");
  expression.setOperator(StateAlarmOperator.isEqual);
  expression.setRed("poweredOff");
  return expression;
}


static MethodAction createPowerOnAction()
{
  MethodAction action = new MethodAction();
  action.setName("PowerOnVM_Task");
  MethodActionArgument argument = new MethodActionArgument();
  argument.setValue(null);
  action.setArgument(new MethodActionArgument[] { argument });
  return action;
}
```

```
static SendEmailAction createEmailAction()
{
  SendEmailAction action = new SendEmailAction();
  action.setToList("sjin@vmware.com");
  action.setCcList("admins99999@vmware.com");
  action.setSubject("Alarm - {alarmName} on {targetName}\n");
  action.setBody("Description:{eventDescription}\n"
      + "TriggeringSummary:{triggeringSummary}\n"
      + "newStatus:{newStatus}\n"
      + "oldStatus:{oldStatus}\n"
      + "target:{target}");
  return action;
}


static AlarmTriggeringAction createAlarmTriggerAction(
    Action action)
{
  AlarmTriggeringAction alarmAction =
    new AlarmTriggeringAction();
  alarmAction.setYellow2red(true);
  alarmAction.setAction(action);
  return alarmAction;
}
}
```

With this sample code, you can automatically recover a virtual machine from power-offs so that their impact is minimized. You can apply this alarm on your critical virtual machines. This in no way substitutes VMware HA, which further protects the virtual machines against host failures.

Finding Existing Alarms

You can find existing alarms on a specific managed entity using the getAlarm() method, which takes in a ManagedEntity object and returns an array of Alarm objects.

The returned alarms do not include inherited alarms that are associated with parent entities. To discover all the alarms that can be triggered on a managed entity, including inherited ones, check out the `declaredAlarmState` property of the managed entity. It does not include the alarms defined by the children of the entity. The type of the property is shown in Figure 12-6.

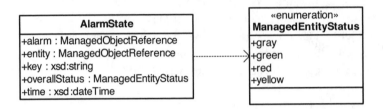

Figure 12-6 The `AlarmState` data object

Getting Alarm State

`getAlarmState()` is the method to get a list of `AlarmState` objects on a specified `ManagedEntity`. As shown in Figure 12-6, the `AlarmState` has references to the `Alarm` and the `ManagedEntity`, the time of last triggering, and the overall status.

The same information is actually held in the `triggeredAlarmState` property of the `ManagedEntity`. Retrieving that property can return the same result.

The returned `AlarmState` objects include not only the alarms triggered by this entity but also those by its descendants. Triggered alarms are propagated up the inventory hierarchy so that a user can tell whenever a descendant has triggered an alarm.

Summary

This chapter introduced the various types of events which are data objects. They signal different kinds of events that happen in the system. The `EventManager` manages the events, including posting new events to the system. With the `EventHistoryCollector`, you can retrieve historical events on a given server with criteria you specify.

The second half of this chapter introduced `Alarm`, which is the managed object that monitors the system with predefined conditions. After an alarm is triggered, it can take different actions such as running a shell script or sending an e-mail. The `AlarmManager` is the managed object that creates and manages the alarms.

Chapter 13

Performance Monitoring

This chapter introduces performance management using the VI SDK. It first introduces several basic concepts used in performance statistics: counters, intervals, rollup types, and real-time statistics. Then it introduces the PerformanceManager managed object, focusing on how to retrieve performance metadata and how to retrieve the system performance data, including the historical data and real-time data. Along the way, this chapter also includes tips on how to avoid common problems and how to monitor performance without hurting performance too much.

Managed Object: PerformanceManager

Basic Terminologies

Before discussing the managed object, let's look at the basic concepts in performance statistics. Once these are clear, the related interfaces should be relatively easy. If you are familiar with VI Client performance monitoring or esxtop,[1] they help as well.

---

[1] This is the command used to monitor performance in ESX.

Performance Counter

A performance counter is a unit of information like CPU usage that can be collected about a managed entity. The PerfCounterInfo data object, shown in Figure 13-1, represents a performance counter. The property key is an integer that uniquely identifies a performance counter, like a primary key of a table in a relational database, and nothing more. It's not guaranteed that a performance counter will have a fixed number. In fact, the same performance counter can have different values in ESX and VirtualCenter. Even for the same type of server, the number could change from version to version. Do not use the performance counter outside the context of the server you connect to.

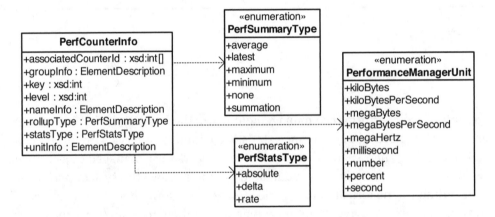

Figure 13-1   PerfCounterInfo data object

The performance counter can be represented by the following dotted string notation:

```
[group].[counter].[rollupType]
```

One sample for such an expression is the following:

```
disk.usage.average
```

This is the performance counter for the average usage of a disk.

In the VI SDK, performance counters have seven predefined groups: CPU, ResCpu, Memory, Network, Disk, System, and ClusterServices. Inside different groups are different counters. For example, the system group has `uptime`, `resourceCpuUsage`, and `heartbeat` counters.

Rollup refers to the process of aggregating statistics so that they can be used at a later time. There are six rollup types, as defined in the `PerfSummaryType` enumeration type: average, latest, maximum, minimum, none, and summation. Each rollup type represents a different mathematical aspect of the same performance data. You can choose the rollups based on your interests. For example, if you are developing a charge-back solution, you might be more interested in the summation than any other type.

The performance counters are not simple permutations of these three dimensions. Some counters may not have all the rollup types. For example, the `system.uptime` has only a summation type, not the other six rollup types.

Moreover, a performance counter contains other information about the unit, type of statistics and description, level, and so on. The available units are listed in the `PerformanceManagerUnit` enumeration type. The type of statistic is listed in the `PerfStatsType` enumeration type. Both of these enumeration types are included in Figure 13-1.

The level of a performance counter is an integer valued from 1 to 4, indicating its importance. The lower the level, the more important it is, the more likely it is collected, and the longer it is kept in the VirtualCenter database.

Here is a list of four levels and what counters are included:

- **Level 1**—Includes basic metrics: average usage for CPU, memory, disk, and network; system uptime; system heartbeat; and DRS metrics. It does not include statistics for devices.

- **Level 2**—Includes all counters with rollup types of average, summation, and latest for CPU, memory, disk, and network; system uptime; system heartbeat; and DRS metrics. It does not include statistics for devices.

- **Level 3**—Includes all metrics (including device metrics) for all counter groups except those with rollup types of maximum and minimum.

- **Level 4**—Includes all metrics supported by VirtualCenter, including maximum and minimum rollup types.

Invoking the `queryPerfCounterByLevel()` method can easily return a list of performance counters in a specific level.

On an ESX server, the level is not set for performance counters; likewise, the `queryPerfCounterByLevel()` is not supported.

All performance counters have their own meanings. When used effectively, they can provide insight into the system performance. For example, when used CPU time approximates ready time, it may signal contention and possible over-commitment due to workload variability.

Appendix B, "The Performance Counters," lists all the performance counters in VI SDK 2.5. Note that VI SDK does not help to interpret the performance statistics. Check out VMware technical notes on performance for more details.[2]

Performance Metric

The performance metric represents the actual information being collected. The counter defines only the type of performance statistic and does not take into account the target device instances. There might be multiple instances of the device for which the same performance counter can be used. Each combination of performance counter and device instance is a performance metric. The relationship of the performance counter and the performance metric is very much like that of the class and object instance in object-oriented programming.

Let us take a look at a quick example. The `cpu.usage.average` is a performance counter for average CPU utilization. When the counter is collected on CPU No. 1 of a host, a performance metric is formed.

The performance metric is represented by the `PerfMetricId` data object, which consists of two parts:

- **`counterId`**—The integer that identifies the performance counter.
- **`instanceId`**—The name of the instance, such as `0`, `vmnic1`, or `vmhba0:0:0`.

Intervals

After it's clear which aspect of a device to collect performance data for, you need to decide the interval with which the performance data is collected and stored. The interval has to be longer than the sampling interval, which can be found as

---

[2] http://www.vmware.com/files/pdf/technote_PerformanceCounters.pdf

refreshRate in the PerfProviderSummary data object returned by the queryPerfProviderSummary() method.

Given the constraints of storage, you don't want to save all the sampled statistics you collect, especially when the statistics are becoming outdated. The more recent ones are normally stored in a finer grain. When the data becomes older, you combine it into longer intervals.

PerfInterval is the data object that represents a historical interval, as shown in Figure 13-2.

PerfInterval
+enabled : xsd:boolean
+key : xsd:int
+length : xsd:int
+level : xsd:int
+name : xsd:string
+samplingPeriod : xsd:int

Figure 13-2   The PerfInterval data object

Historical intervals are identified by an interval ID, the number of seconds for which the performance statistics are calculated. For example, for the 30-minute interval, the interval ID is 1800 (60×30).

Each configured interval has a name, such as PastDay, PastMonth, provided to users. The name does not affect system behavior. The configuration of historical intervals in VirtualCenter specifies the scheme that aggregates performance statistics data in VirtualCenter.

Table 13-1 lists the default configuration of historical intervals at VC server, as documented in the VI SDK API reference.[3] The default levels are subject to change, and you can modify them in the VI Client connecting to the VirtualCenter by clicking Administration, VirtualCenter Management Server Configuration. Select Statistics from the left pane, and change these on the right pane. Beneath the configuration is the database size part, which shows how much data it uses in the database with the change.

---

[3] http://www.vmware.com/support/developer/vc-sdk/visdk25pubs/ReferenceGuide/vim. HistoricalInterval.html. It's actually different from what is observed in the VirtualCenter servers, which all default to level1.

Table 13-1

Default Historical Intervals Defined in the VC Server

Name	Sampling Period	Length	Level	Enabled
PastDay	300 (5 min)	86,400 (1 day)	4	True
PastWeek	1,800 (30 min)	604,800 (1 week)	4	True
PastMonth	7,200 (2 hour)	2,592,000 (30 days)	2	True
PastYear	86,400 (1 day)	31,536,000 (365 days)	2	True

Alternatively, you can change the interval setting with the `updatePerfInterval()` method, which is discussed in the final section of this chapter, "Configuring Historical Intervals."

Under the default settings, a VC server keeps all performance statistics counters (level 4 and above) at 5-minute intervals for the previous day and 30-minute intervals for the previous week. After one week, only counters at level 2 are stored at 2-hour intervals for the previous month and 1-day intervals for the previous year. All performance data older than one year is removed from the VirtualCenter database.

In ESX, there is only one historical interval `PastDay`, similar to the one in VirtualCenter except that you actually have a length of 129,600 (1.5 days), and the level is not set. Since ESX is the source of many performance statistics for VirtualCenter, longer history can help to guard against performance data loss caused by various issues.

As of SDK 2.5, you should neither create a new performance interval nor delete an existing one. You can change the existing intervals to some extent. The rule is a little complicated. In general, you should avoid changing the intervals as much as possible, with the exception of the levels.

Real-Time versus Historical Performance Statistics

The system has two categories of performance data. One is the raw performance samples collected at a pretty fast pace, such as every 20 seconds for a new sample. The interval can be found using the `queryPerfProviderSummary()` method and can vary from managed entity to managed entity. You cannot retrieve performance data more frequently than the real-time samples.

Given the fast pace, you have a one-hour time window to limit the total number of samples. When a new sample comes in, the oldest is removed.

The real-time samples are processed on a regular basis to generate the historical performance statistics with different intervals defined in PerfInterval. On ESX, only 5-minute interval statistics are supported, whereas on VirtualCenter four different intervals, as listed in Table 13-1, are pre-configured.

You can retrieve both the historical statistics and real-time samples using the same interfaces but with different combinations of arguments. You will see how to do both with samples shortly.

PerformanceManager Managed Object

This managed object provides all the services related to performance data. It has three properties, as listed in Table 13-2.

Table 13-2

Properties of PerformanceManager

Name	Type	Description
description	PerformanceDescription	The static description strings for rollup and statistic types enumeration. They can be used in user interfaces. They don't change and should be retrieved no more than once in your application.
historicalInterval	PerfInterval[]	All the configured historical intervals.
perfCounter	PerfCounterInfo[]	All supported performance counters in the system.

Retrieving the historicalInterval and perfCounter properties can provide good information on what performance counters can be collected and at what intervals. Listing 13-1 shows a sample that retrieves all these properties and prints them to the console.

Not all the properties change much, and you can cache them for looking up the detailed information locally. The performance counters, for example, are referenced with their keys. Caching them up can reduce both server workload and network traffic. In general, you shouldn't use them across different targets or persist them into local files or databases for later usage.

Listing 13-1

PrintPerfMgr.java

```java
package vim25.samples.mo.perf;
import java.net.URL;

import com.vmware.vim25.ElementDescription;
import com.vmware.vim25.PerfCounterInfo;
import com.vmware.vim25.PerfInterval;
import com.vmware.vim25.PerformanceDescription;
import com.vmware.vim25.mo.PerformanceManager;
import com.vmware.vim25.mo.ServiceInstance;

public class PrintPerfMgr
{
  public static void main(String[] args) throws Exception
  {
    if(args.length != 3)
    {
      System.out.println("Usage: java PrintPerfMgr"
        + "<url> <username> <password>");
      return;
    }

    ServiceInstance si = new ServiceInstance(
      new URL(args[0]), args[1], args[2], true);

    PerformanceManager perfMgr = si.getPerformanceManager();

    System.out.println("***Print All Descriptions:");
    PerformanceDescription pd = perfMgr.getDescription();
    printPerfDescription(pd);

    System.out.println("\n***Print All Historical Intervals:");
    PerfInterval[] pis = perfMgr.getHistoricalInterval();
    printPerfIntervals(pis);

    System.out.println("\n***Print All Perf Counters:");
    PerfCounterInfo[] pcis = perfMgr.getPerfCounter();
```

```
      printPerfCounters(pcis);

   si.getServerConnection().logout();
}


static void printPerfIntervals(PerfInterval[] pis)
{
   for(int i=0; pis!=null && i<pis.length; i++)
   {
      System.out.println("\nPerfInterval # " + i);
      StringBuffer sb = new StringBuffer();
      sb.append("Name:" + pis[i].getName());
      sb.append("\nKey:" + pis[i].getKey());
      sb.append("\nLevel:"+ pis[i].getLevel());
      sb.append("\nSamplingPeriod:" + pis[i].getSamplingPeriod());
      sb.append("\nLength:" + pis[i].getLength());
      sb.append("\nEnabled:" + pis[i].isEnabled());
      System.out.println(sb);
   }
}


static void printPerfCounters(PerfCounterInfo[] pcis)
{
   for(int i=0; pcis!=null && i<pcis.length; i++)
   {
      System.out.println("\nKey:" + pcis[i].getKey());
      String perfCounter = pcis[i].getGroupInfo().getKey() + "."
            + pcis[i].getNameInfo().getKey() + "."
            + pcis[i].getRollupType();
      System.out.println("PerfCounter:" + perfCounter);
      System.out.println("Level:" + pcis[i].getLevel());
      System.out.println("StatsType:" + pcis[i].getStatsType());
      System.out.println("UnitInfo:"
            + pcis[i].getUnitInfo().getKey());
   }
}


static void printPerfDescription(PerformanceDescription pd)
{
```

```
  ElementDescription[] eds = pd.getCounterType();
  printElementDescriptions(eds);

  ElementDescription[] statsTypes = pd.getStatsType();
  printElementDescriptions(statsTypes);
}

static void printElementDescriptions(ElementDescription[] eds)
{
  for(int i=0; eds!=null && i<eds.length; i++)
  {
    printElementDescription(eds[i]);
  }
}

static void printElementDescription(ElementDescription ed)
{
  System.out.println("\nKey:" + ed.getKey());
  System.out.println("Label:" + ed.getLabel());
  System.out.println("Summary:" + ed.getSummary());
  }
}
```

When the code runs against VirtualCenter, the following printouts show in the console. Most of the performance counters are not included given the size limit. The same code can run on ESX, but there will be only one historical performance counter, and a different key and no level will be set for the counter.

```
***Print All Descriptions:
Key:average
Label:Average
Summary:Average performance counter value collected

Key:maximum
Label:Maximum
Summary:Maximum performance counter value collected

Key:minimum
```

Label:Minimum
Summary:Minimum performance counter value collected

Key:latest
Label:Latest
Summary:Latest performance counter value collected

Key:summation
Label:Summation
Summary:Summation performance counter value collected

Key:none
Label:None
Summary:No rollup performed

Key:absolute
Label:Absolute
Summary:Absolute statistic collection

Key:delta
Label:Delta
Summary:Delta statistic collection

Key:rate
Label:Rate
Summary:Rate statistic collection

***Print All Historical Intervals:

PerfInterval # 0
Name:Past Day
Key:1
Level:1
SamplingPeriod:300
Length:86400
Enabled:true

PerfInterval # 1
Name:Past Week

```
Key:2
Level:1
SamplingPeriod:1800
Length:604800
Enabled:true
```

......

PerformanceManager has nine methods defined: createPerfInterval(), queryAvailablePerfMetric(), queryPerf(), queryPerfComposite(), queryPerfCounter(), queryPerfCounterByLevel, queryPerfProviderSummary(), removePerfInterval(), and updatePerfInterval().

Only two methods, queryPerf() and queryPerfComposite(), retrieve real performance data. All others are for querying metadata and configuring the performance collection behaviors.

Querying Performance Metadata

You can get several types of metadata from PerformanceManager, mainly the PerfProviderSummary, the performance counters, metrics, and intervals. You can also retrieve the performance counters and intervals from the properties defined in PerformanceManager.

Besides direct retrieving of properties of PerformanceManager, you can use the following methods for metadata:

- **queryPerfProviderSummary()** returns a PerfProviderSummary data object for a specific managed object that is capable of providing performance statistics. As shown in Figure 13-3, PerfProviderSummary provides a capability summary of the provider (for example, whether real-time statistics are provided and whether it supports summarized statistics). It also includes the previously mentioned refreshRate, which is the number of seconds between two updates of system statistics. All the intervals should be longer than this value.

PerfProviderSummary
+currentSupported : xsd:boolean
+entity : ManagedObjectReference
+refreshRate : xsd:int
+summarySupported : xsd:boolean

Figure 13-3   PerfProviderSummary data object

- `queryPerfCounter()` looks up the `PerfCounterInfo` array based on an array of counter IDs. It provides convenience over retrieving all the `PerfCounterInfo` using the `perfCounter` property defined on `PerformanceManager`. If you need to look up a lot, you should cache `PerfCounterInfo` and look up locally.

- `queryPerfCounterByLevel()` is another convenient method to look up `PerfCounterInfo` by the level. Both this and `queryPerfCounter()` return an array of `PerfCounterInfo` objects. As mentioned, level is not set on ESX, so this method is not useful there.

- `queryAvailablePerfMetric()` retrieves available performance metrics for the specified managed object between beginning time and end time at an optional interval. These metrics are needed while creating a `PerfQuerySpec` object to further limit the retrieved result.

  If the interval is not provided, the system returns available metrics for historical statistics. If the end time is omitted, it defaults to the time of the most recent metric. If the beginning time is omitted, the system defaults to the time of the oldest available metric in the system.

Querying Performance Statistics

There are two methods to query performance data: `queryPerf()` and `queryPerfComposite()`. The first method queries the managed entities; the second method queries not only the managed entities but also their child entities.

Using the `queryPerf` Method

The `queryPerf()` method takes in an array of `PerfQuerySpec` objects and returns an array of `PerfEntityMetricBase` objects. As shown in Figure 13-4, `PerfQuerySpec` has seven properties, each of which specifies one criterion, such as the starting time and ending time,[4] the interval, the maximum number of samples, the managed entity for which the performance data is retrieved, and the format. The managed entity can only be host, virtual machine, cluster, and resource pool. The starting time, if specified, must be earlier than the ending time. The intervals must be one of the historical intervals or the real-time refresh rate.

---

[4] You should use the time corresponding to the server, not the time from your client. The time is ignored in real-time case.

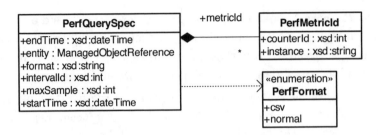

Figure 13-4   `PerfQuerySpec` and related data objects

All seven properties except the entity are optional. When omitted, they default to a value with rules in Table 13-3.

Table 13-3

Default Value of Properties in `PerfQuerySpec`	
Name	**Default Value When Omitted**
startTime	The time of the first available metric. When `startTime` is specified, the returned samples do not include the sample at `startTime`.
endTime	The time of the most recent metric. When `endTime` is specified, the returned samples include the sample at `endTime`. Note: Unlike `startTime`, `endTime` must not be out of the boundary of available historical data, and it must be later than `startTime`.
Format	The format of returned performance data. Can be either normal or "csv."
intervalId	The interval of the samples, for example, 300—PastDay.
maxSample	This parameter should be used only when querying for real-time statistics by setting the `intervalId` parameter to the provider's `refreshRate`. If the user specifies a `maxSample` of 1 but not a given time range, the most recent sample collected is returned.
metricId	All the metrics available on the entity. Sometime it cannot be omitted, or `InvaidArgumentFault` is thrown.

The `format` property is important here because it specifies the returned data type. The valid string is either `csv` or `normal`. When it's not specified, it defaults to `normal`. Because the returned data result format depends on this argument, you should handle your result accordingly. In general, the comma-separated values (CSV)[5] format requires less serialization/deserialization and conversion, so it performs better than the normal format. Consider CSV over the normal array format whenever possible.

The return type `PerfEntityMetricBase` is a supertype that is extended by two subtypes—`PerfEntityMetric` and `PerfEntityMetricCSV`—as shown in Figure 13-5. The returned objects are either one of the subtypes depending on what format you specified in the `PerfQuerySpec` parameter.

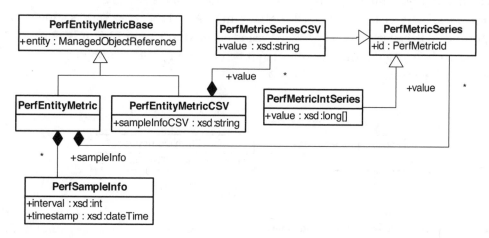

Figure 13-5   The `PerfEntityMetricBase` and related data objects

To get something meaningful, you have to cast the returned object to either subtype. These two subtypes are different presentations of the same set of data. Note that `PerfEntityMetric` holds a reference to `PerfMetricSeries`, meaning the real object could be either `PerfMetricIntSeries`[6] or `PerfMetricSeriesCSV`.

`PerfEntityMetricCSV` contains only `PerfMetricSeriesCSV`. The data inside `PerfEntityMetricCSV` is CSV which is widely used by spreadsheet and database applications. You can export the data as it is or parse it. The `sampleInfoCSV` holds the metainformation of the samples with both the intervals and time like the following. Note that this CSV string has twice as many items in the value string.

---

[5] http://en.wikipedia.org/wiki/Comma-separated_values

[6] Note: `PerfMetricIntSeries` actually holds an array of long integer instead of normal integer.

```
20,2008-11-05T06:18:40-08:00,20,2008-11-05T06:19:00-08:00,20,2008-11-05T06:19:20-
08:00
```

While navigating the results for the information, you need to watch out for the type. Always check the real type before you cast it.

Using the `queryPerfComposite` Method

The `queryPerfComposite()` method gets the aggregated performance statistics for a managed entity. It takes in one `PerfQuerySpec` object and returns a `PerfCompositeMetric` object. The UML diagram of `PerfCompositeMetric` is shown in Figure 13-6. Because `PerfEntityMetricBase` is covered in Figure 13-5, it is not expanded here. Again, the real object can be either one of the subtypes of `PerfEntityMetricBase`.

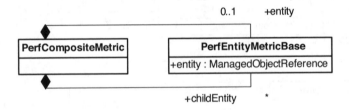

Figure 13-6   The `PerfCompositeMetric` data object

The `entity` is the aggregated statistics, and the `childEntity` is the list of statistics for the entities contained in the aggregated entity. This data structure implies that you can get only one level down from a managed entity for the performance data.

Listing 13-2 shows a sample that uses the `queryPerfComposite()` method to retrieve performance metrics from multiple managed entities. The sample first gets the virtual machine whose name is provided in the command-line parameter and goes up to the host on which the virtual machine is running. Then it retrieves performance data of the host and all the virtual machines associated with it. If there are no metrics during the search period for an entity, the entity is still included in the result but with no performance data.

This sample runs only against VirtualCenter because the `PastWeek` interval is not supported on ESX. But you can change the interval to 300 (`PastDay`) to retrieve historical data on ESX.

Listing 13-2
GetMultiPerf.java

```java
package vim25.samples.mo.perf;
import java.net.URL;
import java.util.Calendar;

import com.vmware.vim25.PerfCompositeMetric;
import com.vmware.vim25.PerfEntityMetric;
import com.vmware.vim25.PerfEntityMetricBase;
import com.vmware.vim25.PerfEntityMetricCSV;
import com.vmware.vim25.PerfMetricId;
import com.vmware.vim25.PerfMetricIntSeries;
import com.vmware.vim25.PerfMetricSeries;
import com.vmware.vim25.PerfMetricSeriesCSV;
import com.vmware.vim25.PerfQuerySpec;
import com.vmware.vim25.PerfSampleInfo;
import com.vmware.vim25.mo.InventoryNavigator;
import com.vmware.vim25.mo.PerformanceManager;
import com.vmware.vim25.mo.ServiceInstance;
import com.vmware.vim25.mo.VirtualMachine;

public class GetMultiPerf
{
  public static void main(String[] args) throws Exception
  {
    if(args.length != 4)
    {
      System.out.println("Usage: java GetMultiPerf "
        + "<url> <username> <password> <vmname>");
      return;
    }

    ServiceInstance si = new ServiceInstance(
      new URL(args[0]), args[1], args[2], true);

    String vmname = args[3];
    VirtualMachine vm = (VirtualMachine) new InventoryNavigator(
      si.getRootFolder()).searchManagedEntity(
```

```
      "VirtualMachine", vmname);

  if(vm == null)
  {
    System.out.println("Virtual Machine " + vmname
        + " cannot be found.");
    si.getServerConnection().logout();
    return;
  }


  PerformanceManager perfMgr = si.getPerformanceManager();


  int perfInterval = 1800; // 30 minutes for PastWeek


  // retrieve all the available perf metrics for vm
  PerfMetricId[] pmis = perfMgr.queryAvailablePerfMetric(
      vm, null, null, perfInterval);


  Calendar curTime = si.currentTime();


  PerfQuerySpec qSpec = new PerfQuerySpec();
  qSpec.setEntity(vm.getRuntime().getHost());
  //metricIDs must be provided, or InvalidArgumentFault
  qSpec.setMetricId(pmis);
  qSpec.setFormat("normal"); //optional since it's default
  qSpec.setIntervalId(perfInterval);


  Calendar startTime = (Calendar) curTime.clone();
  startTime.roll(Calendar.DATE, -4);
  System.out.println("start:" + startTime.getTime());
  qSpec.setStartTime(startTime);


  Calendar endTime = (Calendar) curTime.clone();
  endTime.roll(Calendar.DATE, -3);
  System.out.println("end:" + endTime.getTime());
  qSpec.setEndTime(endTime);


  PerfCompositeMetric pv = perfMgr.queryPerfComposite(qSpec);
  if(pv != null)
```

```
    {
      printPerfMetric(pv.getEntity());
      PerfEntityMetricBase[] pembs = pv.getChildEntity();
      for(int i=0; pembs!=null && i< pembs.length; i++)
      {
        printPerfMetric(pembs[i]);
      }
    }
    si.getServerConnection().logout();
}

static void printPerfMetric(PerfEntityMetricBase val)
{
    String entityDesc = val.getEntity().getType()
        + ":" + val.getEntity().get_value();
    System.out.println("Entity:" + entityDesc);
    if(val instanceof PerfEntityMetric)
    {
      printPerfMetric((PerfEntityMetric)val);
    }
    else if(val instanceof PerfEntityMetricCSV)
    {
      printPerfMetricCSV((PerfEntityMetricCSV)val);
    }
    else
    {
      System.out.println("UnExpected sub-type of " +
        "PerfEntityMetricBase.");
    }
}

static void printPerfMetric(PerfEntityMetric pem)
{
  PerfMetricSeries[] vals = pem.getValue();
  PerfSampleInfo[]  infos = pem.getSampleInfo();

  System.out.println("Sampling Times and Intervales:");
  for(int i=0; infos!=null && i<infos.length; i++)
  {
```

```
      System.out.println("sample time: "
        + infos[i].getTimestamp().getTime());
      System.out.println("sample interval (sec):"
        + infos[i].getInterval());
  }


  System.out.println("\nSample values:");
  for(int j=0; vals!=null && j<vals.length; ++j)
  {
    System.out.println("Perf counter ID:"
        + vals[j].getId().getCounterId());
    System.out.println("Device instance ID:"
        + vals[j].getId().getInstance());

    if(vals[j] instanceof PerfMetricIntSeries)
    {
      PerfMetricIntSeries val = (PerfMetricIntSeries) vals[j];
      long[] longs = val.getValue();
      for(int k=0; k<longs.length; k++)
      {
        System.out.print(longs[k] + " ");
      }
      System.out.println("Total:"+longs.length);
    }
    else if(vals[j] instanceof PerfMetricSeriesCSV)
    { // it is not likely coming here...
      PerfMetricSeriesCSV val = (PerfMetricSeriesCSV) vals[j];
      System.out.println("CSV value:" + val.getValue());
    }
  }
}


static void printPerfMetricCSV(PerfEntityMetricCSV pems)
{
  System.out.println("SampleInfoCSV:"
      + pems.getSampleInfoCSV());
  PerfMetricSeriesCSV[] csvs = pems.getValue();
  for(int i=0; i<csvs.length; i++)
  {
    System.out.println("PerfCounterId:"
```

```
            + csvs[i].getId().getCounterId());
        System.out.println("CSV sample values:"
            + csvs[i].getValue());
    }
  }
}
```

> Try to keep performance measurement and retrieval from impacting server perform-
> ance. Depending on the query specification, the performance data could be huge, and
> retrieving it could cause performance problems. For better performance of the target
> server and your application, retrieve this data only when really necessary; limit your
> retrieval results only to the entities and their metrics you really want, to the smallest
> time period you really care about, and to the coarsest grain you can accept.
>
> Format wise, consider CSV format over the normal array. For the same performance
> data, you should retrieve it once and save it locally to avoid second retrieval.

Monitoring Performance in Real Time

The raw performance data is collected at a pace that the provider defines. You can
easily find the frequency by calling the `queryPerfProviderSummary()` method. Just
check out the `refreshRate` property in the returned `PerfProviderSummary` data
object. It's defined as an integer representing the interval in seconds between two
samples.

As mentioned earlier, because raw performance data is collected at a fast pace,
the system has a window of 1 hour for this data. When a new sample comes in,
the oldest sample is pushed out. The number of samples available is limited. For
example, if the refresh rate of the virtual machine is 20 seconds, the maximum
number of samples is 180.[7] If you specify a number bigger than the maximum in
the `PerfQuerySpec`, the server returns just the maximum samples.

The real trick for real-time monitoring is setting up `intervalId` in the
`PerfQuerySpec` exactly as the refresh rate of the managed entity. `intervalId` is a
tricky property in that you must set it to either refresh rate or one of the historical

---

[7] 20s×180 = 3600S, equivalent to 1-hour time window for raw samples.

intervals; otherwise, the server rejects the API call by throwing an
InvalidArgumentFault.

Listing 13-3 shows a sample code to monitor all the real-time performance data
of a virtual machine. It collects the data every minute for three performance samples for each metric.

Listing 13-3
RealtimePerfMonitor.java

```java
package vim25.samples.mo.perf;
import java.net.URL;

import com.vmware.vim25.PerfEntityMetric;
import com.vmware.vim25.PerfEntityMetricBase;
import com.vmware.vim25.PerfEntityMetricCSV;
import com.vmware.vim25.PerfMetricId;
import com.vmware.vim25.PerfMetricIntSeries;
import com.vmware.vim25.PerfMetricSeries;
import com.vmware.vim25.PerfMetricSeriesCSV;
import com.vmware.vim25.PerfProviderSummary;
import com.vmware.vim25.PerfQuerySpec;
import com.vmware.vim25.PerfSampleInfo;
import com.vmware.vim25.mo.InventoryNavigator;
import com.vmware.vim25.mo.ManagedEntity;
import com.vmware.vim25.mo.PerformanceManager;
import com.vmware.vim25.mo.ServiceInstance;

public class RealtimePerfMonitor
{
  public static void main(String[] args) throws Exception
  {
    if(args.length != 4)
    {
      System.out.println("Usage: java RealtimePerfMonitor "
        + "<url> <username> <password> <vmname>");
      return;
    }

    ServiceInstance si = new ServiceInstance(
```

```
    new URL(args[0]), args[1], args[2], true);

  String vmname = args[3];
  ManagedEntity vm = new InventoryNavigator(
    si.getRootFolder()).searchManagedEntity(
      "VirtualMachine", vmname);
  if(vm == null)
  {
    System.out.println("Virtual Machine " + vmname
        + " cannot be found.");
    si.getServerConnection().logout();
    return;
  }

  PerformanceManager perfMgr = si.getPerformanceManager();

  // find out the refresh rate for the virtual machine
  PerfProviderSummary pps = perfMgr.queryPerfProviderSummary(vm);
  int refreshRate = pps.getRefreshRate().intValue();

  // retrieve all the available perf metrics for vm
  PerfMetricId[] pmis = perfMgr.queryAvailablePerfMetric(
      vm, null, null, refreshRate);

  PerfQuerySpec qSpec = createPerfQuerySpec(
      vm, pmis, 3, refreshRate);

  while(true)
  {
    PerfEntityMetricBase[] pValues = perfMgr.queryPerf(
      new PerfQuerySpec[] {qSpec});
    if(pValues != null)
    {
      displayValues(pValues);
    }
    System.out.println("Sleeping 60 seconds...");
    Thread.sleep(refreshRate*3*1000);
  }
}
```

```java
static PerfQuerySpec createPerfQuerySpec(ManagedEntity me,
    PerfMetricId[] metricIds, int maxSample, int interval)
{
  PerfQuerySpec qSpec = new PerfQuerySpec();
  qSpec.setEntity(me.getMOR());
  // set the maximum of metrics to be returned
  // only appropriate in real-time performance collecting
  qSpec.setMaxSample(new Integer(maxSample));
  qSpec.setMetricId(metricIds);
  // optionally you can set format as "normal"
  qSpec.setFormat("csv");
  // set the interval to the refresh rate for the entity
  qSpec.setIntervalId(new Integer(interval));

  return qSpec;
}


static void displayValues(PerfEntityMetricBase[] values)
{
  for(int i=0; i<values.length; ++i)
  {
    String entityDesc = values[i].getEntity().getType()
        + ":" + values[i].getEntity().get_value();
    System.out.println("Entity:" + entityDesc);
    if(values[i] instanceof PerfEntityMetric)
    {
      printPerfMetric((PerfEntityMetric)values[i]);
    }
    else if(values[i] instanceof PerfEntityMetricCSV)
    {
      printPerfMetricCSV((PerfEntityMetricCSV)values[i]);
    }
    else
    {
      System.out.println("UnExpected sub-type of " +
              "PerfEntityMetricBase.");
    }
  }
}
```

```
static void printPerfMetric(PerfEntityMetric pem)
{
  PerfMetricSeries[] vals = pem.getValue();
  PerfSampleInfo[]  infos = pem.getSampleInfo();

  System.out.println("Sampling Times and Intervales:");
  for(int i=0; infos!=null && i <infos.length; i++)
  {
    System.out.println("Sample time: "
        + infos[i].getTimestamp().getTime());
    System.out.println("Sample interval (sec):"
        + infos[i].getInterval());
  }
  System.out.println("Sample values:");
  for(int j=0; vals!=null && j<vals.length; ++j)
  {
    System.out.println("Perf counter ID:"
        + vals[j].getId().getCounterId());
    System.out.println("Device instance ID:"
        + vals[j].getId().getInstance());

    if(vals[j] instanceof PerfMetricIntSeries)
    {
      PerfMetricIntSeries val = (PerfMetricIntSeries) vals[j];
      long[] longs = val.getValue();
      for(int k=0; k<longs.length; k++)
      {
        System.out.print(longs[k] + " ");
      }
      System.out.println("Total:"+longs.length);
    }
    else if(vals[j] instanceof PerfMetricSeriesCSV)
    { // it is not likely coming here...
      PerfMetricSeriesCSV val = (PerfMetricSeriesCSV) vals[j];
      System.out.println("CSV value:" + val.getValue());
    }
  }
}
```

```
static void printPerfMetricCSV(PerfEntityMetricCSV pems)
{
  System.out.println("SampleInfoCSV:"
      + pems.getSampleInfoCSV());
  PerfMetricSeriesCSV[] csvs = pems.getValue();
  for(int i=0; i<csvs.length; i++)
  {
    System.out.println("PerfCounterId:"
        + csvs[i].getId().getCounterId());
    System.out.println("CSV sample values:"
        + csvs[i].getValue());
  }
}
}
```

Part of the printouts look like the following:[8]

```
Entity:VirtualMachine:128
SampleInfoCSV:20,2008-11-05T06:18:40-08:00,20,2008-11-05T06:19:00-08:00,20,2008-
11-05T06:19:20-08:00
PerfCounterId:131078
CSV sample values:0,0,0
...
PerfCounterId:196612
CSV sample values:262,205,241
...
```

The sample prints out the performance counter ID, but you can easily look up the performance counter information based on the ID. You can use two approaches: employ the queryPerfCounter() method, or first retrieve the perfCounter for all the performance counters and then look up locally. If you look up performance counters quite often, the latter is preferred because it saves you network traffic and should be much faster.

---

[8] It ran against an ESX server 3.5. 196612 is the counter ID for net.packetsRx.summation, and 131078 is the counter ID for disk.read.average. It works with VirtualCenter as it is, but the performance counter ID will be different.

When `PerfQuerySpec` is created in the `createPerfQuerySpec()` method, the `metricId` can be omitted because it defaults to all the performance metrics when not set. But it is included to make it explicit. You can easily change the sample to limit the metrics to the subset in which you are interested.

You don't want to collect performance data too often or get more than what you really need. That would hurt server performance because serving performance query costs system resources like CPU and bandwidth. This is especially true for this real time performance data collecting.

Configuring Historical Intervals

You can configure the performance intervals using `updatePerfInterval()` in SDK 2.5. Previous methods `createPerfInterval()` and `removePerfInterval()` are deprecated as of 2.5, so you cannot create new and remove existing historical intervals. The deprecated methods are not covered here.

You use the `updatePerfInterval()` method to modify the current intervals. It takes in the `PerfInterval` parameter and returns `none`. As shown in Figure 13-2, `PerfInterval` has six properties. With the `PerfInterval` parameter, you can change any of the following:

- The sampling period of the `PastDay` interval can be reduced from 5 minutes to 1, 2, or 3 minutes (60, 120, or 180 in value, respectively).

- The length of the `PastDay` interval can be increased from 1 day up to 3 days (259,200 in value).

- The length of the `PastYear` interval can be increased from 1 year up to 3 years (94,608,000 in value).

- The statistics level of an interval can be changed. However, the level of a smaller historical interval cannot be less than the level of a larger historical interval. For example, you cannot change the `PastDay` level to 1 if the `PastWeek` level is 2.

- An interval can be enabled or disabled.

The last change works in some ways like removing the interval. Note that when an interval is disabled, all the higher intervals are also disabled because a higher interval relies on statistics of its lower interval as input data source.

The performance intervals are highly coupled; therefore, adding and removing an interval can be error prone. That explains why the two methods are deprecated as of SDK 2.5.

Summary

This chapter introduced the basic concepts in performance management using the VI SDK. Then it discussed `PerformanceManager`, which is the singleton managed object in focus in this chapter. You learned how to retrieve the performance metadata and statistics, how to monitor performance in real time, and how to manage the intervals. You also learned tips for better-performing performance management.

Chapter 14

Task and
ScheduledTask

This chapter introduces tasks and scheduled tasks. It describes how to manage and monitor tasks, how to retrieve results from asynchronized API calls, and how to retrieve historical tasks. The introduction of task management covers three managed objects: Task, which represents a running operation; TaskManager, which manages the Task objects; and TaskHistoryCollector, which provides interfaces to retrieve previous tasks.

The second half of this chapter introduces how to schedule an operation to run in the future, once or repetitively. ScheduledTask represents a scheduled task to be activated in the future. ScheduledTaskManager manages all the ScheduledTask objects.

Managed Objects: Task, TaskManager, TaskHistoryCollector, ScheduledTask, ScheduledTaskManager

Task Managed Object

Task is an important managed object. For each command execution or method invocation on the server, a corresponding Task is created. Most Task objects are not exposed to the client directly as a result of method invocation, simply because they take almost no time to finish; therefore, it's meaningless to track progress. To get hold of these hidden Task objects, you need the TaskManager managed object, which is discussed in the next section.

It's a different story for a long-running method invocation, such as cloning a virtual machine. Whenever there is a long-time operation on the server side, a Task object is returned. As a naming convention, these methods normally have _Task suffixes in their names. In VI SDK 2.5, more than 50 such methods are defined with various managed objects.

As you would expect for a long-running method, you can monitor the progress and even cancel the operation if needed. These options are made possible with the Task managed object.

The Task managed object has only one property info of TaskInfo type. Figure 14-1 shows the data structure of TaskInfo.

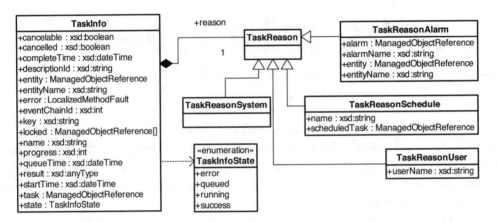

Figure 14-1   TaskInfo and related data objects

As shown in Figure 14-1, the TaskInfo data object has many variables, including whether it's cancelable, whether it has been canceled, the task state, progress, completeTime, started time, associated managed entity, locked managed entities, and reason for running the task.

The TaskReason is a superclass for other four subclasses, each of which represents a specific reason for the Task to run, started automatically by the system (TaskReasonSystem), initiated by a user (TaskReasonUser), fired in response to an alarm (TaskReasonAlarm), or started as a scheduled task (TaskReasonSchedule).

Another important subproperty in TaskInfo is result, whose type is defined as anyType. As its type suggests, it could be any type of data. But why is it defined as any type? Because it must be able to hold many types of data objects as a result. The typical use case is for a long operation that is supposed to return a result besides success or failure when it's done. The long operation returns a Task without waiting, so the result has to be attached to the Task object when it's done. That is the only clue for the client to get a result. Defining it as any type makes life easier, but not so when you use it. Methods have different result types. Check out the API reference for help in figuring out what type you should cast to.

One example of using the result variable is the createVM_Task() method, which returns a Task immediately. When it's done, the virtual machine's ManagedObjectReference is stored in the result. Another example is searchDatastoreSubFolders_Task, defined with HostDatastoreBrowser, which stores the HostDatastoreBrowserSearchResults in the result.

When you want to retrieve the result in this way, check the API reference to find out what the real type is supposed to be for the result property for the long-running operation and cast it accordingly in your application. (Listing 14-1 shows how to get the TaskInfo from a Task and access its properties.)

Three methods are defined with the Task: cancelTask(), setTaskState(), and updateProgress(). The last two methods are really for server-side extensions, not for client applications. Such a server extension can use the interfaces to update the Task so that any VI Client or VI SDK application can monitor the task.

Upon completion, a Task object is valid for about 10 minutes. After that, it's disposed and its property is persisted into the database. Although you still have the ManagedObjectReference to it, do not use it. Instead, retrieve it as one of the historical tasks using the TaskHistoryCollector managed object, which is introduced in the section, "Retrieving Historical Tasks with TaskHistoryCollector."

Monitoring a Task

You can monitor the status of a task by polling its info property, which lets you further examine the subproperty state for the overall state of the task, and the subproperty progress for the percentage of work done. From the info property, you can also find other information (such as what time the task started, what managed entity the task is related to, and so on). Refer to Figure 14-1 for the details.

Canceling a Task

You can cancel a running or queued task by invoking `cancelTask()`. Multiple cancel requests are treated as a single cancelation request. Canceling a completed or already canceled task has no effect on the task.

After a task is canceled, its `info.state` property is set to `error`, and `info.error` includes a `RequestCanceled` fault. The `cancelTask()` operation is asynchronous and may return before the task is canceled.

A task might not be canceled if it is marked as not cancelable with the `info.cancelable` property as `false`.

Fixing Task Timeout

If a task takes too long (for example, more than 15 minutes to create a virtual machine snapshot from VirtualCenter), it can time out before it finishes.

You can easily fix this issue by changing the configurations. On the ESX server, add the following to the `/etc/opt/vmware/vpxa/vpxa.cfg` file:

```
<task>
<timeout>7200</timeout>
</task>
```

and

```
<vmomi>
<soapStubAdapter>
<blockingTimeoutSeconds>7200</blockingTimeoutSeconds>
</soapStubAdapter>
</vmomi>
```

Remember to restart the service:

```
$ service vmware-vpxa restart
```

On the VirtualCenter server, add the following to the `C:\Documents and Settings\All Users\Application Data\VMware\VMware VirtualCenter\vpxd.cfg` file:

```
<task>
```

```
<timeout>7200</timeout>
</task>

<vmomi>
<soapStubAdapter>
<blockingTimeoutSeconds>7200</blockingTimeoutSeconds>
</soapStubAdapter>
</vmomi>
```

After you save the configuration file, don't forget to restart the VMware VirtualCenter Server service from the Control Panel.

The change increases the timeout to 2 hours, and you can increase it as needed.

TaskManager Managed Object

TaskManager is a singleton managed object closely attached to ServiceInstance. It's intended to track all the tasks executed on the specific server.

TaskManager has three properties, which are defined in Table 14-1. The recentTask property shows you recent tasks that have happened on the server.

Table 14-1

Properties Defined in TaskManager		
Name	**Type**	**Explanation**
description	TaskDescription	Static descriptive strings used to represent task information to users. These strings, except the keys, are locale-specific. You should use them instead of localizing by yourself.
		The contents of the property normally don't change, so you only need to retrieve it once in each session. More descriptive strings can be added by server extensions using ExtensionManager.

continues...

Table 14-1   continued

Properties Defined in TaskManager

Name	Type	Explanation
maxCollector	xsd:int	For each client, the maximum number of task collectors that can exist simultaneously. It's 32 on VirtualCenter and 0 on ESX. You cannot create a collector on ESX.
recentTask	ManagedObjectReference[] to Task[]	Tasks that completed recently, are currently running, or are queued to run. A task is only "recent" for about 10 minutes upon completion.
		This list contains only tasks visible to the client. Visibility depends on the login user's permissions to access the task's managed entity.

TaskManager is not the only managed object from which you can get Task objects. The ManagedEntity type also contains a property called recentTask. You can retrieve that property of an entity for the recent tasks on it, which are a subset of what TaskManager gives you.

The TaskManager has two methods defined.

- **createCollectorForTasks()** creates a TaskHistoryCollector object with which you can retrieve the historical data regarding previous tasks. You can provide a TaskFilterSpec to filter out only what you really want. This method is implemented only on VirtualCenter, not ESX. NotImplementedFault is thrown if the method is called against ESX.

- **createTask()** creates a new Task with parameters such as target object, task type, initiator of the task, and whether the task is cancelable. It doesn't return a ManagedObjectReference as you might expect, but a TaskInfo object. Because TaskInfo has a property holding ManagedObjectReference pointing back to the Task object, it is even better. Again, the createTask() method is intended for the server-side extension, not for a typical client application.

Listing 14-1 shows a sample that prints all the properties of the TaskManager, including the maximum number of historical task collectors, task descriptions, and recent tasks.

Listing 14-1
PrintTaskManager.java

```java
package vim25.samples.mo.task;
import java.net.URL;

import com.vmware.vim25.ElementDescription;
import com.vmware.vim25.TaskDescription;
import com.vmware.vim25.TaskInfo;
import com.vmware.vim25.TypeDescription;
import com.vmware.vim25.mo.ServiceInstance;
import com.vmware.vim25.mo.Task;
import com.vmware.vim25.mo.TaskManager;

public class PrintTaskManager
{
  public static void main(String[] args) throws Exception
  {
    if(args.length != 3)
    {
      System.out.println("Usage: java PrintTaskManager "
        + "<url> <username> <password>");
      return;
    }

    ServiceInstance si = new ServiceInstance(
      new URL(args[0]), args[1], args[2], true);

    TaskManager taskMgr = si.getTaskManager();

    int maxCollector = taskMgr.getMaxCollector();
    System.out.println("Maximum number of collectors to " +
      "retrieve historical tasks: " + maxCollector);
```

```java
      System.out.println("\nTask description:");
      TaskDescription td = taskMgr.getDescription();
      printTaskDescription(td);

      System.out.println("\nRecent tasks:");
      Task[] recentTasks = taskMgr.getRecentTasks();
      for(int i=0; recentTasks!=null && i<recentTasks.length; i++)
      {
        TaskInfo ti = recentTasks[i].getTaskInfo();
        System.out.println("\nName:" + ti.getName());
        System.out.println("Key:" + ti.getKey());
        System.out.println("State:" + ti.getState());
      }
      si.getServerConnection().logout();
    }

    static void printTaskDescription(TaskDescription td)
    {
      ElementDescription[] methodInfos = td.getMethodInfo();
      System.out.println("\n***Method descriptions:" + methodInfos.length);
      printElementDescriptions(methodInfos);

      System.out.println("\n***Reason descriptions:");
      TypeDescription[] reasons = td.getReason();
      for(int i=0; reasons!=null && i<reasons.length; i++)
      {
        System.out.println("\nKey:" + reasons[i].getKey());
        System.out.println("Label:" + reasons[i].getLabel());
        System.out.println("Summary:" + reasons[i].getSummary());
      }

      System.out.println("\n***Task state enum descriptions:");
      ElementDescription[] states = td.getState();
      printElementDescriptions(states);
    }

    static void printElementDescriptions(ElementDescription[] eds)
    {
```

414

```
   for(int i=0; eds!=null && i<eds.length; i++)
   {
     printElementDescription(eds[i]);
   }
 }

 static void printElementDescription(ElementDescription ed)
 {
   System.out.println("\nKey:" + ed.getKey());
   System.out.println("Label:" + ed.getLabel());
   System.out.println("Summary:" + ed.getSummary());
 }
}
```

When Listing 14-1 runs, it prints out several hundred (400+) method descriptions similar to the following:

```
Key:TaskManager.createCollector
Label:Create Task Collector
Summary:Creates a task collector to retrieve all tasks that have executed on the
server based on a filter
```

From its key, you can tell that it's related to the `createCollectorForTasks()` method, but the name is slightly different. Most of the time, the keys have a common pattern with managed object name plus method name. In some other cases, the key pattern is different.

```
Key:alarm.AlarmManager.getAlarm
Label:Retrieve Alarm
Summary:Get available alarms defined on the entity
```

The descriptions for the reasons and state enumeration are all listed here:

```
***Reason descriptions:
Key:TaskReasonSystem
Label:System Task
Summary:Task started by the server
```

```
Key:TaskReasonSchedule
Label:Scheduled Task
Summary:Task started by a scheduled task


Key:TaskReasonAlarm
Label:Alarm Task
Summary:Task started by an alarm


Key:TaskReasonUser
Label:User Task
Summary:Task started by a specific user


***Task state enum descriptions:


Key:queued
Label:Queued
Summary:Task is queued


Key:running
Label:Running
Summary:Task is in progress


Key:success
Label:Success
Summary:Task completed successful


Key:error
Label:Error
Summary:Task completed with a failure
```

Retrieving Historical Tasks with `TaskHistoryCollector`

The `TaskHistoryCollector` managed object retrieves historical tasks. It is a subtype of `HistoryCollector`, and it is returned by the `createCollectorForTasks()` method defined with `TaskManager`. As mentioned earlier, `createCollectorForTasks()` is not supported on ESX, so neither is `TaskHistoryCollector`.

You can specify the criteria to filter out only the `Task` objects you want. After the object is returned, however, you cannot change your selection again. But you can always create new collector objects with new criteria. There is a limitation on how many collectors you can have at a time as specified in the maxCollector property in TaskManager, which defaults to 32 on VirtualCenter. So it's always a good practice to destroy the collectors no longer needed with the inherited destroyCollector() method.

HistoryCollector was discussed in Chapter 12 in the section "HistoryCollector Managed Object." If you haven't read the section, read it before you continue this chapter.

Going back to Figure 12-3 in Chapter 12, the TaskHistoryCollector is similar to its peer type EventHistoryCollector.

TaskHistoryCollector has one property, lastestPage, defined as TaskInfo[]. The array holds the TaskInfo objects of the latest Tasks that satisfy the criteria specified when the collector is created. The maximum length of the array defaults to 10 and can be changed via the setCollectorPageSize() method.

> You can only change the maximum length of the array to a number from 10 to 62, and higher than the current value. Any number outside this range sets it to either a lower or upper limit. For example, if you set the limit to 100, the real maximum length will be 62, and then you cannot lower it.

The TaskHistoryCollector has two methods: readNextTasks() and readPreviousTasks(). Both methods take in an integer parameter to specify the maximum TaskInfo objects to be returned and return an array of TaskInfo objects.

In some sense, TaskHistoryCollector works like an Internet search engine in that the viewable result page can be clicked forward and backward as needed.

Listing 14-2 shows you how to retrieve all the historical tasks that were successfully run by the administrator or system against all the inventory entities within the past month. The tasks in the latest page are printed twice, just to illustrate the related APIs. In the end, the sample prints the total number of historical tasks. You can modify the code to factor in any criteria in your applications.

Listing 14-2
TaskHistoryMonitor.java

```
package vim25.samples.mo.task;
package vim25.samples.mo.task;
```

```java
import java.net.URL;
import java.util.Calendar;
import java.util.Date;

import com.vmware.vim25.TaskFilterSpec;
import com.vmware.vim25.TaskFilterSpecByEntity;
import com.vmware.vim25.TaskFilterSpecByTime;
import com.vmware.vim25.TaskFilterSpecByUsername;
import com.vmware.vim25.TaskFilterSpecRecursionOption;
import com.vmware.vim25.TaskFilterSpecTimeOption;
import com.vmware.vim25.TaskInfo;
import com.vmware.vim25.TaskInfoState;
import com.vmware.vim25.TaskReason;
import com.vmware.vim25.TaskReasonAlarm;
import com.vmware.vim25.TaskReasonSchedule;
import com.vmware.vim25.TaskReasonSystem;
import com.vmware.vim25.TaskReasonUser;
import com.vmware.vim25.mo.Folder;
import com.vmware.vim25.mo.ManagedEntity;
import com.vmware.vim25.mo.ServiceInstance;
import com.vmware.vim25.mo.TaskHistoryCollector;
import com.vmware.vim25.mo.TaskManager;

public class TaskHistoryMonitor
{
  public static void main(String[] args) throws Exception
  {
    if(args.length != 3)
    {
      System.out.println("Usage: java TaskHistoryMonitor "
        + "<url> <username> <password>");
      return;
    }

    ServiceInstance si = new ServiceInstance(
      new URL(args[0]), args[1], args[2], true);

    TaskManager taskMgr = si.getTaskManager();
```

```java
    if(taskMgr!=null)
    {
      Folder root = si.getRootFolder();
      TaskFilterSpec tfs = createTaskFilterSpec(root);
      TaskHistoryCollector thc =
          taskMgr.createCollectorForTasks(tfs);

      // Note: 10 <= pagesize <= 62
      thc.setCollectorPageSize(15);

      System.out.println("Tasks in latestPage:");
      TaskInfo[] tis = thc.getLatestPage();
      printTaskInfos(tis);

      System.out.println("\nAll tasks:");
      int total = 0;

      while(true)
      {
        tis= thc.readNextTasks(50);
        if(tis==null)
        {
          break;
        }
        total += tis.length;
        printTaskInfos(tis);
      }
      System.out.println("\nTotal number " +
        "of tasks retrieved:" + total);
      thc.destroyCollector();
    }
    si.getServerConnection().logout();
}

static void printTaskInfos(TaskInfo[] tis)
{
  for (int i = 0; tis!=null && i < tis.length; i++)
  {
```

```
      printTaskInfo(tis[i]);
  }
}

static void printTaskInfo(TaskInfo ti)
{
  System.out.println("\nName:" + ti.getName());
  System.out.println("Key:" + ti.getKey());
  System.out.println("Entity:" + ti.getEntityName());
  System.out.println("Reason:" + taskReason(ti.getReason()));
  System.out.println("QueueTime:"
        + ti.getQueueTime().getTime());
  Calendar calStart = ti.getStartTime();
  Date dateStart = calStart==null? null : calStart.getTime();
  System.out.println("StartTime:" + dateStart);
  Calendar calStop = ti.getCompleteTime();
  Date dateStop = calStop==null? null : calStop.getTime();
  System.out.println("CompleteTime:" + dateStop);
  System.out.println("Cancelable:" + ti.isCancelable());
  System.out.println("Cancelled:" + ti.isCancelled());
}

static String taskReason(TaskReason tr)
{
  if(tr instanceof TaskReasonAlarm)
  {
    return " -- Alarm";
  }
  else if(tr instanceof TaskReasonSchedule)
  {
    return " -- ScheduledTask";
  }
  else if(tr instanceof TaskReasonSystem)
  {
    return " -- System";
  }
  else if(tr instanceof TaskReasonUser)
  {
    return " -- User : " + ((TaskReasonUser)tr).getUserName();
```

```java
    }
    return "Unknown";
}

static TaskFilterSpec createTaskFilterSpec(ManagedEntity ent)
{
  TaskFilterSpec tfs = new TaskFilterSpec();

  // only the root initiated tasks
  TaskFilterSpecByUsername nameFilter
    = new TaskFilterSpecByUsername();
  nameFilter.setUserList(new String[] {"Administrator"});
  // include tasks initiated by non-users,
  // for example, by ScheduledTaskManager.
  nameFilter.setSystemUser(true);
  tfs.setUserName(nameFilter);

  // only the tasks with one entity itself
  TaskFilterSpecByEntity entFilter =
    new TaskFilterSpecByEntity();
  entFilter.setEntity(ent.getMOR());
  entFilter.setRecursion(TaskFilterSpecRecursionOption.all);
  tfs.setEntity(entFilter);

  // only successfully finished tasks
  tfs.setState(new TaskInfoState[]{TaskInfoState.success });

  // only tasks started within past month
  // strictly speaking, time should be retrieved from server
  TaskFilterSpecByTime tFilter =new TaskFilterSpecByTime();
  Calendar cal = Calendar.getInstance();
  cal.roll(Calendar.MONTH, -1);
  tFilter.setBeginTime(cal);
  //we ignore the end time here so it gets the latest.
  tFilter.setTimeType(TaskFilterSpecTimeOption.startedTime);
  tfs.setTime(tFilter);

  // Optionally, you limits tasks initiated by scheduled task
  // with the setScheduledTask() method.
```

```
    return tfs;
  }
}
```

ScheduledTask Managed Object

ScheduledTask represents an operation to be run in the future either once or in a repeated pattern. It is a subtype of ExtensibleManagedObject. It can be created via invoking the createScheduledTask() method of ScheduledTaskManager, which is available only on VirtualCenter.

Like Task, ScheduledTask has only one property info defined of type ScheduledTaskInfo, whose UML diagram is shown in Figure 14-2. As you can see, ScheduledTaskInfo is a subtype of ScheduledTaskSpec, which holds information such as name, scheduling and actions, and so on. In addition, it adds the associated managed entity, time for previous and next run, and so on.

In terms of possible actions, you can define five types of actions: SendSNMPAction, SendEmailAction, RunScriptAction, MethodAction, and CreateTaskAction.[1] The first two actions are easy to understand: They send out either SNMP message or e-mails. RunScriptAction allows you to run a shell script whose path is specified by the script property that runs on the VC server. MethodAction invokes a method on the server with parameters passed in an argument variable typed as MethodActionArgument. CreateTaskAction invokes the createTask() method on the TaskManager.

The scheduling side is complicated, because different types represent different scheduling patterns. TaskScheduler is the supertype for all these schedulers. Underneath it are AfterStartupTaskScheduler, for a scheduled task to run after a delay of starting up; OnceTaskScheduler, for a scheduled task to run only once at a specific point of time; and RecurrentTaskScheduler, for repetitive tasks. RecurrentTaskScheduler is further extended by HourlyTaskScheduler, which is then

---

[1] As it stands in 2.5, only MethodAction is supported for scheduled tasks on VirtualCenter. This is evidenced that you can set up only a limited number of scheduled tasks in VI Client.

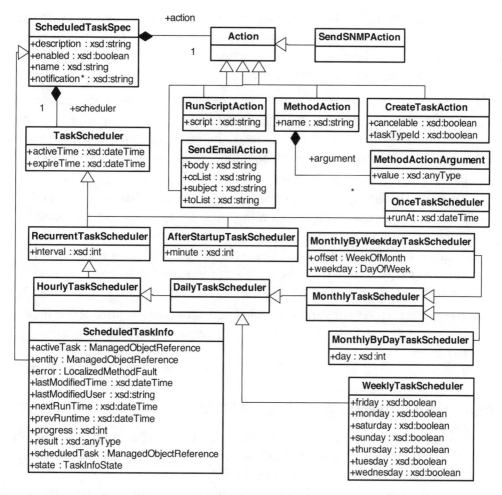

Figure 14-2 ScheduledTaskInfo, ScheduledTaskSpec, and related data objects

extended by DailyTaskScheduler. From DailyTaskScheduler, two types are extended: WeeklyTaskScheduler and MonthlyTaskScheduler, the latter of which is then extended to MonthlyByWeekdayTaskScheduler and MonthlyByDayTaskScheduler. These six types under RecurrentTaskScheduler should satisfy your various needs. They cannot be combined in a single ScheduledTask, but you can always create two ScheduledTasks to accommodate your special needs.

When it comes to the scheduled time, a Task is created and starts to run. While the task is running, ScheduledTaskInfo also holds a ManagedObjectReference to the actively running Task object. The Task object activated by ScheduledTask is the same as any other Task except the reason code is TaskReasonSchedule, which holds a ManagedObjectReference back to the ScheduledTask.

ScheduledTask defines three methods:

- **reconfigureScheduledTask()** takes in a new ScheduledTaskSpec object, which is the same type to the createScheduledTask() method of ScheduledTaskManager. With the information in the parameter, the managed object can morph into a new ScheduledTask with new scheduling, new action, and even a new name, except its ManagedObjectReference.

- **removeScheduledTask()** removes the managed object. It has to be invoked while the ScheduledTask is not running; otherwise, an InvalidState fault is thrown. If a scheduled task is no longer needed, you should remove it. That's especially true for a one-time scheduled task after it runs once. But you don't have to remove it, because you can run it again any time later by explicitly calling runScheduledTask().

- **runScheduledTask()** runs the scheduled task immediately once regardless of the scheduling defined. Running the task doesn't affect the future runs thereafter.

ScheduledTaskManager Managed Object

This managed object is similar to the TaskManager. It's a singleton managed object per service instance that is intended to manage all the scheduled tasks in the scope of the VC server. It's not supported in ESX.

It has two properties defined: description of type ScheduledTaskDescription, and an array of ManagedObjectReference to all the ScheduledTask objects within that service instance. The ScheduledTaskDescription provides static locale-specific strings as descriptions of the scheduled tasks. They don't change, so you need to retrieve them only once when needed.

The two methods are defined:

- **createScheduledTask()**—Has two parameters: one for the target entity and the other for ScheduledTaskSpec, discussed earlier. The target entity can be any managed entity. If it has no child in the inventory tree, it only applies to itself; otherwise, it can apply to all the descendants. The name of the scheduled task must not be the same as any existing one, or

DuplicatedNameFault is thrown. It's recommended that you follow a naming convention to avoid naming conflicts.

- **retrieveEntityScheduledTask()**—Retrieves all the scheduled tasks attached to a specific managed entity. As expected, it takes in a managed entity as its parameter and returns an array of ManagedObjectReference objects pointing to ScheduledTask objects.

Specifying Task Schedule

The scheduling of a scheduled task is defined within the ScheduledTaskSpec data object with the embedded TaskScheduler data object. The TaskScheduler and its subtypes are shown in Figure 14-2. Although TaskScheduler is defined as a type inside the spec object, you can pass in any subtype.

To define a schedule, first decide whether the task is to be a one-time task, a task that runs once after each startup, or a recurring task. If the task fits into the first two cases, create a new OnceTaskScheduler or AfterStartupTaskScheduler object. If the task fits into the last case, it is complicated. You need to pick one from the six subtypes that fit your requirement and create an instance of that type.

All the times involved must be the times of VirtualCenter. You must not use your local client time. It's always a good practice to sync up the clients and servers.

After you have the object ready, assign it to the scheduler property of ScheduledTaskSpec, which will be passed to the createScheduledTask() method.

Having a schedule is not enough. Let the scheduled task do something useful for you. It's defined by the Action in the following section.

Specifying an Action

The action property of ScheduledTaskSpec holds the specification on what actions should be taken once the scheduled time comes. The Action type is an abstract one extended by five subtypes, each of which represents a specific type of action to take place.

Figure 12-5 (in Chapter 12) illustrates Action and its five subtypes. The section "Alarm Managed Object" provided a detailed introduction on what these subtypes are and how to use them. Although the actions are defined separately for alarms, they are trying to define the same behaviors when either a specific condition happens or a timer fires. Therefore, content is not repeated in this section.

When scheduling a task in the VI Client, you have limited choices related to virtual machine and host operations like powering on/off, cloning, creating snapshots, and adding a host. When you select one type of task, a wizard guides you through various specifications.

In theory, you can achieve much more with the SDK than with the VI Client. As it turns out, by testing code, only MethodAction works with the SDK, which is consistent with what you can do with the VI Client. The scheduled tasks created using the SDK can show up in the VI Client just like other created from the GUI. You may or may not edit these from the GUI,[2] though.

The MethodAction, when associated with a method, works only with the managed entities that have the method defined. Be clear about this when calling createScheduledTask().

Now look at Listing 14-3, which creates two tasks. One is a one-time task with a simple operation to power off a virtual machine. The other is a recurring task that runs once every two weeks on Saturday night.

Listing 14-3
CreateScheduledTasks.java

```
package vim25.samples.mo.scheduling;
import java.net.URL;
import java.util.Calendar;

import com.vmware.vim25.MethodAction;
import com.vmware.vim25.MethodActionArgument;
import com.vmware.vim25.OnceTaskScheduler;
import com.vmware.vim25.ScheduledTaskSpec;
import com.vmware.vim25.WeeklyTaskScheduler;
import com.vmware.vim25.mo.Folder;
import com.vmware.vim25.mo.InventoryNavigator;
```

---

[2] You may not be able to edit some tasks created using API in the VI Client because they are not supported there.

```java
import com.vmware.vim25.mo.ScheduledTask;
import com.vmware.vim25.mo.ScheduledTaskManager;
import com.vmware.vim25.mo.ServiceInstance;
import com.vmware.vim25.mo.VirtualMachine;

public class CreateScheduledTasks
{
  public static void main(String [] args) throws Exception
  {
    if(args.length != 4)
    {
      System.out.println("Usage: java CreateScheduledTasks "
          + "<url> <username> <password> <vmname>");
        return;
    }

    ServiceInstance si = new ServiceInstance(
          new URL(args[0]), args[1], args[2], true);
    Folder rootFolder = si.getRootFolder();

    InventoryNavigator inv = new InventoryNavigator(rootFolder);
    String vmname = args[3];
    VirtualMachine vm = (VirtualMachine)inv.searchManagedEntity(
          "VirtualMachine", vmname);
    if(vm==null)
    {
      System.out.println("Cannot find the VM " + vmname
        + "\nExisting...");
      si.getServerConnection().logout();
      return;
    }

    ScheduledTaskManager stm = si.getScheduledTaskManager();
    if(stm!=null)
    {
      //to save space, we just check one name here
      if(taskNameExists(stm, "ViMaster_OneTime"))
      {
        si.getServerConnection().logout();
```

```
      return;
  }

  // Note: the time should be fetched from the server,
  // just to make sure it's synchronized.
  ScheduledTaskSpec oneSpec = createOneTimeSchedulerSpec(
      "ViMaster_OneTime", si.currentTime());

  ScheduledTaskSpec weekSpec = createWeeklySchedulerSpec(
      "ViMaster_Weekly");

  ScheduledTask st = stm.createScheduledTask(vm, oneSpec);
  ScheduledTask st1 = stm.createScheduledTask(vm, weekSpec);
  // sleep two minutes before deleting
  // the one time-scheduled task.
  // A one-time scheduled task does not have to be deleted after
  // it's run. It can be run any time again by calling the
  // runScheduledTask() method.
  Thread.sleep(2*60*1000);
  st.removeScheduledTask();
  }
  else
  {
    System.out.println("SchduledTaskManager is not "
      + "available on this target.");
  }
  si.getServerConnection().logout();
}

static ScheduledTaskSpec createOneTimeSchedulerSpec(
    String taskName, Calendar runTime)
{
  // specify the action
  MethodAction action = new MethodAction();
  action.setName("PowerOffVM_Task");
  action.setArgument(new MethodActionArgument[] { });

  // specify the schedule
  runTime.add(Calendar.MINUTE, 01);
```

```
OnceTaskScheduler scheduler = new OnceTaskScheduler();
scheduler.setRunAt(runTime);

// create a spec for the scheduled task
ScheduledTaskSpec scheduleSpec = new ScheduledTaskSpec();
scheduleSpec.setName(taskName);
scheduleSpec.setDescription("PowerOff VM in 1 minutes");
scheduleSpec.setEnabled(true);
scheduleSpec.setAction(action);
scheduleSpec.setScheduler(scheduler);

return scheduleSpec;
}

static ScheduledTaskSpec createWeeklySchedulerSpec(
  String taskName)
{
  // create an action to take snapshot
  MethodAction action = new MethodAction();
  action.setName("CreateSnapshot_Task");
  MethodActionArgument nameArg = new MethodActionArgument();
  nameArg.setValue("My Snapshot");
  MethodActionArgument descArg = new MethodActionArgument();
  descArg.setValue("My Description");
  MethodActionArgument memArg = new MethodActionArgument();
  memArg.setValue(true);
  MethodActionArgument quieArg = new MethodActionArgument();
  quieArg.setValue(true);
  action.setArgument(new MethodActionArgument[]
    {nameArg, descArg, memArg, quieArg });

  // run the task only once every week at Saturday midnight
  WeeklyTaskScheduler scheduler = new WeeklyTaskScheduler();
  scheduler.setSaturday(true);
  scheduler.setHour(23);
  scheduler.setMinute(59);
  scheduler.setInterval(1);

  ScheduledTaskSpec scheduleSpec = new ScheduledTaskSpec();
```

```
    scheduleSpec.setName(taskName);
    scheduleSpec.setDescription(
       "Run a command at 23:59PM every other Saturday.");
    scheduleSpec.setEnabled(true);
    scheduleSpec.setAction(action);
    scheduleSpec.setScheduler(scheduler);

    return scheduleSpec;
}

static boolean taskNameExists(ScheduledTaskManager stm,
    String vmname)
{
  ScheduledTask[] tasks = stm.getScheduledTasks();
  boolean found = false;
  for(int i=0; tasks!=null && i<tasks.length; i++)
  {
    if(vmname.equals(tasks[i].getInfo().getName()))
    {
      found = true;
      System.out.println("The task name " + vmname
          + " exists. \nPlease pick a new one.");
      break;
    }
  }
  return found;
}
}
```

Summary

This chapter introduced Task, which represents a running operation on the server side. Some of the long-running VI SDK methods return Task objects so that you can track their statuses and progresses, cancel them if allowed, and even get the additional results upon the success of the tasks.

TaskManager is the managed object that can create either a new Task on behalf of server-side extensions or a TaskHistoryCollector for retrieving the historical tasks.

`ScheduledTask` represents an operation to be run in the future either once or on a recurring schedule. It has two important dimensions: scheduling and actions. The `ScheduledTaskManager` is the managed object for creating the `ScheduledTask` and retrieving all the scheduled tasks on a specific managed entity.

`ScheduledTask` and its related manager provide a powerful way to plan future tasks on a predefined schedule. This is useful in data center automation, where you can preschedule maintenance tasks and let the system do the rest.

Chapter 15

User and License Administration

This chapter introduces the security and license management using the VI SDK. It first discusses the operation privileges, roles, and permissions as the model for access control. The managed object involved is the `AuthorizationManager`. It then moves on how to manage users (groups) in the hypervisor, how to look up existing users, and so on. This chapter then covers the user session management using `SessionManager`.

The last part of this chapter introduces the license management and related concepts like feature and edition, and how to use the provided VI SDK to configure and query licensing information.

Managed Objects: `AuthorizationManager, HostLocalAccountManager, UserDirectory,` `SessionManager, LicenseManager`

Security Model

In the VI SDK, the security model consists of three types of components: privileges, roles, and permissions.

Privileges

A privilege is the basic individual right required to perform an operation. It is statically defined and never changes in a single version of a product. Given the many operations in VI, there are many privileges (for example, the privilege to "power on a virtual machine"). These privileges are represented as strings separated by dots, such as `VirtualMachine.Interact.PowerOn`.

The operations and privileges are not one-to-one mapping. Many operations do share common privileges like `System.View`. Therefore, there are many fewer privileges defined than methods. In some exceptional cases, a method requires different privileges depending on the target it operates on and the nature of the operation. The `CloneVM_Task()` method, for example, requires `VirtualMachine.Provisioning.Clone` for cloning from one virtual machine to another, `VirtualMachine.Provisioning.DeployTemplate` for cloning from a template to a virtual machine, and so on.

Roles

The role groups privileges from a user's perspective. A role is normally named and defined for a group of people who have common responsibilities in the system (for example, administrators). Each role can include zero to multiple privileges. The extreme cases are the predefined `Admin` role, which by default, includes all the privileges and the `NoAccess` role, which includes no privileges.

The permission is the actual access-control rule that associates a user or user group with a specific role on a managed entity. The rule could be propagated and applied on the descendent managed entities as well. You could group managed entities with similar requirements on access control under a container entity, such as a `Folder`.

VirtualCenter doesn't create new users or new groups. You can create them in VC server's Windows Domain. On the ESX server, you can create and manage users in the console OS with Linux commands, or you can use the `HostLocalAccountManager` managed object. Use the `UserDirectory` managed object to retrieve them from the system.

Permissions

Permissions are the associations of roles with privileges on a given managed entity. ManagedEntity may have multiple permissions, but it may have only one permission per user or group. When logging in, if a user has both a user permission and a group permission (as a group member) for the same entity, the user-specific permission takes precedence. If there is no user-specific permission but two or more group permissions are present, and the user is a member of the groups, the privileges are calculated as the union of the specified roles.

Managed entities may be grouped together into a "complex" entity (for example, a Datacenter, ComputeResource, or ClusterComputeResource) for the purpose of applying permissions consistently. A Datacenter's child objects are the root virtual machine and host folders. A ComputeResource's child objects are the root ResourcePool and HostSystem. A ClusterComputeResource has only the root ResourcePool as a child object.

Child entities in a complex entity are forced to inherit permissions from the parent object. When you query the permissions on child objects of complex entities, different results may be returned for the owner of the permission. In some cases, the child entity is returned as the object that defines the permission. In other cases, the parent from which the permission is propagated is returned as the object that defines the permission. In both cases, the information about the owner of the permission is correct, because the entities within a complex entity are considered equivalent. Permissions defined on complex entities are always applicable on the child entities, regardless of the propagation flag.

Privilege, role, and permission are represented by AuthorizationPrivilege, AuthorizationRole, and Permission data objects, as shown in Figure 15-1.

AuthorizationPrivilege	AuthorizationRole	Permission
+name : xsd:string	+info : Description	+entity : ManagedObjectReference
+onParent : xsd:boolean	+name : xsd:string	+group : xsd:boolean
+privGroupName : xsd:string	+privilege : xsd:string[]	+principal : xsd:string
+privId : xsd:string	+roleId : xsd:int	+propogate : xsd:boolean
	+system : xsd:boolean	+roleId : xsd:int

Figure 15-1 AuthorizationPrivilege, AuthorizationRole, and Permission

The AuthorizationPrivilege's privId is a unique string consisting of privGroupName and name with a dot in between (for example, System.View). These unique strings can be included in the array of privileges in the `AuthorizationRole`. That is how they are associated.

The `AuthorizationRole` is identified by the `roleId`, an integer that is referenced in the `Permission` object. You can think of the `roleId` in the `AuthorizationRole` as the primary key, and the `roleId` in `Permission` as the foreign key in SQL databases.

AuthorizationManager Managed Object

The `AuthorizationManager` managed object manages the access control in the VI SDK. It has three properties:

- **description (type: AuthorizationDescription)**—It holds static description strings for system roles and privileges.

- **privilegeList (type: AuthorizationPrivilege[])**—It holds all the system-defined privileges.

- **roleList (type: AuthorizationRole[])**—It holds all the currently defined roles in the system, including system default roles.

Retrieving the last two properties can return the complete lists of privileges and roles. Table 15-1 lists the predefined roles in both ESX and VirtualCenter.

Table 15-1

Predefined Roles in ESX and VirtualCenter	
ESX	**VirtualCenter**
NoAccess, Anonymous, View, ReadOnly, Admin	NoAccess, Anonymous, View, ReadOnly, Admin
	VirtualMachineAdministrator, DatacenterAdministrator
	VirtualMachinePowerUser, VirtualMachineUser
	ResourcePoolAdministrator, VMwareConsolidatedBackupUser

Listing 15-1 retrieves all three properties and prints them. You can run it against ESX or VirtualCenter without code changes, but with different results.

Listing 15-1
ListAuthorization.java

```java
package vim25.samples.mo.security;
import java.net.URL;
import com.vmware.vim25.AuthorizationDescription;
import com.vmware.vim25.AuthorizationPrivilege;
import com.vmware.vim25.AuthorizationRole;
import com.vmware.vim25.ElementDescription;
import com.vmware.vim25.mo.AuthorizationManager;
import com.vmware.vim25.mo.ServiceInstance;

public class ListAuthorization
{
  public static void main(String[] args) throws Exception
  {
    if(args.length != 3)
    {
      System.out.println("Usage: java ListAuthorization <url> "
        + "<username> <password>");
      return;
    }

    ServiceInstance si = new ServiceInstance(
        new URL(args[0]), args[1], args[2], true);

    AuthorizationManager am = si.getAuthorizationManager();
    AuthorizationDescription ad = am.getDescription();

    System.out.println("Descriptions of all privileges:");
    printDescriptions(ad.getPrivilege());

    System.out.println("Descriptions of all privilege groups:");
    printDescriptions( ad.getPrivilegeGroup());

    System.out.println("List of all privileges with details:");
    printPrivileges(am.getPrivilegeList());

    System.out.println("List of all the roles with details:");
    printRoles(am.getRoleList());
```

```
  si.getServerConnection().logout();
}

static void printDescriptions(ElementDescription[] eds)
{
  for(int i=0; eds!=null && i< eds.length; i++)
  {
    System.out.println("\nKey:" + eds[i].getKey());
    System.out.println("Label:" + eds[i].getLabel());
    System.out.println("Summary:" + eds[i].getSummary());
  }
}

static void printPrivileges(AuthorizationPrivilege[] aps)
{
  for(int i=0; aps!=null && i< aps.length; i++)
  {
    System.out.println("\nName:" + aps[i].getName());
    System.out.println("onParent:" + aps[i].isOnParent());
    System.out.println("Group:" + aps[i].getPrivGroupName());
    System.out.println("ID:" + aps[i].getPrivId());
  }
}

static void printRoles(AuthorizationRole[] ars)
{
  for(int i=0; ars!=null && i<ars.length; i++)
  {
    System.out.println("\nName:" + ars[i].getName());
    System.out.println("Role ID:" + ars[i].getRoleId());
    System.out.println("Sys Role:" + ars[i].isSystem());
    System.out.print("Privileges: ");
    String[] privs = ars[i].getPrivilege();
    for(int j=0; privs!=null && j < privs.length; j++)
    {
      if(j==0)
      {
        System.out.print(privs[j]);
      }
      else
      {
```

```
        System.out.print(", " + privs[j]);
      }
    }
  }
 }
}
```

`AuthorizationManager` has ten methods defined. Three of them manage roles, and the rest manage permissions.

Managing Roles

As mentioned earlier, the role is a convenient way to group a set of privileges for users who share common responsibilities. You can create a new role, update an existing role, and delete an existing role.

To create a new role, use the `addAuthorizationRole()` method, which requires the name of the new role and a list of strings for privilege names. The name cannot be empty or already existing. Each privilege string must be a `privId` of an existing privilege. Upon success, it returns with an integer as the `roleId` for the newly created role.

> By default, the `addAuthorization()` method adds three privileges (`System.Anonymous`, `System.View`, and `System.Read`) even if you pass in an empty list of privileges.

To remove an existing role, use the `removeAuthorizationRole()` method. It takes in an integer as the `roleId` of the role to be deleted, and a Boolean parameter whether to force deletion when the role is still used by permission. It returns `none`.

> You cannot remove a system predefined role, like Admin, whose ID is –1, or an `InvalidArgument` fault is thrown.

To update an existing role, use the `updateAuthorizationRole()` method. It takes in `roleId` as the key to the `AuthorizationRole` object, and `name` as the new name, an array of strings of `privId`. Just like deleting, you cannot update a system predefined role.

Managing Permissions

Permission is defined on a managed entity to grant a user or a group with privileges included in a specific role. You can set, reset, remove, or merge permissions.

To set permission, use the `setEntityPermissions()` method. It takes a parameter as the entity on which permission is to be set, and an array of `Permission` objects. If a permission is specified multiple times for the same user or group, the last one is set.

The operation is applied transactionally per permission to the entity in the order of the elements in the permission array parameter. This means that if a failure occurs, the method terminates leaving at least one, and possibly all, permissions unapplied.

`setEntityPermissions()` fails with an `InvalidArgument` fault if it's called on the direct child folders (`hostFolder`, `vmFolder`) of a datacenter managed object or the root resource pool of a `ComputeResource`, `ClusterComputeResource`, or `HostSystem` that is part of a `ComputeResource` (standalone host). These entities always have the same permissions as their parent.

You cannot set permissions to the extreme case that no administrator permission on the root node or an `AuthMinimumAdminPermission` fault will be thrown.

The `resetEntityPermissions()` method is similar to the `setEntityPermissions()` method except that it removes all the existing permissions on an entity and replaces them with the specified array of `Permission` in the parameter. Other than this, these two methods take the same parameters and throw the same faults.

To remove a permission, use the `removeEntityPermission()` method. It takes in the entity on which the `permission` is removed, the user or group that has the permission, and a boolean indicator whether it's for a user group or a normal user. As previously mentioned, a given user or group on an entity has only one permission, so the user or group name string is good enough to locate the `permission` and remove it. Similar to adding permission, you cannot remove a permission that results in no administrator permission being on the root node.

By default, the root user has an administrator role on the inventory root `ha-folder-root`. Normally you cannot remove the permission from the root because there must be at least one user with an administrator role on the root. If the ESX server is managed by a VirtualCenter, a new user called `vpxuser` is created and has the same administrator permission as root. Then it becomes possible to accidentally remove the root's permission on the inventory root. When that happens, you cannot log in into the ESX server directly using the VI Client or VI SDK under the root account. That means you cannot perform many administration tasks.

To solve the problem, you can log in on the ESX service console as root. Then you need to modify /etc/vmware/hostd/authorization.xml and make sure the following or similar is in the file. Notice that the –1 inside the ACEDataRoleId represents the administrator role. After the change, don't forget to restart the agent service by running the service mgmt-vmware restart command.

```
<ACEData id="10">
      <ACEDataEntity>ha-folder-root</ACEDataEntity>
      <ACEDataId>10</ACEDataId>
      <ACEDataGroup>false</ACEDataGroup>
      <ACEDataPropagate>true</ACEDataPropagate>
      <ACEDataRoleId>-1</ACEDataRoleId>
      <ACEDataUser>root</ACEDataUser>
</ACEData>
```

The mergePermissions() method reassigns all the permissions of one role to another role. It takes the role IDs of both source and destination. Of course, the source and destination must not be the same.

Querying Permissions

You can use three methods to query the permissions using different criteria:

- **retrieveAllPermissions()**—As its name suggests, the method retrieves all the permissions defined in the system. The return is an array of Permission objects.

- **retrieveEntityPermissions()**—Gets all the permissions defined with a specified managed entity, with an option whether to include propagated permissions from parent entities. The return is an array of Permission objects.

- **retrieveRolePermissions()**—Finds all the permissions that use a particular role. It takes roleId as the parameter.

    As Figure 15-1 showed, the Permission has a roleId as a foreign key pointing to the AuthorizationRole, but not the other way around. So the underlying retrieving is not a simple lookup, because you have to iterate through all the permissions and pick out only those whose role ID is specified by the parameter.

Listing 15-2 shows a sample that creates a new role and updates it. It then assigns the role to an existing user vimaster with the root of the inventory. So that you can verify the permission, all the permissions on the root are printed to the console.

Listing 15-2
CreateRole.java

```
package vim25.samples.mo.security;
import java.net.URL;

import com.vmware.vim25.Permission;
import com.vmware.vim25.mo.AuthorizationManager;
import com.vmware.vim25.mo.ServiceInstance;

public class CreateRole
{
  public static void main(String[] args) throws Exception
  {
    if(args.length != 3)
    {
      System.out.println("Usage: java CreateRole <url>"
        + " <username> <password>");
      return;
    }

    ServiceInstance si = new ServiceInstance(
        new URL(args[0]), args[1], args[2], true);

    AuthorizationManager am = si.getAuthorizationManager();

    int roleId = am.addAuthorizationRole("master1",
        new String[] { "System.View", "System.Read",
        "System.Anonymous", "Global.LogEvent" } );
```

```
//even if you just want to rename the role, you
// still need to provide a full list of privileges
am.updateAuthorizationRole(roleId, "master",
    new String[] { "System.View", "System.Read",
    "System.Anonymous", "Global.LogEvent",
    "Global.Diagnostics", "Folder.Create"} );

System.out.println("The new role ID: " + roleId);


Permission perm = new Permission();
perm.setGroup(false); // false for user, true for group
perm.setPrincipal("vimaster"); // the vimaster must exist
perm.setPropagate(true); // propagate down the hierarchy
perm.setRoleId(roleId);


am.setEntityPermissions( si.getRootFolder(),
    new Permission[] {perm} );


Permission[] ps = am.retrieveEntityPermissions(
    si.getRootFolder(), false);


System.out.println("print the permissions on root:");
printPermissions(ps);



    si.getServerConnection().logout();
}


static void printPermissions(Permission[] ps)
{
  for(int i=0; ps!=null && i< ps.length; i++)
  {
    System.out.println("\nEntity:"
        + ps[i].getEntity().getType() + ":"
        + ps[i].getEntity().get_value());
    System.out.println("IsGroup:" + ps[i].isGroup());
    System.out.println("Principal:" + ps[i].getPrincipal());
    System.out.println("Propogated:" + ps[i].isPropagate());
    System.out.println("RoleId:" + ps[i].getRoleId());
  }
```

```
    }
}
```

Looking Up Users with `UserDirectory`

`UserDirectory` is the managed object that helps you to retrieve users from the server side. It's a simple type with only one property and one method defined.

The property `domainList` is an array of strings used to save the Windows domain names available for the users' searches. On the ESX server, it is not applicable and is, therefore, not set. When retrieving it from the ESX server, you get `null` instead of an empty list. Therefore, you should handle it against `NullPointerException` in your code.

The only method defined is `retrieveUserGroups()`, which searches the users or groups. It takes several parameters, ranging from the domain, search string, whether user or group only, and so on. To match all, just leave the search string empty. Don't use the wildcard (*) as you would do with a regular expression.

The return is an array of `UserSearchResult` data objects. Within the `UserSearchResult` data object are three properties for the user's full name, whether it's a group name, and the login principal name by which the user logs in.

Although a VC server can manage an ESX server, the user profiles are independent. You cannot see what users are on the ESX server from the VC server, let alone assign permissions using the users from the ESX server.

Listing 15-3 shows a sample code to retrieve and print all the domains and all the users and groups that use this managed object. This sample works with both the ESX server and the VC server.

Listing 15-3
`ListAllUsers.java`

```
package vim25.samples.mo.security;
import java.net.URL;

import com.vmware.vim25.UserSearchResult;
import com.vmware.vim25.mo.ServiceInstance;
import com.vmware.vim25.mo.UserDirectory;
```

```
public class ListAllUsers
{
  public static void main(String[] args) throws Exception
  {
    if(args.length != 3)
    {
      System.out.println("Usage: java ListAllUsers <url> "
        + "<username> <password>");
      return;
    }

    ServiceInstance si = new ServiceInstance(
        new URL(args[0]), args[1], args[2], true);

    UserDirectory ud = si.getUserDirectory();

    //print out the domain names
    String[] domains = ud.getDomainList();
    System.out.println("domains:" + domains);
    for(int i=0; domains!=null && i<domains.length; i++)
    {
      System.out.println("Domain:" + domains[i]);
    }

    UserSearchResult[] usrs = ud.retrieveUserGroups(
        null, // only local machine is searched
        "", // blank means matching all
        "users", null, // all the groups
        false, //not exact match for the search
        true, // include users
        false // include groups
        );

    // print out the results
    for(int i=0; usrs!=null && i < usrs.length; i++)
    {
      System.out.println("===============================");
      System.out.println("Full name: " + usrs[i].getFullName());
      System.out.println("IsGroup:" + usrs[i].isGroup());
```

```
    System.out.println("Principal: " + usrs[i].getPrincipal());
  }

  si.getServerConnection().logout();
 }
}
```

There are differences in the results when you run Listing 15-3 against ESX or VirtualCenter. For example, you don't have domain names printed out against ESX server, but you do get domains against the VirtualCenter server. Even though you can see the domain, it doesn't necessarily allow you to pull the usernames and group names from that domain. In the sample, `null` is used in place of the domain name, meaning it searches from the local server.

There is another big difference. You can search the users under a specific group (for example, "users" as in the following code) against the ESX server, but not the VirtualCenter server where the `NotSupported` fault is thrown.

```
UserSearchResult[] usrs = ud.retrieveUserGroups(
        null, // only local machine is searched
        "", // blank means matching all
        "users", null, // all the groups
        false, //not exact match for the search
        true, // include users
        false // include groups
    );
```

Managing ESX Users with **HostLocalAccountManager**

`HostLocalAccountManager` is a managed object that is closely attached to `ServiceInstance`, not `HostSystem`.[1] Therefore, it is available only on the ESX server. It provides services to manage local ESX accounts.

---

[1] It would be better if the `HostLocalAccountManager` were attached to the `HostSystem`.

The `HostLocalAccountManager` managed object does not have properties, but seven methods are defined:

- `createGroup()` and `createUser()` methods create a new group or a new user based on the `HostAccountSpec` parameter. `HostAccountSpec` is a simple data object that includes the ID, a password, and a brief description for the account. As expected, you cannot create a group or a user whose ID already exists in the system; otherwise, the `AlreadyExists` fault is thrown. The user or group ID and password are subject to the underlying platform limitation.

  You can replace `HostAccountSpec` with its subtype `HostPosixAccountSpec`, which defines two extra properties: `posixId`, which is an integer as the user ID; and `shellAccess`, which is a boolean specifying whether shell access is allowed. By default, shell access is not allowed. The `posixId` must not conflict with an existing user ID. For example, you must not specify `0`, which is the user ID for the super user. To be safe, just ignore this and let the system assign you one.

- `removeGroup()` and `removeUser()` remove either an existing group or user. They each take in a string for either username or group name.

- `assignUserToGroup()` assigns a user to a group. Both the user and the group have to exist before this method is called.

- `unassignUserFromGroup()` does the reverse of `assignUserToGroup()`. It removes a user from a group. After the method, both the user and the group still exist, but the membership association is removed.

- `updateUser()` updates an existing user with a new password or description as specified in the `HostAccountSpec` parameter. Even though you can provide a new user ID in `HostAccountSpec` while calling `updateUser()`, it will fail at runtime with `UserNotFoundFault`.

Most methods can be mapped to Linux commands that run in the console OS. For example, the `createUser()` method is similar to the following commands.[2]

```
useradd <username>
passwd <username>
```

---

[2] The `passwd` command doesn't have the password in the command line. But when you run the command, you will be prompted to enter the password.

Now look at a sample on how to use these methods. Listing 15-4 creates a user account and a user group and then assigns the user to the group. To verify that the user account and user group are created, UserDirectory is used to search them. In the end, the user and group are removed from the system. Pay attention to the comments, which explain the misuses of the API that might cause you problems.

Listing 15-4

`EsxAccountManager.java`

```java
package vim25.samples.mo.security;
import java.net.URL;
import com.vmware.vim25.HostAccountSpec;
import com.vmware.vim25.HostPosixAccountSpec;
import com.vmware.vim25.UserSearchResult;
import com.vmware.vim25.mo.HostLocalAccountManager;
import com.vmware.vim25.mo.ServiceInstance;
import com.vmware.vim25.mo.UserDirectory;

public class EsxAccountManager
{
  public static void main(String[] args) throws Exception
  {
    if(args.length != 3)
    {
      System.out.println("Usage: java EsxAccountManager <url> "
          + "<username> <password>");
      return;
    }

    ServiceInstance si = new ServiceInstance(
            new URL(args[0]), args[1], args[2], true);
    HostLocalAccountManager hlam = si.getAccountManager();
    if(hlam==null)
    {
      System.out.println("This sample works ONLY with ESX. "
          + "Please try it again.");
    }

    //create a new POSIX account
```

```
HostPosixAccountSpec has = new HostPosixAccountSpec();
has.setId("vimaster");
has.setDescription("The POSIX account for VI Master");
has.setPassword("password");
has.setShellAccess(true);
hlam.createUser(has);

//create a new group called masters
HostAccountSpec grpSpec = new HostAccountSpec();
grpSpec.setId("masters");
// DON'T CALL the following two lines! NOT supported.
// grpSpec.setDescription("The Group for VI Masters");
// grpSpec.setPassword("grppass");
hlam.createGroup(grpSpec);

//assign the new user to the new group
hlam.assignUserToGroup("vimaster", "masters");

//let's check their existence
UserDirectory ud = si.getUserDirectory();
UserSearchResult[] usrs = ud.retrieveUserGroups(
      null, // only local machine is searched
      "master", // search string
      null, null,
      false, //not exact match for the search
      true, // include users
      true // include groups
      );
// print the results
for(int i=0; usrs!=null && i < usrs.length; i++)
{
  System.out.println("\n===============================");
  System.out.println("Full name: " + usrs[i].getFullName());
  System.out.println("IsGroup:" + usrs[i].isGroup());
  System.out.println("Principal: " + usrs[i].getPrincipal());
}

//delete the new user and group
//Note: you have to delete the user before you delete the group
hlam.removeUser("vimaster");
```

```
    hlam.removeGroup("masters");

    si.getServerConnection().logout();
  }
}
```

When the sample runs, it prints the following in the console:

```
================================
Full name: The POSIX account for VI Master
IsGroup:false
Principal: vimaster


================================
Full name:
IsGroup:true
Principal: masters
```

This sample code removes the user and group after it's created. You can change your flow as needed or just remove part of the flow in your own applications.

Instead of using `UserDirectory`, you can use the Linux command in the console OS to verify the new user like the following:[3]

```
cat /etc/passwd ¦ cut -d: -f1
```

For the group:

```
cat /etc/group ¦ cut -d: -f1
```

Managing Sessions Using `SessionManager`

`SessionManager` is the managed object that controls user access to the server through the APIs. It includes methods to log users on and off and query current user sessions.

---

[3] Running commands after the sample as it is won't show you the newly created user and group, because they are removed at the end. You can comment out the code, removing the user and group, and then run the commands to verify them.

The user sessions use system resources and create locks on the server side. Too many concurrent sessions can slow down the server. For better performance, use as few sessions as possible. This includes the VI Clients and your applications, which should be closed when they're no longer needed. The server terminates your session after a period of time. (The default for VirtualCenter is 30 minutes.)

The `SessionManager` managed object has six properties, which are listed in Table 15-2.

Table 15-2

Properties of `SessionManager`

Name	Type	Explanation
currentSession	UserSession	The data object containing information about the client's current session.
defaultLocale	xsd:string	The default server locale.
message	xsd:string	The system global message from the server.
messageLocaleList	xsd:string[]	The list of locales for which the server has localized messages.
sessionList	UserSession[]	The list of currently active sessions.
supportedLocaleList	xsd:string[]	The list of locales that the server supports. Listing a locale ensures that some standardized information such as dates appear in the appropriate format. Other localized information such as error messages are displayed, if available. If localized information is not available, the message is returned using the system locale.

To tell whether an ESX is managed by VirtualCenter, just retrieve the `sessionList` to see if any `UserSession`'s property `userName` equals `vpxuser`, which is the standard username VirtualCenter uses for connecting to ESX.

From the HostSystem's `summary.managementServerIp` property, you can get the IP address of the VirtualCenter server that currently manages it.

The definition of UserSession is shown in Figure 15-2. The UserSession is also the return type of several methods to be discussed next.

UserSession
+fullName : xsd:string
+key : xsd:string
+lastActiveTime : xsd:dateTime
+locale : xsd:string
+loginTime : xsd:dateTime
+messageLocale : xsd:string
+userName : xsd:string

Figure 15-2   The UserSession data object

The property key is a string that has the same format as the HTTP session discussed earlier, but they are two different things and have different values. It's possible that one username is used in more than one client and therefore is associated with two UserSession data objects. One UserSession can be shared by two clients on different machines. Chapter 18, "Advanced Topics," introduces sharing of a session among multiple clients.

The SessionManager defines nine methods:

- **login()** authenticates the user and password and establishes the session.

- **logout()** terminates the session and removes all the related resources.

- **sessionIsActive()** verifies the session with sessionID and determines whether the username is currently active. It returns a Boolean value as a result.

- **setLocale()** sets the locale of the current session and takes in a string for the new locale. The locale string is a two-character ISO-639[4] language ID (like en) optionally followed by an underscore and a two-character ISO 3166[5] country ID (like US). Examples are de (German), fr_CA (French with Canada flavor), zh (Chinese), zh_CN (simplified Chinese), and zh_TW (traditional Chinese). The same standards are used in the Java standard library, so if you are familiar with Java, you should be comfortable with these locales.

---

[4] http://en.wikipedia.org/wiki/ISO_639
[5] http://en.wikipedia.org/wiki/ISO_3166

setLocale() uses the server default locale when a locale is not provided. This default can be configured in the server configuration file. If it is not configured, it defaults to the locale of the server environment or English (en) if unsupported.

- **terminateSession()** forcefully terminates a list of sessions. It's only transactional for each session ID. The sessions are terminated sequentially in the order as specified in the list. If a failure occurs because of an unknown sessionID, for example, the method aborts with a fault. When the method aborts, any sessions that have not yet been terminated are left in their current states. This method requires the Sessions.TerminateSession privilege. Given the potential consequences, you should take extra caution while trying this method.

- **updateServiceMessage()** sets the message property of the SessionManager and takes a string as the new global message. After the message is set, it's immediately displayed to the currently logged-on users. The VI Client, for example, displays an information dialog box titled Message of the Day upon the invocation. While not null, the message is shown to any user right after successful login later.

If you want to broadcast anything to all the users who are using the VI Client now, this is an excellent way to do so. The message, however, does not appear to users on virtual machines and guest OSes.

Notice that the SessionManager is attached to ServiceInstance. The message is sent to the VI Clients connecting to the server directly. A VI Client connecting to an ESX server directly does not get a message on the VirtualCenter even though the ESX server is managed by the latter. The same is true the other way.

Given this convention, consider checking the message and displaying it to users in your application.

- **acquireLocalTicket()** gets you a one-time ticket for one login. The return is a SessionManagerLocalTicket data object that includes a username and the absolute path to the file that contains the password. The caller can use the username and password arguments for login operation. The local ticket becomes invalid after it is used or after a server-determined ticket expiration time.

This operation can be used by servers and clients to avoid re-entering user credentials. For example, service console utilities that connect to a host agent should not require users to re-enter their passwords every time the utilities run. Because the one-time password file is readable only by the given user, the identity of the one-time password user is protected by the operating system file permission.

The challenge for a remote caller is how to read the password from the file saved in the server. In the ESX server, the file is under the `/var/run/vmware-hostd-ticket` directory.

- `impersonateUser()` converts the current session to impersonate the specified user. The current session takes on the identity and privileges of that user who must have a currently active session. It takes a string as the name of the user to impersonate, and an optional locale string with the same format just discussed in the `setLocale()` method. It returns a `UserSession` data object.

- `loginBySSPI()` is experimental and subject to change in future releases. It's used to log on to the server using Security Support Provider Interface (SSPI) pass-through authentication. This method provides support for passing credentials of the calling process to the server without using a password, by leveraging the Windows SSPI library. It is, as you might have guessed, not supported on ESX server. If you still call it, a `NotSupported` fault is thrown.

The client on Windows first calls the `AcquireCredentialsHandle()` function to get a handle to the preexisting credentials of a specified user. If Kerberos is used, this should include the desired credential to pass. The client then calls `InitializeSecurityContext()`. The resulting partially formed context is passed in Base-64 encoded form to this method.

If the context has been successfully formed, the server proceeds with login and behaves like the `login()` method. If further negotiation is needed, the server throws an `SSPIChallenge` fault with a challenge token, which the client should again pass to `InitializeSecurityContext()`, followed by calling this method again.

For more information, see the MSDN documentation on SSPI.[6]

---

[6] http://msdn.microsoft.com/en-us/library/aa380493(VS.85).aspx

License Management

LicenseManager is the managed object that controls the license for the server. It exposes the interfaces to configure where to look for license, query availability and usage, enable/disable features, and so on.

The LicenseManager managed object defines five properties, which are shown in Table 15-3.

Table 15-3

Properties of LicenseManager

Name	Type	Explanation
diagnostics	LicenseDiagnostics	Current diagnostic information. See Figure 15-3 for more on the type.
featureInfo	LicenseFeatureInfo[]	The list of features that can be licensed. Deprecated as of version 2.5, you should use the QuerySupportedFeatures method instead. See Figure 15-4 for more information on the type.
licensedEdition	xsd:string	The product's license edition key. The edition defines which product license the server requires. This, in turn, determines the core set of functionalities provided by the product and the additional features that can be licensed. If no edition is set, the property is set to an empty string.
source	LicenseSource	The source of license, either from server, local, or evaluation. See Figure 15-5 for more info on the subtypes.
sourceAvailable	xsd:boolean	Current state of the license source. License sources that are LocalSource are always available.

LicenseManager defines eight methods, which are described in the following list. All the methods take an optional host parameter; this identifies a host against which you want to manage license while connecting to a VirtualCenter server.

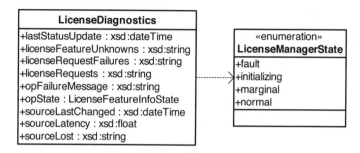

Figure 15-3 LicenseDiagnostics data object

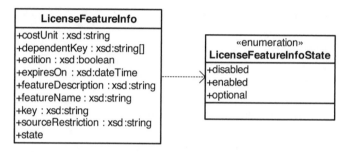

Figure 15-4 LicenseFeatureInfo data object

- **checkLicenseFeature()** verifies whether a specific feature represented by a key is enabled. It returns a boolean value. The feature key has to be valid; otherwise, an InvalidArgument is thrown. Tables 15-4 and 15-5 list the feature keys in both the ESX and VirtualCenter servers.

Table 15-4

Features in ESX		
Key	**Feature Name**	**Edition?**
esxFull	ESX Server Standard	Yes
esxExpress	ESX Server Foundation	Yes
vsmp	Up to 4-way virtual SMP	No
nas	NAS Usage	No
iscsi	iSCSI Usage	No

continues...

Table 15-4 continued

Features in ESX		
Key	Feature Name	Edition?
san	SAN Usage	No
backup	VMware Consolidated Backup	No

Table 15-5

Features in VirtualCenter		
Key	Feature Name	Edition?
vc	VirtualCenter Management Server	Yes
vcExpress	VirtualCenter Foundation Management Server	Yes
das	VMware HA (High Availability)	No
drs	VMware DRS	No
drsPower	VMware DRS Power Management (a.k.a DPM)	No
esxHost	VirtualCenter Agent for ESX Server	No
serverHost	VirtualCenter Agent for VMware Server	No
svmotion	Storage VMotion	No
vmotion	VMotion	No

- **configureLicenseSource()** allows you to reconfigure the license manager with a new license source, whether local, evaluation, or from server (see LocalLicenseSource, EvaluationLicenseSource, and LicenseServerSource in Figure 15-5). Note that the VirtualCenter server supports only the license server as the source. If the license server becomes unavailable, licenses are unaffected for a 14-day grace period. The method actually checks the availability of the license server. You must provide a valid and reachable license server, or you will get a LicenseServerUnavailableFault.

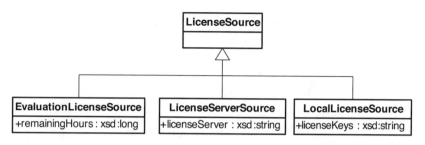

Figure 15-5 The LicenseSource and its subtypes

Before changing the license source location property, the license manager checks the number of licenses available at the new potential source to make sure there are at least as many licenses as have been issued by the current source. If there are enough licenses at the new source, all licenses on the current source are released and then reacquired from the new source. If there are not enough licenses available on the new source to reissue all licenses, the method fails.

- **enableFeature()** enables a feature identified by the feature key parameter.

- **disableFeature()** disables a feature identified by the feature key parameter.

- **queryLicenseSourceAvailability()** gets you a list of LicenseAvailabilityInfo data objects, each of which corresponds to a feature and includes total unit and available unit from the license source.

- **queryLicenseUsage()** returns the license usage data object LicenseUsageInfo, as shown in Figure 15-6. The license usage is a list of supported features and the number of licenses that have been reserved. On a VirtualCenter, an empty string returns the usage of non-host-specific features.

- **querySupportedFeatures()** queries the current license source for a list of available licenses that can be licensed from this system. It returns an array of LicenseFeatureInfo.

- **setLicenseEdition()** sets the product's license edition. The edition defines which product license the server requires. This, in turn, determines the core set of functionalities provided by the product and the additional features that can be licensed. To determine what featureKey the current platform accepts, call querySourceAvailablity() at runtime or consult the documentation for the current platform.

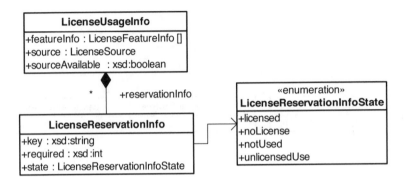

Figure 15-6 `LicenseUsageInfo` data object

Now look at two samples. The first sample, shown in Listing 15-5, retrieves the properties and calls three query methods to print the related information, such as diagnostic information, license sources, available licenses from the sources, all the features and corresponding descriptions, the license usage, and so on.

You can run this sample against both ESX and VirtualCenter. When you are running it against a VirtualCenter, the sample prints out the license information of the VirtualCenter. Optionally, you can specify a real host instead of `null` in the `query*` methods so that you can get host-based license information. The host is ignored when the sample runs against an ESX; therefore, you just put `null` there.

Listing 15-5
PrintLicense.java

```java
package vim25.samples.mo.lic;

import java.net.URL;

import com.vmware.vim25.EvaluationLicenseSource;
import com.vmware.vim25.LicenseAvailabilityInfo;
import com.vmware.vim25.LicenseDiagnostics;
import com.vmware.vim25.LicenseFeatureInfo;
import com.vmware.vim25.LicenseReservationInfo;
import com.vmware.vim25.LicenseServerSource;
import com.vmware.vim25.LicenseSource;
import com.vmware.vim25.LicenseUsageInfo;
import com.vmware.vim25.LocalLicenseSource;
import com.vmware.vim25.mo.LicenseManager;
```

```java
import com.vmware.vim25.mo.ServiceInstance;

public class PrintLicense
{
  public static void main(String[] args) throws Exception
  {
    if(args.length != 3)
    {
      System.out.println("Usage: java PrintLicense <url> "
        + "<username> <password>");
      return;
    }

    ServiceInstance si = new ServiceInstance(
        new URL(args[0]), args[1], args[2], true);

    LicenseManager lm = si.getLicenseManager();

    System.out.println("License edition:"
      + lm.getLicensedEdition());

    System.out.println("Licnese source available:"
      + lm.getSourceAvailable());

    printLicenseSource(lm.getSource());

    System.out.println("License Diagnostic Info:");
    printDiagnostics(lm.getDiagnostics());
    // The featureInfo property is deprecated as of 2.5.
    // Use the querySupportedFeatures as follows.
    System.out.println("\nLicense Features:");
    printLicenseFeatures(lm.querySupportedFeatures(null));

    System.out.println("\nLicense Usage:");
    printLicenseUsage(lm.queryLicenseUsage(null));

    System.out.println("\nLicense source availability:");
    printLicenseAvailable(
      lm.queryLicenseSourceAvailability(null));
    si.getServerConnection().logout();
  }
```

```java
static void printLicenseAvailable(LicenseAvailabilityInfo[] ls)
{
  for(int i=0; ls!=null && i<ls.length; i++)
  {
    System.out.println("Feature:"
        + ls[i].getFeature().getFeatureName());
    System.out.println("Total licenses:" + ls[i].getTotal());
    System.out.println("Available licenses:"
      + ls[i].getAvailable());
  }
}

static void printLicenseUsage(LicenseUsageInfo ui)
{
  System.out.println("The list of feature reservations:");
  LicenseReservationInfo[] ris = ui.getReservationInfo();
  for(int i=0; ris!=null && i< ris.length; i++)
  {
    System.out.println("Feature key :" + ris[i].getKey());
    System.out.println("Required license:"
      + ris[i].getRequired());
    System.out.println("State:" + ris[i].getState());
  }

  System.out.println("All the features that are referenced"
    + " in reservation:");
  printLicenseFeatures(ui.getFeatureInfo());

  System.out.println("License source:");
  printLicenseSource(ui.getSource());

  System.out.println("License source available:"
    + ui.isSourceAvailable());
}

static void printLicenseSource(LicenseSource src)
{
  if(src instanceof EvaluationLicenseSource)
```

```
    {
      System.out.println("Evaluation license: will expire in "
        + ((EvaluationLicenseSource)src).getRemainingHours()
        + " hours.");
    }
    else if(src instanceof LicenseServerSource)
    {
      System.out.println("License from server:"
        + ((LicenseServerSource)src).getLicenseServer());
    }
    else if(src instanceof LocalLicenseSource)
    {
      System.out.println("Local license key:"
        + ((LocalLicenseSource)src).getLicenseKeys());
    }
  }

  static void printLicenseFeatures(LicenseFeatureInfo[] fis)
  {
    for(int i=0; fis!=null && i<fis.length; i++)
    {
      String prtStr =
        "\nFeatureName:" + fis[i].getFeatureName() +
        "\nCostUnit:" + fis[i].getCostUnit() +
        "\nDependentKey:";

      String[] dep = fis[i].getDependentKey();
      for(int j=0; dep!=null && j<dep.length; j++)
      {
        prtStr += dep[j] + " ";
      }

      prtStr +=  "\nEdition:" + fis[i].getEdition() +
        "\nExpiresOn:" + fis[i].getExpiresOn() +
        "\nFeatureDescription:"
          + fis[i].getFeatureDescription() +
        "\nKey:" + fis[i].getKey() +
        "\nSourceRestriction:" + fis[i].getSourceRestriction() +
        "\nState:" + fis[i].getState();
      System.out.println(prtStr);
    }
```

```
}

static void printDiagnostics(LicenseDiagnostics ld)
{
  if(ld==null)
    return;
  String prtStr =
    "LastStatusUpdate:" + ld.getLastStatusUpdate().getTime() +
    "\nLicenseFeatureUnknown:"
      + ld.getLicenseFeatureUnknowns() +
    "\nLicneseRequestFailures:"
      + ld.getLicenseRequestFailures() +
    "\nLicenseReqeusts:" + ld.getLicenseRequests() +
    "\nOpFailiureMessage:" + ld.getOpFailureMessage() +
    "\nOpState:" + ld.getOpState() +
    "\nSourceLastChanged:" + ld.getSourceLastChanged().getTime() +
    "\nsourceLatency:" + ld.getSourceLatency() +
    "\nsourceLost:" + ld.getSourceLost();
  System.out.println(prtStr);
  }
}
```

The program prints available licenses in the source like the following:

```
Feature:NAS Usage
Total licenses:1
Available licenses:0
```

Notice that features such as NAS usage have total as 1 and available as 0. These non-edition features are actually not tracked by the license server. Just ignore them when checking the result from running against ESX.

Listing 15-6 shows how to configure the server to a license server and then set up the edition and disable/enable the iSCSI feature. This sample is written for the ESX server, but you can easily change the feature keys by checking Table 15-5.

Listing 15-6
SetLicenseSource.java

```
package vim25.samples.mo.lic;
import java.net.URL;
```

```java
import com.vmware.vim25.LicenseServerSource;
import com.vmware.vim25.mo.LicenseManager;
import com.vmware.vim25.mo.ServiceInstance;

public class SetLicenseSource
{
  public static void main(String[] args) throws Exception
  {
    if(args.length != 3)
    {
      System.out.println("Usage: java SetLicenseSource <url> "
        + "<username> <password>");
      return;
    }
    ServiceInstance si = new ServiceInstance(
      new URL(args[0]), args[1], args[2], true);
    LicenseManager lm = si.getLicenseManager();

    LicenseServerSource lss = new LicenseServerSource();
    // please change it to a license server you can access
    lss.setLicenseServer("27000@lic-serv.acme.com");

    lm.configureLicenseSource(null, lss);
    lm.setLicenseEdition(null, "esxFull");

    boolean enabled = lm.checkLicenseFeature(null, "iscsi");
    System.out.println("ISCSI enabled:" + enabled);

    lm.disableFeature(null, "iscsi");
    enabled = lm.checkLicenseFeature(null, "iscsi");
    System.out.println("ISCSI enabled:" + enabled);

    lm.enableFeature(null, "iscsi");
    enabled = lm.checkLicenseFeature(null, "iscsi");
    System.out.println("ISCSI enabled:" + enabled);

    si.getServerConnection().logout();
  }
}
```

Summary

This chapter first introduced role-based access control, user directory service. You can use the SDK to create and manage users (groups) with the hypervisor but not the VirtualCenter; and you can use UserDirectory to retrieve the users and groups from the OS or Windows domain controller.

Access permission is granted to a user or group on an entity with a predefined role. The permission can be optionally propagated down to the hierarchy below the entity. The privilege is the finest control that is associated with a specific operation. For easy management, privileges are grouped as roles that can be granted to users on managed entities.

The chapter then discussed session management, which allows a client to log in, log out, list active sessions, and perform other advanced features, such as impersonating users, creating one-time local login ticket, logging in using SSPI, and so on.

Finally, this chapter introduced license management, particularly the LicenseManager managed object. With LicenseManager, you can change the license source, enable/disable a specific feature, query license availability and license usage, and change the license edition.

Chapter 16

Extending the VI Client

Extending the VI Client allows you to integrate your software with VMware products for a better user experience. This chapter explains the extensibility story and how to take advantage of the `ExtensionManager` API to develop a VI Client plug-in. The development process involves writing configuration XML, registering the plug-in, and optionally designing backend Web applications.

Managed Object: `ExtensionManager`

VMware Infrastructure Extensibility Story

VMware VI is designed with a flexible and extensible architecture. It allows you to add more management functionality in three ways:

- Add more components into the VI Client using C#. This is not based on the official interface but is reverse-engineered by the community.[1] In the vSphere, VMware has limited support for .NET plug-ins.

- Add more components into the VI Client using XML-based scripts and backend Web applications. This is an experimental feature in VI 3.5.

---

[1] http://akutz.files.wordpress.com/2008/05/vi3progplugin-rev13.pdf

- Extend the VirtualCenter server by linking your server application so that your application can take advantage of the existing infrastructure. For example, your server application can have operations tracked using Task, which can be monitored in the VI Client like any other tasks. VMware products such as Site Recovery Manager use this mechanism for integration. There is no document about this from VMware or the community.

The first way does not require interaction with either ESX or the VirtualCenter server. The last two ways do require interaction with the server using the VI SDK. The specific managed object is ExtensionManager, which is discussed next. After introducing ExtensionManager, this chapter introduces how to develop a plug-in of a second type, which is referred to as the VI Client plug-in.

ExtensionManager Managed Object

ExtensionManager is a singleton managed object attached to the ServiceInstance. It's only available on a VirtualCenter server, not the ESX server. It has one property, extensionList, which is an array of the Extension data object.

The Extension data object contains all the information about an extension. Several methods depend on it as a parameter or return type. As shown in Figure 16-1, it includes 12 properties ranging from the key to localized resources. The key is the ID for the extension and should be unique with the same VirtualCenter server.

ExtensionManager defines six methods:

- findExtension() looks up an extension whose key is the same as the input parameter. If successful, it returns the Extension data object.

- getPublicKey() retrieves the public key of the VirtualCenter server. The return is a string encoded in private-enhanced mail (PEM) format, like the following:

```
"---BEGIN PUBLIC KEY---
MIGfMA0GCSqGSIb3DQEBAQUAA4GNADCBiQKBgQDS/F57dQ7dAgncQOpeEVqPMLhl
TJ50iFNPlHo1B6Q9xYvbaOxr15l2JCA/Qo66mF9RbGbCrYxSEpB7ucT16ILa1ms
vuJtM0mx/Xkf+saPw23jf8WZhtofgmmMHc99hNw5btLrGLYLXADwHyQeN3omgXdR
g4bQbdDMTrwyvS+ThwIDAQAB ---END PUBLIC KEY--- "
```

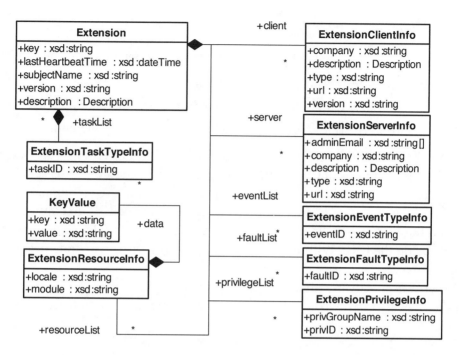

Figure 16-1 Extension data object

- **registerExtension** registers an Extension with the VirtualCenter server. If successful, it returns none, or a fault is thrown. The InvalidArgument fault can be thrown if the extension description is incomplete or an extension is already registered with the given unique key.

- **setPublicKey()** sets an extension's public key. It takes both a string as the extension key and a PEM-encoded public key. If successful, it returns none. An InvalidArgument fault can be thrown if the public key is invalid.

- **unregisterExtension()** unregisters an existing extension. Upon success, the extension is removed from the ExtensionManager's extensionList array.

- **updateExtension()** updates an existing extension. It takes the same parameter as registerExtension(). The difference is really on the precondition. You can achieve the same result if you delete the extension and register it again.

How a VI Client Plug-In Works

A VI Client plug-in allows you to add the following components into the VI Client:

- New icon buttons onto the global toolbar
- New menu items, including the normal drop-down menu and context menu
- New tabs to the right pane associated with an inventory element

A VI Client plug-in needs to be registered with a VirtualCenter server before it can be displayed in the VI Clients that connect to the VirtualCenter server. The registration is one-time only, and you can update an existing registration.

After the registration is done, the VI Client retrieves the URL to configuration file from the VC Server when it starts up. The VI Client then fetches the configuration file using the URL. With the configuration file, the VI Client adds new GUI components.

When a user activates an extended menu item or button, the VI Client pulls pages as specified in the configuration and renders them in an embedded or pop-up browser.

Figure 16-2 shows a typical environment where the VI Client plug-in works.

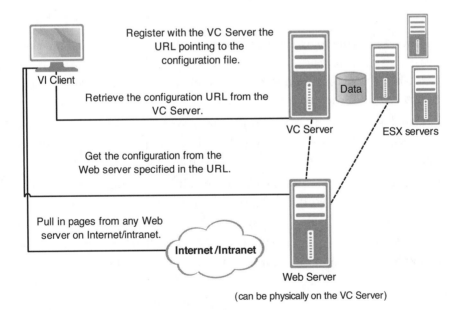

Figure 16-2   The VI Client plug-in architecture

The Web server serving the URL can be on either the same physical host as the VC server or any other connected server.

Understanding Extension Configuration

The extension configuration plays an important role. The following simple configuration file gives you a sense of what it looks like. This configuration adds a button, MapIt, on the toolbar. When it's clicked, an embedded browser displays the Google map site.

```
<scriptConfiguration version="1.0.0">
 <key>com.acme.demo</key>
 <description>VI Extensibility Demo</description>

 <view parent="Inventory.Datacenter">
 <title locale="en">MapIt</title>
 <url>http://maps.google.com</url>
 </view>
</scriptConfiguration>
```

Here are the explanations of the tags used in the configuration file.

- **scriptConfiguration**—Requires `version` attribute. The VI Client can choose to accept or reject based on versions it understands. The element contains one `key` element, zero or one `description` elements, and zero or more `command` and `view` elements.

- **key**—Required. *Must* be a unique identifier for this collection of script configuration elements. The Java package naming convention is recommended.

- **description**—Optional. Describes this collection of script configuration elements.

- **command**—Defines a menu item to add. A command tag in turn can have a command tag and so on to support nested menu-items. The `parent` attribute is required because it defines the parent menu or menu item to which this new menu item is appended. Contains a single `url` element and one or more `title` elements.

- **view**—Defines a view to add. The `parent` attribute is required because it defines the parent to which this view is attached. If `parent` is `Inventory.Global`, the view is a new top-level, toolbar view. In this case, you should also specify an `icon` element; otherwise, a default image is displayed. The `treestyle` attribute controls in which UI view this view is displayed. By default, the view is added everywhere, but if `treestyle` is specified as `Virtual`, it is visible only in VMs and Templates view.

- **url**—The `url` that serves the UI element. For menu extensions, the `display` attribute determines the action that needs to be taken on its click, as listed here:

  - **display=browser**—`url` is launched in a separate Web browser independent of the VI Client

  - **display=window**—`url` is launched in a new window (form), which has a browser embedded in it

  - **display=none**—Just execute the script at the given `url`

  If nothing is specified, `url` defaults to `browser`.

- **title**—Text to display for the UI element. If the `locale` attribute is specified, the label applies only when the client is running with that locale. Only one label may be provided for each locale. You must specify at least one locale.

- **icon**—The URL to load the icon associated with this UI element on the toolbar.

- **customAttribute**—If specified, conditionally adds the extension (menu or view) to the specified managed object. However, currently the VI Client only allows adding custom values for a host and a vm. Has a name and value that need to map exactly to the custom attribute defined on that managed object. If the custom attribute tag is not specified, the extensions are always added, which is the default case.

For a complete document and schema definition of the configuration, check out the VI Client plug-in site (www.vmware.com/support/developer/vc-sdk/vcplugin-exp/).

Registering and Managing Your Plug-In

When you're finished with the configuration file, you can post it to a Web server that the VI Client can access. Write down the URL to the configuration file and double-check it with a browser on the same machine as your VI Client.

> The configuration file is *not* stored in the VirtualCenter server, but a separate Web server accessible anywhere from the VI Client.

Then you can go ahead with registering your extensions with the VirtualCenter. Listing 16-1 shows a utility program that you can use to register and manage the extensions with the `ExtensionManager`. Before you run the utility, modify the `extension.properties`, which is shown in Listing 16-2, to your own settings. Inline comments in the extension properties tell you how to change it.

When you are done, just run the Java program:

```
java ExtMgrUtil c:\myproject\ext\extension.properties
```

Listing 16-1
ExtMgrUtil.java

```
package vim25.samples.mo.ext;
import java.io.FileInputStream;
import java.io.FileNotFoundException;
import java.io.IOException;
import java.net.URL;
import java.util.Calendar;
import java.util.Properties;


import com.vmware.vim25.Description;
import com.vmware.vim25.Extension;
import com.vmware.vim25.ExtensionClientInfo;
import com.vmware.vim25.ExtensionServerInfo;
import com.vmware.vim25.mo.ExtensionManager;
import com.vmware.vim25.mo.ServiceInstance;
```

```
public class ExtMgrUtil
{
  public static void main(String[] args) throws Exception
  {
    // get the properties file for parameters
    String filename = null;
    if(args.length==0)
    {
      System.out.println("Usage: java ExtMgrUtil " +
          "[properties_file_path]");
      System.out.println("Since no properties file is " +
          "specified, we will search for it in current path.");
      filename = "extension.properties";
    }
    else
    {
      filename = args[0];
    }

    // Read in parameters from the properties file
    Properties props = readProperties(filename);
    if(props==null)
    {
      System.exit(-1);
    }

    // Assign the values to the corresponding variables
    URL url = new URL(props.getProperty("url"));
    String userName = props.getProperty("userName");
    String password = props.getProperty("password");
    String operation = props.getProperty("operation");
    String keyStr = props.getProperty("keyStr");

    ServiceInstance si = new ServiceInstance(
        url, userName, password, true);
    ExtensionManager extMgr = si.getExtensionManager();
```

```
if("register".equalsIgnoreCase(operation))
{
  if(extMgr.findExtension(keyStr)!=null)
  {
    System.out.println("Plugin key: " + keyStr +
        " is used. Please try with a new key.");
  }
  else
  {
    Extension ext = createExtensionObject(props);
    extMgr.registerExtension(ext);
    System.out.println("Plugin: " + keyStr +
        " has been successfully registered.");
  }
}
else if ("update".equalsIgnoreCase(operation))
{
  if(extMgr.findExtension(keyStr)!=null)
  {
    Extension ext = createExtensionObject(props);
    extMgr.updateExtension(ext);
    System.out.println("Plugin: " + keyStr +
        " has been successfully updated.");
  }
  else
  {
    System.out.println("The plugin doesn't exist. " +
        "Please register it before updating it.");
  }
}
else if("listall".equalsIgnoreCase(operation))
{
  printAllExtensions(extMgr.getExtensionList());
}
else if("unregister".equalsIgnoreCase(operation))
{
  if(extMgr.findExtension(keyStr)!=null)
  {
    extMgr.unregisterExtension(keyStr);
    System.out.println("Plugin: " + keyStr +
```

```
              " has been successfully un-registered.");
    }
    else
    {
      System.out.println("Plugin: " + keyStr +
          " does NOT exist. No need to unregister it.");
    }


  }
  else if("find".equalsIgnoreCase(operation))
  {
    if(extMgr.findExtension(keyStr)!=null)
    {
      System.out.println("Plugin: " + keyStr +
          " is registered.");
    }
    else
    {
      System.out.println("Plugin: " + keyStr +
          " can NOT be found.");
    }
  }
  else
  {
    System.out.println("Operation is not valide. " +
        "Please try again.");
  }

  si.getServerConnection().logout();
}

static Properties readProperties(String filename)
{
  Properties props = new Properties();
  FileInputStream fis = null;
  try
  {
    fis = new FileInputStream(filename);
    props.load(new FileInputStream(filename));
```

```
    } catch (FileNotFoundException fnfe)
    {
      System.out.println("Properties file " + filename +
          " does NOT exist. Please double check." );
      return null;
    }
    catch (IOException ioe)
    {
      ioe.printStackTrace();
      System.out.println("Please check the parameters " +
          "in the properties file " + filename);
      return null;
    }
    finally
    {
      if(fis!=null)
      {
        try
        {
          fis.close();
        } catch (IOException cioe)
        {}
      }
    }
    return props;
}

static Extension createExtensionObject(Properties props)
{
  String companyStr = props.getProperty("companyStr");
  String descStr = props.getProperty("descStr");
  String keyStr = props.getProperty("keyStr");
  String extUrl = props.getProperty("extUrl");
  String adminEmail = props.getProperty("adminEmail");
  String version = props.getProperty("version");

  Description description = new Description();
  description.setLabel(keyStr);
  description.setSummary(descStr);
```

```
    ExtensionServerInfo esi = new ExtensionServerInfo();
    esi.setDescription(description);
    esi.setUrl(extUrl);
    esi.setCompany(companyStr);
    // the following type must NOT be changed
    esi.setType("com.vmware.vim.viClientScripts");
    esi.setAdminEmail( new String[] { adminEmail } );

    ExtensionClientInfo eci = new ExtensionClientInfo();
    eci.setCompany(companyStr);
    eci.setUrl(extUrl);
    eci.setType("com.vmware.vim.viClientScripts");
    eci.setVersion(version);
    eci.setDescription(description);

    Extension ext = new Extension();
    ext.setServer(new ExtensionServerInfo[]{esi});
    ext.setClient(new ExtensionClientInfo[] {eci});
    ext.setDescription(description);
    ext.setKey(keyStr);
    ext.setVersion(version);
    ext.setLastHeartbeatTime(Calendar.getInstance());
    return ext;
}

static void printAllExtensions(Extension[] exts)
{
  System.out.println("There are totally " +
      exts.length + " plugin(s) registered.");

  for(int i=0; exts!=null && i<exts.length; i++)
  {
    System.out.println("\n —- Plugin # " + (i+1) + " —- ");
    System.out.println("Key: " + exts[i].getKey());
    System.out.println("Version: " + exts[i].getVersion());
    System.out.println("Registration Time: " +
        exts[i].getLastHeartbeatTime().getTime());
    System.out.println("Configuration URL: " +
        exts[i].getServer()[0].getUrl());
```

```
    }
  }
}
```

Listing 16-2

`extension.properties`

```
################################################
# The info needed to connect to the VC server.
# Please change these to your Virtual Server setting.
################################################
url = https://192.168.8.208/sdk
userName = administrator
password = mypass
################################################
# The operation you would like to happen
# Possible operations are:
# listall, register, update, unregister, find
################################################
operation = listall
################################################
# The info about the extension itself.
# Some of them are optional, depending on the operation.
# register, update: all required.
# listall: none is required.
# find and unregister: keyStr is required.
################################################
# The company name
companyStr = Acme Inc.
# A brief description of the plugin itself
descStr = VC extensibility Demo
# Version number
version = 1.0.0
# Unique id for this extension
keyStr = com.acme.demo
# Link to configuration file
extUrl = http://192.168.8.8:8000/demo.xml
# The email of administrator
adminEmail = admin@acme.com
```

The key string for a plug-in must be unique within the VC server it registers. It's recommended that you follow Java naming conventions to prefix your plug-in name with your company name and product/project name.

You can also use the MOB to register the VI Client plug-in. Chapter 2, "VI SDK Basics," discussed how to use the MOB to invoke a method. The XML for the extension parameter is as follows:

```
<extension>
    <description>
        <label>com.acme.demo</label>
        <summary>This is my Plugin description!</summary>
    </description>

    <key>com.acme.demo</key>
    <version>1.0.0</version>
    <subjectName>/O=ACME/OU=DEV/CN=VI Client plugin</subjectName>

    <server>
        <url>http://192.168.8.8:8000/demo.xml</url>  <!-- Replace this URL with
the URL to your plugin config XML -->
        <description>
            <label>com.acme.demo</label>
            <summary>This is my Plugin description!</summary>
        </description>
        <company>ACME Inc.</company>
        <type>com.vmware.vim.viClientScripts</type>
        <adminEmail>admin@acme.com</adminEmail>
    </server>

    <client>
      <version>1.0.0</version>
        <description>
            <label>com.acme.demo</label>
            <summary>This is my Plugin description!</summary>
        </description>
        <company>ACME Inc.</company>
        <type>Script Plugin</type>
        <url></url>
    </client>
```

```
<lastHeartbeatTime>2008-12-18T12:59:26.234375Z</lastHeartbeatTime>
</extension>
```

You can change the related values to your own settings (for example, the company name, description, and configuration URL). You must not change the value of extension.server.type, which should always be com.vmware.vim.viClientScripts. You also should not change the structure and order of elements organized in the XML parameter.

Using MOB for registration can save you time, but it's error prone with XML manipulation. Before invoking the method, validate the XML with Internet Explorer or other tools.

Developing Your Backend Web Application

The URL in the configuration could be a simple one that points to anywhere on the Internet, but that doesn't provide useful information about your VMware Infrastructure. Most of the time, you want a URL that goes back to a Web application that connects to VirtualCenter server.

This section does not introduce how to design a generic Web application, because that is clearly out of the scope of this book. Instead, it focuses on two important aspects that are special for backend Web applications for VI Client.

If you already have an existing Web application, you can just place it in a tab. For a smooth user experience, you should modify your Web application to assume the credential of the current VI Client login user.

Parsing Information from the VI Client

Let's first look at the URL pattern from the VI Client plug-in. In addition to the URL you provide in the configuration file, the VI Client plug-in attaches more information to the URL sent to the Web server, including the following:

- **sessionid**—The same string used by VI Client with VC server after login. With this information, anyone can connect to VC with the same privilege as the VI Client's current login user.

- **morof**—The reference to a managed object if it's selected in the inventory. It has both type and value, separated by a ":".

- `serviceUrl`—The URL to access the VirtualCenter server's Web service interface.
- `locale`—The name of the locale currently in use on the client, to be used for localizing content.

For example, if you have a URL like the following in your configuration file:

```
http://dev:8000/vmAction.cgi?cmd=powerOn
```

the real URL sent to the Web server could be as follows, depending on the context in which the URL is sent.

```
http://dev:8000/vmAction.cgi?cmd=powerOn&moref=VirtualMachine:16&sessionId=9241E7
B8-A37B-4264-A8D2-945628F9E0D6&locale=en&serviceUrl=https://vc-101/sdk
```

From this URL, your Web application should be able to parse all the needed information to connect back to the VirtualCenter server.

> When you log in the VI Client connecting to a VC Server on the same machine, do *not* use the default IP address/name `localhost`. Whatever you enter or choose here is going to be passed on to the Web application. Unless the Web server is located on the same VC Server, the Web server has no way to resolve the correct IP address when it gets `localhost` in the URL string from the VI Client.

Connecting Back to the VirtualCenter

Now let's see how to use the information from the URL to connect back to the VirtualCenter server in your Web application. There is actually not much difference for your application to use the VI SDK from other applications. The tricky part is how to set up the connection. Instead of using a username and password, you use the session ID.

Listing 16-3 shows how to do this. This sample just connects back to the VirtualCenter and prints the name of the managed object and timestamp. To run this sample, have a servlet container like Tomcat.[2] Optionally, you can have the

---

[2] http://tomcat.apache.org/. Version 6.0.16 is used to test this servlet.

Sysdeo plug-in[3] for Eclipse, which helps you to develop a Web application with Tomcat.

To access the servlet, you can use a URL like the following:[4]

```
http://192.168.8.8:8080/ViClientWebApp/TestServlet
```

Listing 16-3
TestServlet.java

```java
import java.io.IOException;
import java.io.PrintWriter;
import java.net.URL;
import java.text.DateFormat;
import java.util.Date;
import javax.servlet.ServletException;

import javax.servlet.http.HttpServlet;
import javax.servlet.http.HttpServletRequest;
import javax.servlet.http.HttpServletResponse;

import com.vmware.vim25.ManagedObjectReference;
import com.vmware.vim25.mo.ManagedEntity;
import com.vmware.vim25.mo.ServiceInstance;
import com.vmware.vim25.mo.util.MorUtil;

public class TestServlet extends HttpServlet
{
  public final static String MOREF = "moref";
  public final static String SESSION_ID = "sessionId";
  public final static String SERVICE_URL = "serviceUrl";
  public final static String LOCALE = "locale";

  protected void service(
      HttpServletRequest request, HttpServletResponse response)
        throws ServletException, IOException
```

---

[3] www.eclipsetotale.com/tomcatPlugin.html. Version 3.2.1 is used to develop the sample.
[4] The actual URL depends on your Web server IP address/port and the configuration pointing to the servlet.

```
{
  PrintWriter out = response.getWriter();

  String morStr = request.getParameter(MOREF);
  String type = morStr.substring(0, morStr.indexOf(":"));
  String value = morStr.substring(morStr.indexOf(":")+1);

  ManagedObjectReference mor = new ManagedObjectReference();
  mor.setType(type);
  mor.set_value(value);

  String sessionStr = "vmware_soap_session=\""
    + request.getParameter(SESSION_ID) + "\"";

  System.out.println("morStr:" + morStr);
  System.out.println("serviceUrl"
      + request.getParameter(SERVICE_URL) );
  System.out.println("session:" + sessionStr);

  ServiceInstance si = new ServiceInstance(new URL(
      request.getParameter(SERVICE_URL)),sessionStr, true);

  ManagedEntity me = MorUtil.createExactManagedEntity(
      si.getServerConnection(), mor);

  String name = me.getName();
  out.println("name:" + name);
  out.println(DateFormat.getDateTimeInstance().format(
      new Date()));
  }
}
```

In your Web application, you should *never* log out of the current session. Doing so terminates the VI Client who shares the session.

Security Discussion

As you have noticed, `sessionid` is sent back to the Web application in a URL. With the `sessionid`, you can log back into the vCenter server as the currently logged in user of VI Client, and then have all her privileges.

Because the `sessionid` is in the URL without protection, it's easy for a malicious party to steal it. The `sessionid` remains the same as long as the VI Client is still alive; it allows enough time to compromise the system. Even worse, there is no easy way to detect when it's been compromised.

In light of these facts, you should be careful when implementing a plug-in. In vSphere 4, you can use a one-time session ticket to mitigate the security risk.

Summary

The VI extensibility allows you to extend the platform by integrating third-party products. This chapter introduced the extension story of VMware Infrastructure and showed how you can develop a VI Client plug-in using the `ExtensionManager` API.

Chapter 17

Scripting the VI SDK with Jython, Perl, and PowerShell

Because the VI SDK is built on top of Web Services interfaces, you can use any programming languages that support Web Services to develop your applications or utilities. Java is the primary language in this book so far, but it's not the only choice.

This chapter shows you how to write code in scripting languages like Jython (Python), Perl, and PowerShell. The introductions show you how to get started, but they're not intended to be a complete in-depth tutorial. For detailed information, read the related documents recommended in the section "Further Reading."

Jython scripting comes as a by-product of the VI Java API. As long as you know how to program Python, you can easily use it to script the VI SDK.

Perl and PowerShell scripting are based on VMware-released products. They have additional features and a slightly different object model.

Scripting with Jython

According to the Jython Web site:

> Jython is an implementation of the high-level, dynamic, object-oriented language Python written in 100% Pure Java, and it's seamlessly integrated with the Java

platform. It thus allows you to run Python on any Java platform.[1]

Given its unique characteristics, Jython has the best of both Python and Java languages.

To understand the rest of this section, you need some basic Python/Jython programming knowledge. Because this is out of scope of this book, if you are new to Jython/Python programming, read the Jython project home page for more information.

What Is Needed?

To script VI SDK in Jython, you need the following software components: Jython interpreter, Jython IDE plug-in, VI SDK 2.5, and VI Java API. Installing the VI SDK and VI Java API was covered in Chapter 3, "Hello VI," so they are not covered here.

Assume you have the VI SDK and VI Java API installed already. You will need

- **Jython runtime**—You can download the Jython runtime from the project download page.[2] Jython 2.2.1 is used here.

- **JyDT (optional)**—If you like an IDE, you can use the JyDT plug-in for Eclipse. You can download it[3] and install it with the Install/Update wizard, or you can go to the online update site[4] directly. The version 1.4.15 is used in this section. Check out a good article on the Internet[5] explaining how to create and configure a Jython project using JyDT.

After you install all these, you can get started with your first Jython code.

HelloVM.py

To script the VI SDK in Jython, follow these steps:

1. Create a new Jython project with a wizard shown in Figure 17-1.

---

[1] www.jython.org
[2] www.jython.org/downloads.html
[3] www.redrobinsoftware.net/jydt/
[4] www.redrobinsoftware.net/jydt/installation/installation.html
[5] www.redrobinsoftware.net/jydt/projects/creatingproject.html

2. Create a `HelloVM.py` and type the sample code as follows:

```
from java.net import *
from com.vmware.vim25.mo import *


si = ServiceInstance(URL("https://192.168.8.8/sdk"),
    "root", "password", True)
vms = InventoryNavigator(si.rootFolder)
    .searchManagedEntities("VirtualMachine")
print "Hello " + vms[0].name


si.getServerConnection().logout()
```

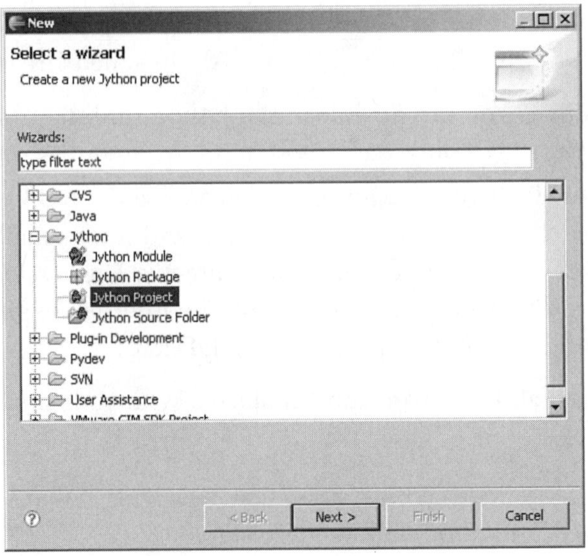

Figure 17-1 The wizard to create a Jython project with JyDT

When you are done, you see a screen similar to Figure 17-2.

3. Go to the project Property dialog and configure the class path. Include all the JAR files you need to run an application using the VI Java API. Figure 17-3 shows how it looks while configuring the Jython class path.

4. Run `HelloVM.py` as any other program in the IDE, and see the printout in the console view.

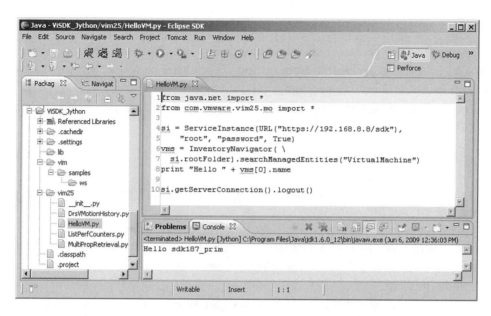

Figure 17-2 Created project

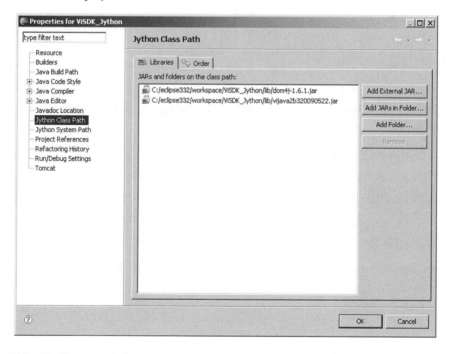

Figure 17-3 The Property dialog box to add a Jython class path

Further Discussion

Because Jython has provided seamless integration with Java, whatever is available in the VI Java API is accessible from Jython. That means if you know how to use the VI Java API and how to program Python, you are ready to go.

You can use the getter methods as they are in Java, or in a simplified manner, such as this:

```
vm.name for vm.getName()
```

This is more readable and more natural for accessing properties than the more wordy way we did this with Java code.

Given the extra layer added by the Jython interpreter, the performance of the Python program is a little slower than the equivalents in Java. But you can get fewer lines of code and dynamic binding. It's really a trade-off between performance and simplicity.

In general, Jython scripting is a great tool for system administrators who want to automate management tasks with the VI, especially when you are already familiar with Python.

VI Perl Toolkit

The VI Perl Toolkit is the first official toolkit built on top of the VI SDK from VMware. Version 1.6 was released in July 2008. It's based on VI SDK 2.5.

The toolkit includes the following components:

- A complete Perl binding, which provides the full VI API on the client side.
- VMware Perl modules (VIRuntime.pl, VILib.pl) with basic subroutines.
- Utilities that you can use directly to manage your VMware Infrastructure.
- Sample scripts that illustrate how to use the APIs. You can adapt them to your own needs.

If you are new to Perl, you may want to read a basic tutorial about Perl online[6] or buy a book.[7]

---

[6] http://perldoc.perl.org/index-tutorials.html
[7] Check out http://books.perl.org/topx for top-rated Perl books

Installing VI Perl Toolkit

The VI Perl Toolkit can be installed on both Windows and Linux. The official supported platforms are

- Windows XP SP2, both 32 bit and 64 bit
- Windows Vista SP1, both 32 bit and 64 bit
- Red Hat Enterprise Linux (RHEL) 5.1, both 32 bit and 64 bit
- Ubuntu Desktop 7.10

If you don't want the hassle of installing and configuring the VI Perl Toolkit, you can use the Virtual Infrastructure Management Assistant (VIMA), which can be imported and run on any ESX 3.5 host. The appliance also includes the VI Remote command-line interface (RCLI), which is the remote version of the CLI on the console OS that has the same syntax.

The installation of the VI Perl Toolkit varies from platform to platform. Let's use Windows as an example. For others, you can read the *Installation Guide: VMware Infrastructure Perl Toolkit 1.6.*[8]

To get the toolkit, visit the SDK download page[9] and follow the instructions to download the VI Perl Toolkit—Windows Installer (.exe) 1.6. The executable includes the ActivePerl runtime from ActiveState and all the required modules/libraries.

After you download it, you can run the executable and follow the wizard. If an earlier version exists, the installer offers upgrading if compatible; otherwise, it prompts you to uninstall the existing version. The default directory is as follows, but you can change it:

```
C:\Program Files\VMware\VMware VI Perl Toolkit\Perl
```

After the installation is finished, you can try a few samples under the `samples` directory; for example:

```
perl discovery/datacenterlisting.pl --server 192.168.8.8 --datacenter
ha-datacenter --username root --password mypass
```

---

[8] www.vmware.com/support/developer/viperltoolkit/viperl16/doc/viperl_install.pdf
[9] www.vmware.com/download/sdk/index.html

Be sure to change the IP address and root password when running it in your environment.

HelloVM.pl

When you are finished with the installation, you can start to write your first Perl code. Listing 17-1 lists all the virtual machines in an inventory.

Listing 17-1
HelloVM.pl

```perl
use strict;
use warnings;
use VMware::VIRuntime;

$Util::script_version = "1.0";

# read/validate options
Opts::parse();
Opts::validate();

# connect to the server
Util::connect();

# get all virtual machines in the inventory
my $vm_views = Vim::find_entity_views(view_type => 'VirtualMachine');

# print vm's names
foreach (@$vm_views)
{
    print $_->name . "\n";
}

# disconnect from the server
Util::disconnect();
```

You can run the code using the command line as follows:

```
C:\Program Files\VMware\VMware VI Perl Toolkit\Perl\workspace>perl
hellovm.pl --server 192.168.8.8 --username root --password mypass
```

Application Flow Using VI Perl

In general, a VI Perl program has the following workflow:

1. Get command-line options. The VI Perl has several default options defined; you don't need to specify them in your code. The most common default options are server, username, and password.[10]

   To add more options, you can incorporate code like the following. The datacenter option specifies the type as string and the description as the datacenter name; this is required. When you run the script, provide the datacenter option as shown in the last section in the command line.

   ```
   my %opts = (
       datacenter => {
           type => "=s",
           help => "Datacenter name",
           required => 1,
       },
   );


   # read/validate options and connect to the server
   Opts::add_options(%opts);
   Opts::parse();
   Opts::validate();
   ```

2. Connect to the server with the Util::connect() method. The parameters are passed onto this method implicitly for setting up the connection and logging in.

3. Create view objects and use them for retrieving information or conducting operations.

4. Disconnect from the server using the Util.disconnect() method.

---

[10] VI Perl does not support PKI keys to authenticate the target server, so there is no option to specify key stores. The communication between the client and server is still secure with HTTPS, but the client cannot tell if the server it connects to is faked.

Perl View Objects for Managed Entities

A Perl View object is a client-side Perl object that has a local copy of properties of the managed object it corresponds to.

> The Perl View objects have nothing to do with the View managed object and its subtypes in the VI SDK. They are two different things.

To get one or more Perl View objects for managed entities, use `Vim::find_entity_view()` or `Vim::find_entity_view()` as follows. To get other types of managed entities, replace the `VirtualMachine` with type names such as `HostSystem`.

```
my $vm_views = Vim::find_entity_views(view_type => 'VirtualMachine');
```

You can also add a filter to fine-tune the result. The following code gets all the virtual machines whose guest OS has Windows in the name. You also specify from which entity to start searching for the entity views.

```
my $vm_views = Vim::find_entity_views(
            view_type => 'VirtualMachine',
            filter => { 'config.guestFullName' => qr/Windows/ }
            );
```

After you get the Perl View object, you can access the property of Perl View objects with a single call as follows. The second line prints the `powerState`, which is an enumeration type; therefore, `->val` is used to access its value.

```
print $vm->name . ": " . $vm->config->guestFullName . "\n";
print $vm->name . ": " . $vm->runtime->powerState->val . "\n";
```

Remember, whatever properties you get as above are actually from the local cache, not directly from the server. It's highly possible that you can access a property that is already out of date. If you need up-to-date property values, you should update the view as follows before you access any property in the Perl View object. When the view is being updated, property values are retrieved again from the corresponding managed entities in the server side.

```
$vm->update_view_data();
```

The Perl View object also defines all the methods corresponding to the managed object. For example, you can power off a virtual machine using the Perl View object for the virtual machine:

```
$vm->PowerOffVM_Task();
```

When parameters are needed for a method, just provide them in the call. These parameters are similar to the way you use them in Java.

```
$vm->Rename_Task(name=> 'myVM');
```

In addition to all the methods that are included in VI SDK, Perl View objects have added peer-blocking methods for the long-running operations whose method names have _Task suffixes. For example, `PowerOffVM_Task()` is a nonblocking call. It has an equivalent version to the `PowerOffVM()` method, which returns only when the operation is complete.

These blocking methods are Perl-only methods that are used more than the nonblocking ones in typical utility applications. Don't confuse them and expect the same in other language bindings. In fact, it's easy to monitor the returned `Task` object and block the execution by yourself.

Using Data Objects

The data objects are mainly for properties and method parameters/returns. After you have a data object, you can access its properties as you would any other objects. For example:

```
my $cfg = $_->config;
print $cfg->guestFullName;
```

When a data object is needed for a method call, create it as follows before invoking the method:

```
my $host_connect_spec = (HostConnectSpec->new(force => 0,
                                       hostName => $host,
                                       userName => $username,
                                       password => $password,
```

```
                                          ));
$folder->AddStandaloneHost(spec => $host_connect_spec,
                           addConnected => 1);
```

If you have an existing data object, you can change its properties like this:

```
$ host_connect_spec->force('true');
```

Working with Non-Entity View Objects

Previous discussions didn't mention ServiceInstance or any other non-entity managed objects. As we mentioned in Chapter 2, "VI SDK Basics," ServiceInstance is the starting point of the managed object hierarchy. Most of the time, it's transparent from the developers in Perl. To get it, just use the following code after Util::connect():

```
my $service_instance = Vim::get_service_instance();
```

From the service instance object, you can call its methods or access its property as follows:

```
$service_instance->CurrentTime();
print $service_instance->serverClock;
```

You can get all other singleton managed objects, such as TaskManager, as follows. The key is to use Vim::get_service_content() for the ManagedObjectReference of the TaskManager object.

```
my $scheduled_task_mgr = Vim::get_view(
mo_ref => Vim::get_service_content()->taskManager);
```

If you know the ManagedObjectReference value from the management information base (MOB) or another source such as the VI Client Plugin, you can create a new object with the previous method:

```
my $moref = ManagedObjectReference->new(
     type => 'HostSystem',
     value => 'host-41'
);
my $host = Vim::get_view(mo_ref => $moref);
```

Further Reading

This introduction provides an overview of VI Perl and gets you started with simple VI Perl programming. It doesn't cover advanced features like saving and using sessions, specifying untyped arguments in scheduled tasks, and callbacks. You can find all these in the *VI Perl Toolkit Programming Guide 1.6.*[11] Also helpful is the *VI Perl Toolkit Utility Applications Reference*, which you can find in the same page with the programming guide.

The most important thing in learning programming is to give it a try. After successfully installing it, you can find many samples covering aspects of VI management, including virtual machine, host system, performance, and scheduled tasks. It is helpful to try these samples and modify them to your requirement as part of the learning process.

The VMware developer center (http://developer.vmware.com/) also has a discussion forum and more sample scripts either by the company or the community, for example William Lam's vGhetto Script Repository (http://communities.vmware.com/docs/DOC-9852). You should periodically visit the forum for new updates.

VI Toolkit (for Windows)

Microsoft PowerShell is a scripting language that targets system administrators. It is similar to the familiar DOS command or the shell script in UNIX/Linux. The standard PowerShell has more than 130 standard command-line tools. It runs on Windows XP, Windows Vista, Windows Server 2003, Windows Server 2008, and Window 7.

What really sets PowerShell apart from other shell environments is that applications are being built with manageability expressly in mind. In the Windows world, PowerShell becomes increasingly important for managing large numbers of servers and applications. Using PowerShell, you can manage all Microsoft server products, such as Exchange Server 2007 and System Center Operations Manager 2007.

The VI Toolkit (for Windows) is a VMware offering for system administrators to use PowerShell to manage the VMware infrastructure. The toolkit version 1.5, released in January 2009, includes 173 cmdlets (the command in PowerShell terminology). Most of the cmdlets are task-driven utilities, but two are .NET cmdlets

---

[11] www.vmware.com/support/developer/viperltoolkit/

exposed through PowerShell. You can use these cmdlets like any command or group them into script files. For a list of cmdlets, see Appendix C, "Cmdlets in the VI Toolkit (for Windows)."

The toolkit version 1.5 supports VMware ESX server 3.5, ESX Server 3i, VirtualCenter 2.5, and ESX Server 3.0/VirtualCenter 2.0.

Installing VI Toolkit (for Windows)

To use the VI Toolkit, you need to install .NET 2.0 SP1 and Windows PowerShell 1.0. Check out the Microsoft Web site[12] to install these first.

Then download the toolkit from its VMware Web site.[13] Just follow the instructions and save the installer to a local directory.

After double-clicking the installer, it starts the installation process, which is straightforward. By default, it is installed to the following directory; you can always change to a directory of your choice.

```
C:\Program Files\VMware\Infrastructure\VIToolkitForWindows\
```

After a successful installation, the console window opens. To launch the toolkit later on, choose Start, Programs, VMware, VMware Infrastructure Toolkit, VMware VI Toolkit (for Windows).

To validate the installation, type a `Connect-VIServer` command in the console:

```
Connect-VIServer -Server 192.168.8.8 -Protocol https -User root -Password mypass
```

The host IP address and root password should be changed while running in your environment.

Common Cmdlets

This section discusses eight basic cmdlets. The first five cmdlets are generic PowerShell cmdlets, and the last four are VMware-specific. Appendix C lists all the cmdlets and their syntaxes for your reference. The PowerShell cmdlets are not case sensitive:

---

[12] www.microsoft.com/windowsserver2003/technologies/management/powershell/download.mspx
[13] www.vmware.com/support/developer/windowstoolkit/

- **ForEach-Object**—Executes a script block for each input object. Input objects are usually piped in to this cmdlet. This cmdlet is usually abbreviated as either foreach or %. The following cmdlet prints the name of each file and directory in the current directory:

```
dir | ForEach-Object { $_.name }
```

- **Select-Object**—Selects certain properties of input objects. Select-Object also provides a means of executing a script block to populate a column. This powerful feature allows you to execute code that uses the object as input and display the results alongside properties from the object. The following example selects only the mode of the files (including directories) in the current directory:

```
dir | Select-Object mode
```

- **Where-Object**—Executes a script block against each object, and if the script block returns true, it emits the input object as an output object. The Where-Object cmdlet is usually used in a pipeline. The Where-Object cmdlet is usually abbreviated as either where or ?. The following cmdlet returns all subdirectories of the current directory:

```
dir | Where-Object { $_.mode -eq "d----" }
```

- **Get-Member**—A reflection that allows you to inspect an object to determine what methods and properties are defined by the method. It is often abbreviated as gm. The following example shows what methods and properties are defined for file or directory objects:

```
dir | gm
```

- **Measure-Object**—Counts the number of objects in a data structure. The following cmdlet counts the number of files and directories in the current directory:

```
dir | Measure-Object
```

- **Connect-VIServer (VMware)**—Before you can do any VMware management from PowerShell, you must connect to a VC server or ESX host. The following cmdlet, for example, connects to the VI server at 192.168.8.8. To complete the connection, you are prompted for a username and password:

```
Connect-VIServer 192.168.8.8
```

Optionally, you can add a username and password in the command to avoid further user interaction.

- **Get-VM (VMware)**—Retrieves managed virtual machines. For example, the following example displays all the names and memories of virtual machines in the VI:

```
Get-VM | select name, memorymb
```

You can also pipeline it with cmdlets to do other things, such as powering it up:

```
Get-VM myVM | Start-VM
```

- **Get-VMHost (VMware)**—Retrieves the hosts. The following cmdlet, for example, prints the names of all the hosts that are available in the VI:

```
Get-VMHost | select name
```

You can get help for any cmdlet by typing the `help` command. For more detailed help, include the `-full` option:

```
help <cmdlet_name> [-full]
```

To list all the VMware cmdlets, you can type the following:

```
Get-Command –PSSnapin VMware.VimAutomation.Core | more
```

Cmdlet Pipeline

Just like UNIX shell commands, PowerShell cmdlets can be pipelined and pass on the output objects of one cmdlet as the input object of the next cmdlet. It's a powerful feature that is used a lot in PowerShell scripting.

This example takes a snapshot of all VMs in your VMware Infrastructure:

```
get-vm | new-snapshot
```

To determine what arguments can be piped into a cmdlet, just issue the following command:

```
help <cmdlet_name> -full
```

In the help, all parameters are explained. For example, the help for the Set-VM cmdlet indicates that the –VM argument can be passed in as pipeline input. Therefore, the following example can pass the virtual machine object to the Set-VM cmdlet and rename it to NewName:

```
Get-VM <my_VM> | Set-VM –Name "NewName"
```

Running the Cmdlets in a Script File

To use the cmdlets, you can either type in the cmdlets directly or group them into a script file with the .ps1 extension. You can also record what you typed in the console and have a script.

To run a script, just type in the valid path either absolute or relative:

```
C:\MyScripts\test.ps1
```

or

```
.\test.ps
```

To work efficiently, you can use a GUI tool similar to the IDE, such as PowerGUI,[14] which helps to develop, edit, run, and manage the scripts. To download the tool, check out its Web site. PowerShell 2.0 CTP3 provides an IDE as well.

---

[14] www.powergui.org

It is even more powerful when the VI Toolkit cmdlets are used with other shell scripts. For example, the following script[15] generates a report in CSV format for all the virtual machines with their name, description, power state, and so on:

```
Connect-VIServer -Server 192.168.8.8 -Protocol https `
-User Administrator -Password myPass

get-vm | select Name, Description, PowerState, Num*, Memory*, `
@{Name="Host"; Expression={$_.Host.Name}} | export-csv output.csv

Disconnect-VIServer
```

Web Service Access Cmdlets

There are two Web Services–related cmdlets in the toolkit: Get-View and Get-VIObjectByVIView. They can be used to access the underlying .NET objects. The .NET objects are much like the Perl View objects in that they are static copies of the server-side managed objects. They keep a local copy of properties but don't sync them up with the remote server. All the methods defined on the corresponding managed object are available on the .NET objects. Using the lower-level .NET objects allows you more flexibility and more programmatic control.

The Get-View cmdlet returns a .NET View object by specified search criteria. The following cmdlets, for example, get the .NET View objects based on the power state and guest OS name, and then shut them down:

```
$filter = @{ "Runtime.PowerState" = "poweredOn";
        "Config.GuestFullName" = "Windows" }
Get-View -ViewType "VirtualMachine" -Filter $filter
        | foreach { $_.ShutdownGuest() }
```

The Get-VIObjectByVIView cmdlet converts a .NET View object to a PowerShell VIObject based on ID. The following code converts a virtual machine View object and powers up the virtual machine:

```
$vm = Get-VIObjectByVIView $vmView | Start-VM
```

---

[15] Thanks to Carter Shanklin for sharing the script.

Although you can work on the .NET View objects, the strength of the VI Toolkit (for Windows) is really on the cmdlets. They are highly management task oriented and don't need to know the underlying .NET object model.

Further Reading

This introduction covers the basics of the VI Toolkit (for Windows) with which you can start to use the cmdlets for your management works. To find out more on the toolkit, look at the Administrator's Guide and Developer's Guide.[16] The latter document also discusses details on using the object model in .NET. Hal Rottenberg's book *Managing VMware Infrastructure with Windows PowerShell* is also a great resource for you to learn the toolkit.[17]

Like VI Perl, there is also an active PowerShell community[18] and VMware Product Manager Carter Shanklin's Blog[19] from which you can find many more samples and updates on new developments. You can also post your scripts to help the community.

Summary

This chapter introduced how to develop scripts using Jython, Perl, and PowerShell. The Jython enablement is a by-product of the VI Java API. As long as you can program the Python and VI Java API, you can easily get started with it. The focus in the section was mainly on the installation and configuration.

The VI Perl is an official offering from VMware that adds slightly different Perl View objects, which are static copies of a managed object on the client side. These View objects define a similar set of interfaces, as in the VI Java API. R-CLI is built on top of the VI Perl Toolkit.

The VI PowerShell binding is highly administrative and task oriented, with 100+ cmdlets in the latest offering. The underlying .NET object model in VI PowerShell is similar to the Perl View objects, but it is not highlighted or heavily promoted. In this sense, it's significantly different from the other two scripting bindings.

---

[16] www.vmware.com/support/developer/windowstoolkit/

[17] http://www.amazon.com/Managing-VMware-Infrastructure-Windows-PowerShell/dp/0982131402

[18] http://communities.vmware.com/community/developer/windows_toolkit

[19] http://blogs.vmware.com/vipowershell/

Chapter 18

Advanced Topics

This chapter discusses several topics that do not quite fit into the previous chapters. However, you may find them useful in your application development:

- Managing global settings with `OptionManager`
- Collecting logs using `DiagnosticManager`
- Sharing sessions with multiple clients
- Using single sign-on from the VI SDK to CIM
- Downloading and uploading files using HTTP access
- Versioning VI SDKs
- Multithreading with the VI SDK
- Following best practices for performance and scalability
- Considering internationalization

Managed Objects: `OptionManager, DiagnosticManager, HostSystem`

Managing Global Settings with OptionManager

OptionManager manages key/value pairs as a mechanism for flexible settings. It can be reached from both ServiceInstance and HostSystem.

When connecting directly to an ESX server, you can get the OptionManager object from the ServiceInstance, but it doesn't have much information. The OptionManager object from the HostSystem has a real data setting that you can find and modify from the Advanced Setting dialog box of the ESX system in the VI Client.

When connecting to a VirtualCenter server, you can get an OptionManager object from the ServiceInstance with VirtualCenter server settings. You can find and change these settings in the VirtualCenter Management Server Configuration dialog box in the VI Client. The OptionManager object from a HostSystem is the same that you would get from the HostSystem on ESX.

The OptionManager type has two properties defined:

- **supportedOption**—List of OptionDef objects. The OptionDef data object, whose UML diagram is shown in Figure 18-1, is extended from ElementDescription. The ElementDescription has a string property key, which normally uses a dot-separated notation to indicate its position in the whole hierarchy, such as mail.smtp.port for the SMTP port option under the Mail section.

  OptionDef includes OptionType, which has one property indicating whether the option is read-only. OptionType has six subtypes, each of which represents a data type of the option. Most of them include defaultValue for the option. FloatOption, IntOption, and LongOption have the same structure but different data types for the properties.

- **Setting**—List of OptionValue data objects to hold real key/value pairs. The key is one of the keys in the OptionDef objects in supportedOption. The value, as you expect, is defined as xsd:anyType because it can be any value as defined in the six types in OptionDef.

The optionManager defines two methods:

- queryOption() retrieves a specific node or nodes in the option hierarchy. It takes in a string parameter name as the key to the OptionDef. You can provide a full key, or the starting part of the key ending with dot, such as snmp,

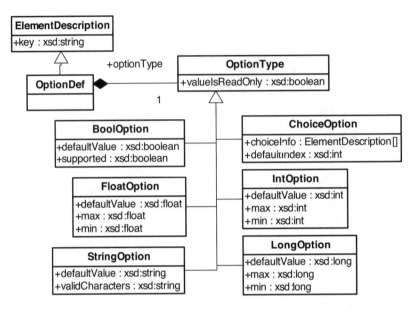

Figure 18-1 The OptionDef and its subtypes

which returns all the OptionValue objects under the snmp node. You must include the dot for the parameter to be valid.

- updateOptions() updates one or more options specified by the OptionValue[] parameter. The changes are done atomically; they are all changed, or none are changed.

For both methods, the option key must be valid, or the InvalidName fault is thrown. For updateOptions(), you must provide a valid value for the option as required in the OptionDef; otherwise, the InvalidArgument fault is thrown.

These two methods do not change the available OptionDef objects. In fact, you cannot add a new OptionDef or remove an existing OptionDef. You can add a new OptionValue without matching OptionDef, but that is not a typical use case.

In the VirtualCenter Management Server Configuration dialog box of the VI Client, you can add more key/value pairs when you select Advanced Settings. Whatever key you enter in is prefixed with config in the OptionManager object. Just use the Managed Object Browser (MOB) to check it out. Awkwardly, the next time you bring back the same dialog box, the newly added key/value pair doesn't display.

Collecting Logs Using `DiagnosticManager`

The `DiagnosticManager` provides services to access low-level debugging logs or generate diagnostic bundles for either the VirtualCenter server or ESX server.

The managed object defines no property but three methods:

- `queryDescriptions()` provides a list of diagnostic files for a given system. It takes in an optional parameter `host` for specifying the `HostSystem` to extract information from. When you connect to the ESX server directly, the parameter isn't needed. When you connect to the VirtualCenter server and the parameter isn't specified, the method assumes you're looking for VirtualCenter logs. The return of this method is an array of `DiagnosticManagerLogDescriptor` data objects. The data object includes six properties, as shown in Figure 18-2.

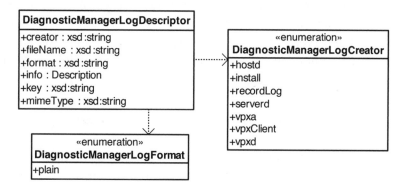

Figure 18-2   The `DiagnosticManagerLogDescriptor` data object

The `creator` property represents the component that creates the log; the value has to be one of the string values defined in the `DiagnosticManagerLogCreator` enumeration type. The filename is the full path to the log file on the ESX server, such as `/var/log/vmware/hostd.log`, or a simple filename on the VirtualCenter server, such as `vpxd-0.log`. The format has only one choice—`plain`—as defined in the `DiagnosticManagerLogFormat` enumeration type. The property `key` is used by other methods for browsing or downloading; it can have values like `vpxd:vpxd-0.log` on VirtualCenter, or `hostd`, `messages`, `vmkernel`, `vmksummary`, `vmkwarning`, or `vpxa` on the ESX server.

The `mimeType` is Multipurpose Internet Mail Extensions (MIME). With the format as `plain`, the `mimeType` is limited to `text/plain`.

- `browseDiagnosticLog()` allows you to "browse" a log file that is identified by the key as returned from the `queryDescriptions()` method. In addition to the key parameter, you can optionally specify two integers as the starting line and the number of lines in the log file you want to browse. If not specified, the starting line defaults to the top, and the number of lines defaults to the total from the starting to the end of the log. To browse the entire log, just leave the two optional parameters empty.

  The return from the method is a `DiagnosticManagerLogHeader` data object, which has properties such as `lineStart` for the starting line and `lineEnd` for the ending line, as well as an array of strings as log entries in the log file.

- `generateLogBundles_Task()` creates diagnostic bundles on the server side to be downloaded. A diagnostic bundle includes log files and other configurations, such as a virtual machine configuration that can be used to investigate potential server issues. The method has a boolean parameter, `includeDefault`, that specifies whether to include the default server, and optionally an array of `HostSystems` while connecting to a VirtualCenter server.

  The return of the method, as its name suggests, is a `Task`. When it's done successfully, the `info.result` property contains a list of `DiagnosticManagerBundleInfo` data object. The data object includes two properties: a system pointing to the `HostSystem` from which the diagnostic bundle is generated; and `url`, which represents the location where you can download the bundle. When you connect to the ESX server directly, `url` might have `*` as a placeholder for the real host name. Just replace it with the real host name or IP address before downloading it.

```
https://*:443/downloads/esxsupport-5224f0a4-becc-cf30-0d30-1bc28a26f7ce.tgz
```

As the file extension suggests, the bundle is a compressed archive file. Use tools like 7-Zip to extract the files inside. Depending on your environment, the bundle could have thousands of files for you to do a thorough analysis of the system.

Sharing Sessions Among Different Applications

When a client first logs into VC or ESX server, a username and password are required to authenticate the user and grant access privileges. In the successive interactions with VC server, no username and password are needed. The HTTP session ID is instead used to track the user.

This HTTP session is different from the UserSession discussed earlier. Their session IDs are in the same format, but they have different values. You can find one sample in the following code.

The HTTP session ID is essentially an HTTP cookie that is pushed from the server when the connection with the server is established. A UserSession is created after the login succeeds. There is mapping from the HTTP session to the user session on the server side so that the consecutive SOAP requests carrying an HTTP session ID automatically assume the privileges of a user. In other words, if your request has the same HTTP session ID as a current user, the system takes you as the user. There won't be a new UserSession for the new client.

In some of the cases, different clients need to share a user session. For example, in a VI Client plug-in, a Web application needs to use the session ID passed in from the VI Client in URL so that it can interact with the VC Server as if from the login user in the VI Client.

Now let's look at how to get the session ID and how to use it from another client.

Getting the Session ID

The code to get the session ID is as follows:

```
...
VimPortType vimService = null;
ManagedObjectReference mor =  null;
ServiceContent serviceContent = null;

VimServiceLocator serviceLocator = new VimServiceLocator();
serviceLocator.setMaintainSession(true);
```

```
try
{
    vimService = serviceLocator.getVimPort(new URL(urlStr));
    ManagedObjectReference serviceRef = new ManagedObjectReference();
    serviceRef.setType("ServiceInstance");
    serviceRef.set_value("ServiceInstance");
    serviceContent = imService.retrieveServiceContent(serviceRef);

    if(serviceContent.getSessionManager()!=null)
    {
        vimService.login(serviceContent.getSessionManager(), username,
password, null);
    }
}
catch (Exception e)
{
    System.err.println("Exception: " + e.getMessage() );
}

VimBindingStub vimStub = (VimBindingStub) vimService;
org.apache.axis.client.Call call = vimStub._getCall();
org.apache.axis.MessageContext msgContext = call.getMessageContext();
String sessionString = (String) msgContext.getProperty(
org.apache.axis.transport.http.HTTPConstants.HEADER_COOKIE);

System.out.println(sessionString);
...
```

Notice that after logging in, the code converts the VimPortType to VimBindingStub and gets the Call, MessageContext objects. From the MessageContext, the session ID is extracted and printed.

In most cases, you only use the interface com.vmware.vim.VimPortType for operations in the VI SDK. This is, however, not enough to access the session information. The VimPortType interface provides a login service, but it does *not* expose session information.

To share a session, just grab the real implementation class, which is com.vmware.vim.VimBindingStub. With this implementation class, you can get and set session information, as shown in the previous samples.

```
public class com.vmware.vim.VimBindingStub extends org.apache.axis.client.Stub
implements com.vmware.vim.VimPortType ()
```

The content of sessionString looks like this:

```
vmware_soap_session="B3240D15-34DF-4BB9-B902-A844FDF42E85"
```

This sample code is not always needed. In the case of the VI client plug-in, the VI client extracts the session ID and passes it in the URL to the Web application, which can use it to interact with the VC Server.

Using Session ID

Now, let's see how another client can use the session ID:

```
VimPortType vimService = null;
ManagedObjectReference mor = null;
ServiceContent serviceContent = null;

VimServiceLocator serviceLocator = new VimServiceLocator();
serviceLocator.setMaintainSession(true);

try
{
      vimService = serviceLocator.getVimPort(
              new URL("https://localhost/sdk"));
}
catch (Exception e)
{
      System.err.println("Exception: " + e.getMessage() );
}

VimBindingStub vimStub = (VimBindingStub) vimService;
vimStub._setProperty(
org.apache.axis.transport.http.HTTPConstants.HEADER_COOKIE,
"vmware_soap_session=\"B3240D15-34DF-4BB9-B902-A844FDF42E85\"");
...
```

This code's flow differs from the last code's flow because it doesn't require you to log in. The VimPortType is casted to VimBindingStub, and the session ID is set as the HTTP cookie.

Essentially, the session ID is a cookie string. It can be sent from one client to others in string format, in a local file, a URL, or messaging through the network. When setting the session, include "vmware_soap_session."

From the last line on, the consecutive code can send SOAP requests as if they were from the previous client, which prints the session ID.

While sharing the session, it's critical for the user of the session *not* to log out of the session. As a rule of thumb, whoever logs in first should close the session—nobody else. It's up to the designer of the client applications to track the numbers of clients who are sharing the same session.

Further Discussion

This introduction covers how to share the sessions in the code samples using Java. The previous samples actually assume using AXIS as the underlying Web Services engine. If you are using a different Web Services engine, find out how to retrieve the HTTP session and change the code accordingly.

Although the sample is only in Java, clients that share a session can write in any language that Web Services supports. For example, the session ID can be extracted by a Java client and consumed by a Perl client. If Perl is used for a re-use session, refer to the *VI Perl Toolkit Programming Guide*.[1]

Note that the session file format used in the VI Perl Toolkit is not simply the session ID string, but something more. The format of the session file is as follows:

```
#LWP-Cookies-1.0
Set-Cookie3: vmware_soap_session="\"52dc490b-a6e7-0e65-65a7-a926b924e72c\"";
path="/"; domain=192.20.143.205; path_spec; discard; version=0
```

I leave it to you to figure out how to construct such a session file with a known session ID and how to use a session file saved in Perl.[2] You might have similar exercises with other language bindings.

---

[1] www.vmware.com/support/developer/viperltoolkit/doc/perl_toolkit_guide_idx.html
[2] Hint: Consider the load_session() method. Check out the VI Perl programming guide, pages 35–36, for details (www.vmware.com/support/developer/viperltoolkit/viperl16/doc/viperl_proggd.pdf).

As mentioned, passing the session ID poses a security risk especially over the wire. The session ID is enough for a client to carry over all the privileges of the original user—whatever operation the user can do, the consumer client is able to do the same. This session cookie can also be used to access files over HTTP. Even worse, the session ID does not expire, so it allows enough time to prepare an attack. To avoid security issues, carefully consider whom to share a session with and how to send the session ID.

Using Single Sign-On from the VI SDK to CIM

When a client connects to the ESX server via the VI SDK, it has to log in. If it wants to further access the Common Information Model (CIM), it has to log in again using the same username and password. So the client has to either get input from users again or save the username/password somewhere. Neither of these two approaches is good for system security.

In some cases, like VI Client plug-in development, the Web application gets only the session string. It's impossible to get the password, which presumably can also be used for CIM access. So it is necessary for the VI SDK to provide a mechanism to issue tokens that can be used for CIM service login.

Starting with VI 3.5, VMware provides a new API to make possible single sign-on from the VI SDK to CIM. The following discusses how to get it done with sample Java code.

VI SDK 2.5 provides `acquireCimServicesTicket()` on a `HostSystem` managed object to get a `HostServiceTicket` object. The definition of the `HostServiceTicket` data object and related classes are shown in Figure 18-3. Some of its properties, such as `host`, `port`, and `sslThumpprint`, could be `null` because the API reference indicates "need not to be set."

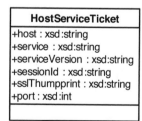

Figure 18-3   The `HostServiceTicket` data object class and related classes

The `sessionId` is a string with a format as follows. It can be used as both user-name and password for CIM access login.

```
5259c389-9891-c650-b108-e10a0ff5c781
```

Now let's look at a Java program that shows how it can be done (see Listing 18-1).

Listing 18-1
CimTicket.java

```java
package vim25.samples.mo.cim;
import java.net.URL;
import java.util.Enumeration;

import org.sblim.wbem.cim.CIMNameSpace;
import org.sblim.wbem.cim.CIMObject;
import org.sblim.wbem.cim.CIMObjectPath;
import org.sblim.wbem.client.CIMClient;
import org.sblim.wbem.client.PasswordCredential;
import org.sblim.wbem.client.UserPrincipal;

import com.vmware.vim25.HostServiceTicket;
import com.vmware.vim25.mo.Folder;
import com.vmware.vim25.mo.HostSystem;
import com.vmware.vim25.mo.InventoryNavigator;
import com.vmware.vim25.mo.ServiceInstance;

public class CimTicket
{
  public static void main(String[] args) throws Exception
  {
    if(args.length!=3)
    {
      System.out.println("Usage: java CimTicket <url> " +
          "<username> <password>");
      return;
    }
```

```
    String urlStr = args[0];
    String username = args[1];
    String password = args[2];

    ServiceInstance si = new ServiceInstance(new URL(urlStr),
        username, password, true);
    Folder rootFolder = si.getRootFolder();

    HostSystem host = (HostSystem) new InventoryNavigator(
        rootFolder).searchManagedEntities("HostSystem")[0];

    System.out.println(host.getName());
    HostServiceTicket ticket = host.acquireCimServicesTicket();
    System.out.println("\nHost Name:" + ticket.getHost());
    System.out.println("sessionId=" + ticket.getSessionId());
    System.out.println("sslThumpprint="
        + ticket.getSslThumbprint());
    System.out.println("serviceVersion="
        + ticket.getServiceVersion());
    System.out.println("service=" + ticket.getService());
    System.out.println("port=" + ticket.getPort());
    retrieveCimInfo(urlStr, ticket.getSessionId());
    si.getServerConnection().logout();
}

private static void retrieveCimInfo(
    String urlStr, String sessionId)
{
    String serverUrl = urlStr.substring(0,
        urlStr.lastIndexOf("/sdk"));
    String cimAgentAddress = serverUrl + ":5989";
    String namespace = "root/cimv2";
    UserPrincipal userPr = new UserPrincipal(sessionId);
    PasswordCredential pwCred = new PasswordCredential(
        sessionId.toCharArray());

    CIMNameSpace ns = new CIMNameSpace(
        cimAgentAddress, namespace);
    CIMClient cimClient = new CIMClient(ns, userPr, pwCred);
    CIMObjectPath rpCOP = new CIMObjectPath(
```

```
        "CIM_RegisteredProfile");

    System.out.println("Looking for children of " +
        "CIM_RegisteredProfile");

    long enumerationStart = System.currentTimeMillis();
    Enumeration rpEnm = cimClient.enumerateInstances(rpCOP);
    long enumerationStop = System.currentTimeMillis();
    System.out.println("Enumeration completed in: " +
        (enumerationStop - enumerationStart) / 1000 + " sec.\n");

    while (rpEnm.hasMoreElements())
    {
        CIMObject rp = (CIMObject) rpEnm.nextElement();
        System.out.println(" Found: " + rp);
    }
    }
}
```

The console printout is shown here. Given the size limit, only the first several lines are listed:

```
test.acme.com
Host Name:test.acme.com
sessionId=5259c389-9891-c650-b108-e10a0ff5c781
sslThumpprint=null
serviceVersion=1.0
service=CimInterfaces
port=null
Looking for children of CIM_RegisteredProfile
Enumeration completed in: 0 sec.

 Found: instance of OMC_RegisteredSensorProfile {
     string AdvertiseTypeDescriptions[];

     uint16 AdvertiseTypes[] = {3};

     string Caption;

     string Description;
```

This API is supported by default in ESXi 3.5, but not in classic ESX. Users can manually enable it by tweaking a configuration file in classic ESX. In classic 3.5 U2, it's enabled as default. You can also use this API with VC server as long as the `HostSystem` it manages supports the feature.

The SBLIM Java client[3] is used instead of the one[4] used with the VI SDK CIM sample. The latter has a bug whereby it truncates the password after 16 characters, so it fails the CIM login.

Downloading and Uploading Files Using HTTP Access

In VI 3.5, VMware introduced a new feature to enable applications to download a file from and upload a file to the datastores of ESX servers.

The syntax of the URLs is as follows:

```
http(s)://<hostname>/folder[/<path>]?dcPath=<datacenter_path>[&dsName=<datastore
_name>]
```

Following are some sample URLs:

```
https://18.17.218.228/folder?dcPath=Datacenter
```

which lists all the datastores in the datacenter whose path is `Datacenter`.

```
https://18.17.218.228/folder?dcPath=Datacenter&dsName=storage1%20(1)
```

which lists all the folders in the datastore named `storage1 (1)` whose path is `Datacenter`.

```
https://18.17.218.228/folder/SuSe_server10/SuSe_server10-
flat.vmdk?dcPath=Datacenter&dsName=storage1%20(1)
```

which points to the vmdk file called `SuSe_server10-flat.vmdk`.

---

[3] http://sblim.wiki.sourceforge.net/CimClient
[4] http://sourceforge.net/projects/wbemservices

VMware has shipped a sample code with VI SDK 2.5 showing how to upload a virtual machine to an ESX server (com.vmware.samples.httpfileaccess.ColdMigration). The sample code works by uploading files whose sizes are 40MB or smaller. In most of the cases, virtual machine disk files are much bigger than 40MB; therefore, an OutOfMemoryError is almost always thrown for such an execution.

Given the average virtual disk size, the ColdMigration sample is almost useless if it cannot work with files bigger than 40MB.

An easy solution seems to be increasing the Java heap size using a parameter to the Java virtual machine. But that is not a good solution given the size of the virtual machines, sometimes 100GB or bigger. It would be hard to find such a large memory and assign it to a Java virtual machine. So let's pin down the root cause of the problem and find an alternative solution.

After debugging the sample, the following section of code is found to throw exceptions.

```
OutputStream out = conn.getOutputStream();
FileInputStream in = new FileInputStream(
    new File(localFilePath));

byte[] buf = new byte[1024];
int len = 0;
while ((len = in.read(buf)) > 0) {
    out.write(buf, 0, len);
}
conn.getResponseMessage();
conn.disconnect();
out.close();
```

Simply reading the code, it seems okay. To figure out in which iteration the problem happens, a conditional breakpoint is set to catch OutOfMemoryError.

The next run reveals the stack shown in Figure 18-4 when the exception happened.

Arrays.copyOf(byte[], int) line: 2786
PosterOutputStream(ByteArrayOutputStream).write(byte[], int, int) line: 94
PosterOutputStream.write(byte[], int, int) line: 61

Figure 18-4   Partial calling stack when OutOfMemoryError happens

The error was thrown at the following highlighted line. The argument `newLength` is 67,108,864. No wonder we have a problem with this huge array.

```java
public static byte[] copyOf(byte[] original, int newLength)
{
    byte[] copy = new byte[newLength];
    System.arraycopy(original, 0, copy, 0,
        Math.min(original.length, newLength));
    return copy;
}
```

Further reading discloses that `PostOutputStream(ByteArrayOutputStream).write()` tries to buffer all the data to be sent. It's not going to work with big size uploading.

The question becomes whether it can use a different output class. The `PosterOutputStream` is returned from the `getOutputStream()` method:

```java
public synchronized OutputStream getOutputStream()
    throws IOException
{
    return delegate.getOutputStream();
}
```

Because the source code of Sun's `HttpURLConnection` class is not available in the `src.zip`, a search on the Web finds code samples like the following. It shows that the `getOutputStream()` method can actually return subtypes of `OutputStream` other than `PosterOutputStream` depending on the variable `fixedContentLength` and `chunkLength`.

```java
public synchronized OutputStream getOutputStream()
{
...
  if(streaming())
  {
   if(fixedContentLength != -1)
     strOutputStream = new StreamingOutputStream(
       ps, fixedContentLength);
   else if(chunkLength != -1)
     strOutputStream = new StreamingOutputStream(
       new ChunkedOutputStream(ps, chunkLength), -1);
   return strOutputStream;
  }
```

```
...
  if(poster == null)
      poster = new PosterOutputStream();
  return poster;
}
```

By exploring the `HttpURLConnection` class, you can find the methods to set the two variables: `setFixedLengthStreamingMode(int)` and `setChunkedStreamingMode(int)`, respectively.

Because the file size is known beforehand, just use the first method and get `StreamingOutputStream`. It works fine by inserting the following line before `conn.getOutputStream()`:

```
conn.setFixedLengthStreamingMode(fileSize);
```

The issue with the sample code is not a bug of VMware Infrastructure per se. The root cause of the issue is the misuse of Java APIs.

You could argue that `PosterOutputStream` should *not* be the default `OutputStream`. In practice, uploading a huge file is not a typical use case of the `HttpConnection`. Most API users use it to download content of any size and upload a relatively small file. After all, the `HttpURLConnection` class has provided an alternative to solve the problem.

Note that the argument to `setFixedLengthStreamingMode` is an integer, meaning it can only hold up to about 2.14GB, which is not enough for a disk file. Uploading bigger files requires using `setChunkedStreamingMode(int)`. As of SDK 2.5, the chunked streaming is not supported on the ESX server side.

Multithreading with the VI SDK

Multithreading is the norm in application development, especially GUI-related applications and server applications. In these applications, you might need several threads, each of which is assigned a specific task. When you develop your application that uses VI SDK, you need to consider using multithreading.

Overall, the AXIS generated VI SDK stubs are thread-safe, meaning you can safely issue multiple calls in different threads. For each call, a new `Call` object is created and not shared with other method invocations.

While using multiple threads, be aware (and careful) of the following:

- There normally shouldn't be more than one operation currently running with one entity. Most of the invocations are fast, so you don't notice there is such a limitation. But some operations are slow. When a second call comes in before the first finishes, a `TaskInProgress` fault might be thrown. In that fault type, you get the first running task's `MOR`.

  To avoid this, you can put a `synchronized` keyword on every operation in your Java code. This prevents the same application from issuing the second call on the same entity before the first finishes. The `synchronized` keyword cannot prevent other applications, either running on the same machine or not, from issuing a second call to the same managed entity on the server side. When that happens, you can do nothing about it but catch the fault and try again. The lock is essentially on the server side.

- Pay extra attention to the `PropertyCollector`. The `waitForUpdate()` defined there is a synchronized method that reports the result as specified by the `PropertyFilter` objects from version to version. You get all the results for all the `PropertyFilter` objects. If you have multiple threads calling the `waitForUpdate()`, you get multiple duplicated updates. It then makes sense to have one backend thread to call the `waitForUpdate()`.

  You can implement the Publisher-Subscriber design pattern, in which the backend thread is the publisher and any other objects/threads are subscribers who can receive notifications when interested updates come. This implementation requires more effort, but it is worthwhile in big-server applications.

Versioning

The VI SDK exposes the features of the VMware Infrastructure. With the rapid changes of the VI, the VI SDK has evolved accordingly. As it stands today, there are three major versions of the VI SDK: 2.0, 2.5, and 4.0 (a.k.a vSphere SDK). The version 2.0 is not compatible with the other two.

Namespace

As discussed earlier, the most important component in the SDK is the WSDL file from which the client stubs can be generated. The two versions' WSDLs use two different namespaces: VI SDK 2.0 uses urn:vim, and VI SDK 2.5 uses urn:vim25. Interestingly, the VI SDK 2.5 package also includes a previous version of WSDL. Therefore, you can use the VI SDK 2.5 package to develop applications with 2.0 interfaces.

When client-side stubs are generated, the package names are up to the developers. The pregenerated stubs use com.vmware.vim in SDK 2.0 and com.vmware.vim25 in SDK 2.5. If your application needs to work with two versions of platforms, you have two package names even though the class definitions are similar, if not the same.

Tying the version with a namespace complicates the application development. If you have to work with two versions of VI in your application, you must include two JARs. These JARs actually include many duplicated classes that are essentially the same, even though they end up in two package names. For example, there are two ManagedObjectReference types. When you enter the type name, the compiler cannot easily decide which one to use. To avoid the confusion, just include the full package name in your code.

The following code detects the version of the target. The basic idea is to get the vimService.wsdl file, as shown in Listing 18-2, with the following URL, and then parse the XML file for the version number.

```
https://<server-name>/sdk/vimService?wsdl
```

When you want to discover the namespace of a target server, simply call the utility like the following. If the target supports SDK 2.5, the version is urn:vim25Service.

```
String version = VerUtil.getTargetNameSpace("192.168.143.209");
```

Listing 18-2
VerUtil.java

```java
package vim25.samples.mo.util;
import java.io.BufferedReader;
import java.io.InputStreamReader;
import java.net.HttpURLConnection;
import java.net.URL;
import java.security.KeyManagementException;
import java.security.NoSuchAlgorithmException;
```

```java
import java.security.cert.CertificateException;
import java.security.cert.X509Certificate;

import javax.net.ssl.HostnameVerifier;
import javax.net.ssl.HttpsURLConnection;
import javax.net.ssl.SSLContext;
import javax.net.ssl.SSLSession;
import javax.net.ssl.TrustManager;
import javax.net.ssl.X509TrustManager;

public class VerUtil
{
  /**
    * Retrieve the target server's namespace
    * @param target, either IP or host name
    * @return the namespace, e.g. urn:vim25Service
    */
  public static String getTargetNameSpace(String target)
  {
    String version = "";
    try
    {
      trustAllHttpsCertificates();
      HttpsURLConnection.setDefaultHostnameVerifier(
          new HostnameVerifier()
          {
            public boolean verify(String urlHostName,
                SSLSession session)
            {
              return true;
            }
          });

      String urlStr = "https://"+ target
          + "/sdk/vimService?wsdl";
      HttpURLConnection conn = (HttpURLConnection) new URL(
          urlStr).openConnection();
      conn.connect();
      BufferedReader in = new BufferedReader(
          new InputStreamReader(conn.getInputStream()));
```

```
      StringBuffer xmlWSDL = new StringBuffer();
      String line;
      while ((line=in.readLine())!= null)
      {
        xmlWSDL.append(line);
      }

      int start = xmlWSDL.indexOf("targetNamespace")
                  + "targetNamespace".length();
      start = xmlWSDL.indexOf("\"", start);
      int end = xmlWSDL.indexOf("\"", start+1);
      version = xmlWSDL.substring(start+1, end);
    }
    catch (Exception e)
    {
      e.printStackTrace();
    }
    return version;
  }


  private static void trustAllHttpsCertificates()
    throws NoSuchAlgorithmException, KeyManagementException
  {
    TrustManager[] trustAllCerts = new TrustManager[1];
    trustAllCerts[0] = new TrustAllManager();
    SSLContext sc = SSLContext.getInstance("SSL");
    sc.init(null, trustAllCerts, null);
    HttpsURLConnection.setDefaultSSLSocketFactory(
        sc.getSocketFactory());
  }


  private static class TrustAllManager
    implements X509TrustManager
  {
    public X509Certificate[] getAcceptedIssuers()
    {
      return null;
    }
    public void checkServerTrusted(X509Certificate[] certs,
```

```
        String authType)
      throws CertificateException
    {
    }
    public void checkClientTrusted(X509Certificate[] certs,
        String authType)
    throws CertificateException
    {
    }
  }

  public static void main(String[] args)
  {
    String ver = getTargetNameSpace("10.20.143.205");
    System.out.println("ver:" + ver);
  }
}
```

Compatibility

Can the applications developed with 2.0 still work with the newer VI product? Yes. The newer version of VI supports both the current and older versions of WSDL generated stubs.

Because the application still uses the old interfaces, they cannot, however, retrieve the new properties and call the newly added methods. So how can you access new properties and methods?

There could be two different solutions. First, rewrite the application to the newer version of SDK. Then the application no longer works with lower versions of VI platforms. For example, the application built on top of SDK 2.5 does not work with ESX 3.0 or VirtualCenter 2.0.

The second solution is to keep the old code as it is and choose to access new properties and new methods after detecting that the target is newer. Of course, the logic could be more complicated and the code could be less straightforward. But the gain would be application compatibility, which allows it to work with both older and newer versions of VI.

In the second solution, to access the newly defined properties or methods, you must convert the old ManagedObjectReference to the newer ManagedObjectReference. Because the definitions are the same except for the package name and name space, the conversion is straightforward. With the new MOR object, you can retrieve new properties and invoke new methods.

There is an easier way: Put all the ESX, old or new versions, under the newer VC2.5 and then connect to it. VC 2.5 handles the versioning for you, and you don't need to worry about it. Only VC needs an upgrade. The newer version of VC can manage the old version of ESXes.

API Deprecation

With the evolution of the VI SDK, some of the interfaces are deprecated in favor of new ones. As a simple naming convention, the new interfaces normally have an Ex suffix in their names. For example, the old interface to create a cluster was createCluster(), and the new interface is createClusterEx().

These new interfaces normally come with new data objects with similar Ex suffixes. The createClusterEx() method, for example, has a new parameter type ClusterConfigSpecEx instead of ClusterConfigSpec for the old method.

Because of interface changes, some of the managed objects might have new properties of new types. For instance, the ComputeResource has a configrationEx property of ClusterConfigInfoEx.

Although for compatibility reasons the new interfaces are still supported, you should use the new interfaces especially for new development for better compatibility and more features.

Note that not all the deprecated methods have replacements. The destroyNetwork() method is such a case. When the network is no longer in use, the system removes it automatically like the garbage collection in Java, thereby making it unnecessary.

Following Best Practices for Performance and Scalability

This section is not intended to be a general guide for improving performance and scalability; instead, it focuses on how to get better performance and scalability from the VI SDK.

The general principles for performance and scalability still hold; for example, don't optimize your code unless you have to.

When designing a VI SDK application, consider the following:

- Use VirtualCenter instead of individual hypervisors as a target server for the VI SDK. VirtualCenter has more functionalities than ESX. From a scalability point of view, your application can scale with VirtualCenter.

  If your application tries to manage 100 hosts, for instance, you must have 100 connections if you're talking to individual hosts. When a virtual machine is moved from one host to the other, you have to track it down from host to host. If you use a VirtualCenter managing these ESXes, you can shift the burden to the VirtualCenter. One connection to VirtualCenter saves almost all the tedious work for you.

  There is a limitation with VirtualCenter server in terms of the number of hypervisors and virtual machines it can manage.[5] Your application can always connect to multiple VirtualCenter servers to scale beyond one VirtualCenter coverage.

- Use as few sessions as possible. The sessions take system resources and use locks on the server side. The slowdown ultimately affects all the VI SDK clients in that the calls to the server are slower to return. This is, of course, out of the control of a single client. Even if your client behaves perfectly well, it might still be affected by others.

  If your application is deployed with many concurrent clients, the one-client, one-session approach doesn't scale, especially when your target is VirtualCenter. Instead, consider having your own backend server that connects to a server with a single session.

- Avoid a big dataset in a single call. Most of the time, you should be fine. It can be a problem when it comes to retrieving performance data, which could be several megabytes of data returned. This puts the pressure on both the server and the client, where the data has to be marshaled to and unmarshaled from SOAP XML. If the client side uses the DOM parser, it also uses a lot of memory.

  In general, specify as much criteria as possible to restrict your dataset as small as possible. In the performance statistics case, you should use the CSV format over the array for better performance.

---

[5] Normally 200 ESX hosts and 2,000 virtual machines in VI3. When the clustering feature is on, numbers will be fewer.

- Use batch processing methods when possible. Some operations can have batch processing in which multiple entities can be manipulated. For example, the `ClusterComputeResource` has two methods: `moveHostInto_Task()` and `moveInto_Task()`. The former moves one host into a cluster at a time, and the latter moves multiple hosts at a time. The latter works faster, in that it causes fewer rounds of communication.

  There is a problem with batch processing methods in the VI SDK: they are not atomic. If something goes wrong, the VI SDK just stops there and returns. Whatever is or is not yet processed stays as it is. The VI SDK doesn't roll back the already processed one. So when faults happen, you need to take care of the half-baked cake by yourself. Or, just go with the one-call, one-entity scheme. This is a trade-off between performance and atomicity.

You can always pass in one item in a method that expects an array of items; just avoid the complexity to handle the atomicity. For example, you want performance data for a list of managed entities, but you don't know which of them might no longer be valid. Instead of retrieving them all, you can simply retrieve one at a time. Just remember to catch the exception so that it doesn't exit the loop.

- Design and implement your local cache. It's not worthwhile if it is a simple utility application. But for a big application that requires extensive interaction with VirtualCenter or ESX, it makes a lot of sense.

  First, your application can have instant access of cached information. Second, it saves the number of calls to the server as well as the workload on the server. The same server can work faster and serve more clients.

  Whenever you have a cache and care about freshness, you must consider how to sync it with the server. The VI SDK has a `waitForUpdate()` method that blocks the current thread and returns when updates come up on the server. Clearly, you shouldn't have multiple threads waiting for update, but one to keep the cache synchronized with the server. Be careful with the synchronization of multiple threads on the client application.

  VI Java API 2.0 includes a caching framework that handles most of the burden for you. All you need to do is specify what properties to cache and monitor on what managed objects, and then retrieve the properties in the same way as from a hash table. It's multithread safe and can be used in large applications.

> The caching framework is designed for caching, mainly speeding up the second time retrieval. A big company reported three times performance gain by retrieving the properties using the caching framework even the first time. Nice surprise.

Considering Internationalization

With today's global market, a software vendor has to consider the internationalization (I18N) issue to better serve users in different areas and maximize the return on the product investment.

There are two basic meanings. First, you have to design your software so that it is localizable. In other words, you have to use the right APIs that can handle double byte characters. Sometimes people call this globalization (G11N).

Second, you should provide localized versions of your software so that users can read and use their native languages. Sometimes people call this localization.

In most cases, you externalize all the text strings that are visible to end users from the code to the resource files and translate them into different languages. Then localizing the software is as easy as combining the code and localized resource files. This is the way VirtualCenter server is localized. Depending on the programming language and platform, the resource files can be organized differently and might have another format. For example, Java uses properties files, yet C++ on Windows uses resource dlls.

That said, I18N is a broad topic that does much more than what is briefly covered here. Further discussion is beyond the scope of this book, but you can find more detailed information online.

As discussed, the VI SDK is essentially a set of Web Services interfaces. The WS-I18N[6] summarizes four internationalization patterns[7] that can be applied with Web Services when deployed.

---

[6] www.w3.org/TR/ws-i18n/

[7] Copyright © 2008 World Wide Web Consortium, (Massachusetts Institute of Technology, European Research Consortium for Informatics and Mathematics, Keio University). All Rights Reserved. http://www.w3.org/Consortium/Legal/2002/copyright-documents-20021231

- **Locale neutral**—Most aspects of most services are not particularly locale affected. For example, a service that adds two integers is locale neutral.

- **Data driven**—Aspects of the data determine how it is processed, rather than the configuration of either the requester or the provider.

- **Service determined**—The service has a particular setting built into it. For example, this service always runs in the French for France locale. Or, commonly, the service will run in the host's default locale. It may even be a deployment decision that controls which locale or preferences are applied to the service's operation.

- **Client influenced**—The service's operation can use a locale preference provided by the end user to affect its processing. This is called "influenced" because not every request may be honored by the service. (The service may only implement behavior for certain locales or international preference combinations.)

If the VI SDK has to be put into a category, it's client influenced because the service provider tracks the client locale and responds accordingly. The VI SDK is indeed complicated, and most of the services and properties of managed objects are locale neutral.

When you first log into the system using the `SessionManager`, you can provide your locale so that the server knows your locale and responds in successive requests/responses. Your locale is held in the `currentSession.locale` of `SessionManager`.

The locale mainly affects the properties in some managed objects, such as the description properties of `TaskManager`, `AlarmManager`, `AuthorizationManager`, `EventManager`, `PerformanceManager`, and `ScheduledTaskManager`. Although they are all named `description`, they are different data object types inherited from the `Description` data object that includes two string properties: `label` and `summary`. These two properties can be displayed as they are at the client side; therefore, they should be localized.

Besides the subtypes, the `Description` data object can be included in other data objects. For example, the `DiagnosticManagerLogDescriptor` data object, which is a return type of the `queryDescriptions()` method defined in `DiagnosticManager`, includes `Description` as a localized description.

If your applications need to display any description about the task, alarm, and so on, you should always get it from the description properties. This not only saves you the time to write the descriptions, but it saves you the time to translate them when localized. The only exception is when you want to localize your application to a locale that the VirtualCenter Server does not support.

From the SessionManager, you can find out the server default locale and a list of locales for which the server has localized the messages. You can tell easily whether the server supports your locale.

Beyond these messages, the error message can be localized. The LocalizedMethodFault is a wrapper around MethodFault that provides a localized message for the wrapped fault. As already emphasized, LocalizedMethodFault is not a fault type, but a data object type.

So far, the discussion has mainly focused on the localized information from the server side. You can also send localized text from the client to the server side. For example, you can change the virtual machine name through the VI SDK. Even if you are working with an English-only version of VirtualCenter/ESX server, you can set a virtual machine's name as a double-byte character string. On the English-only VI Client, you might see just rectangles because they don't render well. If you open MOB to the virtual machine page, you might see the name show up correctly. That means the double-byte name has been saved correctly and your application can retrieve it using the VI SDK.

In general, you should be a little conservative with sending non-English text to the server from the API. Unless necessary, try to restrict to ASCII characters only. Some of the text should never be localized. For example, the keys in the system that identify certain resources should never be localized. Most of the time, they are not visible anyway.

The VI SDK is only part of your I18N story. To have a truly localized VI SDK application, make sure your client-side language, Web Services stub, and application are ready to handle the double-byte character. If you are using a language such as Java, it's less of a problem because it's built from the ground up to handle a double-byte string.

Summary

In this chapter we discussed several topics that do not fit into previous chapters but are important for a successful VI SDK application. Among them are how to manage global settings; how to collect logs; how to share sessions; how to download and upload files to datastores; how to sign on from the VI SDK to CIM without a password; how to handle different VI SDK versions; how to use multithreads with the VI SDK; how to achieve performance and scalability; and how to localize your VI SDK applications.

Appendix A

The Managed Object Types

Table A-1 lists the 63 managed objects in VI SDK 2.5. Table A-2 lists the additional 23 managed object types that are new in vSphere SDK 4.

Table A-1

Managed Object Types in VI SDK 2.5	
Managed Object Type	**Explanation**
Alarm	Defines an alarm that is triggered and an action that occurs due to the triggered alarm when certain conditions are met on a specific ManagedEntity object.
AlarmManager	Represents a singleton object for managing alarms within a service instance.
AuthorizationManager	Provides operations to query and update roles and permissions.
ClusterComputeResource	Represents a cluster of HostSystem objects as a unified compute resource for virtual machines.
ComputeResource	Represents a set of physical compute resources for virtual machines.

Table A-1   continued

Managed Object Types in VI SDK 2.5

Managed Object Type	Explanation
ContainerView	Represents a view convenient for monitoring the contents of a single container.
CustomFieldsManager	Adds and removes custom fields to managed entities.
CustomizationSpecManager	Manages customization specifications stored on the VirtualCenter server.
Datacenter	Represents the interface to the common container object for hosts and virtual machines. Every host and virtual machine must be under a distinct datacenter in the inventory, and datacenters may not be nested under other datacenters.
Datastore	Represents a storage location for virtual machine files. A storage location can be a VMFS volume, a directory on Network Attached Storage, or a local file system path.
DiagnosticManager	Provides an interface to get low-level debugging logs or diagnostic bundles for a server. For VirtualCenter, this includes the log files for the server daemon. For an ESX host, this includes detailed log files for the VMkernel.
EnvironmentBrowser	Provides access to the environment that a ComputeResource presents for creating and configuring a virtual machine.
EventHistoryCollector	Retrieves historical data and updates when the server appends new events.
EventManager	Provides properties and methods for event management support. Event objects are used to record significant state changes of managed entities.
ExtensibleManagedObject	Represents the extensible managed object base interface, mainly for managing custom fields.
ExtensionManager	Provides registration and basic management services for all extensions.

continues...

Table A-1 continued

Managed Object Types in VI SDK 2.5

Managed Object Type	Explanation
FileManager (*)	Manages and manipulates files and folders on datastores.
Folder	Represents the container object type to manage entities in the inventory.
HistoryCollector	Retrieves historical data and receives updates when the server appends new data to a collection.
HostAutoStartManager	Invokes and sets up the auto-start/auto-stop order of virtual machines on a single host.
HostBootDeviceSystem	Queries and changes the current system boot device configuration.
HostCpuSchedulerSystem	Gathers and configures the host CPU scheduler policies that affect the performance of running virtual machines.
HostDatastoreBrowser	Provides access to the contents of one or more datastores. The items in a datastore are files that contain configuration, virtual disk, and other data associated with a virtual machine.
HostDatastoreSystem	Creates and manages datastores from the host.
HostDateTimeSystem	Provides service to query and manage date/time-related configuration on a host.
HostDiagnosticSystem	Configures the diagnostic mechanisms specific to the host.
HostFirewallSystem	Manages the firewall configuration of the host.
HostFirmwareSystem (*)	Provides access to the firmware of an embedded ESX host to back up/restore/reset the configuration.
HostHealthStatusSystem	Manages the health state of the host.
HostLocalAccountManager	Manages local accounts on a host.

Table A-1   continued

Managed Object Types in VI SDK 2.5

Managed Object Type	Explanation
HostMemorySystem	Configures and gathers the host memory management policies that affect the performance of running virtual machines.
HostNetworkSystem	Represents the networking system in a host.
HostPatchManager	Represents the path manager of a host that can scan and patch the host.
HostServiceSystem	Queries and manages the configuration of host services.
HostSnmpSystem	Queries and configures SNMP agent configuration on a host.
HostStorageSystem	Represents the storage subsystem in a host. It can be used to query and manage the storage attached to a host.
HostSystem	Represents a virtualization host platform. It can be used to operate and manage the host.
HostVMotionSystem	Queries and configures the VMotion configuration of a host.
InventoryView	Browses the inventory and tracks changes to open folders.
LicenseManager	Queries and manages license configuration.
ListView	Gets updates on an arbitrary set of managed objects.
ManagedEntity	Represents the abstract base type for all managed objects in the inventory tree.
ManagedObjectView	Represents the base type for view objects that expose a set of managed objects.
Network	Represents a network accessible by either hosts or virtual machines.

continues...

Table A-1   continued

Managed Object Types in VI SDK 2.5	
Managed Object Type	**Explanation**
OptionManager	Manages key/value pair options.
PerformanceManager	Queries performance statistics.
PropertyCollector	Retrieves and monitors a set of properties from one or more managed objects.
PropertyFilter	Controls the properties that a collector retrieves and observes changes.
ResourcePool	Represents a set of physical resources: a single host, a subset of a host's resources, or resources spanning multiple hosts. Resource pools can be subdivided by creating child resource pools. To run, a virtual machine must be associated as a child of a resource pool.
ScheduledTask	Schedules a task to run in the future.
ScheduledTaskManager	Creates and retrieves a ScheduleTask.
SearchIndex	Provides fast search service to obtain an item, typically a virtual machine or a host, in the inventory by UUID, IP address, and so on.
ServiceInstance	Represents the singleton server-side root object for the whole interactive session. From this object, you can obtain the inventory and various services.
SessionManager	Manages client sessions.
Task	Represents an operation that takes time and might be canceled.
TaskHistoryCollector	Retrieves historical data and updates related to tasks.
TaskManager	Retrieves and manages tasks.
UserDirectory	Discovers and verifies users in the underlying user directory.

Table A-1 continued

Managed Object Types in VI SDK 2.5	
Managed Object Type	**Explanation**
View	Represents the base type for all the views that track changes of a set of managed objects.
ViewManager	Provides access to managed objects that make accessing objects and providing updates more convenient for specific use cases.
VirtualDiskManager(*)	Manages and manipulates virtual disks on datastores.
VirtualMachine	Represents the virtual machine.
VirtualMachineSnapshot	Represents a snapshot of a virtual machine.

Note: * Experimental feature in VI SDK 2.5, subject to change in later releases.

Table A-2

Additional Managed Object Types in vSphere SDK 4	
Managed Object Type	**Explanation**
ClusterProfile	Represents the profile for configuring the cluster.
ClusterProfileManager	Manages the cluster profiles.
DistributedVirtualPortgroup	Represents the distributed virtual portgroup objects.
DistributedVirtualSwitch	Represents the distributed virtual switch objects.
DistributedVirtualSwitchManager	Manages the virtual switches.
HostKernelModuleSystem*	Controls the configuration of kernel modules on the host.
HostPciPassthruSystem;	Manages the PciPassthru state of the host.

continues...

Table A-2 continued

Additional Managed Object Types in vSphere SDK 4

Managed Object Type	Explanation
HostProfile	Represents the profile for configuring the hosts.
HostProfileManager	Manages the host profiles.
HostVirtualNicManager	Manages the special v-NIC configuration of the host.
HttpNfcLease	Represents a lease on a VirtualMachine or a VirtualApp that can be used to import or export disks for the entity.
IpPoolManager	Manages and allocates IP addresses to vApps.
LicenseAssignmentManager	Manages licenses in a new licensing model.
LocalizationManager	Provides all the message catalogs for client-side localization of messages.
OvfManager	Provides services to parse and generate OVF descriptors.
Profile	Represents the base type for profiles for configuring the cluster and host.
ProfileManager	Represents the base type for managing profiles.
ProfileComplianceManager	Manages the compliance of entities against profiles.
ResourcePlanningManager	Estimates the database size required to store VirtualCenter data.
VirtualApp	Represents a collection of virtual machines that consist of a software solution.
VirtualMachineCompatibilityChecker	Checks the compatibility of a virtual machine with a host.

Table A-2   continued

Additional Managed Object Types in vSphere SDK 4

Managed Object Type	Explanation
VirtualMachineProvisioningChecker	Checks the feasibility of certain provisioning operations.
VmwareDistributedVirtualSwitch	Represents the VMware implementation of the distributed virtual switch.

Note: * HostKernelModuleSystem was first introduced in VI API 2.5u2.

Appendix B

The Performance Counters

Table B-1 lists all the performance counters that are available in VirtualCenter 2.5. Some of the counters are not supported by the ESX.

Table B-1

Performance Counters in the VI SDK

Group	Full Name	Unit	Level	Description
Cluster	clusterServices. cpufairness.latest	Number	1	Fairness of distributed CPU resource allocation.
	clusterServices. effectivecpu.average	Megahertz	1	VMware DRS Effective CPU resources available.
	clusterServices. effectivemem.average	Megabytes	1	VMware DRS Effective Memory resources available.
	clusterServices.failover. latest	Number	1	VMware HA number of failures that can be tolerated.
	clusterServices. memfairness.latest	Number	1	Fairness of distributed memory resource allocation.

Table B-1 continued

Performance Counters in the VI SDK

Group	Full Name	Unit	Level	Description
CPU	cpu.extra.summation	Millisecond	3	CPU time that is extra.
	cpu.guaranteed.latest	Millisecond	3	CPU time that is guaranteed.
	cpu.idle.summation	Millisecond	2	CPU time spent in idle state.
	cpu.ready.summation	Millisecond	3	CPU time spent in ready state.
	cpu.reservedCapacity.average	Megahertz	2	Total CPU capacity reserved by the virtual machines.
	cpu.system.summation	Millisecond	3	CPU time spent on system processes.
	cpu.usage.average	Percent	1	CPU usage as a percentage over the collected interval.
	cpu.usage.maximum	Percent	4	CPU usage as a percentage over the collected interval.
	cpu.usage.minimum	Percent	4	CPU usage as a percentage over the collected interval.
	cpu.usage.none	Percent	4	CPU usage as a percentage over the collected interval.
	cpu.usagemhz.average	Megahertz	1	CPU usage in MHz over the collected interval. For hosts this can be represented on a per-virtual-machine basis as a stacked graph.
	cpu.usagemhz.maximum	Megahertz	4	CPU usage in MHz over the collected interval. For hosts this can be represented on a per-virtual-machine basis as a stacked graph.

continues...

Table B-1   continued

Performance Counters in the VI SDK				
Group	Full Name	Unit	Level	Description
	`cpu.usagemhz.minimum`	Megahertz	4	CPU usage in MHz over the collected interval. For hosts this can be represented on a per-virtual-machine basis as a stacked graph.
	`cpu.usagemhz.none`	Megahertz	4	CPU usage in MHz over the collected interval. For hosts this can be represented on a per-virtua-machine basis as a stacked graph.
	`cpu.used.summation`	Millisecond	3	CPU time that is used.
	`cpu.wait.summation`	Millisecond	3	CPU time spent in wait state.
Disk	`disk.busResets.summation`	Number	2	Number of bus resets in the period.
	`disk.commands.summation`	Number	2	Number of disk commands issued in the period.
	`disk.commandsAborted.summation`	Number	2	Number of disk commands aborted in the period.
	`disk.deviceLatency.average`	Millisecond	2	Average time taken to complete a command from the physical device.
	`disk.deviceReadLatency.average`	Millisecond	2	Average time taken to complete a read from the physical device.
	`disk.deviceWriteLatency.average`	Millisecond	2	Average time taken to complete a write from the physical device.
	`disk.kernelLatency.average`	Millisecond	2	Average time spent in ESX Server VMKernel per command.

Table B-1   continued

Performance Counters in the VI SDK

Group	Full Name	Unit	Level	Description
	`disk.kernelReadLatency.average`	Millisecond	2	Average time spent in ESX Server VMKernel per read.
	`disk.kernelWriteLatency.average`	Millisecond	2	Average time spent in ESX Server VMKernel per write.
	`disk.numberRead.summation`	Number	3	Number of disk reads in the period.
	`disk.numberWrite.summation`	Number	3	Number of disk writes in the period.
	`disk.queueLatency.average`	Millisecond	2	Average time spent in the ESX Server VMKernel queue per command.
	`disk.queueReadLatency.average`	Millisecond	2	Average time spent in the ESX Server VMKernel queue per read.
	`disk.queueWriteLatency.average`	Millisecond	2	Average time spent in the ESX Server VMKernel queue per write.
	`disk.read.average`	Kilobytes per second	3	Rate of reading data from the disk.
	`disk.totalLatency.average`	Millisecond	2	Average amount of time taken for a command from the perspective of a Guest OS. This is the sum of Kernel Command Latency and Physical Device Command Latency.

continues...

Table B-1 continued

Performance Counters in the VI SDK

Group	Full Name	Unit	Level	Description
	`disk.totalReadLatency.average`	Millisecond	2	Average amount of time taken for a read from the perspective of a Guest OS. This is the sum of Kernel Read Latency and Physical Device Read Latency.
	`disk.totalWriteLatency.average`	Millisecond	2	Average amount of time taken for a write from the perspective of a Guest OS. This is the sum of Kernel Write Latency and Physical Device Write Latency.
	`disk.usage.average`	Kilobytes per second	1	Aggregated storage performance statistics. For hosts this can be represented on a per virtual-machine basis as a stacked graph.
	`disk.usage.maximum`	Kilobytes per second	4	Aggregated storage performance statistics. For hosts this can be represented on a per-virtual-machine basis as a stacked graph.
	`disk.usage.minimum`	Kilobytes per second	4	Aggregated storage performance statistics. For hosts this can be represented on a per-virtual-machine basis as a stacked graph.
	`disk.usage.none`	Kilobytes per second	4	Aggregated storage performance statistics. For hosts this can be represented on a per-virtual-machine basis as a stacked graph.
	`disk.write.average`	Kilobytes per second	3	Rate of writing data to the disk.

Table B-1 continued

Performance Counters in the VI SDK				
Group	**Full Name**	**Unit**	**Level**	**Description**
License	`license.vdiVmAvail.latest`	Number	3	Number of VDI virtual machine licenses that have not yet been checked out. This number is zero if all the purchased VM licenses have been used.
	`license.vdiVmExcess.latest`	Number	3	Number of VDI virtual machine licenses above the number purchased that are currently in use. If the current VM count is less than the number purchased, this is zero.
ManagementAgent	`managementAgent.memUsed.average`	Kilobytes	3	Memory used as percentage of total configured or available memory.
	`managementAgent.swapIn.average`	Kilobytes per second	3	Amount of memory that is swapped in.
	`managementAgent.swapOut.average`	Kilobytes per second	3	Amount of memory that is swapped out.
	`managementAgent.swapUsed.average`	Kilobytes	3	Amount of memory that is used by swap.
Mem	`mem.active.average`	Kilobytes	2	Amount of memory that is actively used.
	`mem.active.maximum`	Kilobytes	4	Amount of memory that is actively used.
	`mem.active.minimum`	Kilobytes	4	Amount of memory that is actively used.

continues...

Table B-1   continued

Performance Counters in the VI SDK			
Group	**Full Name**	**Unit**	**Level**	**Description**
	`mem.active.none`	Kilobytes	4	Amount of memory that is actively used.
	`mem.consumed.average`	Kilobytes	2	Amount of host memory consumed by the virtual machine for guest memory.
	`mem.consumed.maximum`	Kilobytes	4	Amount of host memory consumed by the virtual machine for guest memory.
	`mem.consumed.minimum`	Kilobytes	4	Amount of host memory consumed by the virtual machine for guest memory.
	`mem.consumed.none`	Kilobytes	4	Amount of host memory consumed by the virtual machine for guest memory.
	`mem.granted.average`	Kilobytes	2	Amount of memory granted. For hosts this can be represented on a per virtual machine basis as a stacked graph.
	`mem.granted.maximum`	Kilobytes	4	Amount of memory granted. For hosts this can be represented on a per-virtual-machine basis as a stacked graph.
	`mem.granted.minimum`	Kilobytes	4	Amount of memory granted. For hosts this can be represented on a per-virtual-machine basis as a stacked graph.
	`mem.granted.none`	Kilobytes	4	Amount of memory granted. For hosts this can be represented on a per-virtual-machine basis as a stacked graph.
	`mem.heap.average`	Kilobytes	2	Amount of memory allocated for heap.

Table B-1 continued

Performance Counters in the VI SDK

Group	Full Name	Unit	Level	Description
	`mem.heap.maximum`	Kilobytes	4	Amount of memory allocated for heap.
	`mem.heap.minimum`	Kilobytes	4	Amount of memory allocated for heap.
	`mem.heap.none`	Kilobytes	4	Amount of memory allocated for heap.
	`mem.heapfree.average`	Kilobytes	2	Free space in memory heap.
	`mem.heapfree.maximum`	Kilobytes	4	Free space in memory heap.
	`mem.heapfree.minimum`	Kilobytes	4	Free space in memory heap.
	`mem.heapfree.none`	Kilobytes	4	Free space in memory heap.
	`mem.overhead.average`	Kilobytes	2	Amount of additional host memory allocated to the virtual machine.
	`mem.overhead.maximum`	Kilobytes	4	Amount of additional host memory allocated to the virtual machine.
	`mem.overhead.minimum`	Kilobytes	4	Amount of additional host memory allocated to the virtual machine.
	`mem.overhead.none`	Kilobytes	4	Amount of additional host memory allocated to the virtual machine.
	`mem.reservedCapacity.average`	Megabytes	2	Amount of memory reserved by the virtual machines.

continues...

Table B-1 continued

Performance Counters in the VI SDK

Group	Full Name	Unit	Level	Description
	mem.shared.average	Kilobytes	2	Amount of memory that is shared.
	mem.shared.maximum	Kilobytes	4	Amount of memory that is shared.
	mem.shared.minimum	Kilobytes	4	Amount of memory that is shared.
	mem.shared.none	Kilobytes	4	Amount of memory that is shared.
	mem.sharedcommon.average	Kilobytes	2	Amount of memory that is shared by common.
	mem.sharedcommon.maximum	Kilobytes	4	Amount of memory that is shared by common.
	mem.sharedcommon.minimum	Kilobytes	4	Amount of memory that is shared by common.
	mem.sharedcommon.none	Kilobytes	4	Amount of memory that is shared by common.
	mem.state.latest	Number	2	Memory state.
	mem.swapin.average	Kilobytes	2	Amount of memory that is swapped in.
	mem.swapin.maximum	Kilobytes	4	Amount of memory that is swapped in.
	mem.swapin.minimum	Kilobytes	4	Amount of memory that is swapped in.

Table B-1 continued

Performance Counters in the VI SDK

Group	Full Name	Unit	Level	Description
	mem.swapin.none	Kilobytes	4	Amount of memory that is swapped in.
	mem.swapout.average	Kilobytes	2	Amount of memory that is swapped out.
	mem.swapout.maximum	Kilobytes	4	Amount of memory that is swapped out.
	mem.swapout.minimum	Kilobytes	4	Amount of memory that is swapped out.
	mem.swapout.none	Kilobytes	4	Amount of memory that is swapped out.
	mem.swapped.average	Kilobytes	2	Amount of memory that is swapped.
	mem.swapped.maximum	Kilobytes	4	Amount of memory that is swapped.
	mem.swapped.minimum	Kilobytes	4	Amount of memory that is swapped.
	mem.swapped.none	Kilobytes	4	Amount of memory that is swapped.
	mem.swaptarget.average	Kilobytes	2	Amount of memory that can be swapped.
	mem.swaptarget.maximum	Kilobytes	4	Amount of memory that can be swapped.
	mem.swaptarget.minimum	Kilobytes	4	Amount of memory that can be swapped.

continues...

Table B-1 continued

Performance Counters in the VI SDK

Group	Full Name	Unit	Level	Description
	`mem.swaptarget.none`	Kilobytes	4	Amount of memory that can be swapped.
	`mem.swapunreserved.average`	Kilobytes	2	Amount of memory that is unreserved by swap.
	`mem.swapunreserved.maximum`	Kilobytes	4	Amount of memory that is unreserved by swap.
	`mem.swapunreserved.minimum`	Kilobytes	4	Amount of memory that is unreserved by swap.
	`mem.swapunreserved.none`	Kilobytes	4	Amount of memory that is unreserved by swap.
	`mem.swapused.average`	Kilobytes	2	Amount of memory that is used by swap.
	`mem.swapused.maximum`	Kilobytes	4	Amount of memory that is used by swap.
	`mem.swapused.minimum`	Kilobytes	4	Amount of memory that is used by swap.
	`mem.swapused.none`	Kilobytes	4	Amount of memory that is used by swap.
	`mem.sysUsage.average`	Kilobytes	2	Amount of memory used by the vmkernel.
	`mem.sysUsage.maximum`	Kilobytes	4	Amount of memory used by the vmkernel.
	`mem.sysUsage.minimum`	Kilobytes	4	Amount of memory used by the vmkernel.
	`mem.sysUsage.none`	Kilobytes	4	Amount of memory used by the vmkernel.

Table B-1 continued

Performance Counters in the VI SDK

Group	Full Name	Unit	Level	Description
	mem.unreserved.average	Kilobytes	2	Amount of memory that is unreserved.
	mem.unreserved.maximum	Kilobytes	4	Amount of memory that is unreserved.
	mem.unreserved.minimum	Kilobytes	4	Amount of memory that is unreserved.
	mem.unreserved.none	Kilobytes	4	Amount of memory that is unreserved.
	mem.usage.average	Percent	1	Memory usage as percentage of total configured or available memory.
	mem.usage.maximum	Percent	4	Memory usage as percentage of total configured or available memory.
	mem.usage.minimum	Percent	4	Memory usage as percentage of total configured or available memory.
	mem.usage.none	Percent	4	Memory usage as percentage of total configured or available memory.
	mem.vmmemctl.average	Kilobytes	2	Amount of memory used by memory control.
	mem.vmmemctl.maximum	Kilobytes	4	Amount of memory used by memory control.
	mem.vmmemctl.minimum	Kilobytes	4	Amount of memory used by memory control.

continues...

Table B-1   continued

Performance Counters in the VI SDK

Group	Full Name	Unit	Level	Description
	`mem.vmmemctl.none`	Kilobytes	4	Amount of memory used by memory control.
	`mem.vmmemctltarget.average`	Kilobytes	2	Amount of memory that can be used by memory control.
	`mem.vmmemctltarget.maximum`	Kilobytes	4	Amount of memory that can be used by memory control.
	`mem.vmmemctltarget.minimum`	Kilobytes	4	Amount of memory that can be used by memory control.
	`mem.vmmemctltarget.none`	Kilobytes	4	Amount of memory that can be used by memory control.
	`mem.zero.average`	Kilobytes	2	Amount of memory that is zeroed out.
	`mem.zero.maximum`	Kilobytes	4	Amount of memory that is zeroed out.
	`mem.zero.minimum`	Kilobytes	4	Amount of memory that is zeroed out.
	`mem.zero.none`	Kilobytes	4	Amount of memory that is zeroed out.
Net	`net.packetsRx.summation`	Number	3	Number of packets received in the period.
	`net.packetsTx.summation`	Number	3	Number of packets transmitted in the period.
	`net.received.average`	Kilobytes per second	3	Rate at which data is received.
	`net.transmitted.average`	Kilobytes per second	3	Rate at which data is transmitted.

Table B-1 continued

Performance Counters in the VI SDK

Group	Full Name	Unit	Level	Description
	`net.usage.maximum`	Kilobytes per second	4	Aggregated network performance statistics. For hosts this can be represented on a per-virtual-machine basis as a stacked graph.
	`net.usage.minimum`	Kilobytes per second	4	Aggregated network performance statistics. For hosts this can be represented on a per-virtual-machine basis as a stacked graph
	`net.usage.none`	Kilobytes per second	4	Aggregated network performance statistics. For hosts this can be represented on a per Virtual Machine basis as a stacked graph.
rescpu	`rescpu.actav1.latest`	Percent	3	CPU active average over 1 minute.
	`rescpu.actav15.latest`	Percent	3	CPU active average over 15 minutes.
	`rescpu.actav5.latest`	Percent	3	CPU active average over 5 minutes.
	`rescpu.actpk1.latest`	Percent	3	CPU active peak over 1 minute.
	`rescpu.actpk15.latest`	Percent	3	CPU active peak over 15 minutes.
	`rescpu.actpk5.latest`	Percent	3	CPU active peak over 5 minutes.
	`rescpu.maxLimited1.latest`	Percent	3	Number of CPU resources over the limit that were refused, averaged over 1 minute.

continues...

Table B-1 continued

Performance Counters in the VI SDK

Group	Full Name	Unit	Level	Description
	rescpu.maxLimited15.latest	Percent	3	Number of CPU resources over the limit that were refused, averaged over 15 minutes.
	rescpu.maxLimited5.latest	Percent	3	Number of CPU resources over the limit that were refused, averaged over 5 minutes.
	rescpu.runav1.latest	Percent	3	CPU running average over 1 minute.
	rescpu.runav15.latest	Percent	3	CPU running average over 15 minutes.
	rescpu.runav5.latest	Percent	3	CPU running average over 5 minutes.
	rescpu.runpk1.latest	Percent	3	CPU running peak over 1 minute.
	rescpu.runpk15.latest	Percent	3	CPU running peak over 15 minutes.
	rescpu.runpk5.latest	Percent	3	CPU running peak over 5 minutes.
	rescpu.sampleCount.latest	Number	3	Group CPU sample count.
	rescpu.samplePeriod.latest	Millisecond	3	Group CPU sample period.
sys	sys.heartbeat.summation	Number	1	Number of heartbeats in this period.
	sys.resourceCpuUsage.average	Megahertz	3	Resource CPU usage.

Table B-1 continued

Performance Counters in the VI SDK

Group	Full Name	Unit	Level	Description
	sys.resourceCpuUsage.maximum	Megahertz	4	Resource CPU usage.
	sys.resourceCpuUsage.minimum	Megahertz	4	Resource CPU usage.
	sys.resourceCpuUsage.none	Megahertz	4	Resource CPU usage.
	sys.uptime.latest	Second	1	Total time elapsed since last startup.

Appendix C

Cmdlets in the VI Toolkit (for Windows)

Table C-1 lists all the cmdlets in the VI toolkit (for Windows) version 1.0.

Table C-1

Cmdlets in the VI Toolkit (for Windows)	
Name	**Definition**
Add-VMHost	Add-VMHost [-Name] <String> [[-Location] <VIContainer>] [-Port <Nullable`1>] [-Credential <PSCredential>] [-User <String>] [-Password <String>] [-RunAsync] [-Verbose] [-Debug] [-ErrorAction <ActionPreference>] [-ErrorVariable <String>] [-OutVariable <String>] [-OutBuffer <Int32>] [-WhatIf] [-Confirm]
Connect-VIServer	Connect-VIServer [-Server] <String[]> [-Port <Nullable`1>] [-Protocol <String>] [-Credential <PSCredential>] [-User <String>] [-Password <String>] [-Session <String>] [-Verbose] [-Debug] [-ErrorAction <ActionPreference>] [-ErrorVariable <String>] [-OutVariable <String>] [-OutBuffer <Int32>]
Disconnect-VIServer	Disconnect-VIServer [[-Server] <VIServer[]>] [-Verbose] [-Debug] [-ErrorAction <ActionPreference>] [-ErrorVariable <String>] [-OutVariable <String>] [-OutBuffer <Int32>] [-WhatIf] [-Confirm]

Table C-1 continued

Cmdlets in the VI Toolkit (for Windows)

Name	Definition
Dismount-Tools	Dismount-Tools [[-Guest] <VMGuest[]>] [-Verbose] [-Debug] [-ErrorAction <ActionPreference>] [-ErrorVariable <String>] [-OutVariable <String>] [-OutBuffer <Int32>] Dismount-Tools [[-VM] <VirtualMachine[]>] [[-Server] <VIServer[]>] [-Verbose] [-Debug] [-ErrorAction <ActionPreference>] [-ErrorVariable <String>] [-OutVariable <String>] [-OutBuffer <Int32>]
Get-CDDrive	Get-CDDrive [[-VM] <VirtualMachine[]>] [[-Temp late] <Template[]>] [-Server <VIServer[]>] [-Verbose] [-Debug] [-ErrorAction <ActionPreference>] [-ErrorVariable <String>] [-OutVariable <String>] [-OutBuffer <Int32>]
Get-Cluster	Get-Cluster [[-Name] <String[]>] [-Server <VIServer[]>] [-VM <VirtualMachine[]>] [-VMHost <VMHost[]>] [-Location <VIContainer[]>] [-Id <String[]>] [-NoRecursion] [-Verbose] [-Debug] [-ErrorAction <ActionPreference>] [-ErrorVariable <String>] [-OutVariable <String>] [-OutBuffer <Int32>]
Get-Datacenter	Get-Datacenter [[-Name] <String[]>] [-Server <VIServer[]>] [-VM <VirtualMachine[]>] [-Clus ter <Cluster[]>] [-Location <VIContainer[]>] [-Id <String[]>] [-NoRecursion] [-Verbose] [-Debug] [-ErrorAction <ActionPreference>] [-ErrorVariable <String>] [-OutVariable <String>] [-OutBuffer <Int32>]
Get-Datastore	Get-Datastore [[-Name] <String[]>] [-Server <VIServer[]>] [-Verbose] [-Debug] [-ErrorAction <ActionPreference>] [-ErrorVariable <String>] [-OutVariable <String>] [-OutBuffer <Int32>] Get-Datastore [[-Name] <String[]>] [-Datacenter <Datacenter[]>] [-VMHost <VMHost[]>] [-VM <VirtualMachine[]>] [-Entity <VIObject[]>] [-Verbose] [-Debug] [-ErrorAction <ActionPreference>] [-ErrorVariable <String>] [-OutVariable <String>] [-OutBuffer <Int32>]

continues...

Table C-1   continued

Cmdlets in the VI Toolkit (for Windows)

Name	Definition
Get-FloppyDrive	Get-FloppyDrive [[-VM] <VirtualMachine[]>] [[-Template] <Template[]>] [-Server <VIServer[]>] [-Verbose] [-Debug] [-ErrorAction <ActionPreference>] [-ErrorVariable <String>] [-OutVariable <String>] [-OutBuffer <Int32>]
Get-Folder	Get-Folder [[-Name] <String[]>] [-Server <VIServer[]>] [-Location <VIContainer[]>] [-Id <String[]>] [-NoRecursion] [-Verbose] [-Debug] [-ErrorAction <ActionPreference>] [-ErrorVariable <String>] [-OutVariable <String>] [-OutBuffer <Int32>]
Get-HardDisk	Get-HardDisk [[-VM] <VirtualMachine[]>] [[-Template] <Template[]>] [[-Snapshot] <Snapshot[]>] [-Server <VIServer[]>] [-Verbose] [-Debug] [-ErrorAction <ActionPreference>] [-ErrorVariable <String>] [-OutVariable <String>] [-OutBuffer <Int32>]
Get-Inventory	Get-Inventory [[-Name] <String[]>] [-Server <VIServer[]>] [-Location <VIContainer[]>] [-Id <String[]>] [-NoRecursion] [-Verbose] [-Debug] [-ErrorAction <ActionPreference>] [-ErrorVariable <String>] [-OutVariable <String>] [-OutBuffer <Int32>]
Get-Log	Get-Log [-Key] <String[]> [[-VMHost] <VMHost[]>] [[-StartLineNum] <Int32>] [[-NumLines] <Int32>] [-Server <VIServer[]>] [-Verbose] [-Debug] [-ErrorAction <ActionPreference>] [-ErrorVariable <String>] [-OutVariable <String>] [-OutBuffer <Int32>] Get-Log [-Key <String[]>] [-VMHost <VMHost[]>] [-StartLineNum <Int32>] [-NumLines <Int32>] [-Server <VIServer[]>] [-Verbose] [-Debug] [-ErrorAction <ActionPreference>] [-ErrorVariable <String>] [-OutVariable <String>] [-OutBuffer <Int32>] Get-Log [-DestinationPath] <String> [-Bundle] [-Server <VIServer[]>] [-RunAsync] [-Verbose] [-Debug] [-ErrorAction <ActionPreference>] [-ErrorVariable <String>] [-OutVariable <String>] [-OutBuffer <Int32>]
Get-LogType	Get-LogType [[-VMHost] <VMHost[]>] [-Server <VIServer[]>] [-Verbose] [-Debug] [-ErrorAction <ActionPreference>] [-ErrorVariable <String>] [-OutVariable <String>] [-OutBuffer <Int32>]

Table C-1   continued

Cmdlets in the VI Toolkit (for Windows)

Name	Definition
Get-NetworkAdapter	Get-NetworkAdapter [[-VM] <VirtualMachine[]>] [[-Template] <Template[]>] [-Server <VIServer[]>] [-Verbose] [-Debug] [-ErrorAction <ActionPreference>] [-ErrorVariable <String>] [-OutVariable <String>] [-OutBuffer <Int32>]
Get-OSCustomizationSpec	Get-OSCustomizationSpec [[-Name] <String[]>] [[-Server] <VIServer[]>] [-Verbose] [-Debug] [-ErrorAction <ActionPreference>] [-ErrorVariable <String>] [-OutVariable <String>] [-OutBuffer <Int32>]
Get-ResourcePool	Get-ResourcePool [[-Name] <String[]>] [-Server <VIServer[]>] [-VM <VirtualMachine[]>] [-Location <VIContainer[]>] [-Id <String[]>] [-NoRecursion] [-Verbose] [-Debug] [-ErrorAction <ActionPreference>] [-ErrorVariable <String>] [-OutVariable <String>] [-OutBuffer <Int32>]
Get-Snapshot	Get-Snapshot [[-VM] <VirtualMachine[]>] [[-Name] <String[]>] [-Server <VIServer[]>] [-Verbose] [-Debug] [-ErrorAction <ActionPreference>] [-ErrorVariable <String>] [-OutVariable <String>] [-OutBuffer <Int32>]
Get-Stat	Get-Stat [[-Entity] <VIObject[]>] [-Common] [-Memory] [-Cpu] [-Disk] [-Network] [-Stat <String[]>] [-Start <DateTime>] [-Finish <DateTime>] [-MaxSamples <Int32>] [-IntervalMins <Int32>] [-Realtime] [-Verbose] [-Debug] [-ErrorAction <ActionPreference>] [-ErrorVariable <String>] [-OutVariable <String>] [-OutBuffer <Int32>]
Get-Task	Get-Task [[-Status] <Nullable`1>] [-Server <VIServer[]>] [-Verbose] [-Debug] [-ErrorAction <ActionPreference>] [-ErrorVariable <String>] [-OutVariable <String>] [-OutBuffer <Int32>]
Get-Template	Get-Template [[-Name] <String[]>] [-Server <VIServer[]>] [-Location <VIContainer[]>] [-Id <String[]>] [-NoRecursion] [-Verbose] [-Debug] [-ErrorAction <ActionPreference>] [-ErrorVariable <String>] [-OutVariable <String>] [-OutBuffer <Int32>]

continues...

Table C-1   continued

Cmdlets in the VI Toolkit (for Windows)

Name	Definition
Get-VIEvent	Get-VIEvent [[-Entity] <VIObject[]>] [-Start <Nullable`1>] [-Finish <Nullable`1>] [-Username <String>] [-MaxSamples <Nullable`1>] [-Types <EventCategory[]>] [-Server <VIServer[]>] [-Verbose] [-Debug] [-ErrorAction <ActionPreference>] [-ErrorVariable <String>] [-OutVariable <String>] [-OutBuffer <Int32>]
Get-View	Get-View [-Id] <Object[]> [-Server <VIServer[]>] [-Property <String[]>] [-Verbose] [-Debug] [-ErrorAction <ActionPreference>] [-ErrorVariable <String>] [-OutVariable <String>] [-OutBuffer <Int32>] Get-View [-ViewType] <String> [-Server <VIServer[]>] [-SearchRoot <Object>] [-Filter <Hashtable>] [-Property <String[]>] [-Verbose] [-Debug] [-ErrorAction <ActionPreference>] [-ErrorVariable <String>] [-OutVariable <String>] [-OutBuffer <Int32>] Get-View [-VIobject] <VIObject[]> [-Property <String[]>] [-Verbose] [-Debug] [-ErrorAction <ActionPreference>] [-ErrorVariable <String>] [-OutVariable <String>] [-OutBuffer <Int32>]
Get-VIObjectByVIView	Get-VIObjectByVIView [-VIView] <ViewBase[]> [-Verbose] [-Debug] [-ErrorAction <ActionPreference>] [-ErrorVariable <String>] [-OutVariable <String>] [-OutBuffer <Int32>] Get-VIObjectByVIView [-MORef] <ManagedObjectReference[]> [-Server <VIServer[]>] [-Verbose] [-Debug] [-ErrorAction <ActionPreference>] [-ErrorVariable <String>] [-OutVariable <String>] [-OutBuffer <Int32>]
Get-VirtualPortGroup	Get-VirtualPortGroup [[-VMHost] <VMHost[]>] [-VM <VirtualMachine[]>] [-VirtualSwitch <VirtualSwitch[]>] [-Name <String[]>] [-Server <VIServer[]>] [-Verbose] [-Debug] [-ErrorAction <ActionPreference>] [-ErrorVariable <String>] [-OutVariable <String>] [-OutBuffer <Int32>]

Table C-1 continued

Cmdlets in the VI Toolkit (for Windows)

Name	Definition
Get-VirtualSwitch	Get-VirtualSwitch [[-VMHost] <VMHost[]>] [[-VM] <VirtualMachine[]>] [-Name <String[]>] [-Server <VIServer[]>] [-Verbose] [-Debug] [-ErrorAction <ActionPreference>] [-ErrorVariable <String>] [-OutVariable <String>] [-OutBuffer <Int32>]
Get-VIToolkitConfiguration	Get-VIToolkitConfiguration [-Verbose] [-Debug] [-ErrorAction <ActionPreference>] [-ErrorVariable <String>] [-OutVariable <String>] [-OutBuffer <Int32>]
Get-VIToolkitVersion	Get-VIToolkitVersion [-Verbose] [-Debug] [-ErrorAction <ActionPreference>] [-ErrorVariable <String>] [-OutVariable <String>] [-OutBuffer <Int32>]
Get-VM	Get-VM [[-Name] <String[]>] [-Server <VIServer[]>] [-Datastore <Datastore[]>] [-Location <VIContainer[]>] [-Id <String[]>] [-NoRecursion] [-Verbose] [-Debug] [-ErrorAction <ActionPreference>] [-ErrorVariable <String>] [-OutVariable <String>] [-OutBuffer <Int32>]
Get-VMGuest	Get-VMGuest [-VM] <VirtualMachine[]> [-Server <VIServer[]>] [-Verbose] [-Debug] [-ErrorAction <ActionPreference>] [-ErrorVariable <String>] [-OutVariable <String>] [-OutBuffer <Int32>]
Get-VMHost	Get-VMHost [[-Name] <String[]>] [-Server <VIServer[]>] [-Datastore <Datastore[]>] [-State <VMHostState[]>] [-Location <VIContainer[]>] [-Id <String[]>] [-NoRecursion] [-Verbose] [-Debug] [-ErrorAction <ActionPreference>] [-ErrorVariable <String>] [-OutVariable <String>] [-OutBuffer <Int32>]
	Get-VMHost [[-Name] <String[]>] [-Server <VIServer[]>] [-VM <VirtualMachine[]>] [-ResourcePool <ResourcePool[]>] [-Datastore <Datastore[]>] [-Location <VIContainer[]>] [-Id <String[]>] [-NoRecursion] [-Verbose] [-Debug] [-ErrorAction <ActionPreference>] [-ErrorVariable <String>] [-OutVariable <String>] [-OutBuffer <Int32>]

continues...

Table C-1   continued

Cmdlets in the VI Toolkit (for Windows)

Name	Definition
Get-VMHostAccount	Get-VMHostAccount [[-Id] <String[]>] [-Group] [-User] [-Server <VIServer[]>] [-Verbose] [-Debug] [-ErrorAction <ActionPreference>] [-ErrorVariable <String>] [-OutVariable <String>] [-OutBuffer <Int32>]
Get-VMHostFirmware	Get-VMHostFirmware [[-VMHost] <VMHost[]>] [-Server <VIServer[]>] [-Verbose] [-Debug] [-ErrorAction <ActionPreference>] [-ErrorVariable <String>] [-OutVariable <String>] [-OutBuffer <Int32>]
Get-VMHostModule	Get-VMHostModule [-Name] <String[]> [-Server <VIServer[]>] [-Verbose] [-Debug] [-ErrorAction <ActionPreference>] [-ErrorVariable <String>] [-OutVariable <String>] [-OutBuffer <Int32>]
Get-VMHostNetwork	Get-VMHostNetwork [[-VMHost] <VMHost[]>] [-Server <VIServer[]>] [-Verbose] [-Debug] [-ErrorAction <ActionPreference>] [-ErrorVariable <String>] [-OutVariable <String>] [-OutBuffer <Int32>]
Get-VMHostService	Get-VMHostService [[-VMHost] <VMHost[]>] [-Server <VIServer[]>] [-Refresh] [-Verbose] [-Debug] [-ErrorAction <ActionPreference>] [-ErrorVariable <String>] [-OutVariable <String>] [-OutBuffer <Int32>]
Get-VMHostSnmp	Get-VMHostSnmp [[-Server] <VIServer[]>] [-Verbose] [-Debug] [-ErrorAction <ActionPreference>] [-ErrorVariable <String>] [-OutVariable <String>] [-OutBuffer <Int32>]
Get-VMHostStartPolicy	Get-VMHostStartPolicy [[-VMHost] <VMHost[]>] [-Server <VIServer[]>] [-Verbose] [-Debug] [-ErrorAction <ActionPreference>] [-ErrorVariable <String>] [-OutVariable <String>] [-OutBuffer <Int32>]
Get-VMHostStorage	Get-VMHostStorage [[-VMHost] <VMHost[]>] [-Refresh] [-RescanAllHba] [-RescanVmfs] [-Server <VIServer[]>] [-Verbose] [-Debug] [-ErrorAction <ActionPreference>] [-ErrorVariable <String>] [-OutVariable <String>] [-OutBuffer <Int32>]

Table C-1 continued

Cmdlets in the VI Toolkit (for Windows)

Name	Definition
Get-VMStartPolicy	Get-VMStartPolicy [[-VM] <VirtualMachine[]>] [-VMHost <VMHost[]>] [-Server <VIServer[]>] [-Verbose] [-Debug] [-ErrorAction <ActionPreference>] [-ErrorVariable <String>] [-OutVariable <String>] [-OutBuffer <Int32>]
Mount-Tools	Mount-Tools [[-Guest] <VMGuest[]>] [-Verbose] [-Debug] [-ErrorAction <ActionPreference>] [-ErrorVariable <String>] [-OutVariable <String>] [-OutBuffer <Int32>]
	Mount-Tools [[-VM] <VirtualMachine[]>] [[-Server] <VIServer[]>] [-Verbose] [-Debug] [-ErrorAction <ActionPreference>] [-ErrorVariable <String>] [-OutVariable <String>] [-OutBuffer <Int32>]
Move-Cluster	Move-Cluster [[-Cluster] <Cluster[]>] [-Destination] <VIContainer> [-Server <VIServer[]>] [-RunAsync] [-Verbose] [-Debug] [-ErrorAction <ActionPreference>] [-ErrorVariable <String>] [-OutVariable <String>] [-OutBuffer <Int32>] [-WhatIf] [-Confirm]
Move-Datacenter	Move-Datacenter [[-Datacenter] <Datacenter[]>] [-Destination] <VIContainer> [-Server <VIServer[]>] [-RunAsync] [-Verbose] [-Debug] [-ErrorAction <ActionPreference>] [-ErrorVariable <String>] [-OutVariable <String>] [-OutBuffer <Int32>] [-WhatIf] [-Confirm]
Move-Folder	Move-Folder [-Folder <Folder[]>] -Destination <VIContainer> [-Server <VIServer[]>] [-Verbose] [-Debug] [-ErrorAction <ActionPreference>] [-ErrorVariable <String>] [-OutVariable <String>] [-OutBuffer <Int32>] [-WhatIf] [-Confirm]
Move-Inventory	Move-Inventory [[-Item] <VIObject[]>] [-Destination] <VIContainer> [-RunAsync] [-Verbose] [-Debug] [-ErrorAction <ActionPreference>] [-ErrorVariable <String>] [-OutVariable <String>] [-OutBuffer <Int32>] [-WhatIf] [-Confirm]

continues...

Table C-1 continued

Cmdlets in the VI Toolkit (for Windows)

Name	Definition
Move-ResourcePool	Move-ResourcePool [[-ResourcePool] <ResourcePool[]>] -Destination <VIContainer> [-Server <VIServer[]>] [-Verbose] [-Debug] [-ErrorAction <ActionPreference>] [-ErrorVariable <String>] [-OutVariable <String>] [-OutBuffer <Int32>] [-WhatIf] [-Confirm]
Move-VM	Move-VM [[-VM] <VirtualMachine[]>] -Destination <VIContainer> [-Datastore <Datastore>] [-RunAsync] [-Server <VIServer[]>] [-Verbose] [-Debug] [-ErrorAction <ActionPreference>] [-ErrorVariable <String>] [-OutVariable <String>] [-OutBuffer <Int32>] [-WhatIf] [-Confirm]
Move-VMHost	Move-VMHost [[-VMHost] <VMHost[]>] [-Destination] <VIContainer> [-Server <VIServer[]>] [-RunAsync] [-Verbose] [-Debug] [-ErrorAction <ActionPreference>] [-ErrorVariable <String>] [-OutVariable <String>] [-OutBuffer <Int32>] [-WhatIf] [-Confirm]
New-CDDrive	New-CDDrive [-VM] <VirtualMachine[]> [-IsoPath <String>] [-HostDevice <String>] [-StartConnected] [-Server <VIServer[]>] [-Verbose] [-Debug] [-ErrorAction <ActionPreference>] [-ErrorVariable <String>] [-OutVariable <String>] [-OutBuffer <Int32>] [-WhatIf] [-Confirm]
New-Cluster	New-Cluster [-Name] <String> [-Location <VIContainer>] [-HAEnabled] [-HAAdmissionControlEnabled] [-HAFailoverLevel <Nullable`1>] [-DrsEnabled] [-DrsMode <Nullable`1>] [-Verbose] [-Debug] [-ErrorAction <ActionPreference>] [-ErrorVariable <String>] [-OutVariable <String>] [-OutBuffer <Int32>] [-WhatIf] [-Confirm]
New-CustomField	New-CustomField [-Entity] <InventoryItem> [-Name] <String> [[-Value] <String>] [-Global] [-Verbose] [-Debug] [-ErrorAction <ActionPreference>] [-ErrorVariable <String>] [-OutVariable <String>] [-OutBuffer <Int32>] [-WhatIf] [-Confirm]

Table C-1   continued

Cmdlets in the VI Toolkit (for Windows)

Name	Definition
New-Datacenter	New-Datacenter [-Name] <String> [[-Location] <VIContainer>] [-Verbose] [-Debug] [-ErrorAction <ActionPreference>] [-ErrorVariable <String>] [-OutVariable <String>] [-OutBuffer <Int32>] [-WhatIf] [-Confirm]
New-Datastore	New-Datastore [[-VMHost] <VMHost[]>] [-Name] <String> [-Server <VIServer[]>] -Path <String> [-Local] [-Verbose] [-Debug] [-ErrorAction <ActionPreference>] [-ErrorVariable <String>] [-OutVariable <String>] [-OutBuffer <Int32>] [-WhatIf] [-Confirm] New-Datastore [[-VMHost] <VMHost[]>] [-Name] <String> [-Server <VIServer[]>] -Path <String> -NfsHost <String> [-ReadOnly] [-Cifs] -Username <String> -Password <String> [-Verbose] [-Debug] [-ErrorAction <ActionPreference>] [-ErrorVariable <String>] [-OutVariable <String>] [-OutBuffer <Int32>] [-WhatIf] [-Confirm] New-Datastore [[-VMHost] <VMHost[]>] [-Name] <String> [-Server <VIServer[]>] -Path <String> [-Nfs] -NfsHost <String> [-ReadOnly] [-Verbose] [-Debug] [-ErrorAction <ActionPreference>] [-ErrorVariable <String>] [-OutVariable <String>] [-OutBuffer <Int32>] [-WhatIf] [-Confirm] New-Datastore [[-VMHost] <VMHost[]>] [-Name] <String> [-Server <VIServer[]>] -Path <String> [-Vmfs] [-BlockSizeMB <Int32>] [-Verbose] [-Debug] [-ErrorAction <ActionPreference>] [-ErrorVariable <String>] [-OutVariable <String>] [-OutBuffer <Int32>] [-WhatIf] [-Confirm]
New-FloppyDrive	New-FloppyDrive [-VM] <VirtualMachine[]> [-FloppyImagePath <String>] [-HostDevice <String>] [-StartConnected] [-Server <VIServer[]>] [-Verbose] [-Debug] [-ErrorAction <ActionPreference>] [-ErrorVariable <String>] [-OutVariable <String>] [-OutBuffer <Int32>] [-WhatIf] [-Confirm]
New-Folder	New-Folder [-Name] <String> [[-Location] <VIContainer>] [-Verbose] [-Debug] [-ErrorAction <ActionPreference>] [-ErrorVariable <String>] [-OutVariable <String>] [-OutBuffer <Int32>] [-WhatIf] [-Confirm]

continues...

Table C-1 continued

Cmdlets in the VI Toolkit (for Windows)

Name	Definition
New-HardDisk	New-HardDisk [-VM] <VirtualMachine[]> [[-Persistence] <String>] [[-DiskType] <DiskType>] [-CapacityKB <Nullable`1>] [-Split] [-ThinProvisioned] [-DeviceName <String>] [-Datastore <Datastore>] [-Server <VIServer[]>] [-Verbose] [-Debug] [-ErrorAction <ActionPreference>] [-ErrorVariable <String>] [-OutVariable <String>] [-OutBuffer <Int32>] [-WhatIf] [-Confirm]
New-NetworkAdapter	New-NetworkAdapter [-VM] <VirtualMachine[]> [-MacAddress <String>] -NetworkName <String> [-StartConnected] [-WakeOnLan] [-Type <VirtualNetworkAdapterType>] [-Server <VIServer[]>] [-Verbose] [-Debug] [-ErrorAction <ActionPreference>] [-ErrorVariable <String>] [-OutVariable <String>] [-OutBuffer <Int32>] [-WhatIf] [-Confirm]
New-OSCustomizationSpec	New-OSCustomizationSpec [-OSType <String>] [-Name <String>] [-Server <VIServer[]>] [-DnsServer <String[]>] [-DnsSuffix <String[]>] [-Domain <String>] [-NamingScheme <String>] [-NamingPrefix <String>] [-Description <String>] [-Verbose] [-Debug] [-ErrorAction <ActionPreference>] [-ErrorVariable <String>] [-OutVariable <String>] [-OutBuffer <Int32>] [-WhatIf] [-Confirm]
	New-OSCustomizationSpec -FullName <String> -OrgName <String> [-OSType <String>] [-Name <String>] [-ChangeSid] [-DeleteAccounts] [-Server <VIServer[]>] [-DnsServer <String[]>] [-DnsSuffix <String[]>] [-GuiRunOnce <String[]>] [-AdminPassword <String>] [-TimeZone <String>] [-AutoLogonCount <Nullable`1>] [-Domain <String>] [-Workgroup <String>] [-DomainCredentials <PSCredential>] [-DomainUsername <String>] [-DomainPassword <String>] [-ProductKey <String>] [-NamingScheme <String>] [-NamingPrefix <String>] [-Description <String>] [-Verbose] [-Debug] [-ErrorAction <ActionPreference>] [-ErrorVariable <String>] [-OutVariable <String>] [-OutBuffer <Int32>] [-WhatIf] [-Confirm]

Table C-1 continued

Cmdlets in the VI Toolkit (for Windows)

Name	Definition
New-ResourcePool	New-ResourcePool [-Location <VIContainer>] -Name <String> [-CpuExpandableReservation] [-CpuLimitMhz <Int64>] [-CpuReservationMhz <Int64>] [-CpuSharesLevel <SharesLevel>] [-MemExpandableReservation] [-MemLimitMB <Int64>] [-MemReservationMB <Int64>] [-MemSharesLevel <SharesLevel>] [-NumCpuShares <Int32>] [-NumMemShares <Int32>] [-Verbose] [-Debug] [-ErrorAction <ActionPreference>] [-ErrorVariable <String>] [-OutVariable <String>] [-OutBuffer <Int32>] [-WhatIf] [-Confirm]
New-Snapshot	New-Snapshot [[-VM] <VirtualMachine[]>] [-Name] <String> [-Description <String>] [-Memory] [-Quiesce] [-RunAsync] [-Server <VIServer[]>] [-Verbose] [-Debug] [-ErrorAction <ActionPreference>] [-ErrorVariable <String>] [-OutVariable <String>] [-OutBuffer <Int32>] [-WhatIf] [-Confirm]
New-Template	New-Template [-Name] <String> [[-VM] <VirtualMachine>] [[-Location] <VIContainer>] [-Server <VIServer[]>] [-RunAsync] [-Verbose] [-Debug] [-ErrorAction <ActionPreference>] [-ErrorVariable <String>] [-OutVariable <String>] [-OutBuffer <Int32>] [-WhatIf] [-Confirm]
New-VirtualPortGroup	New-VirtualPortGroup [-Name] <String> [-VirtualSwitch] <VirtualSwitch> [-VLanId <Int32>] [-Verbose] [-Debug] [-ErrorAction <ActionPreference>] [-ErrorVariable <String>] [-OutVariable <String>] [-OutBuffer <Int32>] [-WhatIf] [-Confirm]
New-VirtualSwitch	New-VirtualSwitch [[-VMHost] <VMHost>] [-Name] <String> [[-NumPorts] <Int32>] [[-Nic] <String[]>] [[-Mtu] <Int32>] [-Server <VIServer[]>] [-Verbose] [-Debug] [-ErrorAction <ActionPreference>] [-ErrorVariable <String>] [-OutVariable <String>] [-OutBuffer <Int32>] [-WhatIf] [-Confirm]

continues...

Table C-1   continued

Cmdlets in the VI Toolkit (for Windows)

Name	Definition
New-VM	New-VM [[-VMHost] <VMHost>] -Name <String> [-ResourcePool <ResourcePool>] [-Location <Folder>] [-Datastore <Datastore>] [-DiskMB <Int64[]>] [-DiskPath <String[]>] [-MemoryMB <Int64>] [-NumCpu <Int32>] [-Floppy] [-CD] [-GuestId <String>] [-AlternateGuestName <String>] [-NetworkName <String[]>] [-Server <VIServer[]>] [-RunAsync] [-Description <String>] [-Verbose] [-Debug] [-ErrorAction <ActionPreference>] [-ErrorVariable <String>] [-OutVariable <String>] [-OutBuffer <Int32>] [-WhatIf] [-Confirm] New-VM [[-VMHost] <VMHost>] [[-Template] <Template>] -Name <String> [-ResourcePool <ResourcePool>] [-Location <Folder>] [-Datastore <Datastore>] [-OSCustomizationSpec <OSCustomizationSpec>] [-Server <VIServer[]>] [-RunAsync] [-Verbose] [-Debug] [-ErrorAction <ActionPreference>] [-ErrorVariable <String>] [-OutVariable <String>] [-OutBuffer <Int32>] [-WhatIf] [-Confirm]
New-VMHostAccount	New-VMHostAccount [-Id] <String> [-Password] <String> [-Description <String>] [-UserAccount] [-AssignGroups <String[]>] [-Server <VIServer>] [-Verbose] [-Debug] [-ErrorAction <ActionPreference>] [-ErrorVariable <String>] [-OutVariable <String>] [-OutBuffer <Int32>] [-WhatIf] [-Confirm] New-VMHostAccount [-Id] <String> [-GroupAccount] [-AssignUsers <String[]>] [-Server <VIServer>] [-Verbose] [-Debug] [-ErrorAction <ActionPreference>] [-ErrorVariable <String>] [-OutVariable <String>] [-OutBuffer <Int32>] [-WhatIf] [-Confirm]
New-VMHostNetworkAdapter	New-VMHostNetworkAdapter [[-VMHost] <VMHost>] [-PortGroup] <String> [-VirtualSwitch] <VirtualSwitch> [[-IP] <String>] [[-SubnetMask] <String>] [[-Mac] <String>] [-ConsoleNic] [-VMotionEnabled <Nullable`1>] [-Server <VIServer[]>] [-Verbose] [-Debug] [-ErrorAction <ActionPreference>] [-ErrorVariable <String>] [-OutVariable <String>] [-OutBuffer <Int32>] [-WhatIf] [-Confirm]

Table C-1 continued

Cmdlets in the VI Toolkit (for Windows)

Name	Definition
Remove-CDDrive	Remove-CDDrive [-CD] <CDDrive[]> [-Verbose] [-Debug] [-ErrorAction <ActionPreference>] [-ErrorVariable <String>] [-OutVariable <String>] [-OutBuffer <Int32>] [-WhatIf] [-Confirm]
Remove-Cluster	Remove-Cluster [[-Cluster] <Cluster[]>] [-Server <VIServer[]>] [-RunAsync] [-Verbose] [-Debug] [-ErrorAction <ActionPreference>] [-ErrorVariable <String>] [-OutVariable <String>] [-OutBuffer <Int32>] [-WhatIf] [-Confirm]
Remove-CustomField	Remove-CustomField [-Entity] <InventoryItem> [-Name] <String> [-Verbose] [-Debug] [-ErrorAction <ActionPreference>] [-ErrorVariable <String>] [-OutVariable <String>] [-OutBuffer <Int32>] [-WhatIf] [-Confirm]
Remove-Datacenter	Remove-Datacenter [[-Datacenter] <Datacenter[]>] [-RunAsync] [-Server <VIServer[]>] [-Verbose] [-Debug] [-ErrorAction <ActionPreference>] [-ErrorVariable <String>] [-OutVariable <String>] [-OutBuffer <Int32>] [-WhatIf] [-Confirm]
Remove-Datastore	Remove-Datastore [-Datastore] <Datastore> [[-VMHost] <VMHost>] [-RunAsync] [-Verbose] [-Debug] [-ErrorAction <ActionPreference>] [-ErrorVariable <String>] [-OutVariable <String>] [-OutBuffer <Int32>] [-WhatIf] [-Confirm]
Remove-FloppyDrive	Remove-FloppyDrive [-Floppy] <FloppyDrive[]> [-Verbose] [-Debug] [-ErrorAction <ActionPreference>] [-ErrorVariable <String>] [-OutVariable <String>] [-OutBuffer <Int32>] [-WhatIf] [-Confirm]
Remove-Folder	Remove-Folder [[-Folder] <Folder[]>] [-Server <VIServer[]>] [-Verbose] [-Debug] [-ErrorAction <ActionPreference>] [-ErrorVariable <String>] [-OutVariable <String>] [-OutBuffer <Int32>] [-WhatIf] [-Confirm]

Table C-1   continued

Cmdlets in the VI Toolkit (for Windows)

Name	Definition
Remove-Inventory	Remove-Inventory [[-Item] <InventoryItem[]>] [-RunAsync] [-Verbose] [-Debug] [-ErrorAction <ActionPreference>] [-ErrorVariable <String>] [-OutVariable <String>] [-OutBuffer <Int32>] [-WhatIf] [-Confirm]
Remove-NetworkAdapter	Remove-NetworkAdapter [-NetworkAdapter] <NetworkAdapter[]> [-Verbose] [-Debug] [-ErrorAction <ActionPreference>] [-ErrorVariable <String>] [-OutVariable <String>] [-OutBuffer <Int32>] [-WhatIf] [-Confirm]
Remove-OSCustomizationSpec	Remove-OSCustomizationSpec [[-CustomizationSpec] <OSCustomizationSpec[]>] [-Server <VIServer[]>] [-Verbose] [-Debug] [-ErrorAction <ActionPreference>] [-ErrorVariable <String>] [-OutVariable <String>] [-OutBuffer <Int32>] [-WhatIf] [-Confirm]
Remove-ResourcePool	Remove-ResourcePool [[-ResourcePool] <ResourcePool[]>] [-Server <VIServer[]>] [-Verbose] [-Debug] [-ErrorAction <ActionPreference>] [-ErrorVariable <String>] [-OutVariable <String>] [-OutBuffer <Int32>] [-WhatIf] [-Confirm]
Remove-Snapshot	Remove-Snapshot [-Snapshot] <Snapshot[]> [-RemoveChildren] [-RunAsync] [-Verbose] [-Debug] [-ErrorAction <ActionPreference>] [-ErrorVariable <String>] [-OutVariable <String>] [-OutBuffer <Int32>] [-WhatIf] [-Confirm]
Remove-Template	Remove-Template [[-Template] <Template[]>] [-DeleteFromDisk] [-RunAsync] [-Server <VIServer[]>] [-Verbose] [-Debug] [-ErrorAction <ActionPreference>] [-ErrorVariable <String>] [-OutVariable <String>] [-OutBuffer <Int32>] [-WhatIf] [-Confirm]
Remove-VirtualPortGroup	Remove-VirtualPortGroup [-VirtualPortGroup] <VirtualPortGroup[]> [-Verbose] [-Debug] [-ErrorAction <ActionPreference>] [-ErrorVariable <String>] [-OutVariable <String>] [-OutBuffer <Int32>] [-WhatIf] [-Confirm]

Table C-1   continued

Cmdlets in the VI Toolkit (for Windows)

Name	Definition
Remove-VirtualSwitch	Remove-VirtualSwitch [-VirtualSwitch] <VirtualSwitch[]> [-Verbose] [-Debug] [-ErrorAction <ActionPreference>] [-ErrorVariable <String>] [-OutVariable <String>] [-OutBuffer <Int32>] [-WhatIf] [-Confirm]
Remove-VM	Remove-VM [[-VM] <VirtualMachine[]>] [-Server <VIServer[]>] [-Verbose] [-Debug] [-ErrorAction <ActionPreference>] [-ErrorVariable <String>] [-OutVariable <String>] [-OutBuffer <Int32>] [-WhatIf] [-Confirm] Remove-VM [[-VM] <VirtualMachine[]>] -DeleteFromDisk [-RunAsync] [-Server <VIServer[]>] [-Verbose] [-Debug] [-ErrorAction <ActionPreference>] [-ErrorVariable <String>] [-OutVariable <String>] [-OutBuffer <Int32>] [-WhatIf] [-Confirm]
Remove-VMHost	Remove-VMHost [[-VMHost] <VMHost[]>] [-Server <VIServer[]>] [-Verbose] [-Debug] [-ErrorAction <ActionPreference>] [-ErrorVariable <String>] [-OutVariable <String>] [-OutBuffer <Int32>] [-WhatIf] [-Confirm]
Remove-VMHostAccount	Remove-VMHostAccount [-HostAccount] <HostAccount[]> [-Verbose] [-Debug] [-ErrorAction <ActionPreference>] [-ErrorVariable <String>] [-OutVariable <String>] [-OutBuffer <Int32>] [-WhatIf] [-Confirm]
Remove-VMHostNetworkAdapter	Remove-VMHostNetworkAdapter [-Nic] <HostVirtualNic[]> [-Verbose] [-Debug] [-ErrorAction <ActionPreference>] [-ErrorVariable <String>] [-OutVariable <String>] [-OutBuffer <Int32>] [-WhatIf] [-Confirm]

continues...

Table C-1   continued

Cmdlets in the VI Toolkit (for Windows)

Name	Definition
Restart-VMGuest	Restart-VMGuest [[-VM] <VirtualMachine[]>] [[-Server] <VIServer[]>] [-Verbose] [-Debug] [-ErrorAction <ActionPreference>] [-ErrorVariable <String>] [-OutVariable <String>] [-OutBuffer <Int32>] [-WhatIf] [-Confirm]
	Restart-VMGuest [[-Guest] <VMGuest[]>] [-Verbose] [-Debug] [-ErrorAction <ActionPreference>] [-ErrorVariable <String>] [-OutVariable <String>] [-OutBuffer <Int32>] [-WhatIf] [-Confirm]
Restart-VMHostService	Restart-VMHostService [-HostService] <HostService[]> [-Verbose] [-Debug] [-ErrorAction <ActionPreference>] [-ErrorVariable <String>] [-OutVariable <String>] [-OutBuffer <Int32>] [-WhatIf] [-Confirm]
Set-CDDrive	Set-CDDrive [-CD] <CDDrive[]> [-IsoPath <String>] [-HostDevice <String>] [-NoMedia] [-StartConnected <Nullable`1>] [-Connected <Nullable`1>] [-Verbose] [-Debug] [-ErrorAction <ActionPreference>] [-ErrorVariable <String>] [-OutVariable <String>] [-OutBuffer <Int32>] [-WhatIf] [-Confirm]
Set-Cluster	Set-Cluster [[-Cluster] <Cluster>] [[-Name] <String>] [-HAEnabled <Nullable`1>] [-HAAdmissionControlEnabled <Nullable`1>] [-HAFailoverLevel <Nullable`1>] [-DrsEnabled <Nullable`1>] [-DrsMode <Nullable`1>] [-Server <VIServer[]>] [-RunAsync] [-Verbose] [-Debug] [-ErrorAction <ActionPreference>] [-ErrorVariable <String>] [-OutVariable <String>] [-OutBuffer <Int32>] [-WhatIf] [-Confirm]
Set-CustomField	Set-CustomField [-Entity] <InventoryItem> [-Name] <String> [[-Value] <String>] [-Verbose] [-Debug] [-ErrorAction <ActionPreference>] [-ErrorVariable <String>] [-OutVariable <String>] [-OutBuffer <Int32>] [-WhatIf] [-Confirm]

Table C-1 continued

Cmdlets in the VI Toolkit (for Windows)

Name	Definition
Set-Datacenter	Set-Datacenter [[-Datacenter] <Datacenter>] [-Name] <String> [-Server <VIServer[]>] [-RunAsync] [-Verbose] [-Debug] [-ErrorAction <ActionPreference>] [-ErrorVariable <String>] [-OutVariable <String>] [-OutBuffer <Int32>] [-WhatIf] [-Confirm]
Set-Datastore	Set-Datastore [-Datastore] <Datastore> [-Name] <String> [-Verbose] [-Debug] [-ErrorAction <ActionPreference>] [-ErrorVariable <String>] [-OutVariable <String>] [-OutBuffer <Int32>] [-WhatIf] [-Confirm]
Set-FloppyDrive	Set-FloppyDrive [-Floppy] <FloppyDrive[]> [-FloppyImagePath <String>] [-HostDevice <String>] [-NoMedia] [-StartConnected <Nullable`1>] [-Connected <Nullable`1>] [-Verbose] [-Debug] [-ErrorAction <ActionPreference>] [-ErrorVariable <String>] [-OutVariable <String>] [-OutBuffer <Int32>] [-WhatIf] [-Confirm]
Set-Folder	Set-Folder [-Folder <Folder>] -Name <String> [-Server <VIServer[]>] [-Verbose] [-Debug] [-ErrorAction <ActionPreference>] [-ErrorVariable <String>] [-OutVariable <String>] [-OutBuffer <Int32>] [-WhatIf] [-Confirm]
Set-HardDisk	Set-HardDisk [-HardDisk] <HardDisk[]> [[-CapacityKB] <Nullable`1>] [[-Persistence] <String>] [[-Datastore] <Datastore>] [-Verbose] [-Debug] [-ErrorAction <ActionPreference>] [-ErrorVariable <String>] [-OutVariable <String>] [-OutBuffer <Int32>] [-WhatIf] [-Confirm]
Set-NetworkAdapter	Set-NetworkAdapter [-NetworkAdapter] <NetworkAdapter[]> [-MacAddress <String>] [-NetworkName <String>] [-StartConnected <Nullable`1>] [-Connected <Nullable`1>] [-WakeOnLan <Nullable`1>] [-Verbose] [-Debug] [-ErrorAction <ActionPreference>] [-ErrorVariable <String>] [-OutVariable <String>] [-OutBuffer <Int32>] [-WhatIf] [-Confirm]

continues...

Table C-1   continued

Cmdlets in the VI Toolkit (for Windows)

Name	Definition
Set-OSCustomizationSpec	Set-OSCustomizationSpec [-Spec] <OSCustomizationSpec[]> [-NewSpec <OSCustomizationSpec>] [-Server <VIServer[]>] [-DnsServer <String[]>] [-DnsSuffix <String[]>] [-Domain <String>] [-NamingScheme <String>] [-NamingPrefix <String>] [-Description <String>] [-Verbose] [-Debug] [-ErrorAction <ActionPreference>] [-ErrorVariable <String>] [-OutVariable <String>] [-OutBuffer <Int32>] [-WhatIf] [-Confirm]
	Set-OSCustomizationSpec [-Spec] <OSCustomizationSpec[]> [-FullName <String>] [-OrgName <String>] [-ChangeSID <Nullable`1>] [-DeleteAccounts <Nullable`1>] [-NewSpec <OSCustomizationSpec>] [-Server <VIServer[]>] [-DnsServer <String[]>] [-DnsSuffix <String[]>] [-GuiRunOnce <String[]>] [-AdminPassword <String>] [-TimeZone <String>] [-AutoLogonCount <Nullable`1>] [-Domain <String>] [-Workgroup <String>] [-DomainCredentials <PSCredential>] [-DomainUsername <String>] [-DomainPassword <String>] [-ProductKey <String>] [-NamingScheme <String>] [-NamingPrefix <String>] [-Description <String>] [-Verbose] [-Debug] [-ErrorAction <ActionPreference>] [-ErrorVariable <String>] [-OutVariable <String>] [-OutBuffer <Int32>] [-WhatIf] [-Confirm]
Set-ResourcePool	Set-ResourcePool [-ResourcePool <ResourcePool[]>] [-Name <String>] [-CpuExpandableReservation] [-CpuLimitMhz <Int64>] [-CpuReservationMhz <Int64>] [-CpuSharesLevel <SharesLevel>] [-MemExpandableReservation] [-MemLimitMB <Int64>] [-MemReservationMB <Int64>] [-MemSharesLevel <SharesLevel>] [-NumCpuShares <Int32>] [-NumMemShares <Int32>] [-Server <VIServer[]>] [-Verbose] [-Debug] [-ErrorAction <ActionPreference>] [-ErrorVariable <String>] [-OutVariable <String>] [-OutBuffer <Int32>] [-WhatIf] [-Confirm]

Table C-1   continued

Cmdlets in the VI Toolkit (for Windows)

Name	Definition
Set-Snapshot	Set-Snapshot [-Snapshot] <Snapshot> [-Name <String>] [-Description <String>] [-Verbose] [-Debug] [-ErrorAction <ActionPreference>] [-ErrorVariable <String>] [-OutVariable <String>] [-OutBuffer <Int32>] [-WhatIf] [-Confirm]
Set-Template	Set-Template [[-Template] <Template>] [-Name <String>] [-ToVM] [-Server <VIServer[]>] [-RunAsync] [-Verbose] [-Debug] [-ErrorAction <ActionPreference>] [-ErrorVariable <String>] [-OutVariable <String>] [-OutBuffer <Int32>] [-WhatIf] [-Confirm]
Set-VirtualPortGroup	Set-VirtualPortGroup [-VirtualPortGroup] <VirtualPortGroup> [-VLanId <Nullable`1>] [-Verbose] [-Debug] [-ErrorAction <ActionPreference>] [-ErrorVariable <String>] [-OutVariable <String>] [-OutBuffer <Int32>] [-WhatIf] [-Confirm]
Set-VirtualSwitch	Set-VirtualSwitch [-VirtualSwitch] <VirtualSwitch> [[-NumPorts] <Int32>] [[-Nic] <String[]>] [[-Mtu] <Int32>] [-Verbose] [-Debug] [-ErrorAction <ActionPreference>] [-ErrorVariable <String>] [-OutVariable <String>] [-OutBuffer <Int32>] [-WhatIf] [-Confirm]
Set-VIToolkitConfiguration	Set-VIToolkitConfiguration -ProxyPolicy <Nullable`1> [-Verbose] [-Debug] [-ErrorAction <ActionPreference>] [-ErrorVariable <String>] [-OutVariable <String>] [-OutBuffer <Int32>] [-WhatIf] [-Confirm]

continues...

Table C-1 continued

Cmdlets in the VI Toolkit (for Windows)

Name	Definition
Set-VM	Set-VM [[-VM] <VirtualMachine>] [-Name <String>] [-MemoryMB <Nullable`1>] [-NumCpu <Nullable`1>] [-GuestId <String>] [-AlternateGuestName <String>] [-OSCustomizationSpec <OSCustomizationSpec>] [-Server <VIServer[]>] [-RunAsync] [-Description <String>] [-Verbose] [-Debug] [-ErrorAction <ActionPreference>] [-ErrorVariable <String>] [-OutVariable <String>] [-OutBuffer <Int32>] [-WhatIf] [-Confirm]
	Set-VM [[-VM] <VirtualMachine>] [-Name <String>] [-Snapshot <Snapshot>] [-OSCustomizationSpec <OSCustomizationSpec>] [-Server <VIServer[]>] [-RunAsync] [-Verbose] [-Debug] [-ErrorAction <ActionPreference>] [-ErrorVariable <String>] [-OutVariable <String>] [-OutBuffer <Int32>] [-WhatIf] [-Confirm]
Set-VMHost	Set-VMHost [[-VMHost] <VMHost>] [-State] <Nullable`1> [-Server <VIServer[]>] [-RunAsync] [-Verbose] [-Debug] [-ErrorAction <ActionPreference>] [-ErrorVariable <String>] [-OutVariable <String>] [-OutBuffer <Int32>] [-WhatIf] [-Confirm]
Set-VMHostAccount	Set-VMHostAccount [-GroupAccount] <Object> [-AssignUsers <String[]>] [-UnassignUsers <String[]>] [-Server <VIServer>] [-Verbose] [-Debug] [-ErrorAction <ActionPreference>] [-ErrorVariable <String>] [-OutVariable <String>] [-OutBuffer <Int32>] [-WhatIf] [-Confirm]
	Set-VMHostAccount [-UserAccount] <Object> [-Password <String>] [-Description <String>] [-AssignGroups <String[]>] [-UnassignGroups <String[]>] [-Server <VIServer>] [-Verbose] [-Debug] [-ErrorAction <ActionPreference>] [-ErrorVariable <String>] [-OutVariable <String>] [-OutBuffer <Int32>] [-WhatIf] [-Confirm]

Table C-1 continued

Cmdlets in the VI Toolkit (for Windows)

Name	Definition
Set-VMHostFirmware	Set-VMHostFirmware [[-VMHost] <VMHost>] [-BackupConfiguration] -DestinationPath <String> [-Server <VIServer[]>] [-Verbose] [-Debug] [-ErrorAction <ActionPreference>] [-ErrorVariable <String>] [-OutVariable <String>] [-OutBuffer <Int32>] [-WhatIf] [-Confirm] Set-VMHostFirmware [[-VMHost] <VMHost>] [-ResetToDefaults] [-Server <VIServer[]>] [-Verbose] [-Debug] [-ErrorAction <ActionPreference>] [-ErrorVariable <String>] [-OutVariable <String>] [-OutBuffer <Int32>] [-WhatIf] [-Confirm] Set-VMHostFirmware [[-VMHost] <VMHost>] [-Restore] [-Force] [-Server <VIServer[]>] [-Verbose] [-Debug] [-ErrorAction <ActionPreference>] [-ErrorVariable <String>] [-OutVariable <String>] [-OutBuffer <Int32>] [-WhatIf] [-Confirm]
Set-VMHostModule	Set-VMHostModule [-HostModule] <VmHostModule> [-Options] <String> [-Verbose] [-Debug] [-ErrorAction <ActionPreference>] [-ErrorVariable <String>] [-OutVariable <String>] [-OutBuffer <Int32>] [-WhatIf] [-Confirm]
Set-VMHostNetwork	Set-VMHostNetwork [-Network] <VMHostNetworkInfo> [-ConsoleGateway <String>] [-VMKernelGateway <String>] [-ConsoleGatewayDevice <String>] [-DomainName <String>] [-HostName <String>] [-DnsFromDhcp] [-DnsDhcpDevice <Object>] [-Verbose] [-Debug] [-ErrorAction <ActionPreference>] [-ErrorVariable <String>] [-OutVariable <String>] [-OutBuffer <Int32>] [-WhatIf] [-Confirm]
Set-VMHostNetworkAdapter	Set-VMHostNetworkAdapter -PhysicalNic <PhysicalNic[]> [-Duplex <String>] [-BitRatePerSecMb <Int32>] [-AutoNegotiate] [-Verbose] [-Debug] [-ErrorAction <ActionPreference>] [-ErrorVariable <String>] [-OutVariable <String>] [-OutBuffer <Int32>] [-WhatIf] [-Confirm] Set-VMHostNetworkAdapter -VirtualNic <HostVirtualNic[]> [-IP <String>] [-SubnetMask <String>] [-Mac <String>] [-VMotionEnabled <Nullable`1>] [-Verbose] [-Debug] [-ErrorAction <ActionPreference>] [-ErrorVariable <String>] [-OutVariable <String>] [-OutBuffer <Int32>] [-WhatIf] [-Confirm]

continues...

Table C-1   continued

Cmdlets in the VI Toolkit (for Windows)

Name	Definition
Set-VMHostService	Set-VMHostService [-HostService] <HostService> [-Policy] <HostServicePolicy> [-Verbose] [-Debug] [-ErrorAction <ActionPreference>] [-ErrorVariable <String>] [-OutVariable <String>] [-OutBuffer <Int32>] [-WhatIf] [-Confirm]
Set-VMHostSnmp	Set-VMHostSnmp [-HostSnmp] <VmHostSnmp> [-Enabled] [-Port <Int32>] [-ReadOnlyCommunity <String[]>] [-Verbose] [-Debug] [-ErrorAction <ActionPreference>] [-ErrorVariable <String>] [-OutVariable <String>] [-OutBuffer <Int32>] [-WhatIf] [-Confirm] Set-VMHostSnmp [-HostSnmp] <VmHostSnmp> [-Enabled] [-Port <Int32>] [-ReadOnlyCommunity <String[]>] [-TargetCommunity <String>] [-TargetPort <Int32>] [-TargetHost <String>] -RemoveTarget [-Verbose] [-Debug] [-ErrorAction <ActionPreference>] [-ErrorVariable <String>] [-OutVariable <String>] [-OutBuffer <Int32>] [-WhatIf] [-Confirm] Set-VMHostSnmp [-HostSnmp] <VmHostSnmp> [-Enabled] [-Port <Int32>] [-ReadOnlyCommunity <String[]>] -TargetCommunity <String> [-TargetPort <Int32>] -TargetHost <String> -AddTarget [-Verbose] [-Debug] [-ErrorAction <ActionPreference>] [-ErrorVariable <String>] [-OutVariable <String>] [-OutBuffer <Int32>] [-WhatIf] [-Confirm] Set-VMHostSnmp [-HostSnmp] <VmHostSnmp> [-Enabled] [-Port <Int32>] [-ReadOnlyCommunity <String[]>] [-RemoveTarget] -TrapTargetToRemove <TrapTarget> [-Verbose] [-Debug] [-ErrorAction <ActionPreference>] [-ErrorVariable <String>] [-OutVariable <String>] [-OutBuffer <Int32>] [-WhatIf] [-Confirm]
Set-VMHostStartPolicy	Set-VMHostStartPolicy [-VMHostStartPolicy] <VMHostStartPolicy> [-Enabled] [-StartDelay <Int32>] [-StopAction <Nullable`1>] [-StopDelay <Nullable`1>] [-WaitForHeartBeat <Nullable`1>] [-Verbose] [-Debug] [-ErrorAction <ActionPreference>] [-ErrorVariable <String>] [-OutVariable <String>] [-OutBuffer <Int32>] [-WhatIf] [-Confirm]

Table C-1 continued

Cmdlets in the VI Toolkit (for Windows)

Name	Definition
Set-VMStartPolicy	Set-VMStartPolicy [-StartPolicy] <VMStartPolicy> [-StartAction <Nullable`1>] [-StartOrder <Int32>] [-InheritStopActionFromHost] [-InheritStopDelayFromHost] [-InheritWaitForHeartbeatFromHost] [-InheritStartDelayFromHost] [-UnspecifiedStartOrder] [-StartDelay <Int32>] [-StopAction <Nullable`1>] [-StopDelay <Nullable`1>] [-WaitForHeartBeat <Nullable`1>] [-Verbose] [-Debug] [-ErrorAction <ActionPreference>] [-ErrorVariable <String>] [-OutVariable <String>] [-OutBuffer <Int32>] [-WhatIf] [-Confirm]
Shutdown-VMGuest	Shutdown-VMGuest [[-VM] <VirtualMachine[]>] [[-Server] <VIServer[]>] [-Verbose] [-Debug] [-ErrorAction <ActionPreference>] [-ErrorVariable <String>] [-OutVariable <String>] [-OutBuffer <Int32>] [-WhatIf] [-Confirm] Shutdown-VMGuest [[-Guest] <VMGuest[]>] [-Verbose] [-Debug] [-ErrorAction <ActionPreference>] [-ErrorVariable <String>] [-OutVariable <String>] [-OutBuffer <Int32>] [-WhatIf] [-Confirm]
Start-VM	Start-VM [[-VM] <VirtualMachine[]>] [-RunAsync] [-Server <VIServer[]>] [-Verbose] [-Debug] [-ErrorAction <ActionPreference>] [-ErrorVariable <String>] [-OutVariable <String>] [-OutBuffer <Int32>] [-WhatIf] [-Confirm]
Start-VMHostService	Start-VMHostService [-HostService] <HostService[]> [-Verbose] [-Debug] [-ErrorAction <ActionPreference>] [-ErrorVariable <String>] [-OutVariable <String>] [-OutBuffer <Int32>] [-WhatIf] [-Confirm]
Stop-Task	Stop-Task [-Task] <Task[]> [-Verbose] [-Debug] [-ErrorAction <ActionPreference>] [-ErrorVariable <String>] [-OutVariable <String>] [-OutBuffer <Int32>] [-WhatIf] [-Confirm]

continues...

Table C-1   continued

Cmdlets in the VI Toolkit (for Windows)

Name	Definition
Stop-VM	Stop-VM [[-VM] <VirtualMachine[]>] [-RunAsync] [-Server <VIServer[]>] [-Verbose] [-Debug] [-ErrorAction <ActionPreference>] [-ErrorVariable <String>] [-OutVariable <String>] [-OutBuffer <Int32>] [-WhatIf] [-Confirm]
Stop-VMHostService	Stop-VMHostService [-HostService] <HostService[]> [-Verbose] [-Debug] [-ErrorAction <ActionPreference>] [-ErrorVariable <String>] [-OutVariable <String>] [-OutBuffer <Int32>] [-WhatIf] [-Confirm]
Suspend-VM	Suspend-VM [[-VM] <VirtualMachine[]>] [-RunAsync] [-Server <VIServer[]>] [-Verbose] [-Debug] [-ErrorAction <ActionPreference>] [-ErrorVariable <String>] [-OutVariable <String>] [-OutBuffer <Int32>] [-WhatIf] [-Confirm]
Suspend-VMGuest	Suspend-VMGuest [[-VM] <VirtualMachine[]>] [[-Server] <VIServer[]>] [-Verbose] [-Debug] [-ErrorAction <ActionPreference>] [-ErrorVariable <String>] [-OutVariable <String>] [-OutBuffer <Int32>] [-WhatIf] [-Confirm] Suspend-VMGuest [[-Guest] <VMGuest[]>] [-Verbose] [-Debug] [-ErrorAction <ActionPreference>] [-ErrorVariable <String>] [-OutVariable <String>] [-OutBuffer <Int32>] [-WhatIf] [-Confirm]
Test-VMHostSnmp	Test-VMHostSnmp [-HostSnmp] <VmHostSnmp[]> [-Verbose] [-Debug] [-ErrorAction <ActionPreference>] [-ErrorVariable <String>] [-OutVariable <String>] [-OutBuffer <Int32>]
Update-Tools	Update-Tools [[-Guest] <VMGuest[]>] [-Verbose] [-Debug] [-ErrorAction <ActionPreference>] [-ErrorVariable <String>] [-OutVariable <String>] [-OutBuffer <Int32>] Update-Tools [[-VM] <VirtualMachine[]>] [[-Server] <VIServer[]>] [-Verbose] [-Debug] [-ErrorAction <ActionPreference>] [-ErrorVariable <String>] [-OutVariable <String>] [-OutBuffer <Int32>]

Table C-1   continued

Cmdlets in the VI Toolkit (for Windows)

Name	Definition
Wait-Task	Wait-Task [-Task] <Task[]> [-Verbose] [-Debug] [-ErrorAction <ActionPreference>] [-ErrorVariable <String>] [-OutVariable <String>] [-OutBuffer <Int32>]

Appendix D

Unified Modeling Language

Unified Modeling Language (UML), an open standard modeling language from Object Management Group[1] (OMG), is a fusion of three previously competing methods: Booch (Grady Booch), OMT (Jim Rumbaugh), and OOSE (Ivar Jacobson). Since its release in 1997, UML has gained popularity in documenting high-level and system-level designs and communicating these designs among software professionals and other stakeholders.

A full and deep introduction to UML is out of the scope of this book. Instead, this appendix focuses on the class and object diagrams that are used heavily to model the managed objects and data objects in the VI SDK.

Class Diagram

The class diagram shows how different types are defined and how they are related to each other. The basic unit in the class diagram is a rectangle with three horizontal sections representing a type definition, as shown in Figure D-1.

The top section shows the name of the type, the middle one shows the properties that are defined, and the bottom section shows the operations. The top section for type name must be present, but the properties and operations can be omitted.

---

[1] http://www.omg.org

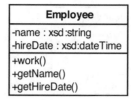

Figure D-1   A typical class diagram in UML

Visibility

Every element can have one of three basic visibilities:

- **Private (-)**—Can be seen only within the class, not even for its subtypes
- **Protected (#)**—Can be seen both itself and its subtypes
- **Public (+)**—Can be seen by anyone

Inheritance/Generalization

A type can be extended to a subtype with extra properties or operations defined. The subtype then inherits all the properties and operations of its supertype. The relationship is called inheritance and represented by a line with an empty arrow head. As shown in Figure D-2, the Manager type is a subtype of the Employee type.

Because a given supertype normally has several subtypes, you can think of inheritance in a different way: The supertype is a generalized type of all the subtypes. Therefore, inheritance is also called generalization. The two are essentially referring to the same thing but in different perspectives. When designing a system, people tend to use more generalization for a concise type hierarchy. When using an existing library or extending a system, however, people tend to use more inheritance for better reuse of software components.

Association

An association represents a structural relationship. Although it links two types, it really means the linkage between the objects of one type and the objects of the other.

On each end of the association, you can specify the number of objects involved. For the Employee/Manager sample, 1 is tagged close to the manager and

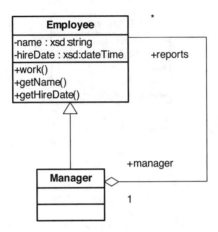

Figure D-2   A UML diagram showing inheritance and association

* close to the employee. Every manager can be related to multiple (including 0) employees, and every employee must have a manager.

In general, you can have one-to-one, one-to-many, and many-to-many associations. The one-to-many association is also called aggregation, with a diamond shape at one end. It represents the relationship of a whole and its parts. If the part cannot exist without the whole, it is called composition, with a black diamond. The difference between composition and normal aggregation sometimes is subtle; you need to evaluate carefully.

Object Diagram

The object diagram looks similar to the class diagram. However, instead of modeling the types and their relationship as in a class diagram, it models the instances of the types and their relationships.

The basic building block in the object diagram is the rectangle with two sections, as shown in Figure D-3. The top section is for the name of the object and the type. To avoid confusion, it has a line under its name. The bottom part denotes the property values; this section is optional and can be omitted.

The objects can have links between each other. These links can help to clarify the associations in the class diagram.

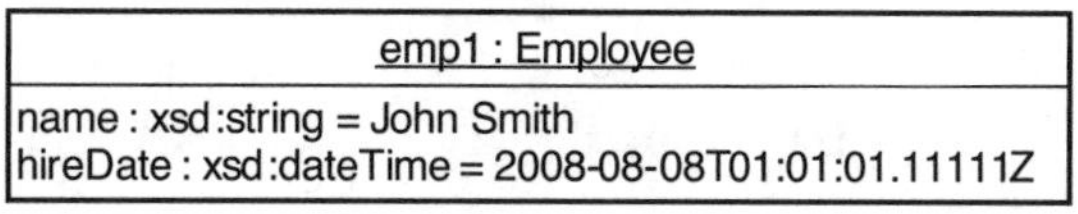

```
                    emp1 : Employee
name : xsd:string = John Smith
hireDate : xsd:dateTime = 2008-08-08T01:01:01.11111Z
```

Figure D-3   A sample object diagram in UML

Modeling XML

Most of our UML diagrams are used to model the data objects that represent the XML data passed over the wire. Each type of message has its equivalent type (class) when the stub files are generated in an object-oriented language.

These types are mainly for holding data and have no useful operation/method associated with them other than the related getter and setter methods. To simplify the diagram, the operations section is omitted for the data objects.

XML has no concept of visibility. Given an XML file, you can obtain any element. In light of this fact, all the elements in the data object type are marked as public. When they are bound to a specific language, however, the related properties might be private while public getter and setter methods are provided.

The data types of the properties are handled differently. Instead of language-specific data types, the original XML data type is used in the class diagram. The thinking behind this is that even though Java is used as the primary programming language in this book, you can always use other languages and find the UML diagrams helpful. After you have the data type mapping of these languages, you can easily map the types in the diagrams to language-specific types. For example, if you use C#, you can check MSDN for the data type mapping as in Table D-1.[2]

---

[2] http://msdn.microsoft.com/en-us/library/xa669bew.aspx

Table D-1

Mapping from WSDL to .NET Data Types

WSDL Type	CLR Type
xsd:base64Binary	Byte[]
xsd:boolean	System.Boolean
xsd:byte	System.SByte
xsd:dateTime	System.DateTime
xsd:decimal	System.Decimal
xsd:double	System.Double
xsd:float	System.Single
xsd:hexBinary	Byte[]
xsd:int	System.Int32
xsd:integer	System.Decimal
xsd:long	System.Int64
xsd:QName	System.XmlQualifiedName
xsd:short	System.Int16
xsd:string	System.String

Appendix E

VI SDK Web Services

This appendix introduces the Web Services interfaces used in the VI SDK, including Simple Object Access Protocol (SOAP) basics, Web Services Definition Language (WSDL), stub code generation, and so on.

The VI SDK Web Services interface complies with the Web Services Interoperability Organization (WS-I) Basic Profile 1.0, which includes XML Schema 1.0, SOAP 1.1, and WSDL 1.1.

SOAP

SOAP is a protocol facilitating client server communications. A SOAP message is encoded as an XML document that has an Envelope element as its root. Optionally, it can contain a Header element and a mandatory Body element. The Fault element within Body is used to report errors. Figure E-1 illustrates the structure of a SOAP message.

To give you a better idea of what a SOAP message looks like, Listings E-1 and E-2 show real SOAP messages sent and received by a VI SDK client. As you can see, the first is a SOAP request message as a result of invoking the RetrieveContent() method; the second is a response message of that method. From the messages, you can find out what parameters and values have been passed back and forth for one invocation.

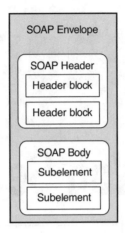

Figure E-1   The structure of a SOAP message

Listing E-1
SOAP Request Message of **RetrieveContent()** *Method*

```
<soapenv:Envelope xmlns:soapenv="http://schemas.xmlsoap.org/soap/envelope/"
xmlns:xsd="http://www.w3.org/2001/XMLSchema"
xmlns:xsi="http://www.w3.org/2001/XMLSchema-instance">
<soapenv:Body><RetrieveServiceContent xmlns="urn:vim25"><_this
type="ServiceInstance" xsi:type="ns1:ManagedObjectReference"
xmlns:ns1="urn:vim25">ServiceInstance</_this></RetrieveServiceContent>
</soapenv:Body>
</soapenv:Envelope>
```

Listing E-2
SOAP Response Message of **RetrieveContent()** *Method*

```
<soapenv:Envelope xmlns:soapenc="http://schemas.xmlsoap.org/soap/encoding/"
xmlns:soapenv="http://schemas.xmlsoap.org/soap/envelope/"
xmlns:xsd="http://www.w3.org/2001/XMLSchema"
xmlns:xsi="http://www.w3.org/2001/XMLSchema-instance">
  <soapenv:Body>
    <RetrieveServiceContentResponse xmlns="urn:internalvim25">
      <returnval>
        <rootFolder type="Folder">ha-folder-root</rootFolder>
        <propertyCollector type="PropertyCollector">ha-property-
collector</propertyCollector>
        <viewManager type="ViewManager">ViewManager</viewManager>
        <about>
```

```
        <name>VMware ESX Server</name>
        <fullName>VMware ESX Server 3.5.0 build-62355</fullName>
        <vendor>VMware, Inc.</vendor>
        <version>3.5.0</version>
        <build>62355</build>
        <localeVersion>INTL</localeVersion>
        <localeBuild>000</localeBuild>
        <osType>vmnix-x86</osType>
        <productLineId>esx</productLineId>
        <apiType>HostAgent</apiType>
        <apiVersion>2.0.0</apiVersion>
      </about>
      <setting type="OptionManager">HostAgentSettings</setting>
      <userDirectory type="UserDirectory">ha-user-directory</userDirectory>
      <sessionManager type="SessionManager">ha-sessionmgr</sessionManager>
      <authorizationManager type="AuthorizationManager">ha-
authmgr</authorizationManager>
      <perfManager type="PerformanceManager">ha-perfmgr</perfManager>
      <eventManager type="EventManager">ha-eventmgr</eventManager>
      <taskManager type="TaskManager">ha-taskmgr</taskManager>
      <accountManager type="HostLocalAccountManager">ha-
localacctmgr</accountManager>
      <diagnosticManager type="DiagnosticManager">ha-
diagnosticmgr</diagnosticManager>
      <licenseManager type="LicenseManager">ha-license-manager</licenseManager>
      <searchIndex type="SearchIndex">ha-searchindex</searchIndex>
      <fileManager type="FileManager">ha-nfc-file-manager</fileManager>
      <virtualDiskManager type="VirtualDiskManager">ha-
vdiskmanager</virtualDiskManager>
    </returnval>
  </RetrieveServiceContentResponse>
 </soapenv:Body>
</soapenv:Envelope>
```

Two WSDL Files

Two WSDL files are included for each version: vimService.wsdl and vim.wsdl. The
first one, shown in Listing E-3, is small compared to the second. The Web Services
directory service uses it to advertise the service.

Listing E-3
vimService.wsdl

```xml
<?xml version="1.0" encoding="UTF-8" ?>
<!--
   Copyright 2005-2007 VMware, Inc.  All rights reserved.
-->
<definitions targetNamespace="urn:vim25Service"
   xmlns="http://schemas.xmlsoap.org/wsdl/"
   xmlns:soap="http://schemas.xmlsoap.org/wsdl/soap/"
   xmlns:interface="urn:vim25">
   <import location="vim.wsdl" namespace="urn:vim25" />
   <service name="VimService">
      <port binding="interface:VimBinding" name="VimPort">
         <soap:address location="https://localhost/sdk/vimService" />
      </port>
   </service>
</definitions>
```

Notice that the address location is https://localhost/sdk/vimService, which points to a local machine. You'll want to change it to a real Domain Name Service (DNS) name or Internet Protocol (IP) address of your ESX or VirtualCenter server if you'll be advertising it for others to use.

Similar URLs are needed for running almost all the sample code hereafter. You can also omit the last part of the URL string to have something like https://localhost/sdk.

The other file, vim.wsdl, is the key WSDL; it's too large to fit into a few pages. It is about 1.326MB in size as of version 2.5. It's impossible to list all its content here. Listing E-4 shows a small piece of each of the major parts of the file:

- Type definition, including those of data objects and faults

- Messages that are to be used in the operations

- portType, which includes all the operation definitions

- Binding, which instructs the stub generator how to create SOAP messages

Listing E-4
partial vim.wsdl

```xml
<?xml version="1.0" encoding="UTF-8" ?>
<!--
   Copyright 2005-2007 VMware, Inc.  All rights reserved.
-->
```

```
<definitions targetNamespace="urn:vim25"
    xmlns="http://schemas.xmlsoap.org/wsdl/"
    xmlns:mime="http://schemas.xmlsoap.org/wsdl/mime/"
    xmlns:soap="http://schemas.xmlsoap.org/wsdl/soap/"
    xmlns:vim25="urn:vim25"
    xmlns:xsd="http://www.w3.org/2001/XMLSchema"
>
    <types>
        <schema
            targetNamespace="urn:vim25"
            xmlns="http://www.w3.org/2001/XMLSchema"
            xmlns:mime="http://schemas.xmlsoap.org/wsdl/mime/"
            xmlns:soap="http://schemas.xmlsoap.org/wsdl/soap/"
            xmlns:wsdl="http://schemas.xmlsoap.org/wsdl/"
            xmlns:vim25="urn:vim25"
            xmlns:xsd="http://www.w3.org/2001/XMLSchema"
            elementFormDefault="qualified">
            <complexType name="DynamicArray">
                <sequence>
                    <element name="dynamicType" type="xsd:string" minOccurs="0" />
                    <element name="val" type="xsd:anyType" maxOccurs="unbounded" />
                </sequence>
            </complexType>
        ...
        </schema>
    </types>
    <message name="HostCommunicationFaultMsg">
        <part name="fault" element="vim25:HostCommunicationFault" />
    </message>
    ...
    <portType name="VimPortType">
        <operation name="DestroyPropertyFilter">
            <input message="vim25:DestroyPropertyFilterRequestMsg" />
            <output message="vim25:DestroyPropertyFilterResponseMsg" />
            <fault name="RuntimeFault" message="vim25:RuntimeFaultFaultMsg"/>
        </operation>
        ...
    </portType>
    <binding name="VimBinding" type="vim25:VimPortType">
        <soap:binding style="document"
transport="http://schemas.xmlsoap.org/soap/http" />
```

```
    <operation name="DestroyPropertyFilter">
       <soap:operation soapAction="" style="document" />
       <input>
          <soap:body use="literal" />
       </input>
       <output>
          <soap:body use="literal" />
       </output>
       <fault name="RuntimeFault">
          <soap:fault name="RuntimeFault" use="literal" />
       </fault>
    </operation>
    ...
  </binding>
</definitions>
```

> Because most people don't use the WSDL directly, there is no need to cover more here. In some rare cases, you might want to closely look at this WSDL. One such case is when you get into performance issues and want to bypass the generated stubs and work on the SOAP message level. That is not recommended, though.

Stub Code Generation

When you develop your application, you don't want to work on a SOAP message directly. Instead, you want to generate client stubs that take care of the tedious work like serialization and de-serialization underneath. The VI SDK has included the stubs, so you can safely skip this section unless you want to customize them.

If you have AXIS 1.x installed, you can use the WSDL2Java utility tool to create all the stubs from a WSDL file as follows:

```
$ java org.apache.axis.wsdl.WSDL2Java (WSDL-file-URL)
```

The generated stubs vary from language to language and from framework to framework. Some frameworks allow you to customize so you can tune your generated stubs. You should always consult the related documentation on the details and make a call whether that is the best choice for your project.

VMware includes the stubs created by AXIS 1.4, which is a leading Web Services framework used in Java. Every type defined in WSDL has its equivalent classes in the generated stubs. These generated classes handle the serialization and deserialization between a method call and the corresponding SOAP message, as well as the message transportation.

You can specify the generated Java package name. The pregenerated JAR file for VI SDK 2.5 has the package name com.vmware.vim25, and the JAR of 2.0 has com.vmware.vim.

Because WSDL has its own data types, they must be converted to Java and vice versa during the serialization and de-serialization. Table E-1 lists the mapping of primitive data types from WSDL types to Java data types in AXIS.

Table E-1

Standard Mappings of Data Types from WSDL to Java

WSDL Type	Java Type
xsd:base64Binary	byte[]
xsd:boolean	Boolean
xsd:byte	Byte
xsd:dateTime	java.util.Calendar
xsd:decimal	java.math.BigDecimal
xsd:double	Double
xsd:float	Float
xsd:hexBinary	byte[]
xsd:int	Int
xsd:integer	java.math.BigInteger
xsd:long	Long
xsd:QName	javax.xml.namespace.QName
xsd:short	Short
xsd:string	java.lang.String

Although we use Java as the main language for samples across this book, we still use WSDL data types to describe data objects and faults. If you are using a language other than Java, just have a similar mapping table ready, and you can easily map the data types to specific language types by yourself.

Note the VI Java API 2.0 includes a high performance Web Services engine and generated stubs, so you don't need AXIS anymore if you're developing your application using the API.

From Managed Object to WSDL to Generated Stub

The methods defined on all managed object types are flattened into one jumbo interface in WSDL and generated stubs. Given the nature of Web Services, this is a step back from object-oriented programming to procedure programming. Therefore, it creates a usability issue. Now given a method, it is not easy to tell on what managed object type the method is defined.

To solve this problem, with any method in generated stub, _this is defined as the first parameter. The type for _this is ManagedObjectReference. In the API reference, it specifies what ManagedObjectReference object should be used for that parameter.

Let's look at a concrete sample here. VirtualMachine has the powerOnVM_Task() method defined. In the generated stub, it is part of the jumbo interface VimPortType with the following signature:

```
public com.vmware.vim25.ManagedObjectReference
powerOnVM_Task(com.vmware.vim25.ManagedObjectReference _this,
com.vmware.vim25.ManagedObjectReference host) throws
java.rmi.RemoteException, com.vmware.vim25.VmConfigFault,
com.vmware.vim25.TaskInProgress, com.vmware.vim25.FileFault,
com.vmware.vim25.InvalidState,
com.vmware.vim25.InsufficientResourcesFault,
com.vmware.vim25.RuntimeFault;
```

Notice the first parameter, _this. From the signature alone, you know you should pass in a ManagedObjectReference, but you have no definitive idea what type of managed object it should point to. You have to check the API reference for the answer. If you pass in a ManagedObjectReference object pointing to a managed object other than a VirtualMachine, the code still compiles but fails at runtime. This basically takes away the benefits of a static typing language like Java even though you are using Java.

What you see in the stubs generated from WSDL is much like a C program that intends to emulate object-oriented programming—you define a struct (class) and pass a pointer to this struct as the first parameter in every function you intend to be a method of the struct (class).

The VI Java API (covered in Chapter 5, "Introducing the VI Java API") reconstructs all managed object types at the client side, as well as getter methods so that you can work with the managed object just like any other objects in Java. Also, the scripting languages covered in Chapter 17, "Scripting the VI SDK with Jython, Perl, and PowerShell," provide some support for managed object types.

Appendix F

What Is New in vSphere 4 SDK?

Besides a brand name change, vSphere 4 has introduced many new features, including new functionalities and capabilities, improved performance, and scalability. To manage these new features, many new APIs are introduced. This chapter goes through important additions and changes of existing APIs as a high-level overview. In the end, we will discuss the migration of your application to the new API.

The next edition of this book will cover the new APIs in detail.

Managed Objects: Profile, HostProfile, ClusterProfile, ProfileManager, ClusterProfileManager, HostProfileManager, ProfileComplianceManager, DistributedVirtualSwitch, VmwareDistributedVirtualSwitch, DistributedVirtualSwitchManager, DistributedVirtualPortgroup, HostVirtualNicManager, HostKernelModuleSystem, HostPciPassthruSystem, OvfManager, HttpNfcLease, VirtualApp, IpPoolManager, ResourcePlanningManager, VirtualMachineCompatibilityChecker, VirtualMachineProvisioningChecker, LicenseAssignmentManager, LocalizationManager

Changes of Existing APIs

Most of the existing APIs are the same, but here are the important changes:

- `Datastore` and `Network` are now subtypes of `ManagedEntity`. This means you have more control over these two types and can apply permission on them.

- Many methods and properties are added into existing managed objects. For example, the `Folder` type has a new method to create a new `DistributedVirtualSwitch`. The `VirtualMachine` has 14 more methods for various operations: `exportVM()`, `extractOvfEnvironment()`, `makePrimaryVM_Task()`, `promoteDisks_Task()`, `queryChangedDiskAreas()`, `queryUnownedFiles()`, `refreshStorageInfo()`, `setDisplayTopology()`, `startRecording_Task()`, `startReplaying_Task()`, `stopRecording_Task()`, `stopReplaying_Task()`, `terminateFaultTolerantVM_Task()`, and `turnOffFaultToleranceForVM_Task()`.

- A few properties and methods have been deprecated.

For all these changes, refer to the new vSphere SDK API reference, which clearly indicates the information with each type and method. The next several sections focus on the newly added managed object types, grouped by new features. The managed objects at the beginning of this chapter list all 23 new types.

Profile Management

A profile captures the blueprint of a known, validated configuration and can be applied to other managed entities. At runtime, the system can also monitor the compliance of profiles across the datacenter. Using profiles greatly simplifies what used to be manual configuration management and can help maintain consistency and correctness of the configurations.

Currently, vSphere supports two types of managed entities: host and cluster. The respective managed object types are `HostProfile` and `ClusterProfile`. The common superclass of these two is the `Profile`.

To manage these profiles, a set of manager types are defined: `ProfileManager`, `HostProfileManager`, and `ClusterProfileManager`. The `ProfileManager` is the supertype of the latter two. The relationship between `Profile` and `ProfileManager` is similar to `Task` and `TaskManager`.

Figure F-1 illustrates the relationships among these six types.

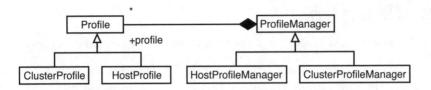

Figure F-1   The relationships of `Profile`, `ProfileManager` and their subtypes

The `ProfileComplianceManager` is a utility type for checking the compliance. It defines four methods:

- `checkCompliance_Task()` checks compliance of an entity against a `Profile`.
- `clearComplianceStatus()` clears the saved `ComplianceResult` based on the `Profile` and `Entity` filtering criteria.
- `queryComplianceStatus()` queries the compliance status based on the `Profile` and `Entity` filters.
- `queryExpressionMetadata()` queries the metadata for the expressions.

Distribute Virtual Switch

Before vSphere 4, a virtual switch is associated with a specific host. It should be configured consistently across many hosts and aligned well with the physical network for cross-host operations such as `VMotion` to happen.

The distributed virtual switch (DVS) simplifies these by abstracting the host-level virtual switch to a centralized datacenter level. When `VMotion` occurs, the corresponding network policies are migrated with the virtual machine. This feature is available only with the vCenter server, not the individual ESX host.

The managed object type for DVS is `DistributedVirtualSwitch`, which is a supertype that is extended by `VmwareDistributedVirtualSwitch`.[1] The `DistributedVirtualSwitch` defines 5 properties and 12 methods in addition to those inherited from `ManagedEntity`.

---

[1] There is another DVS implementation from Cisco: Nexus 1000. It does not have a corresponding type in the API.

To manage these distributed virtual switches, use DistributedVirtualSwitchManager, which is attached to the ServiceInstance object. It defines six methods, mainly for querying information and searching DVS.

To create a new DVS, use the newly added createDVS_Task() method of the Folder managed object.

Host Management

As you have noticed, host management is complicated and has split into many managed object types to cover respective aspects. In vSphere 4, three more managed object types are added to cover the host virtual NIC, kernel, and PCI pass-thru:

- HostVirtualNicManager manages the virtual network interface card (NIC) of a host. It defines one property info (type: HostVirtualNicManagerInfo) and three methods: deselectVnicForNicType(), queryNetConfig(), and selectVnicForNicType().

- HostKernelModuleSystem controls the configuration of kernel modules like vmkernel and usb on the host. It does not define a property but three methods: queryConfiguredModuleOptionString(), queryModules(), and updateModuleOptionString().

- HostPciPassthruSystem manages the PCI pass-thru state of a host. It defines one property, pciPassthruInfo, which is an array of HostPciPassthruInfo objects; and two methods: refresh() and updatePassthruConfig().

OVF Support

Open Virtualization Format (OVF) is an open standard of Distributed Management Task Force (DMTF, http://www.dmtf.org). It provides an open, portable, and flexible format for describing the metadata about virtual machines; therefore, it simplifies packaging and deploying one or more virtual machines. It's different from the disk files that only hold the disk images, but not the information about the virtual hardware like CPU, memory, networking, and storage.

With OVF, virtual machines from different vendors can be provisioned to any hypervisors that support the OVF standard,[2] which is critical for wide adoption of virtualization today.

With vSphere 4, two types are added:

- `OvfManager` provides services to generate and parse OVF descriptors. It does not take care of actual importing or exporting of virtual machines. It defines no property but four methods: `createDescriptor()`, `createImportSpec()`, `parseDescriptor()`, and `validateHost()`.

- `HttpNfcLease` represents a lease on a virtual machine or a `VirtualApp`, which can be used to import or export disks for the entity. While the lease is held, operations that change the state of the virtual machine covered by the lease, such as power on and power off, are blocked. A lease can be in four states: `Initializing`, `Ready`, `Done`, and `Error`.

`HttpNfcLease` defines four properties describing general information, state, initialization progress, and error information. It also defines three methods: `httpNfcLeaseAbort()`, `httpNfcLeaseComplete()`, and `httpNfcLeaseProgress()`.

VirtualApp Support

A `VirtualApp` (a.k.a. vApp) represents a group of virtual machines that consist of a multitiered software solution. In that sense, it would be easier to have named it `VirtualMachineGroup`.

From a management point of view, a `VirtualApp` acts like a virtual machine object. It has power operations, networks, and datastores, and its resources can be configured. It can also be exported and imported. Note that the power operation is on the group of the virtual machines in a predefined order.

On the implementation side, `VirtualApp` is a subtype of `ResourcePool`, so it inherits all the properties and methods from `ResourcePool`. Were multiple inheritances allowed, `VirtualApp` might have been the subtype of both `ResourcePool` and `VirtualMachine`.

---

[2] The OVF does not specify the virtual disk format. VMFS (VMware) and VHD (Microsoft) are two major disk formats used today. A conversion tool must be present if the disk format is different from what hypervisor supports.

In addition to the inherited properties and methods, VirtualApp defines four properties covering the datastore, network, configuration, and parent folder. It also defines six methods.

- cloneVApp_Task() creates a clone of this vApp.

- exportVApp() obtains an export lease on this vApp.

- powerOffVApp_Task() stops this vApp in the order specified in the vApp configuration.

- powerOnVApp_Task() starts this vApp in the order specified in the vApp configuration.

- unregisterVApp_Task() removes this vApp from the inventory without removing any of the virtual machine's files on disk. High-level information stored with ESX or vCenter is removed upon success.

- updateVAppConfig() updates the vApp configuration.

To help the IP allocation to the vApps, IpPoolManager is added. It's a helper type that allocates IPv4 and IPv6 addresses to the VirtualApps. It has no property but four methods.

- createIpPool() creates a new IP pool.

- destroyIpPool() destroys·an IP pool on the given datacenter with a specified ID.

- queryIpPools() returns the list of IP pools for a datacenter.

- updateIpPool() updates an IP pool on a datacenter.

New Compatibility Checkers

Two new compatibility checker types are added:

- VirtualMachineCompatibilityChecker checks the compatibility of a virtual machine with a host.

- VirtualMachineProvisioningChecker checks the feasibility of certain provisioning operations such as migration and relocation.

VirtualMachineCompatibilityChecker has no property but only one method defined: checkCompatibility_Task(). The result is saved in the info.result of the returned Task object upon completion.

`VirtualMachineProvisioningChecker` has three methods defined:

- `checkMigrate_Task()` checks the feasibility of a proposed `migrateVM_Task()` operation.
- `checkRelocate_Task()` tests the feasibility of a proposed `relocateVM_Task()` operation.
- `queryVMotionCompatibilityEx_Task()` investigates the general VMotion compatibility of a set of virtual machines with a set of hosts.

It's highly recommended that you call the respective `check*_Task()` methods before the `migrateVM_Task()` and `relocateVM_Task()` methods for first-time migration or relocation.

Licensing Change

The licensing enforcement changes quite a bit in vSphere 4. It no longer uses the VI 3 licensing model, and it does not require a separate license server to be installed and monitored. The new license key is simply 25 character strings instead of complex text strings.

To reflect the change, a new managed object type `LicenseAssignmentManager` is added. It's accessible from the `LicenseManager`. It does not define a property but does define three methods.

- `queryAssignedLicenses()` gets information about all the licenses associated with an entity.
- `removeAssignedLicense()` removes licenses associated with an entity.
- `updateAssignedLicense()` updates the license associated with an entity.

Localization Support

`LocalizationManager` is added to provide a unified interface for the client-side applications to get localized messages. It's supported only on the vCenter server.

The managed type does not have a method but a property called `catalog`. It is an array of `LocalizationManagerMessageCatalog` data objects that contain the following fields:

- **catalogName**—The name of the catalog.

- **catalogUri**—The relative URI from which the catalog can be downloaded. The user needs to prefix this with a scheme and authority to make a complete URL. For example, if the value is /catalog/en/perf.vmsg, the full URL is https://VC_IP_or_HostName/catalog/en/perf.vmsg.

- **lastModified**—The last-modified time of the catalog file, if available.

- **locale**—The locale for the catalog, such as ja, de, or en.

- **md5sum**—The checksum of the catalog file, if available.

- **moduleName**—The module or extension that provides this catalog. It's empty for core catalogs for the vCenter server.

The contents in the resource pointed by the catalogUri are typical key/value pairs, such as Java property files or Windows .ini files. It should be easy to parse the content.

The following is an excerpt from a German version of the default.vmsg resource:

```
Discovered.VM     = "Virtuelle Maschine erkennt"
Discovered.VMGroup  = "Virtuelle Maschine erkennt"
login.HostAlreadyManaged  = "Dieser Host wird derzeit von vCenter Server mit
der IP-Adresse {1,C} verwaltet. Änderungen, die Sie während dieser Sitzung
am Host vornehmen, werden in aktuellen Clientsitzungen mit vCenter Server
möglicherweise nicht widergespiegelt."
Root.ResourcePool  = "Ressourcen"
Root.Datacenter    = "Datencenter"
Root.UnknownVMName = "{1,C}, unbekannt"
```

Resource Planning

ResourcePlanningManager is a helper type that provides service for estimating the database sizes. It does not have a property but does have one method: estimateDatabaseSize().

The estimateDatabaseSize() method takes in an argument typed as DatabaseSizeParam, which includes two subproperties: one for describing the inventory structure, and the other for describing performance statistic requirements.

The return of the method is the DatabaseSizeEstimate object, which has only one long integer value as the estimated size required in megabytes.

Migrating Your Existing Applications

Because most of the vSphere 4 interfaces are the same as 2.5, you don't need to do anything unless your applications use any of the following ten methods: addHost_Task(), addStandaloneHost_Task(), createTask(), extendVirtualDisk_Task(), findByUuid(), queryVmfsDatastoreExtendOptions(), relocateVM_Task(), revertToCurrentSnapshot_Task(), revertToSnapshot_Task(), or updateInternetScsiAuthenticationProperties().

The changes to these methods are additional parameters that are optional.[3] For example, addHost_Task() has the following signature in 2.5:

```
addHost_Task(ManagedObjectReference, HostConnectSpec, boolean,
ManagedObjectReference)
```

In vSphere 4, the new signature is like the following. As you can see, one additional String type parameter is added as the last parameter.

```
addHost_Task(ManagedObjectReference, HostConnectSpec, boolean,
ManagedObjectReference, String)
```

Because the additional String parameter is optional, you can simply add a new null in your API call.

The VI Java API has patched it up with additional methods; therefore, your applications built on top of it continue to work as they are. If you are using another toolkit, you can check out the source code to see the default values.

---

[3] These new parameters are optional in the WSDL definition. When the stub is generated, they are part of the new method signatures, so they become required.

Index

D

I